PLAIN PATHS AND DIVIDING LINES

EARLY AMERICAN HISTORIES
Douglas Bradburn, John C. Coombs, and S. Max Edelson, Editors

Plain Paths and Dividing Lines

*Navigating Native Land and Water
in the Seventeenth-Century Chesapeake*

Jessica Lauren Taylor

UNIVERSITY OF VIRGINIA PRESS
Charlottesville and London

University of Virginia Press
© 2023 by Jessica Lauren Taylor
All rights reserved
Printed in the United States of America on acid-free paper

First published 2023

9 8 7 6 5 4 3 2 1

Library of Congress Cataloging-in-Publication Data

Names: Taylor, Jessica (Jessica Lauren), author.
Title: Plain paths and dividing lines : navigating native land and water in the seventeenth-century Chesapeake / Jessica Lauren Taylor.
Description: Charlottesville : University of Virginia Press, 2023. | Series: Early American histories | Includes bibliographical references and index.
Identifiers: LCCN 2022048765 (print) | LCCN 2022048766 (ebook) | ISBN 9780813949345 (hardcover) | ISBN 9780813949352 (paperback) | ISBN 9780813949369 (ebook)
Subjects: LCSH: Chesapeake Bay Region (Md. and Va.)—History—17th century. | Chesapeake Bay Region (Md. and Va.)—Boundaries.
Classification: LCC F187.C5 T388 2023 (print) | LCC F187.C5 (ebook) | DDC 975.5/1802—dc23/eng/20230301
LC record available at https://lccn.loc.gov/2022048765
LC ebook record available at https://lccn.loc.gov/2022048766

This book is freely available in an open access edition thanks to TOME (Toward an Open Monograph Ecosystem)—a collaboration of the Association of American Universities, the Association of University Presses, and the Association of Research Libraries—and the generous support of Virginia Tech. Learn more at the TOME website, available at openmonographs.org.

This book is licensed under the Creative Commons Attribution 4.0 International License (CC BY-NC-ND 4.0), https://creativecommons.org/licenses/by-nc-nd/4.0/legalcode.

https://doi.org/10.52156/m.5806

Cover art: Smith Spaulding Map, 20 January 1832, Gloucester County, VA, Surveyor's Book No. 1, 1817–52, p. 38, Gloucester County District Court. (Courtesy Clerk of the Circuit Court, Gloucester County, VA)

CONTENTS

Acknowledgments	vii
Introduction: Connections and Borders in the Chesapeake	1
1. The Moving People and Places of the Powhatan Chiefdom	19
2. Watching Carefully in the Bay, 1607–1614	35
3. New Borders, New Connections, New Fractures, 1615–1644	67
4. Sailors and Rumors in the Bay, 1622–1644	98
5. Trade, Property, and the Meaning of Algonquian Places, 1650–1660	125
6. Neighbors, Local Authority, and Local Violence, 1660–1666	153
7. Rebelling by the Bay, 1670–1680	183
Epilogue: Native History at Dividing Lines	219
Notes	229
Index	301

⁓ACKNOWLEDGMENTS⁓

Any author who says that they did this by themselves is a liar. Acknowledging that we are influenced and edited by others comes with the delight of remembering conversations and people that make this process rich and meaningful. This book was rewritten and edited almost entirely during the COVID-19 pandemic; whether they are about editing history or hopes for the future, those conversations made joyful this isolated work.

I am grateful for the advice and many hours of reading from scholars and editing professionals at the University of Virginia Press, at the Early American Places series, and elsewhere including the anonymous reviewers, David Brown, Max Edelson, Andrew Edwards, Margaret Hogan, Catherine Cotrupi, David Shope, and Mark Guerci. Martha McCartney traveled the last week of this decade-long journey with me, every small last-minute change a gift I will never forget. Cartographers Stewart Scales and Gemma Wessels, and the marketing and art departments at UVA Press, Gloucester County Clerk of the Circuit Court Cathy Dale, and Bill Lawrence have facilitated and created the book cover and maps for which I hope this book will be remembered. I am especially grateful to acquisitions editor Nadine Zimmerli, whose honest friendship and power steering made this process surmountable during COVID.

Before this project reached editors' hands, other people taught me how to research and write. I am especially grateful for the mentorship of Dr. Mrs. and Dr. Mr. Whittenburg, Martin Gallivan, Susan Kern, Carl Lounsbury, David Brown, and Charles McGovern at the College of William and Mary, who made room for me and handed me the tools I needed on my first adventures as an often-overambitious student. My PhD committee at the University of Florida—Jon Sensbach, Paul Ortiz, Elizabeth Dale, and Morris Hylton III—provided invaluable feedback and encouragement.

Members of the Omohundro Coffeehouse and other writing groups reminded me with their own brilliant pieces to keep exploring new sources and frames. Several scholars have taken the time to provide feedback on images, proposals, or chapters, including Buck Woodard, Matt Sparacio, Peter Potter, Camilla Townsend, Karen Kupperman, Lucien Holness, Jason Sellers, Edward Ragan, Joshua Piker, Tom Klatka, Brent Tarter, and Phil Yaure. I received incomparable mentorship and encouragement from members of the Virginia Tech history department. I am most indebted to Juliana Barr, the sort of honest and kind advisor I hope to be.

My gratitude could never match my family's fierce and unstoppable support and love, which reminds me often of the vast, beautiful world beyond academic work where we also live. Members of our church community have since reinforced this lesson. Jeff Flanagan's unending compassion and love has softened my experience of this work and made its brightest moments possible.

So many women whose friendship has shaped life beyond writing and teaching also supported me and this project. They include Danna Agmon, Annemarie Anderson, Sarah Blanc, Diana Dombrowski, Debbie Fine, Carmen Gitre, my mentor Melanie Kiechle, Johanna Mellis, Dominique Polanco, Audrey Reeves, Ashley Reichelmann, Courtney Roberts, Emily Satterwhite, Helen Schneider, Mallory Szymanski, Jennifer Thelusma, Lili Wang, Laura Beth Weaver, and Anna Zeide. I thank Sarah Samples, partner in adventure Desiree Poets, partner in lunch Amanda Demmer, adopted sister Mindy Quigley, and longtime friend Shannon Ralston for texts and loud laughter, or quiet stoop sitting, at any hour. We all faced challenges over the previous half decade, often separately because of the pandemic, inequities in our workplaces, and uncontrollable life circumstances. When lost in the forest alone, it is everything to see other flashlights cut through the dark and know they see yours too.

PLAIN PATHS AND DIVIDING LINES

─ INTRODUCTION ─

Connections and Borders in the Chesapeake

The sands on the Eastern Shore of the Chesapeake Bay are held in place by patches of marsh grasses, but even so the wind and tide pull sand and grass apart from one another. Blue crabs move fast just under the surface of almost still water. Where Nandua Creek appears, its low and flat shoreline is shaded by pines. The winding and crooked path of the main creek obscures the broad bay, where the sun sets behind the moving spits of sand at the mouth.[1]

In the Chesapeake Bay, water becomes deeper, choppier, colder, and cloudier. To the traveler, reassuring landmarks appear on the horizon from the middle of the bay. Due west from Nandua cutting into the mainland is the Rappahannock River, a winding and wooded waterway on the western shore of the Chesapeake. Moving upstream, and tracing the north bank, runs of shad enter Totuskey Creek every spring moving toward where the saltwater turns fresh, between broad swaths of marsh grass and the leaves of arrow arum turned skyward.[2]

On the southern shore of the Rappahannock, opposite Totuskey Creek, roads along marshy Piscataway Creek connect to a network of travel routes along Virginia's broad Middle Peninsula. Canoes left hidden by grass on the shore and bridges built from poles tied together in the shape of an X aid travelers moving south across the marshes. White fog covers the black water of Dragon Run, water rippling around fallen trees. People know the way along runs of low, wet earth that shifts with the creeks across generations.[3]

Algonquian people of the seventeenth century moved among dozens of towns, foraging spots, fishing weirs, and fields along these routes, recognizing local shifts in the vegetation and in the presence of residents along

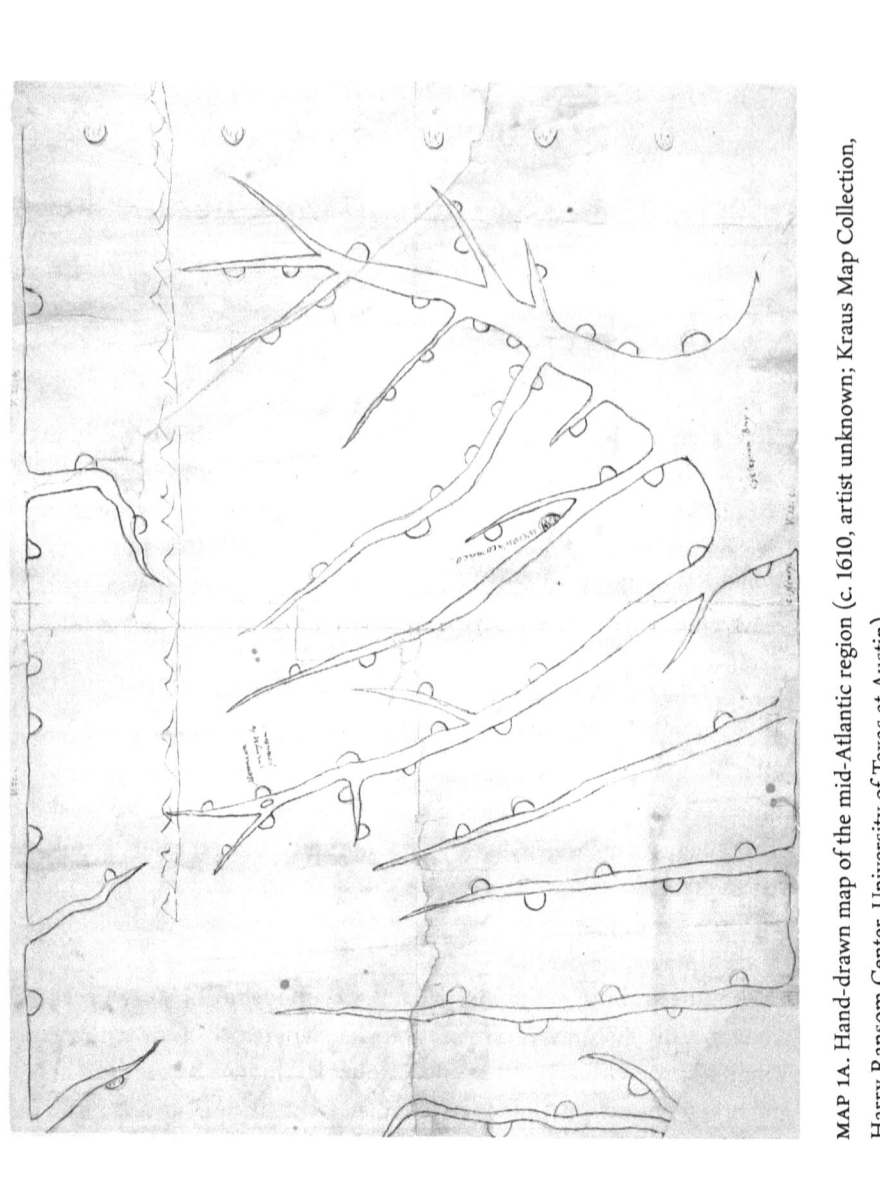

MAP 1A. Hand-drawn map of the mid-Atlantic region (c. 1610, artist unknown; Kraus Map Collection, Harry Ransom Center, University of Texas at Austin)

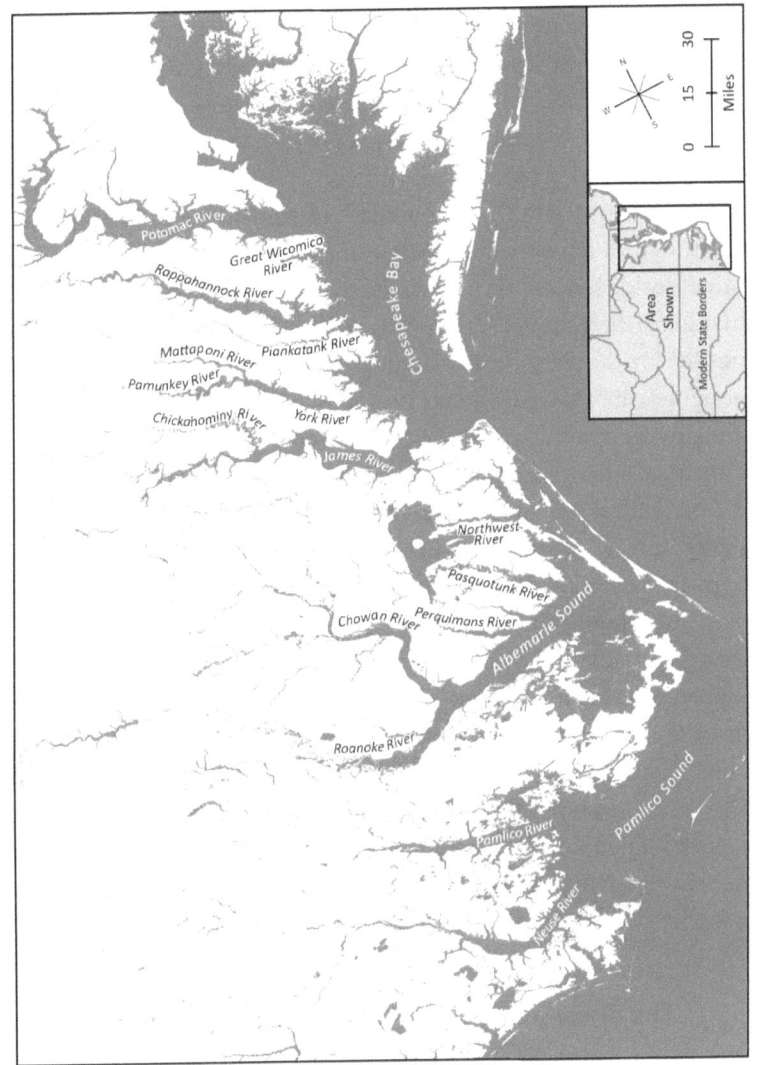

MAP 1B. Reconstruction of early seventeenth-century drawing in map 1a above, with contemporary coastline (Gemma Wessels)

the way. This book follows the people who moved through the Chesapeake's waters in the seventeenth century, Native people who continued to travel and live here, and unfree people and enterprising settlers who relied on Native networks and places to pursue their own ends. It chronicles Native and English leaders' attempts to break river and shoreline, and later land, into governed territories, domains, and private property that would halt their mobility. It then tells the stories of the violent consequences of trespass and transgression over these boundaries, which turned into battles for authority, freedom, and profit.

Over hundreds of years, Algonquians had transformed Chesapeake waterways into lines of connection between their families and towns, and to the Native worlds beyond their territories.[4] The water also defined them, giving chiefdoms their names: "trap-fishing river" for the Appamattucks; "at the mouth" for the Paspaheghs, among many.[5] It gave them a sense of place among neighbors, traders, and hostile outsiders who also traversed the bay, ranging from modern-day Pennsylvania to North Carolina. And it provided their sustenance from open water to managed marshlands.

Toward the end of the sixteenth century, the Powhatan chiefdom, one polity among several in the Chesapeake where Eastern Algonquian languages were spoken, pulled into its networks people of dozens of smaller Algonquian chiefdoms. They and their places in the Chesapeake are at the center of this story. The connections between people and water that had developed over centuries remained strong through the bloodshed and migration of the seventeenth century and the arrival of colonists. When expansionist chiefs and colonial officials attempted to control those connections by marking boundaries and segmenting the Chesapeake landscape, all sorts of people who knew the Chesapeake's waters—people like Native leaders, English traders, and enslaved Africans who absconded—pushed back.[6]

The Stakes of Boundaries and Movement

Native studies scholars emphasize that riverine and oceanic environments supported Native mobility and power over European newcomers. With thorough understanding of aquatic environments and seagoing vessels, Native people had distinct political, economic, and military advantages along North American coastlines. These insights hold true for the Chesapeake landscape as well; the expansionist strategies of the Powhatan chiefdom during Wahunsenacawh's rule, and that of his successor, Opechancanough, demonstrate that Native people were not just on the defensive, holding on to past power, but instead innovated new political relationships and identities in the 1600s. Space is a crucial variable in the study of history and of Anglo-Native relations; after all, the Chesapeake's transformation through colonization relied on connectivity along Algonquian waters and the spread of slavery and tobacco production across the landscape in the seventeenth century.

Seventeenth-century colonial government records, county records, Virginia Land Office books, travel accounts, correspondence, and archaeological research demonstrate that as English colonists arrived in the Chesapeake, founded Virginia, and then planted settlements in Maryland, they navigated a broad-reaching, riverine web of Algonquian connections inside the Powhatan chiefdom and beyond it. Although the waters and landscapes that played host to these connections often served as backdrops for a diverse array of actors, they were themselves multidimensional, not only as physical spaces but also as the grounds for the perceptions and representations of those spaces. They made the complicated successes and failures of initial English expansion visible and measurable, in fields full of tobacco or in houses burned by Native people during war.[7] What archaeologists term "cultural landscapes" and the boundaries of ownership and political control around them changed over time, but the ways in which fields, paths, and especially waterways facilitated communication served to continuously remind new residents of Native power and presence.[8]

At midcentury, as Native people and English settlers encountered one another through spreading settlement and trade with Native people beyond the Chesapeake, movement and conflict reoriented from water to land. Settlement—tobacco plantations and the trade in skins and furs—brought Native people to county courts, surveyors onto Native land, and Native travelers from nations beyond the Chesapeake. This presented new dangers and tensions for Algonquian leaders creating and reaffirming their own claims to land and resources. As surveyors and traders sought to place boundaries on land between English settlement and outsider Native people and Chesapeake Algonquians, they found that Native people at both the fringes of colonial claims and well within English colonial, county, and property bounds moved through them.

In fact, Algonquian people's sustained networks, and their knowledge of the Chesapeake, shaped borders, inequality, access to resources, and political power for English and Native people in the seventeenth century. They also contoured the resistance to colonial authority on the part of elite English factions, other Native people, and bonded laborers. Before and after contact with the English, for example, the Powhatan chiefdom's leaders made war on Native outsiders who threatened their boundaries and trade routes. These leaders surveilled and at times curtailed the movements of people who brought information, rumor, and trade goods valuable to Algonquians. However, the Powhatans were often also challenged and foiled by people within their boundaries, who in some cases used distance from the Powhatans' central location on the York River or nearness to the English to form new alliances and flout Powhatan control over movement.

Meanwhile, English settlers grafted their plantations on top of Native towns and places, seizing Native people's cleared ground, as the stakes of knowing boundaries and keeping laborers within them grew exponentially.[9] Despite their intentional placement of new settlements atop Native landscapes, the English attempted to establish boundaries between Native people and English homes, goods, and riverfront property, counter to the role of Native places within Native networks. As English planters began to claim larger pieces of property and purchase bonded laborers to farm tobacco, their plantations remained connected to not only other plantations and European ships but Native places as well. For many indentured servants and enslaved Africans who helped transform Native places into plantations, the surrounding Algonquian riverine world was not entirely foreign. Indeed, African and English people brought with them their own skills and understandings of riverine landscapes and capacity to engage with surrounding Native people, watercraft, and places.[10] In this book, I therefore detail the ways in which English planters relied on Native networks and knowledge but in so doing inadvertently opened access to them for people like enslaved Africans and indentured servants, who through travel and talk also sought knowledge of the bay and its people beyond the boundaries of enslavers.

Boundaries are the imaginary, geographical places where assertions of property or sovereignty begin and end, made by practices of marking them on trees or measuring them with survey instruments or reminding one another that the line marks a division between at least two different places. Borders include these bounds but are also defined by the ways in which they are policed, marked, discussed, and legitimately or illicitly crossed. Both are and have historically been shifty and uncertain and tied to local customs and regional politics, even inside of a Native or European polity. Even measured and drawn by the most exacting surveyor, boundaries were and are not just mapped lines between governments; they necessitate exclusion and enclosure. They accentuate social and economic difference and differences in identity for people on either side.[11]

However, drawn lines and contemporary efforts to map a boundary, like a "frontier," rarely describe clear divisions in reality. Native people lived in between settler-occupied land across Virginia and remained and are today connected to people and political movement beyond the Chesapeake. This book follows Native people who lived surrounded by other Indigenous people and settlers in Virginia, far inside of settler-occupied territory in the Chesapeake, and who connected the region to the rest of the continent. On the ground in the seventeenth century, most people knew boundaries meant little without actual barriers—palisades, patrols, and corporeal consequences—that fenced people in or out. The English colonists' barriers were often faulty, and planters and officials often understood their most precise boundaries to be aspirational. Fences rotted, lines between colonies and properties remained uncertain, forts faced building delays, and people and animals trespassed or ambled away, frequently unseen. Instead, markers of boundaries like forts and fences became new centers of exchange and settlement rather than isolated outposts, attracting people rather than dividing them.[12] People from Algonquian towns and Virginia settlements, but also Maryland, Dutch, and African contexts, lived in a world crosscut by an array of often incommensurable, often locally defined Native and English boundaries and then chose to risk the consequences of ignoring those boundaries.

At the beginning of the seventeenth century, the Chesapeake's navigability and rich resources made Native and English efforts to police borders worthwhile. In the early seventeenth century, leaders of the Powhatan chiefdom, the Chesapeake's largest Algonquian polity, cultivated kinship ties and employed force to control the movement of people, luxury goods, and food through their domain and to ensure the loyalty of people on the fringes of their territories. For their part, English officials employed officially sanctioned or extralegal violence, physical fortifications, and legal measures to impose borders between their own settlements and Native land.[13] These boundaries often cleaved through roads or waterways or foraging areas belonging to Native people, inviting conflict. At the same time, colonial officials remained anxious about boundary crossing, since trespass over a boundary, however nebulously defined, was trespass on their authority. But neither side could control the people inside of their claimed borders, let alone beyond them. Native people traded corn inside of English forts without permission from Native leaders; English mariners attempted violent takeovers of other English plantations, and servants and enslaved people liberated canoes to run to the next county or a nearby Native town. Failed efforts to cut people off from one another, in a place so intentionally connected, brought territorial claims into question for officials and resistors alike. Violence that attempted to stop movement only accelerated it.

Newcomers in the Chesapeake saw that Native riverine routes and roads—and Native people—crisscrossed between Chesapeake plantations and Native towns, an alluring invitation to cross from one set of worlds into another. However, I argue that the consequences for transgressing boundaries did not apply to everyone equally. Instead, the permeability of borders, and the benefits and risks of crossing them, depended on status, knowledge, and networks.[14] Caught servants faced extended time or physical punishment for attempting to run to a different colony or Native territory, whereas enslaved Native people or Native servants with knowledge of local waterways and kinship networks might be more likely to disappear into Native towns. Enslaved Africans with knowledge of sailing and a partner could make it across the river or bay in a stolen vessel. Planters with political connections, of course, might walk away unscathed by law or violence.

Indeed, in the Chesapeake, those that did the greatest damage to boundaries and colonial authority were in the same class as those who, in erecting them, dealt damage to Native neighbors. Well-heeled and well-resourced traders and planters, representing a variety of visions for the future of the Chesapeake colonies and understandings of how boundaries ought to work, regularly trespassed across colonial and Native boundaries for booty or land. They inflicted violence on Native people (and other colonists) usually without fear of retribution from colonial authorities, all the while ensconcing bonded laborers inside of plantations. And their success encouraged other planters to do the same. As English settlers crept inland from the shoreline and onto Native territory, elites from William Claiborne to Edmund Scarborough to rebel Nathaniel Bacon harnessed overland and riverine networks to their own ends at the expense of the colony, almost severing these connections in the process. Information about these local relationships and violent episodes reached officials in England, Jamestown, and St. Mary's City, creating expensive and embarrassing panic and confusion that shook the English colonies. These crises and other factors, among them disputes over land and social mobility, culminated in small and large bouts of violence over boundaries from the 1620s to the 1670s.[15] Bacon's Rebellion in 1676, a pivotal moment in the history of race and Native history, is a product and extension of these bouts of local, then colony-level violence over border transgressions.

As I started researching the seventeenth-century Chesapeake, I discovered events known to specialists but still not fully part of the wider understanding of the histories of the North American English colonies. Elite Virginians and Marylanders repeatedly demanded that others respect their colonies' and properties' respective borders, when locally they themselves pushed and bent them. What accounts for this inconsistency, and in moments hypocrisy? How did Native people develop diplomacy with knowledge of the broad range of English ideas about boundaries and histories of violence in mind? After starting along the James River with early seventeenth-century colonial records, I followed the fringes of Virginia in the records of the colony's proliferating counties, focusing on the Eastern Shore during the mid-seventeenth century and across the bay to the Rappahannock River as episodes of violence proliferated there. In order to understand transgressions or conflicts, I sought out information about the place where it started: What shipping routes and roads were nearby? What neighbors might have influenced how events unfolded? When available, I used the analyses of archaeologists and geographers to access factors not in the documentary record, like cultural change inside of Native towns and everyday trade between Native and English people. While most of the local conflicts I discovered were Virginian, I soon realized that connectivity of Native networks beyond the colony made this a Maryland story, and a story also belonging to non-Algonquian Native people of the Piedmont, to the west of the Virginia colony. People involved in Native politics crossed relatively new colonial borders, since as the saying goes, the border crossed them. Treaties and law, instability and the growth of settlements, and Native politics in the interior altered by trade in Native captives and animal skins all pulled people toward boundaries in the southern Chesapeake with promises of prosperity and freedom.

The breathtaking Native landscapes crossed by English-imposed borders rendered them complicated and porous—cliffs and swamps, open water and Native towns that moved with the season. From my own southeastern perspective, I saw a complicated network of Native landscapes much broader than the Chesapeake colonies, with migrations, people, and economies intertwined on either side of borders between English settlers and Native people. Sometimes Indigenous, African, and European peoples were entangled before a boundary existed. Meanwhile, Native people consistently pushed against the incursions of colonists, and through their movements across boundaries kept alive and created new networks of people and places. Attempts to shore up colonial authority here only highlighted the futility of stopping their movement, failure that further undermined authority.

Unbounded Local Networks, Unbounded Ambitions

The established story of dispossession along the eastern seaboard and the corresponding disappearance of Native people is often told through a clash of big names, between Wahunsenacawh, leader of the Powhatan chiefdom, and John Smith, or between Governor William Berkeley and rebel Nathaniel Bacon.[16] They fought for power in broad swaths of the Chesapeake. My retelling of the stories of individual Algonquians' shifting personal ambitions and allegiances decenters larger political categories like "the Powhatans" and "the English" and centers local networks. In particular, the negotiating, transgressing, and feuding travelers and occupants of the Chesapeake highlight how connections across borders influenced the strategies of border-crossers living inside and outside the bounds of a colony. The story here is punctuated by tense exchanges between less well-known neighbors like John Catlett and the great man George along the Rappahannock, or the Gingaskins and John Dye on the Eastern Shore, their ambitions informed by local conditions and opportunities. At the local level, Native individuals had in mind regional diplomatic and economic ties when dealing with feuding English elites and indentured and enslaved laborers. Native people and others who transgressed boundaries took advantage of their local piece of the riverine environment in pursuit of commerce, loot, or freedom.

With these local landscapes in mind, I argue that by the third quarter of the seventeenth century, intracolonial and Anglo-Native tensions came not just from English settlers fighting for status or to vent hatred of Native people but also from disparate spatial visions shaped by Native landscapes. Even as they changed life for Native people, plantations and forts became local incubators for Native resistance and resistance on the part of nonelites inside of the colony. And as English people constructed English places from Native ones, some planters used these networks of sites where information, goods, people, and gossip were exchanged to support their visions of economic and political power. Others employed networks toward different visions for the future and different relationships with boundaries, like freedom from servitude beyond the bounds of English settlement or as an assertion of sovereignty over Indigenous land. For people outside of the English planter class, visions of the future in the Chesapeake were made more expansive by the presence and movement of Native people, whose land but also roads and towns they saw as a means of material security, freedom, and independence elsewhere—mobility feared by seventeenth-century enslavers and colony officials.

Scholarship on the Chesapeake has long reinforced this complexity. There was not an "English" and an "Indian" side, but rather many competing ambitions on both sides of the colonial-Indigenous borders clashed and informed one another. Pursuing different avenues for wealth and power in the Chesapeake, planters' understandings of borders and movement varied by political affiliation, class, religion, and ethnicity; indeed, elite infighting and rule-bending also became a primary driver of violence and conflict with Native people at the expense of other elites of, for example, Catholic convictions or the Virginia governor's inner circle. English elites pushed competing and sometimes muddled visions for the future of land and water in the Chesapeake, constructing a fur-trading outpost or planning a riverfront feudal manor or mapping a network of plantations fueled by enslaved labor.[17] Meanwhile, Native people sought to expand their influence over other Indigenous neighbors or people living in English-occupied land, to retain security or stability or to gain an edge in riverine trade. Yet for all this nuance, the traditional story of seventeenth-century Anglo-Virginian conflict still concludes with a decline in population of some Native nations and the annihilation or removal of others, as Virginia's and Maryland's mapped bounds expanded outward from the James River and St. Mary's City like an amoeba.

However, an orientation away from the geographic centers of English and Powhatan power reveals a messier truth: planters and Native people in particular locales, from the Eastern Shore to the Potomac, formed enmities and agreements independent of colonial officials and, if within reach of the Powhatans, Powhatan authorities. These many sides and ambitions were negotiated locally. Although a patent for river-adjacent land might be signed by the governor and a map drawn by a surveyor, it was neighbors who consolidated or broke through one another's boundaries. The people on the borders often decided the nature of the borders, and colonial officials and paramount chiefs could only react. Maps and titles in the hands of elites were hardly indicators of territorial control—or even a unified sense of how that territory was defined by those inside of it. English dependence on Algonquian networks undermined claims to the legitimacy of those borders even as they were mapped. The English themselves were honing the meaning and everyday use of a boundary in the seventeenth century, defining land tenure, legitimacy, and safety from outsiders on paper and in custom. Simultaneously, as historians have demonstrated, success of the colonial project required accumulated knowledge of the claimed territory, not just to farm but to travel, treat, and control the economy. European maps often erased the history and texture of Native places by omitting or claiming Native domains as their own, but maps were, in Juliana Barr and Edward Countryman's words, "expressions of desire, not reality."[18]

Indigenous borders and networks influenced events in the Chesapeake disproportionate to Native numbers and claimed territories. Here, as elsewhere in Native North America, Native and English sailors initially developed relationships with one another on the water and came into conflict over the degree of connection and knowledge rather than the amount of space they shared. In their explorations of the Chesapeake, English settlers were forced to take seriously Native knowledge of productive land. As these colonists moved inland and north along the bay, they grappled with the Native world beyond the Chesapeake and the movements of Algonquians and non-Algonquians who threatened, or contested, the legitimacy of their plantation boundaries.[19] In other words, Algonquians enforced their own boundaries. As described throughout this book, these Indigenous cartographies manifested and reinforced the power of Native polities through conceptual mapping, acts of war, trade along established routes, and diplomacy. Algonquians shaped not only English settlements but also English thinking about the Chesapeake and boundaries.

Just as plantations were shaped by Native people, resistance to enslavement and colonialism started on Native lands and waterways and may have been contoured by Native politics from the start. And rather than fighting for a seat at the table, many indentured servants and enslaved people sought to leave the table. The unrelentingly horrible conditions in Chesapeake settlements, which worsened as social inequality increased, encouraged nonelites inside of English borders to unite and rebel as some did in Bacon's Rebellion. But they also encouraged bonded laborers to think beyond English borders altogether. Scholars who study African and Black fugitivity and mobility note that people who illicitly crossed plantation and colonial boundaries called the authority behind those boundaries into question. Further, they did so on the water: the development of Black history and the category of "Black," scholars argue, is tied to water, the coasts and oceans where the perpetrators of the slave trade wrought death and dispersal but also landscapes with which Black people sustained intimate relationships. Those who self-emancipated or ran away created "rival geographies," new ways of knowing and using the landscapes beyond plantation bounds, in conflict with planters and their oppressive racial structures.[20] The movements of bonded laborers signal yet another set of spatial visions in the Chesapeake that we can only glimpse; often, what was waiting for illicit travelers in Native territory went unrecorded.

However, archaeological and cartographic studies on Black resistance have suggested or confirmed Black uses of Native geographies as they absconded and built new futures, along the same ocean currents and roads and in Chesapeake wetlands. Of course, colonists intentionally employed physical and structural violence, here in the form of legal and geographic boundaries and borders, to discourage African and Native people from engaging and allying with one another.[21] Still, enslaved people and indentured servants took risks using Native roads, towns, and waterways, suggesting the centrality of Native territory to nonelite hopes for the future. Their movements shaped the stakes and the meaning of marking and patrolling boundaries for planters and colonial officials. Because enslaved people and indentured servants harnessed the lasting connections between Native people across the Chesapeake, and because Native-controlled territory provoked their imaginings of a world beyond the English colony, the history of resistance to enslavement and servitude was bound up with Native history and should be told as such.

Overall, mapped and legislated boundaries, meant to provide order to places and people, proved as murky as the Chesapeake's rivers and swamps. Algonquians and Europeans understood that one another's desires were divided, and intercolonial, class, and racial divisions among colonists further destabilized Anglo-Native connections. Because places in the Chesapeake were connected by water to one another, and by roads to other nations in the region, local conflicts and relationships never failed to have far-reaching implications. The mosaic of local interactions developed over the seventeenth century, built on earlier Native places and histories. It demonstrated the evolution of a wide variety of strategies to avoid displacement, escape slavery, and trade, build alliances, and resolve violent conflict. Increasing instability and violence caused by boundary-makers and boundary-crossers brought a reckoning to the Virginia colony over the unsustainable assertions of colonial boundaries. Bringing together reconfigurations in Anglo-Native relationships through small, spatial encounters, as I do in this book, therefore clarifies the configurations and reconfigurations of boundaries between Algonquians and English settlers.[22]

Moving through the Seventeenth Century

Any story of the Chesapeake and Algonquians on the Coastal Plain has to start on the water. In chapter 1, I begin with a specific Native contest over boundaries: the forcible relocation of recalcitrant Algonquians by paramount chief of the Powhatan Wahunsenacawh, in order to consolidate power over the river mouths within his domain. Using the mobility provided by the bay, the Powhatans maintained a network of surveillance and control over trade, when needed creating new boundaries around tributaries. I emphasize the importance of Native leaders' knowledge of human movement on the bay and the centrality of mobility and regional position for seafaring Coastal Plain people. Elites desired the power and goods brought by water and overland from the west but could never fully control how people moved within their bounds, even as they sought to suffocate the ability of outsiders and competitors to move freely.

After the sustained English presence on the bay began in 1607, the Powhatans used their prowess on the water to control English movement and force the English into an appropriate geographical and diplomatic niche. Powhatan people were confronted with English fortifications and acts of violence as ways of marking boundaries and of trading as a form of gathering intelligence. In chapter 2, I follow Wahunsenacawh and others as they took to the waters to control English understandings of and impact on the landscape, its resources, and its boundaries. Internal discord among the English and among Native people contributed to uncontrolled and uncontrollable sailing on the rivers and bays, showing colonists and Native people that assertions of borders provided opportunities for mobile people to delegitimize them. They learned this just as large numbers of servants and the first enslaved Africans arrived along the shores.

After only a few years, Algonquians in the southern Chesapeake and English newcomers confronted the legacy of their interconnectedness and their porous boundaries. In 1618, the Virginia Company's Great Charter established the headright system, increasing access to land for settlers and investors. With a massive attack on English settlements inside of their districts in 1622, the Powhatans' strategy of pushing settlers back toward the mouth of the James River not only rectified English overreach but temporarily stunted colonists' access to land and precipitated the demise of the Virginia Company in 1624. English officials used the Anglo-Powhatan War of 1622–32, discussed in chapter 3, to assert land tenure and boundaries, attempting to move from a fort clinging to the coast, dependent on ships for survival, to transforming Native land into private plantations. The creation of a network of forts and a system of shires were the mappable complements to legal separation. As soon as these boundaries and administrative units were legislated, I argue, they were undermined by both servants and self-interested English settlers who sought trade along creeks and Native roads, revealing divisions among the English to Native neighbors. These nonelites' continued engagement with Native people, and violence against friendly Native groups, undercut attempts to convey authority from James Fort.

At the same time as they pursued war with the Powhatans, English elites also sought wealth beyond plantations. In the 1630s, the maritime pursuit of the trade in beaver furs and other skins in the northern Chesapeake seemed like a promising and lucrative venture. There, traders confronted a whole new set of Native (and English) boundaries informed by the concurrent conflict on the James River. In chapter 4, I show why established Virginian mariners, and their fresh competition from the new colony of Maryland, sailed to compete for Native allies along their shared and nebulous border. The failure of Virginians to control the flow of goods, information, and Marylanders in the bay—in part due to Algonquians, who sought to keep control of the shoreline and information—encouraged Virginians to turn away from the waters as the most lucrative place of Anglo-Native diplomacy and trade toward Native lands.

In chapter 5, I document how the shift in English orientation from the northern Chesapeake to the Piedmont interior, and the corresponding interest in upriver land, put profit-seeking Englishmen in charge of new local governments and in new, uncomfortably close relationships with Native people. Amid conflicts over space and resources required by Algonquians to subsist, leaders turned to the colonial legal systems to secure physically demarcated land. As property claims followed traders in the 1640s and beyond, English conceptions of personal property depended on Indigenous knowledge and colored diplomatic and trade relations with Native people they had never met before. Through the Anglo-Powhatan War of 1644 and the acceleration of land grants, landowners and traders—often one and the same—used Indigenous knowledge, routes, and places to construct plantations and surrounding boundaries from surveys to forts. Their understandings of Native politics changed as they traveled west and south in search of new trading partners beyond Algonquian territories, and as new servants ran away to nearby Algonquian towns. From the English expeditions deep into the Piedmont to local trade on the weekends, Algonquian people treated with these local governments directly, negotiating a series of agreements and boundaries between themselves and landowners.

In the 1660s, Native leaders built on, and English leaders broke with, previous strategies in their negotiations over land, as violent encounters proliferated. Native people protected their access to land with deeds, county courts, and squatters in mind as elite planters exploited the nebulous boundaries defining western and northern Virginia counties. In chapter 6, I emphasize local relationships as recorded in northern Virginia's county courts and detail how Native people contended with surveyors and planters in order to maintain access to land, roads, and water. Officials, who were also often traders and planters with their own agendas, crossed boundaries and committed overt acts of violence, and in doing so demonstrated their unwillingness to play by their own rules in their pursuit of Native land. Instead, they used Native mobility by land and water, well understood by generations of Chesapeake English settlers, to stoke fear and contest both colonial and Native boundaries. The colonial government on the James River far to the south proved ineffectual in resolving these local disputes.

Chapter 7 emphasizes how resistance to colonialism by water and land outlined in earlier chapters—over boundaries between counties, landowners, colonies, subjects under law, and inside and outside of forts and palisades—and the increasing influence of Native outsiders like the Susquehannocks, led to escalating Anglo-Native disputes. Ultimately, I argue that Bacon's Rebellion could have only occurred on Native land marred by decades of boundary disputes. In the 1670s, the English weathered a crisis of authority as colonial officials simply could not keep people in or out along their northern and western bounds as raids from outsider Native people and resistance from nonelites grew more frequent. Strategies to rectify local tensions and injustices, cultivated by settlers, bonded laborers, and Native neighbors and trade partners, proved increasingly ineffectual as connections were strained by destruction of and displacement from Native places. For colonists, local chaos that reigned before and during the rebellion resulted in increased surveillance from Virginia and Maryland authorities over the varied Anglo-Native relationships and formal boundaries that this book tracks. But for Algonquians, outsider Native and English attacks fell into a decades-long pattern of challenges to their place in the Chesapeake, one that continued long after Bacon's Rebellion. I do not discount hardening ideas about race and other reasons for unrest that also contributed to violence, but I add that concerns of Indigenous people aligned with other fears of invasions of English territory, and that bonded laborers had a resource in Native people, towns, and roads should they choose to escape or rebel. Bacon's Rebellion was a moment when fears about boundaries were realized, when the actions of enslaved people and servants, Native people, and uncontrollable elites came together in stark relief.

By 1677, the Treaty of Middle Plantation promised a new relationship between Native and English people, which accounted for the return of enslaved and indentured people who had run away, space between Native and English settlements, and surveillance of Virginians and Native people to back up these promises. Simultaneously, the decline in social mobility, rise in the number of Africans and Native enslaved laborers, and increased legal limitations on mobility changed the relationships among planter elites, Chesapeake Algonquians, and newcomers. But certain things stayed the same: Algonquians remained at the center of the politics and violence surrounding expansion, and their geopolitical knowledge enabled them to continue to transgress borders by foot or boat, navigate the waters, control and convey information, and thereby lay bare the gaps in English authority. The plantation landscape, and the exploitation of indentured and enslaved labor that accompanied it, was built on Native land. Plans and dreams of resistance to the plantation landscape, from inside and out, were also built on Native land.

–1–
The Moving People and Places of the Powhatan Chiefdom

For the people on the Kecoughtan peninsula, one day the sun set on a different horizon. In 1594, news that the longtime leader of the Kecoughtan people had passed traveled from their seat at the mouth of the Powhatan River (later renamed the James River) to the north and inland to paramount chief Wahunsenacawh.

The werowance, or hereditary leader, of the people at Kecoughtan and the surrounding inlets, fields, and marshes had long sustained them and protected them from strife. At their main town at the southern entrance to the Chesapeake Bay, they now sat uncomfortably between long-established trading roads leading to friends to the south and a new and growing threat to the north. With escalating dread the Kecoughtans had heard that distant neighbors on the Eastern Shore and Rappahannock River, and near neighbors like the Weyanokes a day's journey upriver, had added their smaller domains, complete with towns, river access, trade connections, and cornfields, as districts to Wahunsenacawh's expanding Powhatan chiefdom, called Tsenacomoco. The towns inside of these neighbors' domains sent corn and goods in tribute to the capital town of Werowocomoco at the heart of Tsenacomoco. The Kecoughtans hoped to remain independent, but the moment they feared had come. Men from the heart of Tsenacomoco approached by water and took formation in their fields. In their grief and vulnerability, the Kecoughtans watched as the core tribes of the Powhatan chiefdom attacked.

Wahunsenacawh and other werowances inside of the Powhatan chiefdom gathered authority and prestige from gathering tribute. Wahunesenacawh wanted not just tribute in corn and goods from the Kecoughtans' werowance

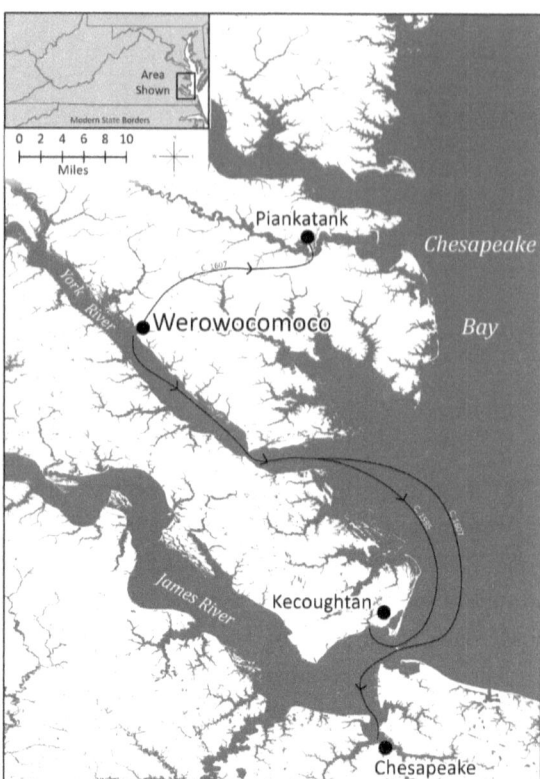

MAP 2. Powhatan invasions and migrations, 1594–1607 (Stewart Scales and Gemma Wessels)

but the place from which tribute would come, specifically the peninsula's sightline onto the bay and its trading roads. To secure these, he needed to separate the people who called themselves Kecoughtan from Kecoughtan, the place. The Kecoughtans saw many of their men and their new leader fall. Those who remained alive departed as captives, women carrying remnants of their homes and contents on their backs, in the conquering Powhatans' fleet of long canoes constructed from the trunks of trees. They moved up the bay and into the core of Powhatan territory away from home, to a different shore. Their intimacy with places to forage, fish, or shelter mattered little now. They were no longer close to trade and talk with kin, nor able to care for the bones of their leaders. Even the water itself was different; the Kecoughtans had never fished in freshwater streams like those to the north. They were no longer at Kecoughtan; they were no longer Kecoughtans. Wahunsenacawh installed his son Pochins on the peninsula, resettling a people loyal and connected by blood to the Powhatan chiefdom as the new Kecoughtans. The bay and Powhatan River, which had connected the former Kecoughtans to their identity and alliances, now became a broad boundary between them and home.[1]

This was one of several moments when the mamanatowick (paramount chief) Wahunsenacawh made war to secure and expand the boundaries of the Powhatan chiefdom. The Powhatans indeed laid claim and defended territory, but as for many Indigenous people across North America, boundaries were built not from hard mapped lines but from incorporation of people and their territories into the chiefdom's political structure, in which district tribes, each with their own leader or leaders, paid tribute to a paramount chief. Surrounding his chiefdom with managed woodlands, agricultural land, and strategic nodes like Kecoughtan, Wahunsenacawh gained control of places by controlling the movement of people and goods.[2] His actions highlight the tension between local places and the regional sources of power to which they were tethered.

Following scholars' calls to take seriously the lethality, strategies, and ambitions behind Algonquian warfare, I show how in the decades preceding the English arrival at Jamestown, the Powhatans absorbed particular sites as key defense points along the Chesapeake's periphery.[3] Here, a focus on local landscapes and connections between towns and districts complements historians' focus on the broader Powhatan chiefdom and emphasizes how the Algonquians' most dynamic leader shared control of territory with local leaders who reflected a myriad of identities. Archaeology and limited ethnographic material helps explain how Algonquians understood and adapted to local landscapes over time and how they developed shared identities based on knowledge and stewardship of a particular place in the centuries before the rise of Wahunsenacawh. In order to better secure their influence, hereditary chiefs along the Chesapeake's tributary rivers created new boundaries around who could live and travel through what places. At the end of the sixteenth century, Wahunsenacawh and the Powhatans then exploited these established communication lines between Algonquians, using canoes to keep watch and pursue war and diplomacy beyond the Chesapeake to secure the constantly shifting edges of their domains.

Finding a Home on the Water

Travel into Weyanoke territory was, for people to the south and west, a familiar and lucrative journey. Approaching Weyanoke towns that lined either side of the winding Powhatan River, visitors anticipated a feast of seafood, with sturgeon during the spring run and corn stews cooked in massive pots in the late summer.[4] Near the confluence of the Appomattox and Powhatan Rivers, people had come downriver by canoe and overland to trade among the Weyanokes for generations. The Weyanokes watched for traffic and for one another from both sides of the river, and could expect visitors and their goods to appear predictably with the seasons, like during fish runs.[5] Traders and diplomats who traveled days from town to town would hear around fires overlapping Algonquian dialects and foreign languages, some spoken in the familiar tones of family members and friends who had moved to these towns for good. Rare metals from the Great Lakes came through the territory of the non-Algonquian Monacans to the west, who controlled access to trade in the interior; from the south, people like the Nottoways traded red dyes called puccoon.[6] The werowance of the Weyanokes and his family, who organized the hospitality for visiting traders and diplomats, would accept these as gifts and provide food and goods from the water, pearls and shell beads in return. Some of these luxury items would become tribute to the Powhatan chiefdom. For Algonquians, rivers served as conduits in multiple ways, connecting them to other people, towns, and nations sharing the same waterways.[7]

People migrated and connected with one another along Chesapeake waterways over thousands of years, even as the waters themselves changed. By 3000 BCE, with the melting of ice floes, the Chesapeake's rivers established their present rhythm and shape. Low-lying marshes, rich in plant and animal life, proliferated. People had already lived on the coast for thousands of years by then, gathering and maintaining knowledge as expert foragers, and as the landscape changed they cared for domesticated plants like sunflower and marsh elder.[8] Between the coastal ecosystems, inland rivers and forests, and transitions in between them, the Chesapeake's people managed and harvested from distinct ecosystems often within sight of one another, or by moving seasonally among them.[9] Archaeologists working along the York River believe that Algonquians migrated into this rich environment from the north or west around 200 CE, clearing forests along riverbanks to make room alongside their hosts.[10] At the same time, residents began to orient toward estuaries for subsistence, adding marsh plants to their pots and incorporating fresh and dried fish and oysters into their diet year-round.[11]

People brought maize east over the Blue Ridge Mountains around 1100 CE and changed how people lived and traveled.[12] With the introduction of maize, many people left smaller settlements to be nearer larger towns, almost always located within a two-minute walk of the waterways.[13] Patterns in agriculture, fishing, hunting, and foraging ordered their lives into five seasons. Hereditary chiefs grasped control of corn surpluses and trade, storing corn paid in tribute and limiting access to foreign goods like sought-after copper used for body adornment. People who paid tribute and received gifts from chiefs were part of a chiefdom, and excavated ceramics are similar between sites within a chiefdom when compared to neighboring chiefdoms beyond, with shared and distinct pottery practices reflecting new cultural borders.[14] Between 1200 and 1500 CE, prosperous southern Chesapeake communities developed the long-distance trade, agricultural economies, and politics that ultimately fed the rise of the Powhatan paramount chiefdom. Indeed, sometime after 1200 Algonquians built what would become the largest town of the chiefdom at Werowocomoco, adjacent to the largest marsh on what is now the York River.[15]

Algonquians developed and maintained alliances, enmities, trading partnerships, dialects, and kinship surrounding the rivers. The switch to maize agriculture in the Chesapeake and beyond meant a shift in how Algonquian people interacted with people beyond their towns: archaeologists have uncovered evidence of less long-range travel and more short-range movement to nearby places, and argue that this led to increased attachment to place and development of territory.[16] As other leaders to the west and along the Chesapeake began to direct military campaigns and the flow of goods through their domains, Algonquian werowances did the same.

Anthropologists disagree about the extent to which werowances, and Wahunsenacawh, ruled through persuasion or might.[17] What is clear is that at the local level, leaders retained power through consent and at least in part through the promise of defense in a crisis. They established rank by controlling and exploiting the movement of food and of luxury goods like those that came through the Weyanoke towns, in particular copper, exchanging valuable goods and redistributing them along lines of alliance or kinship.[18] By 1600, along the rivers' peninsulas, the Chesapeake supported several independent nations representing multiple political and social structures, headed by chiefs or great men. The largest was the Powhatan chiefdom, which at its broadest reach claimed tribute from around thirteen thousand people divided into around thirty-four constituent chiefdoms.

Inside of the Powhatan chiefdom, proximity to the rivers cultivated identity for local Algonquian places. Early European maps of Algonquian districts plot settlements in tandem to rivers; for example, the cartographer of the circa 1610 Kraus map drew towns as a half-moon extension of the closest river or tributary.[19] Waterways were a reference point for identifying places and people. The Kecoughtans knew their neighbors as "People on the Great River" (Chesapeakes) and "Corner Fishing-Place" (Nansemond), acknowledgment of the sustenance and connection the James River provided.[20] The ocean bounded the Algonquians to the east and the falls of the rivers of the Chesapeake Bay watershed to the west. Waterways also led to the wider world. The four major rivers traveled by Powhatans—the Powhatan (later James), Pamunkey (later York), Rappahannock, and Potomac—flowed into the bay, creating the three peninsulas of the lower Chesapeake and tying together the Coastal Plain, Piedmont, and mountains. The waters' length from mouth to head varied from the York River, with headwaters stopping at the core of the Powhatan chiefdom, to the four-hundred-mile Potomac River, with connecting waterways covering fifteen thousand square miles. To explain to a colonist how the rivers came from the mountains, one Algonquian emphasized the unity of the four and their connection to the west, intertwining his fingers to show a traveler how land and water met.[21]

Natives habitually traversed creeks, rivers, and the bay in watercraft to make trade, alliances, and war. Dugout canoes were relatively simple if time-consuming to build, adaptable to a variety of needs from transport to trade and ideal for a spectrum of waterways, from tributary waters to estuaries. Constructed of a single log burned and scraped hollow, these vessels required relatively few tools and only a patient hand to fan the flames. Unlike trees used for ships' masts, canoe logs did not have to be especially straight or tall, and Algonquians chose fallen or burnt trees long enough to hold between ten and forty people.[22] With no keel or ballast, dugout canoes were prone to capsize or flip, yet men and women learned to handle them with ease. They could transport dozens of people toward war or trade, and canoes proved equally important in moving news and diplomatic emissaries.

Rivers connected to overland roads, tying together long-distance trade and short-distance communication.[23] On each peninsula, a set of roads probably ran parallel to the larger rivers, joining each town in every chiefdom and skirting impassable areas, intersecting at the mouths and heads of waterways to connect circuitous roads. Daily traffic made at least some roads sunny, wide, and obvious to outsider travelers, yet the overland routes themselves could also be riverine and pass through or lead to estuaries and marshes affected by the tides.[24] Thus, visitors from beyond the region could expect to make an amphibious approach, floating down one of the major Chesapeake rivers east toward the bay, leaving canoes on a bank or secreted in marsh grass, and walking to a town.[25] With bark and saplings, Algonquians manufactured and maintained bridges over minor waterways and muck with poles nested horizontally on X-shaped struts fixed into the banks or marsh.[26] Algonquians shared similar landscapes and the technologies to traverse them, intelligible to their fellow travelers.

Use of that shared landscape was controlled, at least in part, by werowances, who had a clear obligation to maintain the appropriate flow of information and goods inside of their districts. In 1609, for example, a colonist reported that a Patawomeck man on the Potomac River was put to death for a murder he had only witnessed as a passerby, bribed by the culprits into silence. The man had intelligence—maybe even only traveling from one side of the town to another—but had withheld knowledge of wrongdoing. Another executed man, a robber, was knocked on the head and thrown into the fire not only for stealing from a traveler but specifically for taking trade items of copper and beads, items vested with social power and controlled by werowances. His transgression carried extra weight. To maintain authority over goods and people, perhaps the leader of the Patawomecks needed to assert and reassert authority over goods and people in transit, since these leaders also gained some authority and relationships with trading partners through accruing those goods.[27]

While werowances policed movement and the bounds of acceptable behavior, everyone shaped daily and seasonal movement. The long roads ran from the Great Lakes to the Gulf of Mexico, commingling regional powers, goods, and languages, while local routes connected towns sometimes less than a mile apart and usually very near navigable water.[28] Adult men hunted, traded, conducted diplomacy, and warred seasonally using roads that took them long distances beyond the region—colonists recorded that invaders came and plundered, so Chesapeake residents likely reciprocated—and when trading they took with them goods made by women such as shell beads and processed hides. They also relied on food cooked by women and hospitality provided by women when they stopped.[29] In this and their everyday work foraging and gathering material for mats, rope, and house construction, women developed intelligence about the landscapes and peoples surrounding their towns different from their male counterparts, who brought back knowledge and stuff from more distant destinations.[30]

Algonquians also keyed into natural landscape barriers that protected local communities and served as habitats for natural resources. The fall line running north–south across the major Chesapeake rivers—a boundary line between Algonquians and culturally distinct Siouan people to the west like the Monacans—was only seasonally inhabited at the turn of the seventeenth century, allowing both groups to hunt the deer that flourished there in the periodic absence of human intrusion. The fall line was also the geographical point at which traveling by watercraft from one side to the other became difficult, providing protection from invaders.[31] Closer to home, the woodlands and estuaries on the coastal peninsulas provided women with diverse grounds to forage. Chesapeake people used wetlands on the interiors of the peninsulas and mainland to disappear, or as cover, during counterattacks.[32] According to later European accounts, Algonquians developed foraging skills through movement along water and overland across seasons, mentally mapping the "places most frequented with Deere, Beasts, Fish, Foule, Roots, and Berries" through "their continuall ranging, and travel."[33] Men and women both had extensive knowledge of the grounds uninhabited by people and the waters around them for this purpose, even as they changed seasonally or shifted with nearby watercourses.

Like managed woodlands, sacred places were local; anthropologists note that Algonquian cosmologies and histories imbued nearby landmarks from human-made stone piles to funerary structures with meaning, turning them into places to ask for and give thanks for well-being for their town or district and for safe travel beyond.[34] Algonquian men asked nearby priests about where to hunt deer within their districts, and worried women farmers asked for the aid of conjurers who could divert rain from one place to another.[35] The local and regional geography of the rivers and the act of traveling them gave Algonquians overlapping mental maps of the Chesapeake region and of their spiritual world. Algonquians understood that the rivers bound them together and defined the known and unknown.

By the sixteenth century, the Chesapeake's geography and waterways supported Native people as they cultivated chiefdoms along the shores and sustained new political hierarchies in agricultural towns. Mobility on the Chesapeake's rivers—to trade, hunt and fish, or travel from town to town, supported by technology like canoes—complemented this rootedness. Waterways, roads, and what people did on them became the concern of werowances, who came to power in part through the goods and agricultural bounty supported by the region. Developing knowledge of their locale and surroundings, men and women on the coast decided the nature of their connections to other Algonquians and the people beyond. Algonquian sustenance and safety relied on the riverine geography, even as it connected them to the North American continent and Atlantic seaboard broadly.

Alliances, Rivalries, and Consolidation

Inside of this landscape, networks of smaller chiefdoms coalesced into paramount chiefdoms and alliances. Wahunsenacawh was only one of many leaders in the southeast and on the North American continent to consolidate authority and resources into a chiefdom. Since around 900 or 1000 CE, chiefdoms grew on fertile riverbanks on the eastern seaboard alongside the corn and other farmed foods upon which they depended. To the west of the Powhatans, between 800 and 1500, many kinship-based societies coalesced into culturally diverse towns, with subsistence and cultural practices like growing maize in fertile soil along rivers and building monumental pyramidal mounds. Leaders of Native towns may have joined forces to repel mobile invaders or leaders of chiefdoms who might expand into their territory in pursuit of new resources. Drought and weather changes may have also accelerated conflict, particularly as people who had moved into wooded areas between settlements to forage and hunt encountered one another.[36]

By the 1580s, Wahunsenacawh had orchestrated a complex tribute system built on corn and luxury goods from his capital on the York River at Werowocomoco. As a Powhatan werowance himself, he inherited leadership of Powhatan, Arrohateck, Appamattuck, Pamunkey, Youghtamond, and Mattaponi chiefdoms and districts, all in the fertile areas north of the James River; the other territories he claimed along the rivers were according to English chroniclers attacked or intimidated like the Kecoughtans into accepting tributary status.[37] Influencing polities settled at a greater distance from Werowocomoco also expanded Powhatan control of tribute and trade in luxury goods at the core of their consolidation of power.[38] People made jewelry and other ornaments from shell beads and copper, gifting these goods and corn to the werowances, who then passed them to the paramount chief and his family. Werowances from across the districts over which the Powhatans exerted influence gave them corn, beads, copper, pearls, and meat.[39] The exchange was folded into feasting rituals in single towns and repeated on a grander scale at special places central to the entire chiefdom, like Powhatans' capital at Werowocomoco. Through the gifting rituals at which these goods were exchanged, the Powhatan were able to incorporate strangers and other polities into their world.[40] In exchange, incorporated groups on the periphery received protection comparable to the chiefdoms closer to the Powhatan core and access to goods brought in from different corners of the chiefdom. The consolidation of political power happened nearby the Powhatans too: the Monacans to the west of the fall line had joined into a separate alliance between people who spoke a Siouan language as early as 1000.[41] Along the Potomac River and into the northern Chesapeake, as a seventeenth-century Piscataway leader recounted, Algonquians were pulled into what became the Piscataway chiefdom under a leader from the Eastern Shore who "imbrace[d] and cover[ed] them all" sometime between 1270 and 1400.[42] Archaeology demonstrates that Chesapeake cooking fires during this time held regional types of pottery roughly aligning with the areas occupied by these different chiefdoms. Algonquians had thus long known where one domain ended and another began.[43]

However, changing climate and outsiders proved threatening to Algonquians in the Chesapeake. By the time Wahunsenacawh came to power, many of the chiefdoms to the west had collapsed, perhaps due to resource strain and military encounters with other Native groups or with the Spanish.[44] The Chesapeake region had also experienced extensive droughts that caused famine in the 1560s and 1570s, while outside invaders were an endemic threat. Spanish invaders had first explored in the 1560s and then attempted to colonize Algonquian territory in the 1570s, their missionaries visiting Native towns along the James and York Rivers and mariners sailing to the northern reaches of the bay. The Spanish missionaries were put to death in 1571 by a group of Algonquians led or aided by a man who had been taken captive in the Chesapeake by a Spanish mariner a decade earlier and had returned to his family.[45] The relatively new threats heightened concerns about the future: Wahunsenacawh had heard of or seen himself the toll of European diseases and was certainly aware of the havoc European ships traveling in the region had caused for decades.[46] Up the rivers, seasonal raiding of groups like the Susquehannocks and Massawomecks from the north side of the bay, who excelled at amphibious raids on Algonquian peoples, threatened the safety of all in the densely populated northern Chesapeake.[47] After 1575, the Susquehannocks and Massawomecks began raiding with increased frequency, and the Susquehannocks placed trading outposts in the bay that signaled their long-term interest in the Chesapeake.

When these outsiders traded furs to Europeans like the French to the north, they gained European weaponry and tools. By the turn of the seventeenth century, they began to pull Chesapeake Native people into their sphere of influence, as captives and through intimidation.[48] Outsiders' access to goods and the ease of travel by water threatened Algonquians along the Potomac River and on the Eastern Shore, many of whom abandoned or consolidated towns and leadership by the seventeenth century.[49] The ability of these raids to frighten Algonquians on the fringe of the Powhatan chiefdom demonstrated how the nebulous nature of the chiefdom's boundaries shifted the balance of power locally. Along the Potomac River, werowances paid tribute to Wahunsenacawh in order to gain military alliances against northern neighbors, but as a populous and powerful group themselves, smaller chiefdoms like the Patawomecks maintained their own relations with their neighbors. The Powhatans might have held these people loosely in their orbit, but their separate use of movement through diplomacy and trade emphasized these chiefdoms' autonomy.[50]

Displacing the Kecoughtans in 1594 therefore allowed the Powhatans to simultaneously expand and surveil the edges of their influence over smaller tributary chiefdoms, a central strategy the Powhatans employed on their eastern fringe to secure their border. The Kecoughtans sought independence, so the Powhatans quelled their dissent by bringing survivors to live at the core of their territory. Even more importantly, the location of Kecoughtan allowed the Powhatans to see vessels entering the bay or the Chesapeake's river system. Across the river from the Kecoughtans, Wahunsenacawh also distributed the territory of an independent neighboring chiefdom, the Chesapeakes, to a newly absorbed group, the Nansemonds.[51] Alongside new farming land, their territory allowed a different view of the bay and mouth of the Powhatan River, too wide to reliably and quickly see or cross. Controlling the tip of the southern peninsula protected the inland rivers and trade routes from maritime interlopers or invaders. In 1608, Wahunsenacawh rehomed the remaining Kecoughtans to territory in Piankatank, on the tip of the Middle Peninsula, where Powhatan warriors had annihilated a different group, taking war prizes back to Werowocomoco for display.[52] Through a mix of exchange and threat, the Powhatans attempted to curtail the mobility of their neighbors and establish loyalty and eyes on the boundary.

The Powhatan chiefdom had moving boundaries, but Algonquian people within the chiefdom understood their boundaries with their neighbors through day-to-day life.[53] The Powhatans' growing power was built on and complemented smaller, preexisting economic and social exchanges among districts. Overland routes linked the Powhatans to a continental trade network, but an established network of local water routes and roads proved more important as everyday channels. As Wahunsenacawh brought groups from farther afield into his orbit during the expansion of his empire, members of each smaller chiefdom adjusted their local networks of exchange to accommodate tributes and alliances. John Smith wrote that Powhatans "all knowe their severall landes, and habitations, and limits, to fish, fowle, or hunt in" relative to one another. With each smaller chiefdom operating inside of its respective territory as a cooperative neighbor to others, tribute from each found its way to Wahunsenacawh.[54] The Powhatans' system of territories was built to sustain cooperation and the tribute system into the future.[55]

The Powhatans also harnessed local networks to uphold the tribute system and boundaries between districts and Algonquians beyond the chiefdom, taking advantage of local adaptations to the landscape. Every chiefdom functioned differently based partially on its surrounding resources, from soil quality to trade routes. Anthropologist Helen C. Rountree mentions just a few examples from the core of the chiefdom: "The Appamattucks were a conduit to luxury goods like puccoon [a red dye]. . . . The Pamunkeys were the guardians of the holiest place in the region, Uttamussak. . . . The Youghtanunds, and the Mattaponis could be a breadbasket of the organization."[56] Groups on the fringes that had their own political relationships beyond, like the Weyanokes to the south, served to bring outside trade goods to the core. Likewise, the populous Patawomecks to the north could reinforce a counterattack on outsider invaders with the Powhatans' help. Eastern Shore people's consistent supply of cultivated and gathered foodstuffs, and luxury goods and mediums of exchange like clamshell beads, tied them to the Powhatans despite distance.[57]

At the local level, prestige goods, tribute corn, and people were funneled to old places that had been granted new meaning. The previous generation of Powhatan people no doubt revered both their temple at Uttamussack and their capital town, Werowocomoco, as important places, but the resources of additional chiefdoms transformed them into signals to outsiders of a successful, large-scale polity.[58] Priests stuffed the temple at Uttamussack full of copper, beads, European metal goods, and pearls, all of which were sourced through the extensive riverine trade networks Powhatans worked to strengthen.[59] Traded objects and the routes those objects took placed the Powhatans as a charismatic and geographic node in the prestige goods economy, in which precious objects were traded and possessed primarily by elites as markers of status. By water, smaller chiefdoms reinforced access to and control over treasured places and the things inside of them, a display of power apparent to outsiders as well as other Powhatans.

The trade in luxury goods shaped diplomacy beyond the Powhatans' territory. For example, Algonquians' nearest source of the valuable red dye puccoon was in Nottoway territory, Iroquoian speakers distinct from the Algonquians a three days' journey away from the Pamunkey River.[60] Yet the Powhatans did not challenge the territory of the Nottoway, perhaps because of the Nottoways' ties to the Tuscarora, more powerful neighbors to the south.[61] According to archaeologists, communication was swift along the nearby main fall line road, running north–south; the rocky shoals allowed for relatively dry and quick river crossings useful to war or trade parties of the Powhatans.[62] Desirable resources and nearby roads made these two distinct peoples long-term acquaintances, if not friends. Although not necessary to sustain everyday life, prestige goods shipped north via river roads buttressed Algonquian elites' displays of wealth and power; their ability to redistribute goods to tribute-paying chiefs and elites also brought influence.

Other non-Algonquian neighbors and outsiders provided access to trade that shored up the power of the Powhatan chiefdom's leadership. The Monacans to the west, an alliance of agricultural towns, amassed a large territory surrounding the capital Rassawek at the confluence of the Powhatan and Fluvanna Rivers. Despite little archaeological evidence of earlier enmities with their Algonquian neighbors, the Monacans' relationships with the Powhatans were sometimes hostile in the years when Wahunsenacawh was expanding his chiefdom, perhaps seasonally in cyclical warfare or as deer brought both to hunt in the forests between their territories.[63] But they historically traded goods, pots, and clay pipes from the Shenandoah Valley for shell beads and pendants from Patawomeck peoples to the north of the Powhatan core.[64] Copper sourced through Monacan territory was the most important prestige good for Powhatan leaders.[65] Werowances controlled the flow of this prestige good found nowhere on the Coastal Plain, and Wahunsenacawh was aware of the very distant Great Lakes supply.[66] Maintaining control over and negotiating the movement of goods like copper across territorial boundaries increasingly fell to leaders who negotiated for goods with their neighbors. After all, as archaeologists point out, the

Powhatan chiefdom grew between the ocean and a continental network of nations and in an area relatively bereft of mineral wealth—they relied on this trade for prestige goods.[67]

While the structure and size of the chiefdom was unprecedented in the Chesapeake, it relied on tributaries' preexisting, regional relationships like these with non-Algonquian and Algonquian neighbors. In 1608, for example, a Mannahoac man from the western portions of the Rappahannock River reported that because routine burning of the forests facilitated easy travel into certain territories, he knew the Powhatans, Monacans, and Massawomecks who lived farther into the mountains. He had only heard of an additional three polities beyond the mountains themselves, however.[68] His place on the Rappahannock River dictated his firsthand knowledge, unlikely to be replicated by peoples to the south or east. The Weyanoke to the south had probably heard of the Massawomecks but were much more familiar with the Iroquoian-speaking Meherrins and Nottoways to the immediate south of their own towns with whom they traded. Meanwhile, the Powhatans and the Monacans might harass one another, but people on the Eastern Shore were largely separated from their conflict by the wide bay. They never mentioned the Monacans, even if they enjoyed copper that came from Monacan territory, because they had more reason to worry about Susquehannock canoes.[69] Proximity and relationships predating the expansion of the Powhatan chiefdom decided daily interactions and placed certain groups in either vulnerable or lucrative positions.

At the end of the sixteenth century, Wahunsenacawh and the Powhatans had built Tsenacomoco to its height, a chiefdom ranging from the south side of what is now the south side of the James River north to the Potomac, and parts of the Eastern Shore west to the fall line. They harnessed riverine networks to pull complementary goods and connections from each tributary werowance and redistribute people inside of their domain, entangling Algonquians in tribute, kinship, and military relationships. The resources and places inside of the smaller chiefdoms comprising Powhatan domains provided the Powhatans with their power, not the other way around.[70] Tributary werowances leveraged their access to trade goods and local resources extant before the rise of the Powhatans, who relied on their local networks to gain prestige goods. Even at Tsenacomoco's height, however, incorporation and coercion were never complete processes, and outsiders like the Massawomecks and Susquehannocks threatened the Powhatans' expanding boundaries. The Powhatans, at the center of this riverine landscape, grew powerful from this network, vulnerable as it was to threats.

Visitors to Werowocomoco saw the trappings of well-traveled and well-connected people: an enormous fleet of canoes safely tucked into marsh grass off the York River, scalps of people from a recently defeated chiefdom on display, shell bead embroidery and shell bead necklaces on women, feasts of corn and wild game. These objects, representing military might, trade, and successful farming, demonstrated the regional power of Tsenacomoco.[71] The leadership of the Powhatans addressed outsider threats and harnessed both local and outsider exchange networks to thrive on trade and military force.

That might was built on a web of local networks, as the map on the back of "Powhatan's mantle," or cape, demonstrates. The few seventeenth- and early eighteenth-century Indigenous maps in existence underscore the importance of social, political, and familial relationships and spheres of influence rather than formal geographical borders.[72] Maps are material manifestations of group identity and interdependencies, and of relationships to outsiders. The makers of the Powhatans' only extant map, kept in a museum in the United Kingdom today, distilled the Chesapeake's countless identities and political relationships into a single object. "Powhatan's mantle" is a conceptualization of the Powhatan chiefdom sewn of Powhatan trade goods, featuring four deerskins and thousands of shell beads. A human figure looms large at the center, flanked by animals and surrounded by thirty-four circles created through concentric rings of beading, which, according to John Smith, was the number of districts Powhatan claimed under his control at the time of English contact.[73]

Each circle is nearly identical in size and shape: rather than map rivalries or relationships between diverse Algonquian peoples, they are homogenized in their orbit around a single individual. The designers chose white beads rather than the rarer and more valuable purple beads. Anthropologists postulate that the color white was associated at the time with civil peace, perhaps a reference to the alliance between each district and the safety guaranteed by a powerful new leader.[74] Whether all thirty-four lesser chiefs truly orbited Wahunsenacawh and his heirs cannot be known, but much like other conquerors' assertions, his "mantle" was a claim that they did. His influence crossed rivers, gathered together and channeled resources and goods, and halted invading outsiders.

The Chesapeake Bay environs supported dramatic changes and choices for Indigenous people: a movement to agriculture and an identity tied to place for people who planted corn by the rivers; the rise of chiefdoms alongside surpluses in corn; and by the end of the sixteenth century, a chiefdom of Algonquian-speaking people that grew outward from the James River through persuasion and violence against smaller chiefdoms. The Powhatans were reliant on the connectivity that brought prestige goods like copper to the coast, even as the same connectivity also brought violence. Accordingly, its leaders sought to control how people moved through tributary chiefdoms, and forcibly displaced and surveilled people in strategic positions. Tsenacomoco represented a formidable military and trading presence on the eastern seaboard. Leaders of the Powhatan chiefdom did not maintain hard borders, but they did react to transgressing outsiders and insiders with violence, using rivers as their conduits of influence in order to control access to waterways and shorelines.

When broader Chesapeake politics and diplomacy shifted, some things remained the same. Over centuries, Algonquians had developed particular ways of living by the water, growing maize, harvesting seafood, foraging, traveling, and finding refuge from outsiders in the woodlands and estuaries over centuries. Algonquians maintained networks and boundaries on local levels that complemented neighbors' needs for sustenance and trade. They were no strangers to outsider threats, even as new ones moved into the Chesapeake with European weapons. While they relied on trade connections, the Powhatans also relied on Algonquian networks across the Coastal Plain, and the knowledge of these places, to sustain their expansion as they faced increasingly dangerous and uncontrollable threats.

– 2 –

Watching Carefully in the Bay, 1607–1614

From the shores along the Potomac River in 1613, one of the Patawomecks' lesser werowances, Iopassus, saw the outline of a familiar ship. Algonquians had studied the movements of English ships of different sizes and configurations cutting through their districts across the flat and broad span of water. The watercraft pulled close to shore to trade and visit, dropped anchor to fish, and sounded the depths and explored shallows. Their occupants watched their Native observers from the decks. This was Captain Samuel Argall's vessel, sizable enough to carry forty men and supplies. Iopassus and a young interpreter, Henry Spelman, then living with the Patawomecks, had the previous year exchanged the creation stories of the Bible's Book of Genesis and the Algonquians' Great Hare aboard one of Argall's ships.[1] Iopassus and Argall had become adopted brothers and powerful allies during Argall's previous travels; both were diplomats from their respective nations.[2] The English had come this time with only a few men, to trade for corn with people friendly to them. But a mutual acquaintance, Pocahontas, had come at the same time to the Patawomecks' shores to trade.[3] As Iopassus soon learned, Argall's plan to procure supplies changed abruptly when he learned of Pocahontas's presence.

Argall and Iopassus both understood the vulnerability of English life in Powhatan territory. To the Patawomecks, Argall represented Jamestown, its skilled sailors and military men and their accoutrements made from copper and glass valuable across Algonquian trade networks. An experienced sailor and soldier, Argall used his ship to develop diplomatic ties between Jamestown and the Patawomecks, driven by Jamestown's need for food and people following three years of war with the Powhatans to the south. Invoking their brotherly bond, Argall asked Iopassus to help him capture Pocahontas and purchase a peace with her father, Wahunsenacawh, in exchange for goods and goodwill.[4] Iopassus probably sought out the head werowance of the Patawomecks for input, then agreed to assist Argall. Maybe he was reluctantly fulfilling a familial obligation to Argall, or maybe he calculated that a peace between the Powhatans and the English would relieve the diplomatic and resource pressures on the Patawomecks: both Powhatans and English leaders had turned to the Patawomecks for alliance. The Patawomecks lived at some distance from the Powhatan core to the south but maintained relationships with the Powhatans. Meanwhile, the English in particular sailed up the Potomac River looking for corn. In either case, he, his wife, and Pocahontas boarded Argall's ship for a meal at his suggestion. After dinner the sailors stopped Pocahontas from disembarking with Iopassus, to Pocahontas's visible alarm and despair. Likely hoping to avoid Pocahontas's discovering his involvement and conveying it to her family, the Patawomeck guests feigned a "howle and crie" of protest at their kinsman Argall's "betrayal."[5] The Patawomecks left the ship with a kettle and some other trade goods, and Argall left with his ship laden with corn and with Pocahontas, who was held hostage until the Powhatans could ransom her.

Pocahontas's travels connected disparate places—her father's capital at Werowocomoco, the English settlement at the mouth of the James, the Patawomeck town, the dark and damp interior of the ship—that held residents uncertain of their shifting relationships with people at other places. Pocahontas's movement fueled tension between these places, exactly the type of movement at the fringes of his chiefdom that Wahunsenacawh sought to prevent.

English settlers formally planted Virginia in 1607 in Paspahegh territory in the Powhatan chiefdom's domain, to look for waterways through North America and to gather precious metals and other resources. They were governed by leaders appointed by the Virginia Company, a joint-stock venture with investors who funded the ships and supplies necessary for travel.[6] The Powhatans pulled the English into a trading relationship for weapons, farming implements, and precious goods, and Powhatan guides controlled English movement through their part of the Chesapeake. Here and elsewhere along the eastern seaboard, well-traveled, skilled, and knowledgeable English mariners confronted well-traveled, skilled, and knowledgeable Algonquian mariners. For leaders and sailors with limited knowledge of Tsenacomoco's guts and ditches and the caprices of its weather and wildlife, however, establishing claims to the Chesapeake's rivers meant reliance on Native people and places for understanding and sustenance. The landscape itself complicated attempts to establish communication and authority: while river mouths were established centers of trade, exploration, and European claims to land in the Americas, as settlers spread upriver and up the bay in the first decade of colonization, English leaders could not ignore the difficulty of communicating quickly between outposts and could not totally control the movement and trade between Algonquians and English sailors nearby.[7]

Powhatans maintained the upper hand in the initial decade of Jamestown's settlement by using their superior knowledge about the Chesapeake, orchestrating the experiences of English emissaries and interpreters along the Chesapeake's waterways. Leveraging a network of districts, the Powhatans deployed longstanding strategies for selectively sharing knowledge and bounding the movement of tributaries and strangers like the English. In response, both Powhatan tributaries and other Native people beyond Powhatan control sought their own access to English trade goods and maritime might, while English sailors sought to loosen Powhatan control over waterways. Like Powhatans drawing on earlier experiences in gaining control over their territories in the Chesapeake, the English made sense of the Chesapeake landscape through expeditions in Europe, from cataloging and mapping host populations to pursuing exploration by ship. In order to survive, let alone accrue a profit and wrest some control over exchange and diplomacy from Powhatan leaders, settlers needed to understand their environment and understand the people occupying it.[8] The Powhatans did their best to control that knowledge.

When Argall leveraged his bond with Iopassus, built in part on the sharing of stories, he betrayed a mutually understood ugly truth: the pursuit of knowledge also meant seeking exploitable fissures in "Indian" and "English" politics. When Iopassus howled and cried as he left Pocahontas in Argall's hands, he understood that the ship would take with her news of the capture to the Powhatans. Argall saw the geographical distance between the Patawomecks on the Potomac River and the Powhatans on the York River, and that damaging a Patawomeck-Powhatan alliance helped the English. Argall and the English saw exchange and power in a similar light as their Powhatan hosts, concentrated in local leadership but connected to a continent of networks. For English and Powhatan leadership, their authority in specific localities, particularly on the borders of the Powhatan chiefdom, remained ill-defined and negotiable as people sailed and paddled through them.[9] That made trade and movement, as in the exchange of Pocahontas for a kettle, exploitable by, but also a threat to, elites in both large polities.

While the Powhatans attempted to control the flow of prestige goods and outsiders to maintain authority, English leaders, to ensure their survival in the new colony of Virginia, sought to take control of strategically useful places but also to control the movement and fates of their own discontented people residing in James Fort and Native towns beyond. Even with elite strategies to contain movement on both sides, with access to broader networks people in neither English nor Powhatan domains behaved as they were supposed to. They instead established patterns of illicit movement. Unfree Europeans ran away from the fort and wandered the woods; Native people traded aboard English vessels, behaved violently, spread rumors, and formed alliances beyond Powhatan control. As English outsiders and Algonquians from multiple nations sought intelligence and diplomacy through travel and trade, they revealed internal divisions and weaknesses useful to the other.

Ultimately, English inability to respect Powhatan networks and boundaries and to control their own people led to conflict. In the first Anglo-Powhatan War from 1609 to 1614, Powhatans fought to preserve their control over trade in prestige goods and diplomacy along the rivers that had helped them rise to power.[10] As their settlements expanded, English elites made new efforts to control the movement of people through their domains: evolving policies and settlement patterns broadly excluded non-Christian Native people, and new geographic boundaries threatened local relationships between English and Native Chesapeake residents.[11] Attempts at enforcement of English and Powhatan boundaries would not have occurred without resistance cultivated on the water and in the woods, and would not have been possible without appropriated Native knowledge, networks, and land. Nevertheless, those often risky relationships established by water on the fringes of the chiefdom, like the brotherhood between Iopassus and Argall, helped the settlers survive and find leverage against Wahunsenacawh.

Understanding and Dividing Places in English

For English military men, understandings of the Chesapeake's landscape and people were cast against the background of other European colonization efforts—but on-the-ground knowledge of the Chesapeake Bay itself came through both the violence and hospitality of Native people. Military men comprised a large contingent of the early English arrivals at Jamestown, and their ideas informed the construction of colonial Virginia's built environment along the Powhatan River, what they called the James. Other English people followed as laborers and settlers, with ways of understanding their surrounding landscapes different from those of military commanders, which informed their experience of a new environment. Among the English at Jamestown, ideas about space and boundaries were neither uniform nor uncontested.[12]

Armed with stories of Spanish conquest and the failed Roanoke venture to the south, the English sailed into the bay in April 1607 and scoured the Chesapeake's rivers for Native polities and people that could ensure their survival.[13] In the initial days of the 1607 arrival, Native people met English exploration with either avoidance or violence. Where the English first landed, men with bows in their mouths charged at the settlers, injuring several before the newcomers discharged their firearms. A little over a week after arriving, however, on the north side of the Powhatan River, the colonists met with the werowance of Paspahegh and began diplomatic relations.[14] The English settled on an island they understood to be inside of Paspahegh territory. The site was partway up the Powhatan River, "according to the name of a principall country that lyeth vpon it."[15] Jamestown colonists constructed a wooden triangular fort during the summer of 1607 on a piece of elevated ground on the James, complete with bulwarks and artillery.[16] The Paspahegh werowance allowed it after the English had already begun constructing the fort, since it was hunting-and-gathering land on the edge of his territory.

Within a month of the ships' arrival, Native attacks against English people at the fort showed that relationships with some of the Powhatans had soured as the English began gathering information on the Chesapeake's people in earnest. Leader and skilled negotiator for the English John Smith explored the James River that summer and by September successfully visited non-Powhatan Chickahominy territory in search of more Native food, which either because of drought or bad feelings had ceased to come from the Powhatans. The Powhatans captured Smith on one of these trips and took him through their territory to the capital at Werowocomoco. There, Smith's observations and conversations with the Powhatans earned him a trove of information about the connections between the Chesapeake chiefdoms and Wahunsenacawh's authority. The following year, Smith sailed to the northern Chesapeake to meet outsider Native people like the Massawomecks and Susquehannocks, effectively discovering the outer boundaries of the Powhatan chiefdom and meeting Wahunsenacawh's enemies.[17]

English elites relied on earlier colonial precedents for how to settle the Chesapeake.[18] The Spanish had for a century used the mouths of rivers to gain knowledge and control of Native territory, moving from the coast inward. In doing so, they worked to establish a stake to both waterways and land and to establish themselves at the top of Native political structures in order to dictate the flow of goods and labor.[19] Indeed, instructions from England divorced from the reality of the Powhatans' control of the Chesapeake advised settlers to ally with the Powhatans' neighbors, collect tribute in food from Algonquians using captives as collateral, and bring Native children into English settlements.[20] The English fitfully attempted to follow these instructions, and also erected fortifications in fear of Spanish attacks and Spanish alliances with Native people. Algonquians could share intelligence of the landscape with their enemies too, and the English were advised not to allow Native settlement between the fort and the sea, "least they be guides to your enemies."[21] To prove the promise of extensive English settlement, John Smith discussed the Chesapeake and its inhabitants in descriptive terms—long and flat horizons, bounties of birds and fish, towns by the shore—rather than in precise measurements. Smith's eyewitness account of trade and diplomacy with Indigenous people demonstrated the reach of English exploration upriver but also revealed Native use and control of the same waterways.[22]

English mapmakers created another precedent for English claims on Indigenous land and played a key role in depicting an orderly and understandable landscape. Atlases of counties in the British Isles, like those by Christopher Saxton and John Speed, set a precedent for illustrated and uniform maps depicting major towns, parklands, and county boundaries with mathematical precision, accompanied by a description and history of each county. Mammoth efforts to map the British Isles had served the interests of both landlords in England, who sought with surveys to replace the ambiguous community processes of marking property boundaries, and colonizers in Ireland, who commodified Irish land for Protestant settlers. Viewers of Speed's 1610 map of Cork saw illustrations of a well-ordered town at the center of British occupation, contrasting with stories in the atlas about "the wild Irish" and "Christianitie in Ireland how it decaied."[23] Sir John Davies, an English official working to complete colonization in Ireland, recognized the connection between mapping the lands of Irish rebels and mapping the lands of hostile Indigenous people in the Chesapeake. The point of the survey of County Tyrone, he wrote in 1609, was not only that future investors in stolen land "know what Land he hath heer, & how to distribute it" but also to serve as "a special meane hereafter of . . . suppressing rebellions." The English had been hindered by a lack of knowledge of colonized people's resources and places of defense in a landscape "so obscure & unknown to the English heer, as the most inland part of Virginia." To Davies's mind, the lack of intelligence had been the central hurdle: "Now we know all the passages, have penetrated every thickett & fast place, have taken notice of every notorious Tree or bush, All wch will not only remayne in our knowledge & memory during this Age, but being . . . drawn into Cards & mapps or discovered & layd open to all." Davies knew that Irish people understood the intention of English maps, reporting that Donegal people had beheaded mapmaker Robert Bartlett only a few years earlier because "they would not have their country discovered."[24] Cataloging and bounding resources and people, writing a narrative and drawing a picture that justified colonization, was already a factor in colonization and resistance before Smith began to chart the Chesapeake.

For his part, documenting Native boundaries and movement on water made it easier for Smith to envision colonization. John Smith's account acknowledged that Indigenous people knew their chiefdoms' territorial limits and the Powhatans' authority over those limits. His map of Virginia, notable also for its descriptions of the navigability of the rivers and knowledge of the bay trade among Native people, made the Chesapeake intelligible to English mariners.[25] Even Smith's conversations with Powhatan leadership, relayed to an English audience, detailed how the Powhatans showed interest in the English watercraft, the knowledge of celestial navigation, and King James's military successes through his "innumerable multitude of ships."[26] Later, Dutch traders supplying these plantations (also gathering intelligence) copied a map made by one of Samuel Argall's English sailors in 1619 or 1620 to plot the plantations along the James.[27] A chart for mariners produced by Dutch cartographer Johannes Vingboons, likely from an

English original, reveals not only the locations of soundings and English forts and storehouses but also English boundaries like palisades and lines, perhaps pales, separating marsh from tillable land west of Jamestown.[28] The map also points out possible entrance points to Native communication interspersed between plantations, like the reference to a "Rickahock" path and the "Troking Point" opposite Jamestown Island.[29] These maps and descriptions of Native people together point an English audience toward conquest and access through maritime power.

For English sailors, exploring the possibilities of trade and diplomacy beyond the vicinity of James Fort and across the bay required these maps. Soundings of the Chesapeake's winding waterways might provide steps toward independence from local guides and the spread of knowledge to other English traders. Mapmaker Robert Tindall sailed with other Englishmen on a journey along the James and York Rivers and took measurements of depths along the shores, mapping the mouths and nearby landmarks of both for future navigators. Tindall was careful to measure around the mouths of tributaries to the east and nearby Jamestown, perhaps thinking of future expansion of the English presence. To the west of Jamestown, Tindall documented tributary waterways near capitals belonging to the people they met up the river.[30] His renaming of Native places, such as Tindall's Point and Tindall's Shoals at the center of the map, underscored the outsized influence that mariners held in mapping the Chesapeake for future generations.

Onshore, mapping aided the English in making sense of how they had already physically entered Native power relationships and networks. John Smith, the most likely original author of the 1608 "Zúñiga Map" smuggled to Spain by Spanish ambassador Pedro de Zúñiga, noted the names of Powhatan districts, where werowances lived, and his impressions of the numbers of settlements as he traveled up the James River past the fall line and into Monacan territory.[31] On a trip at the end of 1607, he did his best to map overland routes after he was captured by the Powhatans and carried down to the York River. Throughout, Smith included narrative information useful to English colonists who traveled by ship—that it was two days' journey between the falls of the James and the Monacans, for example, and that Powhatan overland paths ran away from the water into the wooded peninsulas, crossing the rivers at key points clear of marsh. He had also mapped information he had collected about the fate of the Roanoke colonists, where there had been rumors of men "clothed like me" still living on barrier islands to the south.[32] These maps provided a framework for spreading outward not just across a natural landscape but through peopled territories, placing future allies and enemies in the context of history and the river systems.

In their efforts to establish defenses for their newly claimed lands, elites lifted ideas from the built environment along the European coasts. During the reign of the Tudors, engineers and shipbuilders transformed the construction of forts and ships simultaneously. Henry VIII had built the English navy and a coastal defense system in southern England, and Elizabeth I maintained these forts while adding more.[33] While they continued to commandeer merchant vessels during wartime, northern European kingdoms built warships with mounted long-range guns and firing platforms that transformed them into floating fortresses. Advances in maritime technology, alongside advances in artillery technology, allowed the English to sail and make war farther away from home. But their ventures at sea were often disorganized. Military leaders on land remained unsure of how to integrate ships into their campaigns and struggled to communicate in the parlance of ships' captains and sailors.[34]

On land, military leaders had made decisions about fortifications depending on limited intelligence about the environment and people. In occupying territory in Ireland, for example, English commanders found gathering information difficult just as mapmakers had. Military leaders and engineers were overwhelmed by the unreliability of people, supplies, and roads they needed to run communication between English outposts. Weathering a campaign season in the Netherlands, military engineers favored impermanent fortifications. But in Ireland, fortifications might include a combination of temporary earthworks, stone fortresses, and even remains of medieval structures, saving labor.[35] Before reaching the Chesapeake, English attempts to occupy new places had been reliant on and grafted unevenly atop the local landscape, and the lack of predictability in resources and people only underscored their dependence on the people and places they sought to colonize.

Despite how warfare was experienced on the ground, English designs on Virginia were influenced by the circulation of literature about exploration and new strategies in war and mapping in England, Ireland, and continental Europe.[36] Promoter of English exploration Richard Hakluyt published *Divers Voyages Touching the Discoverie of America, and the Ilands Adjacent*, and after the defeat of the Spanish Armada, *The Principall Navigations, Voiages, and Discoveries of the English Nation,* affirming the English nation's military might, navigational prowess, and intimacy with the sea.[37] English elites sought through their published works to encourage investment in colonization, entertain readers, and justify colonialism in Ireland and elsewhere. As they gathered new intelligence through trade, exploration, and local information along the Chesapeake's coast, their accounts reflected both prior experiences as sailors in Europe and their contained and dependent experiences in Powhatan territory. Colonization was haphazard and tentative, reliant on local landscapes and people, but the English collection and distribution of knowledge about the people and places itself fueled support and investment in the messy process.

English leaders' writings emphasized that Indigenous places were ideal for strengthening their vulnerable position at Jamestown. Smith gushed about the five "Faire and delightfull navigable rivers" that comprised the western shore of the Chesapeake.[38] Smith explored the bay as far north as the Susquehanna River by boat with the help of Native people, impressing the English with the size and resources of Wahunsenacawh's domain, the Algonquians' nations beyond it, and outsider Native people even farther afield.[39] Smith also marveled at the defendable terrain and access to trade goods maintained by the Appamatucks, the cornfields of the Nansemonds, Powhatan strengths enmeshed in the Chesapeake landscape, all connected: "The river is enriched with many goodly brookes, which are maintained by an infinit number of smal rundles and pleasant spings that disperse themselves for best service, as doe the vaines of a mans body."[40] Not unlike Wahunsenacawh, the English conceived of mastery over both lands and waters as mutually reinforcing.

Powhatans, for their part, demonstrated their mastery over human movement on land and water. The 1607 journey of Gabriel Archer, mariner Christopher Newport, and Arrohateck men demonstrated how the English were tightly controlled and surveilled in the spirit of Powhatan hospitality. Only weeks after arrival in the Chesapeake Bay, Newport and Archer sailed up the James River and inquired at Native towns along the water. On the second day, Archer called to a group of Native men in a canoe along the James, the Native pilot of which learned the use of Archer's pen and "layd out the whole River from the Shesseian bay to the end of it so farr as passadg was for boates."[41] The falls of the James were impassable for ships like Newport's and marked the far reaches of Wahunsenacawh's dominion, a natural place to stop. The pilot then announced the English ship's presence to neighboring towns, outpacing the heavier and wind-reliant English craft in his canoe. He grabbed provisions, followed Archer's group six miles with dried oysters for the journey, and alerted others to the English arrival. It was the polite and safe thing to do, to report to local werowances the presence of a new vessel on water so heavily trafficked by Powhatan people. Archer saw the man three times that day, each time more amazed at his pace and knowledge of English movements. Through Native transportation, the English mariners were folded into Algonquian news networks with electric speed. Perhaps the English were outstandingly slow in their journey upriver, since by the time they reached the home of the werowance of the Arrohatecks close to the falls, Wahunsenacawh himself was on his way to appoint a high-ranking Arrohateck named Navirans to guide the English through a series of posts through Tsenacomoco. If they missed a post, someone could alert Powhatans that they had strayed off course, but Archer did not notice and was delighted by his hosts.[42] The rapid nature of Powhatan communication lines allowed Powhatans to curate and control the experience of this hospitality.

Powhatan guides also attempted to enforce geographic boundaries by controlling English knowledge of what lay beyond them. It was tricky work, however, since the Powhatans revealed to the English the extent of their domains and their differences with outsiders as they enfolded these strangers into their preexisting alliances and enmities. On his journey with Archer, Navirans halted the English at the fall line, demurring their requests to continue. They would encounter "tedyous travel," he said, and "if wee proceeded any further . . . we should get no victualls and be tyred." Navirans revealed that the people to the west of the falls, the Monacans, were enemies to the Powhatans. The English had reached the western edge of the Chesapeake and the Powhatans' dominion, where they might glimpse evidence of neighboring Monacans, their copper supplies, or defensible bluffs along the falls that could urge the English into new alliances beyond the Powhatans. The Arrohatecks in particular were located near to Monacan territory and would have much to lose from conflict. Archer added the note to a diagram of Native enmities and geography that the English reconstructed along their travels.[43]

Thinking from the perspective of inter-Indigenous relations, individual werowances also deployed knowledge of local alliances and riverine travel to forge diplomacy highlighting their districts' importance to potential English trade partners and allies. On the way back down the James River and away from Monacan country, Navirans refused to enter the Weyanokes' district and then suddenly turned and left them. Archer had previously discovered from an earlier guide that the Weyanokes were at odds with the nearby Paspaheghs, on whose land the English were just then clearing trees to erect James Fort. Newport, with Archer at the time, suspected danger, and he sped back to Jamestown where two hundred men—probably Weyanokes and men from other nearby towns—under their werowance made an assault at the palisade gate, for days shooting at the English whenever they left the fort to relieve themselves. Still playing the role of guide, the Arrohateck werowance sent messengers weeks later to lay out the situation for Newport: the Pamunkeys, Arrohatecks, Mattaponis, and Youghtanunds would help them make peace with "Contracted Enemyes" of the English—the Weyanokes, Rappahannocks, Appamattucks, and Kiskiaks. In the meantime, the English should "Cutt Downe the long weedes rounde about our Forte," helpful advice from people familiar with palisaded towns.[44]

Before the Powhatans' rise to power, Algonquians in the Chesapeake had developed political and social relationships among polities that lasted long past the induction of some groups as tributary nations into Powhatan society, and marine exploration allowed the English to note these histories. The English noticed fractures between the Powhatan core, people separated from them by some distance but still in the Powhatan orbit, and Algonquians who were altogether independent from Tsenacomoco. During John Smith's 1608 explorations of the bay, Algonquian competitors in the region, the Piscataways to the north of the Potomac, were helpful to the expedition. Meanwhile, the Patawomecks on the Potomac and Accawmacks on the Eastern Shore sought independent alliances and trade with the English, revealing their discomfort or disregard for Wahunsenacawh's authority at some distance from their towns.[45] The English knew their independent trading bothered the Powhatans, who controlled the movement of trade goods inside of their domains: the Powhatans conducted a military raid on the Piankatanks shortly after the latter agreed to share food with the English in 1608, for example. When the English visited Werowocomoco, the Piankatanks' locks of hair were prominently displayed. The English dutifully recorded both the attack and the resulting celebration, underscoring the results of unregulated trade in the Powhatans' domains of Tsenacomoco.[46] However, understanding and exploiting the difference between real and expressed limits of Powhatan domains would benefit the English in the future.

Making Sense of the Chesapeake

English colonists were often jarred by the sight of something familiar in an unfamiliar environment: Wahunsenacawh pouring wine given to him by Christopher Newport years before to lubricate a diplomatic discussion; Patawomeck men and women tossing European glass beads at funerals; an English bedstead and crown sitting at a temple to the deity Okeus.[47] English and Powhatan elites like Navirans developed trade in Virginia's initial years, integral to gathering intelligence and political clout. As paramount chief, Wahunsenacawh accumulated power during this period of contact in part because of his ability to control movement of prestige goods, in particular copper and glass beads manufactured by Europeans.[48] The Powhatan trade in European goods was made easier by trading paths established almost a century before the paramount chiefdom was constructed. As he had before the English came, Wahunsenacawh collected and distributed items valuable for their rarity, enhancing his own political and spiritual authority. The goods spread: at the head of the Roanoke River beyond the Powhatans' domain, where Native people processed copper, white glass beads appeared no later than 1615, traded west presumably for copper or other products desirable for Powhatan elites.[49] European goods emerged everywhere but in ways controlled by Wahunsenacawh.

Surrounding the peninsula on which James Fort sat, the Powhatans could choose between trading with and isolating the strangers, who seemed a disorderly and divided group. From initial diplomatic overtures and the construction of the fort from 1607 to 1609, the dismal water quality of Jamestown; the revolving door of leadership; the endemic starvation, disease, and death; and the violent and erratic behavior of the English toward the Powhatans and nearby Algonquians had made clear Jamestown's precarity to the Powhatans.[50] Further, a massive drought, possibly the worst in hundreds of years, began in 1606 and would last until 1612, raising the stakes of subsistence for everyone.[51] English hope lay in the intelligence and food supplies located on the rivers and controlled by Native people. In 1608, the settlement's leaders sent English boys to live with the Powhatans in hopes of establishing long-term relationships and communication lines. Facing food shortages in the summer and fall of 1609, John Smith pushed the settlers from the fort into Native territories to survive on fish in Kecoughtan territory and the smaller chiefdom also called Powhatan at the fall line. Other leaders attempted to purchase land from the Powhatans and to build forts in the territories of the Nansemonds and people of the smaller district also named Powhatan. They were met with violence.[52] The Powhatans pushed back against inappropriate English use of waterways and land and defiance of Powhatan boundaries, even as the English relied on Native guides and interpreters to facilitate their own movement in the Chesapeake.

As the English and Powhatans gathered information on one another, Algonquians relied on generations of social connections and ways of moving around the bay to inform their dealings with the English, and English leaders became uncomfortably aware of the connections surrounding them.[53] Chesapeake Algonquians in and beyond Tsenacomoco were accustomed to linguistically diverse outsiders coming into the bay via watercraft, bearing people, goods, and information.[54] Outsiders like the Massawomecks, who lived many days' distance north, harassed Algonquians like Iopassus's people along the Potomac in their lightweight birch-bark canoes.[55] Diverse outsiders also included Europeans: the English soon discovered that Massawomecks and Susquehannocks, non-Algonquians who lived at the head of the bay, were already trading furs to the French to the north by the time of John Smith's explorations. Smith saw among people in the northern Chesapeake tools and objects more familiar to him: "Many hatchets, knives and pieces of iron and brass" purportedly from Canada and used by women in their cornfields.[56] Some Algonquian towns were semi-palisaded, with family homes surrounding a circular fort for protection from northern groups.[57] Up the James River from the English fort, the Weyanokes maintained a double-walled palisade and "a place called the great market," a feature that no doubt interested English colonists looking to trade with people to the south.[58] Smith and his company of gentlemen were not the only hostile force or trade competition to reckon with on the James River or the Chesapeake.

To the potential detriment of Algonquians, then, Native nations from beyond the southern Chesapeake were interested in the military and trade offerings of the English. Pushed by Virginia Company leaders, voyagers like Samuel Argall followed after Smith to make contact with "those Northern people," but worried that Wahunsenacawh "seeing o[u]r access theither againe . . . might forestall o[ur] Trucking."[59] The rewards might outweigh the risks, though, and Argall had heard "the French have cleered eight thousand pounds of trade with the Indians, for furs, which benefit wil be as easily by us procured" and received an invitation from the Susquehannocks to return north the following season.[60] In 1611, naval captain and deputy governor Thomas Dale suggested hiring mariners to trade for corn with the Patawomecks or the Susquehannocks in spite of the Wahunsenacawh's wishes for control of trade.[61] They hoped moving beyond diplomatic borders would bring them freedom from Powhatan attempts to orchestrate English movement and trade along the rivers.

Simultaneously, everyday life at the fort and surrounding areas was shaped by daily trade with the Powhatans when the Powhatans' supplies were abundant enough to share and were willingly given. In only a short time at the fort, English dependence on Native women's food and Native desire for trade had cultivated daily familiarity. The "supply" ships brought people—in 1609, for example, as many as three hundred men, women, and children—but often few provisions and many people unused to farmwork, creating further need. English people therefore found themselves drawn into the Powhatans' gift exchange economy, which at once marked them as friends but created obligations that English leaders constantly violated by not gifting in return or by taking what was not freely given.[62] Archaeologists at James Fort have found a high proportion of Native ceramics in contexts dating to 1607, including in a hearth where they likely were used to cook as well as store food. Another pot in unfinished form probably made by an English person furthers the idea that Native women shared cooking and ceramic technologies with the new settlers. Bones of fish and wild mammals in archaeological remains, alongside seeds from wild plants, indicate English reliance on Native knowledge of the Chesapeake's maritime resources and the seasonal changes in life in the marshes and on the shores.[63] Use of Native goods continued through hostilities, and ceramics likely used to store food from between 1610 and 1620 outstripped the number of European-produced ceramics in some areas of the fort. Unfinished shell beads, bone tools for processing hides, and stones for grinding corn also point to the constant work and presence of Native women.[64] It was in this context that colonists first got to know children like Pocahontas, who played with the English boys in the fort. In locations near James Fort where the English attempted to farm, a similar pattern of goods and trash again reveals an abundance of Native wares.[65] Archaeology also shows that colonists, for their part, processed the metals they brought with them into pieces marketable to Native people.[66] William Strachey noted that Jamestown's soldiers looted mats made by Algonquian women "to dress their chambers and inward rooms, which make their houses so much more handsome."[67] Algonquian women's presence redefined how fort spaces were used and their wares were found in the most intimate interior spaces of the fort, marking the spaces as not wholly English.

At the same time that the Powhatans increasingly found the English integrated into Powhatan life but difficult to control, English leaders were unable to control the movements of their own sailors and settlers. Initially, leaders gave English colonists "libert to truck or trade at their pleasures," only to find the value of copper among the Powhatans decreased sharply with the flooding of the market. Wahunsenacawh sought to stem this flow as well in order to maintain control of the trade and the luxury value of copper, at times ordering tributary chiefdoms not to trade with the English. But the allure of English metals was strong. The allure of trade was probably also strong for lower-class English people, for whom idleness, hunger, and self-reliance had been the norm in England.[68] The fort's disappearing weapons—pikes, knives, shot, powder, and small arms—taken by colonists for trade irritated John Smith.[69] Sailors traded with Algonquians directly from their ships or traded English goods like butter and cheese with colonists who had access to Algonquian goods. Their reliance on trade fed the now-famous narrative of "distracted lubberly gluttons" who Smith forced back to work.[70] Uncontrolled trade and movement revealed the weakness of the leadership among the English, who could not control the lower sort, a point Smith drove home calling the "gentlemen, and carelesse governours" the "scorne, and shame" of Virginia.[71]

Further, colonists who lived among Native people—whether given permission or not—discomfited English leaders, who could not control their movements or mouths. Initially these arrangements were a benefit to the English; the men "billited among the Salvages" passed on crucial knowledge of Native "passages" between towns and the skills of finding food in Native-managed forests. However, many early chroniclers mentioned men who absconded, or attempted to abscond, to Native towns, in particular during periods of starvation, becoming a liability even as it was one less mouth to feed.[72] Far from simply running "away" or seeking out the nearest Native town blindly, settlers sought Native places they had learned about based on their previous interactions with Native people. In 1608, the English took captive an Algonquian man named Kemps, who probably learned English as he taught colonists how to plant fields and probably hunted for the colonists at a new fort on the south side of the James River. In the months following, Kemps was released, and runaway soldiers followed him, only for Kemps to return them to certain punishment after putting them to work in Native women's fields. Perhaps this was a commentary on English reliance on Native food and labor, or a savvy diplomatic decision to maintain a bond with English leaders like Smith—certainly, a Native observation on colonists' idleness would resonate with Smith.[73] Either way, it fell to Native people, and not the English, to control the limits of roving settlers, a responsibility that demonstrated Powhatan control over boundaries and further underscored the lack of English authority.

Uncontrolled sharing of knowledge and supplies posed an immediate physical threat to the English settlement itself, to the advantage of the Powhatans. Algonquians and English settlers took part in illicit trade in weapons, which made an illicit trade in information about English weaknesses more dangerous. John Smith was particularly irritated with the fort's Dutch or German servants who in 1608 and 1609 repeatedly ferried goods without English permission between the English and Powhatan towns. So much of what bothered Smith was what he did not know: he found the servants' friends skulking in the woods, unsure whether they had run away or not; he knew that the Dutchmen had taken weapons to the Powhatans and assumed that the Powhatans learned how to use them from the gifters. Was there any relation or conspiracy between these maddening free-ranging servants and other people who had run from the English, like he guessed? And what were they telling the Powhatans, or other English servants, about the English situation? Smith blamed the sudden removal of Wahunsenacawh, and his corn supply, from Werowocomoco on information provided by "those damned Dutch-men" of English plans for an ambush, stealing from the colonists the opportunity to steal Native food. The situation escalated when another man tasked with retrieving runaway colonists instead "conveighed them every thing they desired," presumably weapons. Weapons in mind, Smith envisioned that the men had planned no less than an alliance with the Powhatans, if not the Spaniards, to overthrow the English. At the same time, Smith ordered a blockhouse to be built to hem in movement between the fort on one side and Native land on the other. He understood that poor English surveillance and leadership left power in the hands of both lower-ranking servants and Native people.[74]

Interpreters—women, children, diplomats—also complicated the movement of knowledge and goods between the Powhatans and English commanders, establishing kinship ties aligned with Powhatan diplomacy, which promised sustained communication. Smith sailed into a world already full of interpreters, particularly in the northern Chesapeake where traders from multiple nations met with one another.[75] Communication, the English had quickly learned, would be difficult for them because "the language of every government is different from any other, and the farther they are [apart] the greater is the difference."[76] In a 1608 attempt to establish diplomatic communication, the English traded Thomas Savage as an adopted child for an aide to a Powhatan man named Namontack, "one of a shrewd, subtill capacitie."[77] The next year, Namontack left for England with his English adoptive father, Captain Christopher Newport, on a reconnaissance mission for Wahunsenacawh.[78] Upon his return, Namontack provided intelligence to the Powhatans about governance and life in England, and at Jamestown helped the English trade for corn and avoid combat when "the Salvages [were] more readie to fight then trade."[79] To navigate these complex relationships, interpreters crossed borders and provided crucial knowledge for both Powhatans and the English. This initial interaction demonstrated a promising ideal: individuals like Namontack would devote their lives as new kinfolk to English relations, overcoming wide physical and cultural chasms and advancing the knowledge and security of their nations.[80]

But diplomats also revealed and created divisions. In 1609, on his way to Werowocomoco, Smith and his party stopped at a Warraskoyack town along the James River. The werowance, attempting to dissuade him from moving forward, told him not to put his guard or guns down since Wahunsenacawh had sent a so-called messenger to Smith but, in actuality, "sent for you onely to cut your throats." If it was indeed true (friendship, after all, could also be gained from a lie), it was a betrayal of the Powhatans and suggested a separate relationship cultivated with the colonists. Smith also noted the Warraskoyacks' location, on a road connected to independent Native nations beyond the chiefdom to the south, and thoughts of trade in English goods no doubt crossed the werowance's mind. As a token of goodwill to the Warraskoyacks, Smith bequeathed his literate young page Samuel Collier "to learne the Language," establishing a direct tie to a particular district with promising trade relations.[81] Both Powhatans and English realized interpreters were crucial in keeping peace and in gathering intelligence, but they could also use interpreters to undermine established diplomatic channels and create new ones.

English leaders and interpreters also used the intelligence gained through go-betweens to pursue private ends, further revealing internal divisions to Native people and intensifying already heightened suspicions of English colonists against their own. Two years after Thomas Savage's adoption, Smith took young Englishman Henry Spelman to a Powhatan werowance named Parahunt to whom, according to Spelman, "unknowne to me he [Smith] sould me," leaving Spelman in exchange for the rights to a Powhatan town, to learn the language and become an interpreter for the English.[82] Smith insisted his aim was only to buy land and apprentice Spelman, but Spelman reported that Smith traded him for Powhatan land explicitly to undermine Deputy Governor Francis West's choice for a fortified location on the James River nearby, intending to move the fortifications to his new land. This episode caused violence and tension between West's and Smith's men, which Parahunt and surrounding Powhatans used to escalate attacks on West's isolated men in an ultimately successful effort to push the English out of this territory. Soon after, John Smith was hurt in a suspicious gunpowder incident, perhaps the result of political infighting such as this, and sailed back to England.[83] His attempted exchanges of people and land among Parahunt, Spelman, and West ended in the loss of Smith's skills to the company, and more opportunity for Powhatans to curb English settlement.

In their movements along the rivers they now knew well, English-born interpreters like Spelman also threatened Powhatan control of resources and movement among nations as they pursued their own ends. In 1610, Spelman and a Dutch boy named Samuel, also placed with the Powhatans, absconded to Patawomeck territory together. Such a move would serve the Patawomecks in creating separate long-distance trade opportunities with the English and in conveying information about the Powhatans and English alike. Wahunsenacawh responded by sending men to order Spelman and Samuel back to their hosts. Spelman refused, unsure if he could trust these emissaries, and turned to continue walking north. Unwilling to lose control of the interpreters or let the marginal Patawomecks have access to the interpreters' knowledge, a Powhatan man walking behind the boys suddenly cleaved through Samuel's head with an axe. Breaking into a run for the woods, Spelman made it to Patawomeck territory on his own, a feat of orienteering in a riverine environment that spoke to his time traveling between Algonquian domains. Among the Patawomecks he lived in security for a year until he was ransomed back to the English by Captain Samuel Argall with copper.[84]

Like Algonquian guides who met English ships on their journeys on the bay, Powhatan go-betweens folded the English into Algonquian politics.

The obligations of gifting and trade reinforced those bonds. Interpreters included adopted kin like Thomas Savage but also unnamed Algonquian women who cooked and brought goods inside of English living spaces—making them look, sound, and smell like Algonquian spaces. Intimacy developed between English colonists and Algonquians within the Powhatans' framework of acceptable movement and exchange. But deviation from that framework, like Smith's and Spelman's, only possible through accumulation of the knowledge of Native places and politics, threw into stark light the weaknesses and divisions on either side.

Containing the English

Regardless of trade and efforts at relationship-building, by 1608 disputes over the expansion of English fields and fortifications into multiple Powhatan territories, and their claims to food resources, soured the relationship between the English and many of the leaders of neighboring Powhatan districts along the James River. The local conflict precipitating the Anglo-Powhatan War, fought between 1609 and 1614, foreshadowed decades of violence the English would inflict beyond Jamestown, fights over space with neighbors they knew. English desires to gain a stronger foothold and a larger footprint along the river triggered escalating retaliations and counterattacks between the English and surrounding districts. In response, Wahunsenacawh reinforced political boundaries with a siege on Jamestown in the fall of 1609, beginning an unprecedented season of privation inside of the fort.

Combatants often knew each other from their time trading and treating, and often communicated about supplies and space even as they sought to slay each other. Between 1608 and 1609, the English had built fortifications and other works on either side of Jamestown along the James River, as with the purchase of a site at the falls and the establishment of Fort Algernon at the mouth. Facing widespread hunger in 1609, John Smith sent soldiers beyond the walls of the fort to fend for themselves. The soldiers living beyond the confines of Jamestown made a bid to purchase a well-situated island in a bend on the Nansemond River from the Nansemonds that year. Smith and other military men were already intimately familiar with the territory of their neighbors, having raided it for scarce corn supplies the previous year. The site, on elevated land surrounded by marsh, was suited to good fortifications mirroring those in Jamestown, with a prime view of incoming ships and canoes. But Nansemonds lived there, a place for their current werowances to reside (and likely, by extension, a holding place for food gathered in tribute) and a site for the burial of past werowances.[85] A thriving religious and political site, it was not for sale. Either the English messengers dawdled in returning or were killed by the Nansemonds, and in response the English took possession through desecration: they "Beate the Salvages outt of the Island burned their howses ransaked their Temples, Tooke downe the Corpes of their deade kings from their Toambes, and Caryed away their pearles Copper and bracelets whereiwth they doe decore their kings funeralles."[86] The Nansemonds and their neighbors retaliated, shoving bread into the mouths of English dead, a message concerning English hunger for food and the land from which it came.

The Powhatans not only cut off the trade in food in 1609 but lay siege to the colonists inside James Fort. Lacking leadership and the ability to trade for sustenance, food became a scarce commodity while paranoia and restlessness abounded. The same few Paspahegh men guarded their borders from trespass by the colonists who had dined and treated with them in the years before. The strategy surely appeared maddeningly slow and simple to the English, who watched for Paspaheghs waiting outside the fort to pick off English settlers attempting to walk in search of food beyond the palisade. The Powhatans constricted access to water, fish, and hunting and foraging opportunities. By the middle of 1610, only sixty colonists remained alive out of several hundred.[87] A colonist named Powell caught sight of Paspahegh werowance Wowinchapunk, a face he recognized and the man who had allowed the English to settle at Jamestown, and against orders chased him down and stabbed him until he was sure Wowinchapunk was dead. This resulted in a skirmish between the two sides.[88] In desperation and crisis, colonist Hugh Price stalked into the exact center of the fort, "exlameinge and Creyinge outt thatt there was noe god, alledgeinge thatt if there were a god he wolde nott Suffer his Creatures whome he had made and framed to indure thse miseries." Onlooker George Percy considered it an act of God that when Price left the fort the same day, he was killed by Powhatan forces and his body abandoned to be torn apart by wild animals.[89]

The English did their best to hide their weakness, burying the dead inside the fort and retrieving bodies from without so that the Powhatans would not see the tolls of siege and disease.[90] Nevertheless, Wahunsenacawh and other elites understood that English inadequacies lay not only in food procurement but in a lack of understanding of the new place, and he reminded English leaders of that fact. When Smith had threatened violence against Wahunsenacawh in 1608 after bargaining extensively over corn, Wahunsenacawh replied, "What can you get by warre, when we can hide our provisions and fly to the woods? Whereby you must famish by wronging us your friends."[91] Without Native food, relations, and knowledge, the Chesapeake landscape yielded little for the English.

Wahunsenacawh sought to humble the English by confining them inside of the boundaries granted them, a tactic the English had already noted he had used with other Native districts. People of chiefdoms who paid tribute to the Powhatans, however, might not follow instructions on when and how to trade with the English.[92] Wahunsenacawh cut off illicit movement with violence, even inside of his own kinship network, including a wife's brother, "Amarice, who had his braynes knock't out for selling but a baskett of Corne, and lying in the English fort 2. or 3. daies without Powahtans leave."[93] Probably a high-ranking member of a tributary group, Amarice's travel to Jamestown posed as much a threat as Smith's travel out of the fort, both potentially providing intelligence and trade beyond Wahunsenacawh's control. Even as the English remained dependent on Native people's corn, the visible gap between Wahunsenacawh's policy of containing the English and his inability to consistently enforce it during the siege later proved useful to English settlers.

As the war continued, the English relied on other Native people for intelligence about Native movements and places. The Powhatan siege ended in May 1610 after six months, when Algonquians chose to disperse for the season as they would normally, to hunt, fish, forage, and care for crops, rather than fence in the English. Only a month later, English resupply ships sailed into the bay, and under the governorship of Thomas West, Lord de la Warr, the colonists pursued war against the Powhatans with renewed vigor. But rather than sailing to their towns, George Percy led an overland expedition against the Chickahominies and Paspaheghs. When he was unable to find dispersed Native people, Percy had no choice but to rely on the colonists' former captive and interpreter Kemps, who "was Leadinge us outt of the Way the which I [disbelieving him, beat] him with my Tuncheon and threatned to Cutt of his heade."[94] Guidance from Kemps indeed brought the English to an enemy town for colonists to pillage. Given freely or not, Native people's intelligence kept settlers fed and fighting.

Facing deprivation and the violence of a chiefdom united against them, English mariners leveraged their understandings of Algonquian political differences along the bay to seek new alliances and resources farther afield. In 1611, Lord de la Warr reported that Argall had made a peace and trade for corn with the Patawomecks, and referred to their werowance as "a King as great as Powhatan."[95] Tobacco pipes typical of those crafted along the Potomac River to the north were found in James Fort, suggesting that goods created by Algonquians living far from the English traversed great distances in the name of diplomacy.[96] For groups on the periphery like the Patawomecks, providing the English with food, while dangerous, simultaneously cultivated a separate alliance with the English while undercutting Wahunsenacawh's control over the English food supply during a crucial moment.

But while the English expanded their geographic reach, escaped colonists undermined leaders' thin facade of control during wartime as they had before. Sometimes the colonists did so overtly, as when ten men sent to fish off the coast left for England instead in 1612.[97] While their stories are largely unrecorded, settlers who ran to Algonquian towns offered knowledge, labor (even interpreter Henry Spelman farmed next to Patawomeck women), and leverage in diplomatic discussions with colonial leadership. Where gentlemen and Smith sought riverine passages west, people who ran away became experts on their immediate options for survival outside of but near James Fort. Leader Edward Wingfield chuckled that as a sign of goodwill "the wyroances doe likewise send our men runnagates to us home againe, using them well during their beeing with them; so as now they being well rewarded at home at their retorne, they take litle joye to travell abroad without Pasportes."[98] Spelman's traveling companion Samuel may have been one of the Dutch artisans sent to build a house for Wahunsenacawh but who then absconded permanently. Once commanders built settlements beyond Jamestown, the problem compounded; men mining for iron attempted to steal a small boat and break for freedom, and in 1610 Lord de la Warr sentenced one of those caught to death as an example.[99] Servants forced into the work of claiming English dominion over the landscape by altering it for the colony were also given new opportunities by Powhatans to "Runn away unto the Salvages whome we never heard of after."[100] The farther the English extended their claims beyond Jamestown, the more scattered the colonists would become and the more plausible the strategies to escape English control. If Virginia were to permanently expand beyond the triangle of James Fort, more control over the movement of servants, and internal policing of boundaries, would be necessary.

The Anglo-Powhatan War began in 1609 with English claims to the Nansemonds' strategic political center, violating deep-seated understandings of how space was bounded in Algonquian districts. As Native people curtailed English freedom of movement and the English starved, they sought knowledge and resources through new allies like the Patawomecks. For both sides, however, illicit boundary-crossers undermined any hopes of a unified and controlled image that, in the English case at least, hid chaos and suffering. Wahunsenacawh gave the leaders at Jamestown an ultimatum in 1611: "Either we should depart his Country, or confine our selves to James Towne only, without searching further up into his Land, or Rivers, or otherwise, hee would give in command to his people to kill us, and doe unto us all the mischiefe, which they at this pleasure could and we feared."[101]

Reining in Boundary-Crossers

Two men eyed one another on a spit of land on the shores of the James River, each surrounded by a group of men dressed similarly—the one side in breechcloths sewn together with sinew and hemp, adorned with skin mantles, the other in cloth shifts with fine linen threads, wet through from the heat. All were silent as water lapped the marsh grass on its way downriver and the occasional waterfowl splashed. Wahunsenacawh stood waiting. Sir Thomas Dale, acting governor of Jamestown, and Virginia Company investor Sir Thomas Gates stepped forward. Both sets of men followed them with their eyes. The scene was framed by burnt cornstalks and woven mats surrounding the hearths on the ground, once at the center of Native homes, and the mutilated bodies of captured colonists who had attempted to run away, dirty and covered in flies after days hanging from a creaking and unstable gibbet. Together, Wahunsenacawh and Dale proceeded to a giant pine, its roots protruding from the marsh, where one of Gates's companions drew an iron axe and cut a fresh gash in the side, deepening and widening it with multiple strokes. Together, they climbed the bank inland, treading on unstable and waterlogged ground in as straight a line as Gates could make, to the next tree, where they paused as minutes passed and another mark was made. Then from the marsh into the shaded forest—and then the next tree. Members of the parade ignored signs everywhere of past travelers among the giant trees, the rooting marks of hogs, a path to a patch of berry bushes. Gates's men understood and told their friends and newcomers that the new territory was eighty miles in circumference, although none knew how far he had walked that day. What mattered was that each man saw with his own eyes the marks and agreed that the line would separate the Powhatans from the land that had just been named the "Kings Forest."[102]

Thomas Dale's arrival as chief military officer in 1611 marked a key shift in escalating violence between the colonists and Powhatans. Veteran English commanders like Dale and Gates drew on the rigid military models they implemented in continental Europe to upend leaders' haphazard boundary-marking and the Anglo-Native relationships created through interlocutors.[103] Their plan was to create exclusively English spaces by destroying the Powhatan networks leading to them, using English military rules and strategies. Trade, expansion, and diplomacy would be conducted the English way, and illicit movement and trade would stop. Ironically, to implement this strategy, they would first need to use the knowledge and skills acquired through captives and interpreters and gain the cooperation of werowances on the Powhatan fringe. Algonquians uncomfortable with Wahunsenacawh's authority used the chaos to ally with the English, fragmenting the Powhatan chiefdom at its periphery as Jamestown colonists sought to secure their places near the Powhatan core.

Restricting movement but insisting on expanding English territory, Gates and Dale continued the Anglo-Powhatan War by integrating the fights for land, food, and the creation of exclusively English spaces. They oversaw the reorganization of the fort system; new forts at the mouth of the James and upriver defied Wahunsenacawh's command that incorporated communities stay within assigned territories.[104] In search of corn and with plenty of English death to "revenge" on Native people, Gates led English colonists on murderous rampages, forcibly displacing neighboring Powhatan groups. When an Englishman's canoe was blown to the enemy's shore where he was retrieved by Powhatans and executed, Gates destroyed the town of Kecoughtan, whose residents were almost certainly uninvolved in the incident. He turned it over to English plowmen "so much grownd is there Cleered and open, ynough with little Labour alreddy prepared, to receave Corne . . . of 2. or 3000. Acres."[105] Within months of his arrival, Dale marched south against the Nansemonds, who had faced down earlier English invaders, gaining control of the mouth of the James and the nearby food supplies and strengthening fortification at Kecoughtan. On the other end of the chiefdom, Dale cut into the territory of the Arrohatecks, who had guided Archer on the river only a few years before, to build a new fort at the falls their guide had drawn with Archer's pen.[106] He routed the Appamattucks in 1611 and on former Appamattuck land, he founded Bermuda Hundred, the agricultural settlement where colonist John Rolfe first experimented with tobacco and where English mariners began to ship hogsheads of it across the sea.[107] Harnessing powerful places along the James River and reshaping them into defensive and productive nodes connected to maritime trade, Dale rearranged patches of the Powhatans' landscape and established plantation landscapes as the new threat to Powhatan control of the river.

Dale also rearranged the movement of people among forts, plantations, and Native places. New leadership used military violence to enforce Virginia's boundaries by controlling movement to and from the forts. Building on the earlier laws established by Lord de la Warr, Gates and Dale imposed martial law on their arrival in 1611. Their rules, including a ban on all unauthorized trade and the severest punishment for absconded settlers, made radical changes to everyday Anglo-Native interactions. At the new city of Henricus downriver from the falls, a group of men ran away and Dale, the fort's commander, retaliated: "Some he apointed to be hanged some burned some to be broken upon wheles others to be Staked and some to be shott to deathe all theis extreme and crewell tortures he used and inflicted upon them To terrefy the reste for attempteinge the Lyke."[108] Inside Jamestown, Gates also abruptly and violently halted the presence of Native people in the fort, demarcating an exclusively English space to halt the flow of intelligence beyond: "Dyvers Indyans used to come to our foarte at James Towne bringeinge victewalls with them Butt indede did Rather come as Spyes then any good affectyon they did beare unto us." Gates had them "apprehended and executed for a Terrour to the Reste." They even policed the border by altering the architecture of the fort's interior, constructing a building with limited access around a newly dug well and "a block howse to be raised . . . to prevent the Indians (whoe use ordinarily to swimme over unto our Isle at a certaine Creek) from killing o[ur] Cattell."[109] Control over mobility expanded within and beyond the fort, enforcing geographic and behavioral boundaries between English settlers and Algonquians.

Gates and Dale successfully fused their militarization and border expansion aims to finally gain some real control over land and people on the James. In 1613, after the capture of Pocahontas, Dale rode up the Pamunkey

River with her on board and waited to be noticed by people from the Powhatans' town. He shouted to emissaries, "I came to bring him his daughter, conditionall he would . . . render all the armes, tooles, swords, and men that had runne away, and give me a ship full of corne, for the wrong he had done unto us." Pocahontas encouraged her kinsfolk to treat with Dale, who continued, "If not burne all."[110] Powhatan leadership attempted to negotiate, offering to return an Englishman named Simons, "who had thrice plaid the runnagate, whose lies and villany much hindred our trade for corne," but lied that another runaway colonist (who was indeed staying with them) was beyond reach because he was dead. The negotiations devolved and the English burned Powhatan homes, forcing Wahunsenacawh's brother Opechancanough to sue for peace through emissaries to the fort. Wahunsenacawh later returned seven English people and some guns and promised corn to follow.[111] In so doing, he publicly forfeited to English mariners a degree of control over the flow of goods and people in his chiefdom.

Soon other Indigenous groups seized opportunities to chip away at Wahunsenacawh's control of movement. The Chickahominies, loosely allied with the Powhatans but without a tributary relationship inside of the paramount chiefdom, sought a separate peace at James Fort, only a dozen miles from where they lived. The English noticed that "these people presuming upon their owne strength and number (in no one place In those parts, which we know, so many togeather) . . . a long time neglected Powhatan," either not paying tribute or disengaging from military pursuits.[112] During the previous war, Wahunsenacawh actively worked to keep these neighbors from coming to agreement, telling the English the Chickahominies were not to be trusted while urging the Chickahominies "to betray such of our [English] men as should come at any tyme to trade with them for corne."[113] With presents of deer the Chickahominies approached Dale and proposed a similar relationship to the one they had had with Wahunsenacawh previously, to fight and pay tribute in exchange for self-governance. Argall, considered by the English a master negotiator from his time among the Patawomecks, promised them protection, trade, and an engraved copper image of King James. In return, they would help fight the enemies of the English and signal their alliance by calling themselves "Tassantasses," the Algonquian word for "strangers" that the Powhatans used to describe the English.[114] The Chickahominies consulted among each other and "requested further, that if their boats should happen to meet with our boats . . . we would let them passe." In requesting this condition, the

Chickahominies revealed the English mariners' power to disrupt and coopt established trade and communication along the James and Chickahominy Rivers. Mobility remained key to self-determination for Native people who would live nearby English forts. Dale commented, "We agreed unto it, so that they pronounced themselves English men." Proudly, he added, "This people never acknowledged any King, before; no nor ever would acknowledge Powhatan for his King, a stout people they be." As an afterthought, he added, "and a fine seat they have."[115] At the perfect moment, the Chickahominies gained an alliance in exchange for an acknowledgment of English control over the landscape. With the Chickahominies' request of free passage along the rivers, King James was perhaps becoming to some, in John Smith's words to Wahunsenacawh, "king of all the waters."[116]

Through illicit movements and agreements like this, the English transgressed their kinship ties with the Powhatans that had brought them intelligence and political clout. The young English interpreter and adopted Powhatan kin Thomas Savage visited Wahunsenacawh in 1614 for the first time since he had run away in 1610, this time on a diplomatic visit on behalf of the English. Wahunsenacawh gently scolded him, "My childe you are welcome, you have bin a straunger to me these foure yeeres, at what time I gave you leave to goe to Paspahae [to the English, Jamestown] . . . to see your friends, and till now you never returned." He reminded Savage of his symbolic placement inside the bounds of the chiefdom as well, established "by the donative of Captaine Newport, in lieu of one of my subjects Namontacke, who I purposely sent to King James his land, to see him and his country."[117] Savage had abandoned his roles as both an interpreter and a son among Algonquians, each of which carried lifetime obligations. To the Powhatans, Savage's message from the English was also beyond the realm of acceptability from a tribute-paying chiefdom or neighbor. To add insult to injury, on the same mission an Englishman recognized and demanded the return of William Parker, a man captured at one of the forts during the war, apparently adopted, and accordingly reported to the English as dead by Algonquians to halt any search for him. Wahunsenacawh replied to the demand that Parker be returned, "You can no sooner see or know of any English mans being with me, but you must have him away. . . . I will send no guides along with you, so as if any ill befall you by the way, thanke your selves."[118] The English refusal to cooperate with the Powhatans' placement of people and his claims to kinship, strategies at the core of his rise to power, led to Wahunsenacawh's own bitter withdrawal from diplomacy.

Amid these violations of Algonquian kinship, John Rolfe announced his intent to engage in a Christian marriage with Pocahontas a year into her captivity in 1614.[119] Wahunsenacawh agreed since perhaps, like other marriages in Powhatan diplomacy, it could renew an alliance. The marriage ushered in almost a decade of tense peace. While Pocahontas and other go-betweens receive credit for skillful guidance and maintaining strained, shifting relationships, colony leaders effectively harnessed their influence in this case. The harsh leadership of Gates and Dale, and Wahunsenacawh's diplomatic choices, had expanded Virginia's geographical footprint with fortifications and plantations along the James River and transformed Native-English relationships. English success lay in part in deploying resources—ships, discipline, and intelligence—to gain access to Powhatan towns and rivers. It was impossible, of course, without relationships with other Native people like the Patawomecks and the Chickahominies. The Powhatans, however, who had lost key places and allies, still knew those places and people intimately, and could deploy that knowledge and their remaining networks and resources in the future.

English Plans for the Future

In coopting Powhatan fields, trade, laborers, interpreters, and kinship networks, English colonists and their new Native allies chipped away at Powhatan authority but still remained dependent and linked to Algonquians throughout the Chesapeake. They remained a small presence, with only 350 settlers dispersed among six settlements in 1616. To find the extent of English settlements hugging both sides of the river, a ship or canoe could travel past the English settlement on the Eastern Shore and into the bay, then up the James River from Kecoughtan, Jamestown, Bermuda Hundred, and West and Shirley Hundred, to Henricus.[120] The settlements were hard-won by mariners and diplomats, at the fringes of vast Native networks. In the pursuit of profit through furs and tobacco beyond the shore, colonists needed Native guides, Native roads, and Native fields. With such dependency and exchange, controlling mobility on the water became increasingly difficult for both English leaders and Powhatans.

After "a firme peace" was established in 1614, Dale enforced on the colonists English, rather than Algonquian, ideas about appropriate movement through the Chesapeake. Perhaps because they were unwilling to be held liable for illegitimate English movements, Native and English people began to at least make a show of enforcing Dale's requirements that runaways be returned and that traveling colonists carry a passport.[121] But control and separation was never total. Archaeologically, a large amount of Native women's wares and butchered wild game but fewer English-made trade goods at Jamestown probably meant that trade continued.[122] People continued to move too: Ralph Hamor wrote that Native people were working for the English under Dale, perhaps to plant corn and cook at the surrounding forts. English expansion, it appeared, created new room for old patterns of interaction.

Peace also gave the English a chance to pursue potential profits from agriculture with new energy. In 1614, John Rolfe exported four barrels of sweet-scented tobacco, and the company shifted from collective farming to private garden plots. Company servants were freed from their obligations in large numbers and farmed exclusively tobacco, forcing them to rely on supply ships for many of their needs.[123] Men now able to cultivate for themselves could expect a 200–300 percent return on their investment in tobacco.[124] John Pory reported one man who cleared two hundred pounds sterling's worth of tobacco; another with six servants cleared a thousand pounds.[125] This made the land adjacent to English forts and homes, in addition to the trade passages through them, profitable for the first time to the English. Even as they justified "plant[ing] ourselves in their Places," since Native people keep "only a generall recidencie there, as wild beasts have in the forrest," Virginia Company servants understood that the fallow fields they intentionally chose for cultivation were "clear'd here by the Indians to our hands."[126] Native work and knowledge of fertile grounds thus shaped early Virginian tobacco plantations.

The first English planters replicated this pattern upriver from Jamestown as they settled prime agricultural land in Powhatan districts to farm exclusively tobacco. The Virginia Company began to distribute its most important asset of claims to large tracts of Native land to investors, in an effort to encourage settlement and keep the company afloat. With the Great Charter in 1618, the company put in place a "headright" system whereby a settler, or a planter paying for a settler's passage, received fifty acres of land in recompense, encouraging immigration and the importation of laborers—and providing considerable influence to merchants who could claim headrights on their passengers. Forty-four additional patents of over five thousand acres apiece were distributed by the company. Expansion of plantations began in earnest in 1619, and English people settled on twenty particular plantations.

The plantations were beyond the control and supervision of the company in a few key ways: First, most were not surveyed and so placed ten miles from one another and at least five miles from the company-run tracts of so-called Company Land to avoid boundary disputes, meaning that plantation leaders operated with little outside interference in everyday management and at geographic, wooded distances from one another.[127] Second, planters were not subject to the same laws as people under company purview, including in their relationships with Native people. At the foundation of the General Assembly in July and August of 1619, plantations but not planters were originally represented by the burgesses, who established the colony's laws.[128] Free trading with Native people, and sometimes raiding, helped decide local diplomacy.

Interest in agricultural land and in acquiring and controlling the movement of laborers shifted with the meaning of land and created new challenges for would-be planters attempting to control mobility. Enslaved Angolans first arrived on Virginian shores aboard the *White Lion* and Argall's ship, the *Treasurer,* in 1619; the wealthy men like George Yeardley who purchased them probably considered them to be enslaved for life.[129] English elites now understood that they could not rely on Algonquians, who could provide means of escape, if they hoped to control mobility on the shore and rivers.[130] Colonist Sir George Sandys wrote, "I like not this stragelinge" or fanning out of English settlement west, one reason being "two of those [white servants] a little after ran away (I am afraid to ye Indians) & no doubt the other two would have consorted with their companions, if sickness had not fettered them."[131] The dispersal of settlement between and atop Native landscapes, necessary for trade and profit, foreshadowed problems of control over both land and labor.

Interest in keeping servants on plantations also altered the meaning of Native movements for the English. Planters recognized the necessity of controlling and surveilling Natives' whereabouts, especially if they were laboring regularly on English plantations, and if they might entice English and African unfree people to run off to Powhatan towns. English leaders negotiated with Native parents to take Powhatan children into their households to instill in them a Christian education; the children were placed at outlying plantations where their families were supposedly well acquainted with particular settlers. But then it was up to the planters "to after keep them that they runn not to theire parents or frends, and their said Parrents or frends steale them not away wch naturall affeccon may inforce in the one and the other."[132] Planter William Capps made, he thought, a humorous argument for importing and maiming enslaved Native people to solve the endemic runaway problem: "By hap bring you in 3 or 4 score slaves to work about a ffort or other servile worke, but before I deliver them up I will make them sing new Toes, old Toes, no Toes at all, because they shall not outrun me."[133]

Within a decade, English sailors and military men had constructed new legal and geographic boundaries reflecting intentions to surveil and police borders, and when these were defied, to inflict violence on offending Native and unfree people. However, many factors remained in play for both Powhatans and English colonists. English land grabs on the James River relied on Native-derived knowledge of key Powhatan places, gained through mapping, warring, interpreting, and trading. English diplomacy and trade goods undercut Powhatan surveillance and authority and certainly dealt a blow to the Powhatan chiefdom's control over much of the Chesapeake. But Wahunsenacawh's own ability to curtail English movement had indeed defined the first decade of English settlement in the Chesapeake. He had also defined initial resistance from within: the illicit traders, "runnagates," and interpreters were united by little else besides their self-interest and their reliance on Native resources to pursue self-interest. Their movements also helped Native people maintain ties to and knowledge of the places that the English claimed, an advantage they exploited by curating English relationships and ideas about the Chesapeake. Alongside some English people, many Native people ignored or sought to undercut Powhatan and English boundaries to their own ends. They moved through fields and down rivers as before and continued to keep a wary watch on their new neighbors and Native allies.

— 3 —

New Borders, New Connections, New Fractures, 1615–1644

The furnace ate wood faster than he could chop it, urging an Englishman to hack faster into the tall, straight yellow pine on the edge of the woods. In Sussex across the ocean, people might have objected to fueling a fire with wood that could be used for barrel staves and ships' masts, but in Virginia the woods needed to be thinned anyway to see those approaching the settlement. After building a huge furnace and their own quarters by the creek, English craftsmen finally felt the patterns of life had become familiar. In Sussex, the Englishman had been surrounded by ironworkers whom he had known for years, whose fathers and grandfathers had eked out a living producing iron bars for export and ordnance. Most of his fellow workers in Virginia were ironworkers unfamiliar to him, from the West Midlands; they all together found themselves surrounded by Powhatans who hunted and moved through English colonists' clear fields and came to trade. While the ship that brought him here had passed plantations and Native towns on their slow trip up the James River, few English vessels reached this far inland and could go no farther than the rushing, rocky water. He and other settlers had heard rumors of past attacks on English fortifications at the falls. The next English settlement downriver was three miles away; he could see and hear nothing else familiar but the fire in the forge, and it unnerved him.

Then on this early spring morning, the sounds of footfall, crunching piles of charcoal and iron waste, warned him of danger before any English voice reached his ear. In March 1622, Powhatan men entered the clearing as they would any other day, but this time they grabbed the tools of

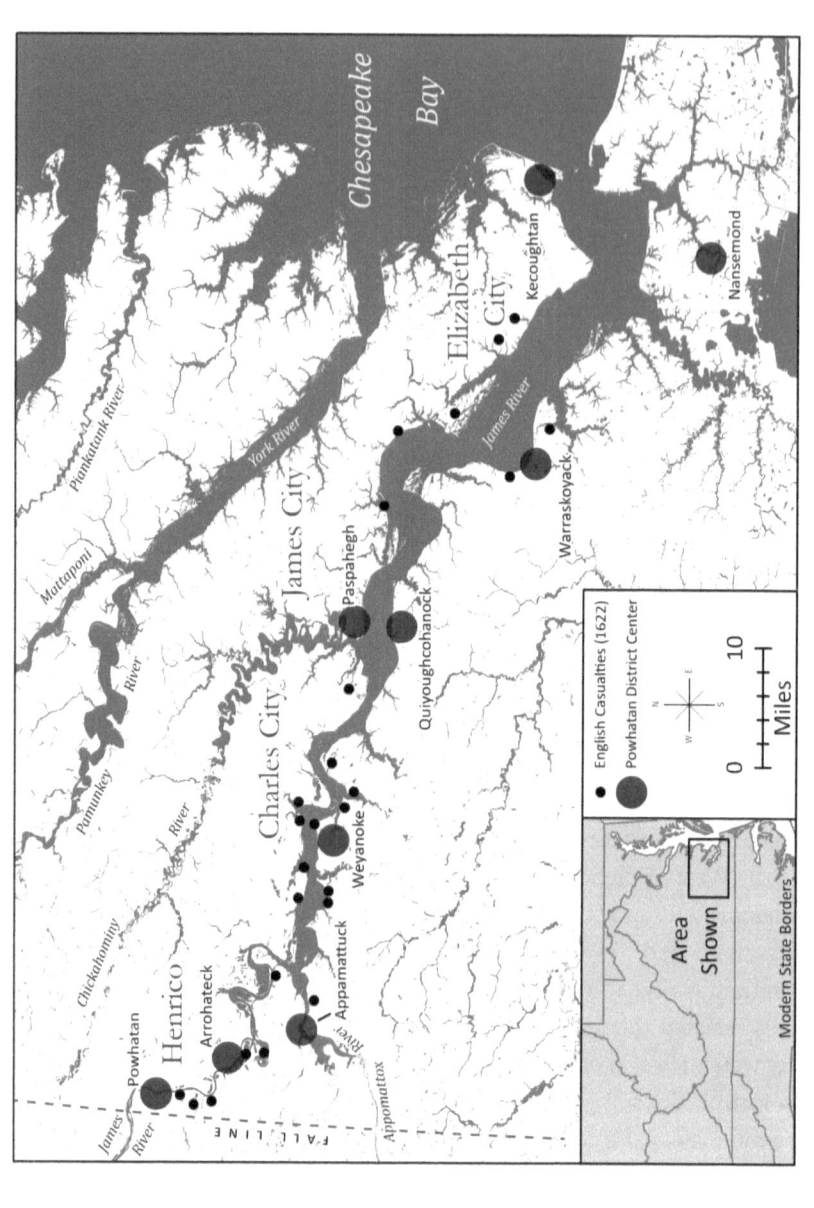

MAP 3. English land claims and casualties in Native districts along the James River, c. 1622 (Stewart Scales and Gemma Wessels)

the forge—the axes and hammers—and killed every English person they saw. The furnace was soon engulfed in the destructive blazes set by the Powhatans. Native people threw equipment and tools brought from Sussex into the river to sink.[1]

The establishment of English plantations miles away from Jamestown like the Falling Creek ironworks were unwelcome changes in the landscape for Powhatan people and portended shifts in power.[2] Leaders Opechancanough and Opitchapam saw in English-made metals and glass a threat to the control of trade, and in English fortifications and farming a threat to Algonquian control of Chesapeake resources. Additionally, English settlements were a threat to control of people's movements. Not only could the English not control their own sailors and servants to the detriment of Native people, but they also made it more difficult for Opechancanough, Wahunsenacawh's brother and eventual successor, to control the movements of goods within his domain. Locations of new English settlements threatened control of waterways and overland communication lines, and therefore threatened the ability to monitor visitors and beat back invaders.

Opechancanough's attack, coordinated to destroy simultaneously several English settlements in response to these threats, revealed how he had reimagined Powhatan spatial and social boundaries since Wahunsenacawh's death in 1618.[3] He understood that knowledge from Native people strengthened the English settlements, and he sought to control the flow of information from Native to English hands and to limit English movement along the James River. To do this, he demanded loyalty from other werowances, something required for an attack of such large magnitude, and distrusted interpreters and other go-betweens. Only with this strategy in place, undergirding a vision of broad Powhatan influence over regional knowledge and political leaders, were the Powhatans able to physically shrink the footprint of the English. The English's increasingly frenetic felling and building and sailing along the Chesapeake's rivers reinforced to the Powhatans something central: that English trade and authority centered at these new settlements represented a spatial vision irreconcilable to theirs.

English visions of expansion were informed by Powhatan strategies for implementing their boundaries. Colonial elites understood that the transition to farming tobacco, and harnessing the labor and land to do it, was key to profit in the Atlantic trade. The establishment of "particular plantations," and ultimately individual landholdings adjacent to the water, made that possible. To occupy not just a fort clinging to the river but to build plantations along the rivers, they needed to successfully tap into Native communication lines and politics. By imprinting English borders and systems of governance on the Powhatan lands they grabbed and by amplifying their impact on the landscape with the large number of new settlers, English leaders asserted control over the Chesapeake—control that Powhatans worked to undermine. This chapter follows people who navigated new legal and spatial boundaries imposed by English authorities before and during the Powhatans' attack on English settlements in 1622, which began the Second Anglo-Powhatan War lasting until 1632. From demolishing Native towns at the beginning of the war to the creation of the shire governments a decade later, English elites attempted to consolidate their authority by drawing lines on the landscape: between Native and English people, between plantations and shires, and between landowners. New laws claimed control over the movement of people as settlements shifted, even as some settlers benefited from war and trade with Native people who crossed these new boundaries.

Meanwhile, Algonquians on the fringes of English and Powhatan reach built on longstanding diplomatic and trade strategies to keep at bay English elites' pursuit of land and plunder. Their relationships with English servants and planters were cultivated locally, varying among districts and territories. As they had during the First Anglo-Powhatan War, their influence and resources, often deployed for English allies, undermined Powhatan claims to control over trade and intelligence. The growing divisions between and among English settlers and Powhatans presented them with the opportunity to cultivate new relationships along established communication lines.

Spread Too Thin

In the couple of years preceding the attack of 1622, the particular plantation of Martin's Hundred was bounded by the James River along which settlers erected fortifications. Inside the compound, despite the abundance of open space all around, many laborers might have felt just as hemmed in and watched over as they had in England: groups of men shared beds in small sleeping quarters, within earshot of the men who directed their labor, in rooms with a fire and a damp smell, perhaps oiled paper or cloth covering small window frames. In the daylight beyond, fences stopped cattle from roaming and stopped animal intruders from poking into the vegetable garden. The concern with defense, the buildings themselves surrounded by palisades, might remind a newcomer of English settlements in Ireland. From a bluff overlooking the river, their safest route to Jamestown ten miles away, English laborers would have felt the river as a boundary different from the fences of the settlement buildings. Besides ships on the rivers, they would have seen few signs of other colonists, while they watched Native people travel by foot and in canoes.[4]

Despite their wariness and the constant sight of Native people, many colonists caught only hints of the changes brewing beyond their compounds. Trade with colonists created a regional shift. Built atop Native seasonal settlements, English plantations intersected avenues of trade and communication among Native people. English copper had glutted the market, and the violence of the English during the First Anglo-Powhatan War disrupted trade and farming. At the same time, the English familiarized themselves with the overland routes and the open water leading beyond the Powhatan chiefdom to the Patawomecks on the Potomac River and Accawmacks on the Eastern Shore, circumnavigating the Powhatans upon whom they had previously relied for food and guidance. John Rolfe reported that for some Algonquians, "now the case is altered, they ... come to our Townes, sell the skins from their shouldiers which are their best garments to buy corne."[5] The previous strategy for maintaining surveillance over newcomers and accruing and distributing goods among Native people was falling apart.

In response, Algonquian leaders with a history of military feats rose in power. Wahunsenacawh himself moved from Werowocomoco to a town and spiritually important site called Orapax at the head of the Chickahominy River in 1616 to avoid English ships.[6] He died soon after as an old man, and his successor, Opitchapam, appears infrequently in the Virginia Company records. In contrast, Pamunkey warrior Nemattanew had distinguished himself against the English in battle in 1611 and gained a following in the years afterward, conducting an additional raid in 1618 to steal English weaponry.[7] "There was at this time a tall handsome well-made Indian, called Nemattanow," one bemused English chronicler explained, "who had gain'd such Esteem amongst his own People in War, that they believ'd him to be invulnerable; for he had hitherto escaped without Hurt, from all the Battles he had ever been engaged in."[8] Whether or not the Powhatans thought their leaders invincible, a decade of endemic tension cultivated assertive and well-organized leaders.[9]

Alongside Opitchapam, Wahunsenacawh's brother Opechancanough rose as the dominant threat to non-Powhatan Native people and English settlers. In his role as a Powhatan werowance, he worked to police the movements of neighboring Native polities to the benefit of the Powhatan chiefdom.[10] While Wahunsenacawh still ruled, for example, a wife of Opechancanough had either been taken captive by or had willingly left with another werowance, who was deposed in retaliation and replaced by one of Wahunsenacawh's own young sons (though the woman remained with the now former werowance).[11] Opechancanough's reputation outlasted him. Almost a century later in 1710, Weyanoke women and a Nansemond werowance cited Opechancanough by name and his wars with the English as the reason for their migration south from the James River, albeit to an English audience.[12] Opechancanough had intimidated or redistributed entire Native nations over decades, or taken part in conflicts that forced migrations, as part of the Powhatans' reinforcement of their boundaries and expansion of their influence. Unsurprisingly, he attempted to contain the English as well.

Searching for allies against the English, Opechancanough made overtures to other Algonquian people who had remained beyond the total control of his brother's chiefdom, namely the Patawomecks and the Accawmacks to the north. He was angered to find that leaders geographically sheltered from Powhatan power had developed their own neighborly relationships with English traders and planters. At the invitation of Esmy Shichans, werowance of the Accawmacks, interpreter Thomas Savage had built a plantation and engaged in the fur trade on a neck of land with navigable waters on what became known as the Eastern Shore across the Chesapeake Bay. Savage himself probably consciously chose this advantageous setting with access to the fur trade by boat but safe within the Accawmack network of towns from the raids of foreign groups. With Savage's help, the English established their first permanent settlement in the east along Old Plantation Creek near Esmy Shichans's district capital in 1619. The werowance had used the gift of land to seal the relationship between himself and the Englishmen he invited, and his corn and intelligence would prove useful.[13]

Opechancanough recognized that Esmy Shichans and the geography of the Eastern Shore provided safety and prosperity to the English and yet another outpost for colonists. During John Pory's stay on the Eastern Shore with interpreter Thomas Savage in the 1620s, Opechancanough sent someone to murder Savage, among other reasons, "because he brought the trade from him to the Easterne shore"—or at least, that is what Esmy Shichans told Savage, thwarting the assassination.[14] Pory also wrote of escalating hostilities facing the Accawmacks, detailing that "they on the West would invade them, but that they want Boats to crosse the Bay."[15] Similarly, Eastern Shore Algonquians warned Savage of Opechancanough's intentions to attack the English and gifted corn to the settlers through Savage's mediation.[16] Like other Algonquians had before, the Accawmacks used geographical distance from and intelligence about Powhatan hostilities to build a relationship with the English. The English, catching on to the divergent interests of Native people, had succeeded to a degree in strengthening their relatively weak position.

Powhatans approaching English settlements, still primarily situated along the James River, no doubt noticed variations in their appearance and political dynamics cultivated by colony leaders. For example, in 1614, acting governor Sir Thomas Dale had encouraged food production by providing colonists with small plots; four years later, Governor Samuel Argall established an estate and moved Martin's Hundred colonists to "Argall Town" just north of Jamestown, along one of the only English-controlled roads that ran between his plantation and Jamestown.[17] Most importantly for the success of the colony, in 1616 individual colonists settled privately owned land for profit. The Virginia Company's 1618 orders to Governor George Yeardley authorized private land grants incentivizing investment and the migration of laborers from Europe.[18] In the ensuing years, new English claims to land stretched to both banks of the James River to the fall line. Some were carefully palisaded to keep safe warehouses of tobacco; others were merely a half-dozen hastily constructed wooden homes.[19] With more investment in tobacco planting than home construction, quarters were often small and intimate. A plantation might be worked by only one free family or several, by several purchased Africans in bondage, or with only a few indentured servants and tenants, or dozens. By 1620, factions within the Virginia Company had engineered a variety of labor regimes and forms of land tenure, influencing the makeup of settlements and their relationships with Native towns and other English settlements.[20]

Plantations were intentionally placed atop Native land, their location and histories informing communication and diplomacy. Transitioning to farming required Native-occupied fertile places, so colonists chose peninsulas of land that had often been recently and noticeably occupied by Native people. The English, like Algonquians, preferred defensible sites bordered by water, the better for navigating the river in trade, fishing, and foraging—and they valued sites that had already been cleared, perhaps by Native people who had planned to return after a seasonal migration away. Archaeology at Flowerdew Hundred on the south side of the James River, for example, revealed that Native people used English bricks in their hearths on that site, indicating recent if not contemporaneous occupation with English settlement. George Yeardley patented Flowerdew Hundred in 1618, and English laborers built palisades on the footprint of Native fortifications—certainly with a different set of intruders in mind.[21]

Hostilities mounted over contested use of Chesapeake towns, fields, and routes, as the construction of plantations along the James River cut into the Powhatan chiefdom's riverine communication lines and farmland. Legislators in James City attempted to modulate Anglo-Native interactions on new settlements with a plethora of new rules about proximity and governing structures. For English lawmakers, a key component of breaking dependence on the Powhatans was the formation of their own political order atop this complicated Native geopolitical landscape. According to instructions from the Virginia Company issued in 1618, implemented by Governor Yeardley in 1619, new Virginians lived either in the "boroughs"—local chartered districts headed by a commander who reported to the company—or on "particular plantations" located within the bounds of boroughs but governed separately and operated by investing planters with patents. The system would have been familiar to a middling or indentured English person, who might have belonged to a borough as large as London or as small as a rural group of farms. It would also have been familiar to English military men, who had watched the imposition of the English borough system on Ireland, or whose landed family members governed everything from alehouses to church attendance on their holdings.[22]

Unlike the Powhatan districts, the English boroughs—from east to west, Kecoughtan, James City, Charles City, and Henrico—each straddled the James River with both company lands and particular plantations scattered nearby with their own settlers and governance. The boroughs themselves had unclear geographical boundaries but were divided into company, church, common, and patented lands, designed to absorb the flow of families and laborers who hoped to eventually own their own few hundred acres.[23] Each borough was headed by a commander responsible for enforcing the rules of the company and for bringing to the governor and council intractable servants and business disagreements.

As Opechancanough worked to consolidate authority over the Powhatan chiefdom, the English governorship also shifted their approach to Anglo-Native relations. George Yeardley, who had worked to court favor with Opechancanough, was relieved by the company in 1617. In his stead, mariner Samuel Argall sought to strengthen trade and alliances with Powhatan werowances and other Algonquians like the Accawmacks and the Patawomecks at the edge of the Powhatans' influence. He also pushed for a diverse economy less dependent on tobacco—a plan that required artisans, infrastructure, and industrial sites throughout the Chesapeake.[24] Native leaders along the James and York Rivers watched as an alternative vision for Virginia materially manifested in the construction of ironworks and saltworks, and in the sight of ships passing Powhatan-controlled banks of the James River for the Potomac and the Eastern Shore.

But a vision of industry and cleared, productive land on both sides of the James was realized only in patches, and the James River remained the only connective tissue between nodes of settlement. English elites seized opportunities for economic and social gain through the availability of headrights, leadership positions, and laborers to work their plantations.[25] Company leaders like Edwin Sandys believed that land ownership was only the beginning, that "the benefit grew not by a bare title to the Land, but by cultivating & peopling it so to reape profit." Unused property was "a matter of opinion, rather then of realty, & a shadowe rather then a substance." Enormous private grants from the Virginia Company could total as much as eighty thousand acres apiece, far more than could be cultivated by a few dozen servants.[26] Into the 1620s and 1630s, private planters and merchants accrued large tracts surrounding existing settlements.[27]

For many leaders who predicted that the colony would become permanently settled, however, land ownership promised access to offices and connections. The company's 1618 charter allowed free settlers to own property and awarded tenants and land to colonial officers. The company intended the establishment of an assembly elected from the boroughs in 1619 to better life in the colony by replacing martial law with a representative governing body.[28] Plantations sent burgesses to the new assembly, but they also needed magistrates and officers. Company lands, on the other hand, needed marshals, who received Company servants, tenants, and lands for their troubles—and perhaps received more, since company officials heard "dayly great Complaints" about their fees.[29] The creation of both private plantations and public boroughs necessitated surveys to demarcate boundaries so that they might be "conveniently divided and known the one from the other." The colony's secretary, William Claiborne, began surveying near Jamestown years later in 1625.[30] Whether shadow or substance, claims to land provided footholds for social advancement to a select few and a replicable structure for local politics run by landed men.[31]

Commanders at the settlements developed or broke diplomacy with nearby Algonquians, and the movements of Algonquian neighbors informed their choices. In 1619, for example, when looking for sites to house and Christianize Native children, a burgess skipped over older, more established spots like Bermuda Hundred and instead pointed to newer settlements at Smith's Hundred and Martin's Hundred, located on the north banks of the James River on either side of Jamestown. Although only a few years old, these sites were "alredie there settled and the Indians well acquainte wth them." Meanwhile, planters and Native people had included one another in everyday commerce, and planters hired Native labor and traded at Native towns nearby.[32] These relationships might be carefully stewarded, or they could turn negative or spiral out of control. In 1619, John Martin (a proprietor of a particular plantation and according to his patent not beholden to Virginian law) undertook direct and nonconsensual "trade" with Native people across the bay. He threw trade goods at the Accawmacks' canoes on the Eastern Shore while confiscating their corn, jeopardizing a precious English alliance and earning the censure of Virginia's brand-new assembly, which spent much of its first session, the first meeting of a representative government in the English colonies, discussing tense Anglo-Native interactions like this one.[33] For Algonquians, inconsistencies demonstrated that the English elites in charge of diplomacy and their own public good could not be trusted. Their actions threatened to turn friendly Algonquian neighbors against the entire colony. At the very least, they exposed the company's lack of control over self-interested planters and traders.

Leaders at outlying settlements were tasked with keeping Native people in designated areas of their plantations and with prescribing appropriate movement inside of English domains.[34] The assembly in 1619 forbade provoking violence with Native people or stealing goods but permitted trade in goods and services, such as "killing of Deere, Fishing, beating Corne, & other works." But Native people's knowledge of the landscape made them difficult to track and surveil. "They are a most treacherous people," the assembly generalized, "& quickly gone [escaped] when they have done a villainy." English settlers were to tread lightly and neither encourage nor discourage Native visits to their plantations. Archaeologists suggest that work in English settlements—tasks like fishing and processing deer—might have been done by Native men and women offsite and products brought to be traded at some plantations.³⁵ For those working at the settlement or coming from a distance, the assembly allowed five or six Native people housed in separate lodgings per settlement, except for those with a "lone" English inhabitant. To facilitate relatively peaceful relationships, each borough was to take part in the education and conversion of male Native children and raise a crop of useful Christian servants and go-betweens; the specification that the children be boys also might imply concern about sexual contact between Englishmen and Native girls and women. Children raised among the English might attend a college to be built for the Christianization of Native youths.³⁶ As non-Christian laborers, as children, and as members of households, these Native people were prescribed role-specific movements within the bounds of English settlement.

Members of the assembly also sought to control English movement in Native places by building an intelligence network of their own. English people were allowed to trade goods with their Native neighbors—with the exceptions of powder, shot, and European-bred dogs—but were required to notify the commander or governor of their intention to visit any Native "townes, habitations, or places of resort."³⁷ Further, colonists leaving the plantation were not to travel more than twenty miles away without specific leave and were to be gone from the settlement no longer than seven days. Such specificity implies that settlers were trading not only in mappable towns but in seasonal dispersal and foraging spots more difficult for planters to find. Plantation leaders decided the trading privileges of their residents.³⁸ This law may have been passed to protect the interests of some burgesses thinking of trading beyond Powhatan territory, but it also discouraged planters like Martin from crossing the bay to raid the Accawmacks and encouraged officials to curtail the movements of liabilities like him. Instead, the commanders of the plantations near to one another were to coordinate and gather intelligence on local trade, diplomacy, and the movement of English and Native people nearby.

While company commanders and landholders might have seen these strategies as in the colony's best interest, English relationships with Native people often revolved around the actions of nonelite settlers uninvested in the colonial officials' visions for their plantations. Tenants and servants were a weak link in the efforts to regulate and monitor contact. Facing privation and brutal work regimens, unfree men had been "forced to flee for reliefe to the Savage Enemy" for over a decade. Planters sought laborers as never before to plant and tend to profitable tobacco, and new customs and laws—passed by assembly members with many bonded laborers of their own—formalized indentured servitude in Virginia, punished breaches of contract and bad behavior, and ensured individual planters' private property rights over their servants' time and eventually over the bodies of enslaved laborers.[39] Planters also had to protect their property from other planters, warned not to "intic[e] awaye the Tenants & Servants of any particular plantation from the place where they are seated." But Native people were under no such obligation, and some indeed harbored fugitive colonists in their towns. Therefore, laws governing the movements and relationships of servants were especially strict. Servants faced physical punishment based on English vagrancy laws for trading with and stealing from Native people, and, perhaps most significantly, using Native canoes to travel.[40] Not only were Native people uncontrollable but their mobility contributed to the possible uncontrollability of non-Native people. Ill-behaved servants, who might illegally trade or brawl with Native people, were a liability to English planters struggling to control English relationships with Native neighbors.

Even in peace, English leaders did not trust that those who could move information across boundaries shared their evolving spatial vision for the Chesapeake. Two Powhatan women who had served as personal attendants to Pocahontas, following their English hosts' complaints that they were too expensive to keep within their households, were sent to Bermuda to find suitable husbands.[41] With so much time spent among the English, perhaps their Algonquian relatives doubted their loyalties and were hesitant to reclaim them, or perhaps officials worried about relevant intelligence they had gathered and were hesitant to return them. Interpreter Robert Poole was never seen as trustworthy by either side.[42] In 1619, interpreter Henry Spelman was tried for treason at Jamestown for confiding in Opechancanough about a "great man [that] should com and putt [the governor] out of his place." The governor, "beinge mercifull in sparinge his life have degraded him from his Capt: Ship . . . made him a servnnt to the Collony for Seaven years in quallytie of an Interpriter."[43] That Spelman was both valuable as an interpreter and disgraced demonstrated an irony for leaders who sometimes valued control over boundaries and at other times valued the profitable possibilities inherent in crossing them.

These types of tensions signaled the many pressures pushing Opechancanough over the course of some months to plan a massive attack on the English in 1622. His most obvious concern was the rapidly expanding

English population.⁴⁴ In early 1622, the English had asked Opechancanough to send a guide with them to mines in Monacan territory to the west, which might threaten the Powhatans' control of access to goods and people beyond the fall line.⁴⁵ Further, recalling tactics of the previous conflict, colonists boarded ships to visit raids on Native trading partners for corn when they were too slow in supplying it. This reneged on established Powhatan trading norms inside of their bounds and perhaps encouraged constituent chiefdoms to agree to Opechancanough's plan.⁴⁶ Finally, English leaders' continued insistence on trading to the north and east of the Powhatans, issuing commissions to planters to travel the bay to trade, threatened the controlled flow of European goods through the Powhatans.⁴⁷ The Powhatans occupied more of the Chesapeake than the English, but it became clear that communication lines and the flow of people and goods were not totally in Opechancanough's control.

Indeed, the Powhatans, like English leaders, faced cracks in control along their periphery. Perhaps because of Savage's presence, Opechancanough ultimately failed to convince the Accawmacks on the Eastern Shore to join in his developing plot to attack English settlements. On English plantations where Native people visited and resided on the western shore, others provided information to the English. One of Reverend George Thorpe's English servants, possibly informed by Thorpe's Native students living at Berkeley Hundred, alerted him to an impending attack and ran away so as not to die at the hands of the Powhatans since "his Master out of his good meaning was so void of suspition and full of confidence."⁴⁸ A Native person of unknown origin named Chauco, or Chanco, gave a warning that was believed but came too late to stop the attack.⁴⁹ Connections, perhaps even familial identities, that had developed through English expansion ran counter to Opechancanough's goals of secrecy and Powhatan unity.

Leaders like Esmy Shichans had allowed settlers like Savage to become neighbors for their mutual benefit, with go-betweens' privileged positions further undermining Powhatan control over goods and other werowances. However, to the west, leaders of English plantations and of the Powhatan chiefdom realized how intricately and uncontrollably they were linked by the Chesapeake, especially as they tried to separate from one another. Their respective attempts to gain an edge over the other, the English over riverfront land and the Powhatans over trade, only underscored their connectedness. The English relied on past and present Native occupation to guide their expansion, feed settlers, and return unhappy laborers. English planters were also caught between a reality of interconnectedness and permeability facilitated by the Algonquian landscape, their own ideal boundary between English and Native people, and Powhatan ideas about appropriate boundaries. Attempts to legislate separation were undercut by self-interested colonists and werowances at every turn. English use of Powhatan information and goods through local relationships helped Algonquians control the dispersal of intelligence, ultimately leading to Opechancanough's successful attack on English outlying settlements.[50]

Putting the Attack in Motion

Powhatan leader Nemattanew walked freely to one of the plantations on the north side of the James, far west of Jamestown. Near the site of the proposed college, in early spring of 1622 some settlements hosted just one house. Glimpsing valuable goods inside the home of a man named Morgan, he offered to guide the settler from his home down a path and across the forested peninsula to trade. Such an offer could mean a day trip to a Powhatan-allied town nearby, or it could mean travel down paths and across rivers where few English people went, and where Morgan would be dependent on his guide. Morgan agreed and told no one he had gone into the woods with an enemy of English expansion. (If he had had permission previously to trade at that town, why would he have accepted such a dubious guide?) Already, Morgan had broken several English laws.[51]

Morgan was gone, and his household did not know where. Nemattanew emerged from the woods into Morgan's plantation several days later, wearing Morgan's hallmark red cap. His servants understood what the sight meant immediately, and Nemattanew confirmed that Morgan was dead. Assuming that he had been murdered along the Native routes by his guide, the servants resolved to bring Nemattanew to the governor of Berkeley Hundred and deputy of the College Lands, Reverend George Thorpe. Powhatan leaders had developed a relationship with Thorpe as he had sought since his arrival in 1620 to convert Native children and Opechancanough. He had brought Native children into English homes and constructed English homes in Native places in an effort to win them over, and so Native intelligence about his household would have been thorough. Nemattanew resisted the Englishmen's efforts to drag him before a magistrate. The assumption that Nemattanew murdered an ordinary Englishman may have been incorrect, but from his perspective someone at the colony, not local, level should have met with him about a developing diplomatic incident. The servants shot him.[52]

Nemattanew did not survive. While Opechancanough had by then probably already determined a violent course against the English, the needless death of a high-ranking Pamunkey leader reinforced its necessity. The English were spread too thin and their governance at crucial moments too ineffective to control their servants and planters, to communicate and conduct consistent diplomacy among themselves and the Powhatans. Opechancanough would turn this diplomatic flaw to his advantage the next year.

In March 1622, the Powhatans' attack facilitated the breakdown of the English settlements and networks that they had only just allowed to flourish. The Powhatans launched the Second Anglo-Powhatan War with a massive coordinated assault on twenty English settlements, the culmination of extensive knowledge of habits and resources on the budding plantations and at places like the Falling Creek ironworks.[53] Otherwise unarmed Native men bearing goods to trade found the English inside of their homes and in the fields, "well knowing in what places and quarters each of our men were, in regard to their daily familiarity."[54] At the predictable midday mealtime, seizing a moment of congregation and vulnerability, "they fell to Work all at once every where, knocking the English unawares on the Head, some with their Hatchets, which they call Tommahauks, others with the Hows and Axes of the English themselves, shooting at those who escap'd the Reach of their Hands."[55] A quarter of the colonists, 350 people, were killed and dozens taken captive.[56] The warriors culled farm animals, cut down tobacco and corn, and mutilated the deceased, horrifying the English as "a fresh murder, defacing, dragging, and mangling the dead carkasses into many pieces, and carrying some parts away in derision."[57] Opechancanough planned for the long term by waiting until Powhatan families were safely dispersed for the season, and by taking women captive to bargain for a ceasefire during corn planting.[58]

Beyond wiping out a quarter of the colony's population in days, the beginning of this second Anglo-Powhatan War contracted English borders. Real horror began in the days and weeks that followed with the collapse of the plantation landscape and economy, and with it any sense of safety at unfortified fringe settlements. The English lost control of promising settlements in Henrico, Charles City, and Martin's Hundred, the last of which saw over seventy deaths alone. Some survivors were evacuated to nearby plantations; Native people returned to burn settlements and harass people who remained, causing additional casualities for years.[59] On either side of English fortifications, many English and Powhatan combatants might have been reminded of the First Anglo-Powhatan War a decade before. English trade with the Powhatans was abruptly severed while Opechancanough anticipated the desperate movements of the colonists. In letters copied for company investors in London, one after another the colonists pleaded for help or rescue. "We are all undone," moaned Lady Wyatt. William Rowlshy tried to buy his wife a single hen, unaffordable because of inflated prices. Christopher Davison's servants and crop of corn on the Eastern Shore were spared by Native people, but he had no way to get there from the mainland. Colonists watched from their doorways as Powhatans slaughtered their cattle in untended fields. They dared not plant corn since once it grew tall enough, Powhatan attackers could hide there. Pigs permitted to propagate in the woods remained there since "we dare scarce stepp out of dores neither for wood nor water."[60]

Death and disorder followed the abrupt population shifts caused by the Powhatan attack. In 1622, the *Abigail*, bearing English servants, brought sudden sickness and more acute hunger to a colony already clustered in James Fort. George Sandys wrote that "the lyveing [are] hardlie able to bury the dead" and continued, "Extreme hath beene the mortalitie of this yeare, wch I am afraid hath double the Nomber of thse wch were massacred."[61] One contemporary estimated that five to six hundred people succumbed to disease in the year following the attack. Sickness faced colonists inside of the forts and war faced people without, and everyone slowly starved "so that out of nessessitie they must have perished either by the Enemye, or famyne."[62] Caribbean sailors stopping in to port were stunned by the bizarre combination of disorganization and inaction greeting them, reporting that no one had unloaded the goods on the *Abigail* two weeks after its arrival at Jamestown, "everie tide being overflowed with water and the trunks readie to bee swallowed." As people remained concentrated at Jamestown, sick and hungry servants spread illness, while those too ill "have died in the streets at James Towne, and so little cared for that they have lien untill the hogs have eaten theyr Corps."[63] The brisk trade of people and goods along the James River had come to a halt and underscored the precariousness of the plantation economy.

With the destruction of the plantations themselves, English labor regimes fell apart and human suffering revealed deepening class divisions. Nonelites learned that they had little control over their location or fate in wartime, exacerbated by the scattered nature of settlement. Servants bore starvation and abandonment disproportionately. "A pinte of meal must serve 3 dayes," wrote home Richard Frethorne, who asked for cheese and a voyage home from his parents and clergyman. He also asked for clothes since a fellow servant, engaged in a trade for foodstuffs, stole Frethorne's cloak and "to his dying hower would not tell mee" where he sold it. These servants also shared meager provisions with captured Powhatans who were enslaved according to the English ideas of just war—enslavement "was by pollicie," wrote Frethorne—and defended themselves and crops from attack knowing full well any call to "the nighest helpe that Wee have" ten miles away would come too late.[64] In need themselves, colonists sold their servants "like a damme Slave," said Thomas Atkins of the man who held him in servitude, and who bartered him for a shirt. Henry Briggs wrote, "My master hath sould me & ye rest of my ffellowes" and packed to leave Virginia.[65] The wealthiest men held on—and became wealthier. During the ongoing war in 1625, half of the remaining colonists were servants, and half of the remaining servants were owned by just ten men. While burgesses claimed otherwise (in response to rumors that servants died alone under hedges, they replied that no one died alone under hedges because "there are none in Virginia"), servants paid the price of English expansion into Algonquian territories.[66] William Capps, himself owner of several indentures, pitied the planter without laborers and land to fend off such catastrophe: "Plants gone, that's 500 waight of Tobacco, yea and what shall this man doe, runne after the Indians?"[67] The 1622 Native attack and following chaos underscored for unfree people the distance between a small number of rich men and everyone else.

With so many displaced and unable to grow crops, securing English landholdings became an "absolute necessitie" and central charge from investors in England.[68] The public commentators on the Second Anglo-Powhatan War dwelled on the dangerous spatial relationships between the attackers and the attacked, drawn to commenting darkly on a history of mornings in which settlers and Native people sat together at the breakfast table. They pointed out the Powhatan betrayal of their "Benefactors" as they justified a scorched-earth English military campaign, but they also condemned the dead. "Yet were the hearts of the English ever stupid," said commentator Edward Waterhouse in hindsight.[69] In William Bullock's judgment years later, "the English, by reporting trust and confidence in the Indian, gave the opportunity.... There is no danger in them, except you give them weapons, and stand still whilst they destroy you."[70] Reverend George Thorpe, who had arrived in 1620 to lead the mission effort and had worked out an agreement with Opechancanough in the months preceding the attack to bring entire Native families into English homes, seemed especially and willfully ignorant. He seemed to overlook the risks of daily familiarity with the Powhatans and had ensured open lines of communication with Powhatan leadership. His story served as a warning to newly arrived colonists. "He thought nothing too deare for them, he never denied them any thing" in his efforts to convert them to Christianity, John Smith said.[71]

The Powhatans recognized how trade increased English vulnerability. Native surveillance was heightened by the predictable English decision to disperse patents inside of Algonquian districts and specifically women's fields.[72] In the aftermath of the attack, Governor Francis Wyatt was surrounded by Native enemies on the James River, a demographic situation that worsened during the first year of the war as planters sailed to Esmy Shichans's Eastern Shore or England for safety and many more English people died of disease. Instead of blaming Anglo-Native intimacy, colony leader Edwin Sandys saw the problem inherent in expanding settlement while patrolling and communicating between plantations: "How is it possible to govern [English] people so dispersed; especially such as for the most part sent over?" His own plantation boundaries and presence in the Chesapeake in question, Sandys called the attack a moment for "reformacon."[73] Planter John Martin pointed out that people of all "ranke" had been trading with Native people, and that "the infinite trade" had in fact strengthened the alliance between the attacking groups because the Powhatans had directed that trade. He also pointed out that the English had not yet stifled the Powhatans' access to corn or goods from Native people south of the Chesapeake, and from other Algonquians on the Eastern Shore. Through their time spent in the forts and on plantations, the Powhatans accumulated "manie peeces [firearms] besides, with Powder and Shott, and knowing too well how to use them."[74] The English leaders on the ground planning retaliation would have to reckon with superior Algonquian understandings of the Chesapeake's alternative food sources, escape routes, and previously acquired English arms and intelligence.

The obvious solution for the English was to change settlement strategies, and the nature of Anglo-Native relations with them. The Virginia Company could end the placement of Native children in English households, the welcoming of Native people at English tables, and the permission for

English traders to sail to Native towns. Commentators posited that expanding English territory through stewardship of the land necessitated removing Native people from it. "The Countrey is not so good," Waterhouse said, "as the Natives are bad, whose barbrous Savagenesse needs more cultivation then the ground it selfe, being more overspread with incivilitie and treachery, then that with Bryers."[75] A successful military campaign could wipe away their presence along the rivers and cut off access to resources: "surprisinge them in their habitations, intercepting them in theire hunting, burninge theire Townes, demolishing theire Temples, destroyinge theire Canoes, plucking upp theire weares, carying away theire Corne." The company recommended the enslavement of Native enemies, to be divided with other trade goods and prizes that enriched the planters turned soldiers.[76]

To separate Native and English people, the English attempted to exert greater control over the footprint of people and plantations, encouraging planned and uniform fortification on the Chesapeake's peninsulas. In the immediate aftermath of the attack English leaders consolidated people and cattle from dozens of outlying settlements into places that remained accessible to one another by ship, near Jamestown and the mouth of the James River, including Kecoughtan and Newport News, and on the south side of the river at Jordan's Journey and the north side at Shirley Hundred.[77] Between 1622 and 1624, plans for connected, defensive boundaries developed, although these were often not executed. In 1623, colonists returned to abandoned settlements; all houses were to be palisaded, and neighbors were ordered to work together to construct shared fence lines.[78] Military expedition labor was pooled from the remaining able-bodied men, to be sent on seasonal marches against the Powhatans. Military engineers organized workers to fortify the core settlements, and colonists coalesced at nearby forts as administrative centers. The settlers fell into the construction, seasonal rhythms, and bureaucracy of a long-term military campaign.[79]

Many English leaders recognized that creating a defensible border was only possible by coopting the Native landscape in new ways. Colonist John Martin, who had attacked the Accawmacks before the conflict despite their friendliness toward the English, submitted a list of suggestions at the end of 1622 about how it might be done. In addition to halting the trade and conducting seasonal marches, he believed the English should resettle the capitals of every original Powhatan district, already situated and cleared for fishing and farming. They would map an English "shire" atop each Algonquian district; Martin even suggested that thirty-two English shires should each send a hundred men to settle in each of the thirty-two Powhatan districts (sparing people on the friendly Eastern Shore). Virginia's new capital would logically be at the center of Powhatan power, Opechancanough's seat on the Pamunkey River. Martin thus recognized that the Powhatan chiefdom's geographic distribution and network, down to land use and relations among districts, provided Opechancanough with resources and military strength and was suited to the environment. Despite new defensive strategies meant to physically separate Powhatan and English places, the practice of mapping English claims onto Native places continued.[80]

Many colony leaders and settlers, some of whom took part in the First Anglo-Powhatan War, adapted with difficulty to this period of heightened threat, especially in how Native settlements in the Chesapeake shaped military engagement. "In Somer time when the corne and weeds are growne high, heer will be much mischief done, as the Attempts of the Indians in these two months of march and Aprill," Captain John Harvey warned in 1624.[81] Thicker foliage in summer forests provided camouflage. Powhatan men could simply kill people and cattle that spent their days beyond the palisades in clearings for crops and pasture. Algonquian families and entire towns might prove difficult to find when Algonquians dispersed inland in late autumn and early spring to forage.[82] Cleared fields meant not just productivity to colonists but some reprieve from danger and better awareness of surroundings.

Transformation of Native land as a path toward victory entered into deliberations in Jamestown. While others proposed burning Native canoes and boats, Martin proposed crippling Powhatan alliances by amphibious attack in the hope of cutting off supplies and subjecting captives to labor on English plantations. The English strategy would require both an army dedicated to "contynuallie harassinge and burneinge all their Townes in winter" and "90 shallopps, that in May, June, July and August may Scoure the Baye and . . . the Rivers [that] are belonginge to Opekankano" to intercept trade and fishing and avoid "a Tedious Warr."[83] Unable to gain the desired decisive victory by 1624, two years after the initial attack, a pessimistic Captain John Harvey guessed that the war would drag on for two or three years more.[84] That year, the Virginia Company's charter was revoked due to conditions in the colony and a host of other problems, placing the colony directly under royal control.[85]

The attack encouraged attempts to sever communication and the sharing of places and trade, but prosecuting a war with a numerous and well-organized enemy required intelligence and alliances across the bay. Native leaders on the Potomac and Eastern Shore proved eager to provide knowledge and trade at the expense of Opechancanough. As English colonists renewed seasonal raids for corn harvests, their survival was dependent on such leaders who had broken alliances with the Powhatans and engaged instead with English traders and interpreters. While they might promote the destruction of Native people nearby, English elites profited from Algonquian networks more distant from Jamestown.

Translators and other boundary-crossers between English and Algonquian places thrust these broader changes in power into stark relief, as they took on the dangerous work of creating new alliances amid fracturing relationships between the Powhatans and English and among Algonquian chiefdoms. One man recognized Henry Spelman aboard an English boat and told him of an imminent attack, which his people had chosen to avoid joining. In perhaps the same episode, Spelman took an informant and a small armed force to a nearby werowance—possibly to the Patawomecks themselves—to verify the story. It was an unfortunate move: "Ye kinge in his presence caused the fellowes head to bee cut of & cast into the fire before the said captain, his face (a bad reward to betray him that had given him so faigthfull a warninge)."[86] After fighting broke out, Thomas Savage continued to serve as an emissary between Esmy Shichans and the colonists. Meanwhile, Henry Spelman returned north to secure an alliance between the English and the Patawomecks, necessary for English survival.[87]

In response to English aggression and new alliances, Powhatans relied on the Chesapeake environment to plan attacks and mitigate risks afterward. The English in turn adapted to Algonquian patterns of surprise attacks, exchange of captives, and periodic truce-making. Powhatans used the landscape to their advantage; wetlands undesirable to English farmers provided shelter against enemies and slowed the progress of colonial expeditions. Supplies of starchy tuckahoe in shallow water meant that Algonquian families ate in wartime.[88] Powhatan tactics also gave them an upper hand over early modern English experience in siege warfare and campaign seasons in densely settled areas. Using that experience to gauge their losses, colonists marveled at how Powhatan raiders "utterlie demolished" two riverside forts in 1622, which like many English castles "stood upon high ground their Cliffs being Steepe."[89] Elsewhere, when colonists ran for nearby palisades, Powhatan men promptly burned vacated English homes, shrinking the English presence on the landscape for a brief time.[90] In perpetual pursuit during the war, the English were perplexed and frustrated at what they viewed as cowardice on the part of the retreating Powhatans, who "flye as so many Hares; much faster then from their tormenting Devill" into the woods.[91] Not just Native knowledge but English ignorance and demoralization made possible the Algonquians' low-risk military strategies.

Captive-taking proved another key Algonquian tactic that mitigated risk, necessitating parleys and periodic truces that facilitated exchanges of people. Sandys promised the destruction of the Powhatans but only "after the restitution of their prisoners," primarily women taken during the initial attack.[92] The Powhatan recognized their leverage and offered to return people taken from Martin's Hundred in spring of the year following the attack in exchange for a ceasefire that would allow them to plant corn without fear.[93] Anne Jackson was taken captive in 1622, repatriated, and transported back to England in 1629; others were forced to sell their labor to other colonists to pay off ransoms made to the Powhatans.[94] The English effort to take captives was opportunistic rather than diplomatic, facilitating intelligence-gathering and short-term financial gain. In 1622, two captured Powhatans provided the whereabouts of missing English prisoners before they themselves were sold into slavery.[95] After an incident during which he slayed friendly Patawomecks for booty, Captain Isaac Maddison caught the werowance "and his sonne, taken prisoners brought to James Towne, brought home agayne, ransomed," effectively terrorizing one of only a few allies.[96] During a temporary truce in 1629, the governor sent an Algonquian man, "who not withstanding wee forebore to kill or punishe," to Opechancanough to negotiate for an end to depredations of livestock.[97] As the war transformed and lengthened, captive-taking ensured that enemies and temporary allies would return to negotiations. Even though captives were caught in power grabs, their role in Native diplomacy underscored ongoing Powhatan power.

Raiding and Trading with Purpose

By the end of 1622, the English elites had adapted to Algonquian warfare by reorienting the goals of their military campaigns from extirpation to profit. Guarding their fields and still wanting for military supplies and food, planters and servants ventured out again to plant tobacco; the Company enticed settlers onto Company land with promises of compensation or improvements to the land.[98] The English recovered from their initial devastation and confusion not through subsequent victories in battle but by food raids, starving Algonquians and enriching themselves. In 1624, alongside men required to march against the Powhatans, the English confiscated the Pamunkeys' central corn supply over a two-day battle, "sufficient to have sustained four thousand men for a twelvemonth."[99] Settlers and Powhatans began to fight seasonally at harvest time, a long-term strategy employed by English elites to benefit from Native agricultural labor.[100] Simultaneously, alliances with Algonquians on the fringes of the Powhatan chiefdom supplemented food stores. In pursuit of booty to sell at inflated prices, English elites profited handsomely from both strategies. Then, they invested their prizes in land and in large numbers of bonded laborers.[101] For almost a decade, Powhatan cornfields directly fueled the growth of English tobacco fields.

To profit and sustain themselves, English leaders integrated trading and raiding along the bay as interchangeable strategies. Immediately after the initial Powhatan attack on outlying English farms, the retaliating English sought corn along every route, "eyther from our freends by trade, or from our enemies by force, though wee will to our uttermost endevor both."[102] Meanwhile, with limited munitions, they focused seasonal raids on the Powhatans in order to weaken the enemy at the center of the Powhatan chiefdom.[103] Employing different strategies, some mariners pushed even farther to the north and south ends of the Chesapeake in pursuit of furs to trade and other sources of income or foodstuffs. In 1626, George Sandys paid an interpreter to seek furs from the Patuxents to the north.[104] He bemoaned Jamestown's location, chosen for its defensibility, so near the Powhatans in the wake of the desolation. Reevaluating Jamestown's safety in light of Powhatan riverine access, Sandys now argued that it should have been built in a more defensible position—against both Native and foreign enemies—on the Eastern Shore and nearer friendly trading Native people.[105] Looking beyond the Powhatan for resources, the English shifted dependence onto Native maritime networks at a distance from the war.

While many settlers proved impatient and turned with ease toward violence, they provided high-risk opportunities for their Native allies. The Patawomecks especially experienced the push and pull of violence and profit during the war. To gain their alliance in 1622, the English helped the Patawomecks to combat nearby enemies in exchange for corn. But the budding relationship with the English, and English inability to police their own men, proved risky to new allies: acting on a rumor of betrayal and on no higher authority, Captain Isaac Maddison killed between thirty or forty allied Patawomecks on an expedition, threatening the buildup of goodwill.[106] From his place on the York River, Opechancanough understood that maintaining control of corn and intelligence during the war relied on stopping traders from circumventing Powhatan influence and traveling into the arms of outside groups. In 1622, the Powhatans brought news of the initial attack to Englishman Raleigh Croshaw and the Patawomecks while they were trading along the Potomac. They sought to pay two baskets of beads to the Patawomecks to have them kill Croshaw, and the messenger told the Patawomeck werowance that "before the end of two Moones there should not be an Englishman in all their Countries." It was probably a lie since the Powhatans were not pursuing an aggressive military strategy in the moment after the initial attack, but it was also a warning not to invest in these new ties with the English at the expense of old ones. The werowance justified his neutrality with kinship, reasoning that "the English were his friends" and Opechancanough's brother and werowance, Opitchapam, "was his brother, therefore there should be no blood shed betwixt them."[107] Opechancanough had reason to worry about English traders who, just like Native interlopers, represented a diplomatic as well as a military and economic threat.

Although Opechancanough's messages failed to have their desired effect, the fears behind them proved true: the Patawomecks chose to ally with the English and took part in their own surprise attack against a core Powhatan group, the Pamunkeys. In the summer of 1623, the Patawomecks invited Pamunkey leadership to a parley at their "neutral" capital and then poisoned them according to a plan they hatched with the English.[108] The Patawomecks, like the English, understood that periodic truces and surprise attacks stretched thin the line between a nominal ally and an enemy, and maintaining even frayed relationships with both Powhatans and English colonists meant surviving and regrouping for the next season of warfare.

Native navigation of water and of English goings-on highlighted the English place in Algonquian diplomacy and English vulnerability to violence. In spring 1623, Potomac River people "woke Mr. Pountis his shallop [small boat] & hewed her too pieces." They regrouped and "came with 60 canouse to take the unlucky ship the *Tyger*," an English transport vessel that had earlier unloaded its second cargo of indentured servants and women intended for Virginia. In October of the previous year, Ralph Hamor had been commissioned with the same ship to gather corn by trade from the Patawomecks, and nearby people at odds with them, like the Piscataways and Nacotchtanks, may have recognized the same watercraft months later.[109] The *Tyger*'s skeleton crew of "4 saylers & some few land men" awoke to somewhere between ten and forty warriors in each of sixty long dugout canoes, intent on capturing the Englishmen's vessel by surprise attack. Acting fast and catching a lucky wind, the sailors "whipped up sayles & went faster [than] theyr Canowes."[110] With the help of the Patawomecks, the English returned to destroy the Nacotchtanks and their homes and corn supply, which they had hidden deep in the woods. In return, the Patawomecks were supposed to join the fight against Opechancanough, but they held back, citing the weather and the need for food in their towns.[111] Perhaps this was true, or perhaps the Patawomecks played the English for their help against their nearby enemies without having to enter the fray further.

Meanwhile, across the bay on the Eastern Shore, an entirely different set of Anglo-Powhatan exchanges continued to develop. Accawmacks sheltered colonists while they and their English neighbors shipped corn to English combatants via traders on the western shore. Algonquians who lived among the English continued to shape English experiences and movements but through long-term alliances rather than wartime captive-taking and plundering. Fewer palisades and a bay separating them from the conflict meant more opportunities for routine interactions. As the war progressed, laws that governed the mainland excluded Accawmacks and their English neighbors. The Virginia Assembly prohibited speaking with Native people in 1631 except on the Eastern Shore, for example, recognizing their developing alliance and trade with the Accawmacks.[112] Over the years, the Accawmacks granted dispersed parcels to the English.[113] Archaeological evidence along Old Plantation Creek near Cape Charles on the tip of the peninsula indicates that settlers tore down or built atop the place where English palisades once stood only decades before, a stark contrast to reflections of defensive strategy to the west.[114]

The difference between Accawmacks' ties to the English and the Patawomecks' more volatile relationships with traders to the west highlights how a spectrum of interpersonal, local relationships kept communication lines open. On the Eastern Shore, mundane hints illuminate everyday life alongside permanently settled English people as it developed over decades: Edward Bestwick's probate inventory at the time of his death, for instance, listed three "Indian bowles," and his accounts noted that two other settlers owed him bowls. Thomas Jolly drowned in a creek with green beads and peake, a form of currency, in his pocket. Anthony Linny's probate inventory reveals that he kept four Native-made reed mats in his home's hall space where company gathered and one by his bed, some Native baskets with his tools, and seven Native-made bowls near the hearth. Cooked meals, salted meats, and aid in travel or in emergencies probably also accompanied Native people to English plantations, though the convenience and permanency of reusable materials like pots and baskets are the only remaining evidence of the food and exchange items once inside them.[115] With fewer palisades or pales around English or Algonquian towns on the Eastern Shore, Accawmacks influenced English settlement patterns and, as Algonquian women at Jamestown had in previous decades, even the most private of English domains. Their interactions demonstrate that as warfare continued and Powhatan control diminished, local diplomacy might thwart the intentions behind broader calls for English-Native boundaries.

From the devastation of the 1622 attack, new settlement patterns and alliances eroded Powhatan abilities to control movement of people and goods. The English were forced to adapt to the Native networks and alter their own settlement patterns to secure people and land, but the fight proved profitable for the mariners who had successfully raided Native foods and cultivated new Native alliances. While officials sought to disentangle the Powhatan and English to secure the colony, planters did not need to annihilate their enemies; they just needed to tap Native alliances and resources along the bay, to control more labor and land. As the English glutted the market with copper through trade and alliances with Algonquians, English tobacco farmers claimed an important toehold in the James River basin, foreshadowing Virginia's embrace of slavery-driven tobacco culture.

Resettling with New Limits

When newly arrived laborers approached the palisaded walls on William Tucker's or Edward Bennett's plantations, or George Yeardley's skiff, shallop, and bark near Jamestown, they looked on Native places reshaped by decades of conflict with colonists and the riches that resulted from that conflict.[116] Using the wealth they accrued from raids and Native alliances to purchase labor and plant tobacco on Native land, English elites began to rebuild a world organized by private property and Atlantic trade along the James River. To many English leaders, the permanent destruction of the Powhatan polity was tied to the transformation and regulation of

Powhatan landscapes. Colonial officials attempted to construct a recognizably English landscape out of palisades and orderly settlement, all while pursuing a fast-paced, geographically broad-ranging war against Powhatan forces. An accompanying transformation of legal authority had profound impacts for local interactions and land use for both Native and English people. The implementation of new physical and legal boundaries, what would become Virginia's counties and fort system, allowed military leaders to consolidate power beyond a state of war. While colonists were barred from interacting with Native people, enslaved people, servants, and Native people adapted to one another anew through continued proximity.

In the years following the 1622 attack, land patents and rents demonstrated English attempts to settle the mouth of the James River piece by piece, settling into the districts of their Algonquian neighbors. The 1625 muster lists five forts, three of which were under company treasurer George Sandys's name. Twenty-three settlements, all to the south and east of Jamestown in Elizabeth City close to the mouth of the James, were palisaded. By 1624, English commander John Utie patented land bordering the Nansemond districts south of the James River, and in 1626 Lieutenant Thomas Flint settled the "Indian howse thickett" on the east side of the Hampton River possibly belonging to the Kecoughtans, a trend in settling on Native settlements cleared by warfare other colonists followed.[117] John Leyden was granted a new tract near Blunt Point in 1628 downriver from Jamestown on the north shore in lieu of his settlements west of Jamestown, which had been obliterated by the Powhatans, "in regard of the great danger of planting the same."[118] By 1629, colonial claims again stretched north and west, and within a year colonists had claimed pieces of core Powhatan territory: for example, brothers Robert and Toby Felgate were granted Kiskiak land on the Pamunkey River, a corn-producing area targeted by English raiders only a few years before. In 1632, colonists claimed more land in Nansemond territory on the south shore of the James, then continued into Chickahominy territory, and on the west side of the Chickahominy River in Paspahegh territory—a crucial place where colonists and Powhatans had parleyed throughout the war.[119] English people continued to claim strategic Powhatan farmland, towns, shoreline, and important nodes of interaction, threatening to cleave core districts apart from one another and usurp land productive for Algonquians.

Meanwhile, Virginia's new governor John Harvey implemented legal separations between Native people and settlers that he hoped would end the conflict, but his new policies threatened to cut into profits. Traders and raiders both developed alliances based on their antagonism toward the new administration. Becoming governor in 1628, the former shipmaster ordered thrice-yearly marches, a halt to all peace talks, and corn cultivation to be undertaken by the colonists themselves.[120] The assembly banned all private Native trade in 1631 (except on the Eastern Shore), and the following year the governor issued a direct order that all merchants "saile directlie to the port of James Citty; and that you unlade no goods nor breake any bulke until you shall come to an anchor there" to halt smuggling.[121] All of these changes eroded enterprising colonists' goodwill toward Harvey, which dissipated altogether after he secured a truce with the Chickahominies and the Powhatans in 1632.[122] Already stretching resources because of this influx and a crop blight, colonists resented the "dangerous peace" prohibiting them from seizing Powhatan corn and retaliating against property and livestock damage inflicted by Powhatan raiders. Although reoccupying Native settlements from both sides of the James River enabled burgeoning numbers of "inhabitants to clear the grounds and lands" and plant their own crops, inflated food prices, a rising population, and the delicate peace meant that trade continued despite Harvey's attempts to shut it down.[123] After all, there were "no meanes left to relieve their wants without transgressing his Commands."[124] Although the initial 1622 attack caused irreparable changes in the colony, it survived because a handful of elites thrived by crossing these types of boundaries, with Native help and resources, in the decade of war.

The truce in 1632 ended the war and allowed Harvey to consolidate a recognizably English landscape very different from Virginia before 1622. The Powhatans moved inland and upriver as settlements with new English, African, and continental European arrivals settled in their territories on the north and south banks of the James River all the way to the fall line. The English population grew. In 1625, the English settlements held 1,300 people; by 1629, there were 2,000 settlers; by 1640, there were 8,000, mostly new English immigrants.[125] Harvey buttressed the English foothold and put in place Governor Wyatt's plans for a much longer palisade, a wall to stretch the length of the lower peninsula between the James and York Rivers. The wall did little for defense since it stopped at the river and rotted in place in the wet Chesapeake climate, but as the colony "began to bee of more plenty and Security . . . the planters then first began to fence their ground, and plant Corne; the few Cattell they had encreased to such numbers that they were able to help their neighbour plantations."[126] He and the council also encouraged settlement to buffer the burgeoning James River plantations against the Powhatans, providing an incentive from 1630 onward "for securing a tract of land called the Forest, bordering on the chief residence of the Pamunkey King, the most dangerous head of the Indian enemy" of "50 acres to all persons the first year and 25 the second year, who should venture to seat on south side of the Pamunkey River."[127] Woodlands on which Native people relied, like other Chesapeake land, would be bounded out as private property.

The spread of settlers, and an influx of more migrants, necessitated a more efficient way for the English to settle disputes with each other and with Algonquians beyond Jamestown. The establishment of the county system assigned authority over local affairs to planters, who translated that responsibility into the creation of a local elite class. County justices stewarded the funding and firepower behind defending borders, collecting ammunition, arms, and taxes to fund future military campaigns and infrastructure like ferries and roads.[128] Local elites gained new powers to adjudicate disputes, and it was with these local elites that many Native people would develop relationships on court days and in paths and fields. The new system encouraged the erasure and replacement of Native places. In 1634, the General Assembly in part realized Martin's vision and divided land by the rivers into "shires" with names that mirrored county seats in England, imposing a firmly English lexicon on the landscape of the Chesapeake. At Weyanoke, Kecoughtan, and Warraskoyack, English settlers continued to use the Algonquian names that had defined places and their former residents. But leaders at Kecoughtan had long protested the district's "savage name" and changed the settlement to Elizabeth City in 1620; in 1634, it became Elizabeth City shire. Warraskoyack became a shire in 1634 and was renamed Isle of Wight in 1637.[129] This aspect of John Martin's plan, to engineer English places on top of Powhatan districts, worked at least in name to separate places from their Native history. Archaeology at some plantations also reflects this increasing separation between peoples: a decline in remains from consumed game and Native wares at some outlying tobacco plantations indicates Algonquians no longer traded many foodstuffs into some English plantations in the second quarter of the seventeenth century. Instead, the English relied on Dutch shipping for continental goods they could buy on credit when the tobacco economy flourished and locally made English ceramics when it did not.[130] The growing number of patents and surveys inside of the shires allowed more planters and elites to participate in commerce along the James River.

While planters profited from the war, their servants' strategies for survival could run counter to the boundary-making ambitions of the people who held them in bondage. Some willingly left the English, like a group of Carib people from the West Indies who escaped in 1627 and made haste to Native towns.[131] Evidence points to continuing interactions and dependence on Algonquians to survive, in spite of the law. At a plantation called Neck-of-Land, primarily occupied by low-status people, evidence of the consumption of deer meat was ubiquitous—but not evidence of processing and butchering, suggesting that these functions were performed off the plantation by someone else, perhaps Algonquian people.[132] A palisaded complex owned by Councilman Sandys revealed that the bones of wild game, and especially fish, comprised 78 percent of faunal remains—but no fishing gear was found onsite, further signifying potential trade in vital proteins. Copper and glass beads were also found on a site dated to the Second Anglo-Powhatan War and after, supporting the idea that someone on the plantation hoped to trade with nearby Native people.[133] Although cattle and tobacco had quickly come to dominate the English Chesapeake landscape, on a local level some people—and perhaps especially unfree people—persisted in Anglo-Native trade for survival while they transformed the James River.

The Second Anglo-Powhatan War permanently transformed the relationship between plantation and Native spaces in ways that legal efforts to establish boundaries did not. Algonquian men took advantage of the integration of English plantations as nodes within larger Native trade and communication networks, walking through English fields, yards, and kitchens without suspicion for months before using that knowledge to destroy the occupants. Native people living near plantations coordinated for weeks but still continued to trade, sleep, and eat among English settlers. The everyday entanglements kept the English alive but gave an edge to the Powhatans.

The reenvisioning of the Chesapeake Bay and riverfronts wiped clean of Native history was only possible because of it: the corn sold by English marauders, the trade that fed servants, the fields cleared by Native women that became tobacco fields. In pursuing military strategies from fortified peninsulas to seasonal raids on towns, the English were the latest aggressors to threaten Chesapeake Algonquians. At the local level, werowances and Native traders had new bureaucracies and leaders to navigate in palisaded places, no longer boroughs but shires and then counties beyond Jamestown. While the Powhatans were never formally defeated, their attempts to contain the English resulted in the acceleration of English movement on Powhatan borders. The English built back from the destruction of 1622 with both established and new ways of marking physical, social, and legal boundaries and violent means of enforcing them. They replicated these practices on plantations connected by the river as their numbers grew.

For Opechancanough and the Powhatans, the war was not a defeat. The English did reduce Powhatan territory, their hold over chiefdoms on the periphery, and total control over the James River. But Opechancanough remained a leader to thousands of Algonquians, who lived in much the same ways as before, whose survival over a decade of depredations on their crops reinforced the value of environmental knowledge. But neither did it help realize a vision of control over goods and movement, including hemming in the English. The future looked equally uncertain for Algonquian people beyond the core of the Powhatan chiefdom, many of whom had thrown their lot in with English traders and interpreters who had become neighbors and allies. The truce of 1632 did not restore Opechancanough's control over information and goods; in fact, the multiple betrayals from the months before the 1622 attack and during the war only highlighted how much the reach of the chiefdom had shrunk. But the English, in their inability to control their own borders and people, were unreliable allies. Drawing advantage from these intimate relationships and the captive-taking and border-crossing caused by a decade of war to the west, a new generation of interlopers carved niches in the fur trade for themselves on the bay.

– 4 –

Sailors and Rumors in the Bay, 1622–1644

William Abram was a servant on Virginia's Eastern Shore, but not for much longer. In 1638, he armed himself with a bolt of cloth and "a booke to learne to speake the Indyan tongue." The cloth might have been stolen from a planter's trunk, the "booke" perhaps a folded paper with a handwritten list of common phrases from a planter's coat pocket.[1] Spreading the word household to household, Abram invited all men who shared his condition within two miles to cross waters, Native territory, and land claimed by Virginia and, more recently, Maryland. They would together seek sanctuary in New Netherland, and Abram reassured the others that he "speake very good dutch." Other servants had also left for Dutch territory, and while Abram could not be sure, the fact they had never returned suggested their success. Abram appealed to the servants' common experiences of violence, starvation, and oppression when he asked of his fellow servants, "Wherefore should wee stay here and bee slaves [when we] may goe to another place and live like gentlemen?"[2]

Knowledge of the wider world informing Abram's escape was available locally. In the 1630s, Abram and other servants saw canoes and ships move along the creeks of the Eastern Shore, where Dutch merchants had a strong trading presence, sailing beside Virginia and Maryland traders and Native people like the Susquehannocks from the head of the Chesapeake Bay. Abram's possessions—cloth and a dictionary—were the tools of trade and communication in the Native nations beyond. Their presence in Abram's sack indicates his hope that Native people would aid his escape. He had learned Dutch, and he could learn to communicate with Algonquians to ensure success in his travels. Using information about the connecting waterways and developing borders between Virginia and the Algonquians, and new neighbors the Marylanders and the Dutch, he hoped to translate the value of his goods and language skills into mobility through multiple colonies and Native places. His plan required imagining a voyage and life outside of the colony, beyond his legal status in stratified Virginian society and as a traveler and trading partner in his own right along Native-dominated Chesapeake waters.

During the 1630s, the waterways in the Chesapeake served both as information channels that strengthened kinship and alliances and at the same time as political borders, often at odds with one another. The Second Anglo-Powhatan War had weakened the Powhatan hold on the larger Chesapeake Bay and provided opportunities for Native people when the English sailed north of Opechancanough's domains. On the fringes of both Powhatan and English places, the water continued to facilitate local communication, more crucial than ever to developing and maintaining diplomacy and trade. Even as violence beween the Powhatans and English waned in the 1630s, Algonquians on the Potomac and the Eastern Shore, the far reaches of the Powhatans' direct influence, maintained safe and prosperous communities by tapping into and controlling the movement of information. As in other colonial contexts atop Native networks, colonists found their broad-ranging colonial ambitions in tension with expressions of Native sovereignty atop the landscape, while Native people found themselves in a unique position to leverage information as potential allies to newcomers.[3]

Despite a growing obsession with property and colonial boundaries, some newcomers believed that the pursuit of trade and knowledge around the Chesapeake's waterways were open and fluid ventures.[4] The Chesapeake's riparian geography, and how Native people used it during and before Abram's time, guided how ungovernable English and Native people moved and communicated with one another. Wielded by Native people and people like Abram using Native networks, information itself proved a force that broke through borders and highlighted the porousness of those borders. Sailing gave wind to this process and the rumor mill among localities. The Piscataways and Patawomecks, for example, leaned on rumors and diplomatic ties to contend with outsiders, from planters to non-Algonquians with claims in the Chesapeake like the Susquehannocks. While Powhatan power devolved and English servants and traders visited more often, Algonquians' intimate knowledge of the Chesapeake's waterways influenced the movement and ideas of unfree people like Abram, people who disregarded English leaders' attempts to make borders where they had little control.⁵

As with Abram's pursuit of freedom, Europeans of higher castes saw the Chesapeake as a passage rather than a barrier toward the fulfillment of a broad range of ambitions—often with little regard for multiplying colonial boundaries. Kent Island off the coast of Abram's Eastern Shore was the eye of the storm for many stakeholders in the trade in beaver pelts and other furs and skins, situated in the contested waters between Maryland and Virginia and between Susquehannock and Algonquian spheres of influence. The struggle over this promising trading post between people from multiple nations demonstrates how, for invested parties, the Chesapeake remained a single, fluid place contoured by extant Native networks.

Back in 1627, the Virginia Council had given soldier and trader William Claiborne, newly arrived in the colony as secretary and a surveyor, permission to explore up to the heads of the bay to "trade with Indians for Corne Skins or any other Comodities" useful to a colony at war, a practice colonists had employed for two decades.⁶ He was not alone, joined by investors, competitors like interpreter Henry Fleet, and a number of servants and bonded Native people and Africans who ran their operations. Meanwhile, Dutch traders entered the bay from their posts on the mid-Atlantic by the 1620s, establishing themselves as prime players in the politics of southern New England and into the Chesapeake, pulled into the politics and geographies of Susquehannock traders. Accelerated movement played a large role in dictating the settlement and experiences of their new Roman Catholic neighbors, Maryland's first settlers, who arrived in 1634 and negotiated for the land that became St. Mary's City on a tributary of the Potomac River. Like Virginians, they established a headright system and began selecting dispersed patches of land suitable for tobacco but also saw promise and threat in their premier location along fur-trading routes.⁷ European merchants and traders understood that sailing farther up (or in the Dutch case, down) the bay helped establish the reach of their respective colonies. But in tapping Native networks they often flouted the boundaries of their own and other colonies, undermining the imperial expanse they represented and promoting mutual distrust—reason to turn information networks against fellow settlers and traders.

As more English settlers arrived in the Chesapeake, the question of boundaries, and fear that information and violence might cross them, became paramount. The boundaries that defined Maryland as a legitimate colony, from the finalization of its royal charter in 1632 to formal permission from neighboring Native people to settle in 1634, were contested from the start by both European and Native people. Native leaders, traders, servants, and colonial officials shared mutual distrust and fear of catastrophe.[8] At a distance, colonial officials often heard too late news of violence and scheming among people in places they could not have witnessed themselves, since information and misinformation spread among localities rather than from the colonial center of authority.[9] Controlling the rumor mill and shoring up authority at places of encounter between distrustful strangers were two parts of the same colonial project, and on both counts authorities in Maryland and Virginia failed.[10] Instead, traders, local leaders, escaped laborers, and interpreters weaponized these connections against one another through unverified information and rumor, run via boats and canoes.[11]

As resistance to servitude, along with Anglo-Native trade and communication, continued across the water, that very movement pushed a reorientation away from water to land. Communication and movement through the fur trade, battles over Kent Island, and Maryland claims to Algonquian territory reveal how a myriad of Native people maintained power in the northern Chesapeake in the 1620s and 1630s. But by the 1630s, Virginia traders' hopes sank as unbounded access to a maritime trade for northern furs diminished. Marylanders and their Native allies pushed the Virginians out violently by enforcing their shared border, and Native traders took their furs elsewhere. Instead, Maryland and Virginia planters invested in new bounded claims on land, where plantation regimes and planters' property boundaries altered Native places along the James River with promises of profit. Algonquians on the Chesapeake's peninsulas not only asserted their control over trade in the Chesapeake's waters; they also created new diplomatic relationships with colonists with whom they shared local resources, further fortifying their influence over colonists' knowledge about the Chesapeake's people and environment.[12] The Algonquian vision of the connected Chesapeake contrasted sharply with some settlers' imposed segmentation through rigid colonial borders on land, where colonial leaders sought to stake a definable claim and fracture the broader Chesapeake into mapped pieces, pulling apart delicate nodes of interaction into colonies and plantations.

From the 1630s and for decades afterward, survival at the border between the two colonies for both Native people and settlers was jeopardized by entangled Native alliances, confused and contradictory information, and bouts of intercolonial violence. Competition for trade and land caused endemic distrust between Catholic St. Mary's City and Anglican Jamestown, and competing traders and their Algonquian allies exacerbated these tensions. As Maryland and Virginia officials attempted to claim sovereignty in overlapping lands along the Chesapeake, the geography of open water and the diverse nations it supported undercut official attempts to pull apart Native connections, limit mobility, and impose borders. When Native people and English traders from servant William Abram to powerful trader William Claiborne took to the water, their adventures in the bay on the ambiguous border between Virginia and Maryland undercut English authority and its place in Native politics across the colony.

Trucking with Servants and Native People

After declining to participate in the initial attacks on the settlers, Algonquians on the periphery of the Anglo-Powhatan War of the 1620s found that English commercial traffic stayed on the bay but oriented northward, in lockstep with the English colonists' violent pursuit of Native corn. By the 1620s, regional chiefdoms had developed exchanges of goods and information with particular traders informed by the war to their south. The Patawomecks, for example, developed independent relationships with colonists like Raleigh Croshaw, who resided near the mouth of the James River but traded along the Potomac to the north for food. Expansive trade brought new opportunities and dangers to Algonquians. They traded beads, copper, illicit weapons, powder, and shot for the basics of survival in the Chesapeake: corn, mats, canoes, travel guidance, and animal furs and skins.[13] Trade goods and new alliances could shore up defenses against marauding northern groups like the Massawomecks and shore up relationships with their longtime Algonquian neighbors. Some strengthened their connections with other Native people living along trade routes: settlers spoke with a Patuxent man from the western shore living with his Wicomiss wife on the Eastern Shore; they probably met through networks also frequented by English traders, who habitually visited both groups during the trading season.[14] Others built rapport with their neighbors, like interpreter Thomas Savage on the Eastern Shore, and it was with these men that Algonquians also shared access to food and precious information, perhaps to cultivate goodwill, keep supply lines open, and maintain close watch over the English.

The trade in beaver pelts expanded in the 1630s, encouraging consistent communication between diverse Native leaders and enterprising settlers.[15] Eyed as potential partners by John Smith, the Susquehannocks traded furs for goods from the English, Dutch, and Swedes from their territory at the head of the Chesapeake Bay. From as far west as perhaps the Great Lakes, the Massawomecks traveled by birch-bark canoe to raid Chesapeake Algonquian enemies and trade with the English; they enriched chosen Native middlemen like the Nacotchtanks on the Potomac River who held the Massawomecks' furs and escorted the English through the trade.[16] Interpreter and former captive to the Nacotchtanks, Henry Fleet built a trade among the Nacotchtanks, who provided him with diplomatic and orienteering assistance and the labor of storing and carrying skins in the trade with the Massawomecks.[17] By 1631, Fleet was trading corn with New Englanders for trade goods to "beate about from town to town for Beaver" along the Potomac River where he was once a captive. Competing with other Virginians for skins saved by Native people, he made diplomatic overtures with gifts to inland town leaders as a potential connection to the English trade.[18] Informed by past conflicts and alliances, the beaver trade brought people of the Chesapeake into frequent, frenetic contact.

To connect with Native people who brought furs to trade, the Dutch established a series of tiny forts between the Connecticut and Delaware Rivers far to the north of Virginia between the 1610s and 1650s and further accelerated the movement of goods and information. Their ships moved south and flooded the Chesapeake during this period.[19] By the 1630s, Dutch merchants had settled on the Eastern Shore and connected to shipping interests in New Netherland, and English traders and planters shipped goods from New Netherland to trade with Native people and colonists.[20] New Amsterdam and short-lived New Sweden supplied the Susquehannocks and other Native people with guns in exchange for pelts, empowering them to conduct devastating raids on their traditional Algonquian southern enemies like the Piscataways and Wicomiss.[21]

During war with the Powhatans, English traders and military men entered the northern Chesapeake as one and the same: the colony relied on soldier-traders for corn violently taken from enemies, and for the whereabouts of Native trading partners and their corn, required to survive and defeat the Powhatans. Unlike earlier commissions to traders in which they were warned to honor "our peace" by trading with Native people for goods "which they can afford," commissions during the war encouraged traders to acquire desperately needed corn "either by trade, or by force of Armes, as occasion shalbe given by the Indians." Certain traders were licensed to take prisoners and other goods from people along any river leading into the bay and were also allowed to sell or keep a surplus of corn.[22] Soldiers developed through violence the geopolitical know-how of traders. In his report from journeying up the Potomac River with Algonquian guides and interpreters, Henry Fleet assessed the numbers and fortifications of non-Algonquian people he met, their preferences in European goods, and from whom they got them. He also assessed his guides' reactions to entering new territories—which people threatened the traders or guides with violence? Which people were protected from violence by more powerful allies?[23] And traders, in turn, relied on Algonquian information for these assessments.

The early career of William Claiborne demonstrated how an accumulation of knowledge about Native places served him well as both trader and raider. As a member of English raiding parties, he stole corn and other resources during campaigns against the Nansemonds and Pamunkeys on the lower James River in 1624.[24] At the same time, as a surveyor, he parceled the Native landscape left behind for himself and other planters. He patented land in formerly bountiful Native fields at Kecoughtan and at English settlements like Blunt Point, a site of well-remembered violent encounter with Native people (William Blount, or Blunt, had died at the hands of the Nansemonds).[25] During the conflict, Claiborne offered to build the palisade between the James and York Rivers to protect the 300,000 acres surrounding Jamestown and the peninsula from future incursions, in exchange for the land surrounding.[26] He accrued enough land and wealth to become secretary for the colony in 1626 and to sail his own craft up the Chesapeake and establish trading relationships in 1627.[27] In just a few short years, Claiborne had played the roles of soldier, officeholder, landowning elite, and cultural broker while also becoming Virginia's foremost fur trader.

Virginia's officials observed traders' successes in the profitable war with Opechancanough and recognized what men like Claiborne might do to establish the colony's territorial boundaries. In 1628, the governor granted Claiborne a license "to trade and trucke with the Indians," both to explore to the south and to seek Native trading partners to the north as traders like Croshaw and Fleet already had. While his commission allowed him to trade within the northern and southern bounds of Virginia established decades earlier—thirty-four and forty-one degrees latitude—they pointed out that the bounds of Virginia "may be far augmented" by travel along the water to include new territory acquired by "search and discovery."[28] The following year, in 1629, Claiborne moved to secure the safety of the settlements surrounding the core of the colony on the James River by expanding the bounds. Placed in charge of the campaign against Powhatan allies in "these territories adjoining . . . by cutting down their corne surprising them in their habitations intercepting them in their hunting, burning their townes distroying their Canoes and [weirs] and depriving them of whatsoever may yeld them succour and relief," Claiborne worked to erase Native presence and means of subsistence in areas adjacent to the settlements, clearing the way for safe passage and expansion.[29] Among other soldier-traders like himself, Claiborne simultaneously asserted new borders through trade with one Native group while pushing borders on land through war with another.

In both trade and war, close to Jamestown and abroad, Claiborne's growing knowledge of the Chesapeake's waterways and Native land use built his wealth and geographic reach. By 1631, William Claiborne was well established politically and at last geographically. To reach the Susquehannock trade, he drew from his experience as a soldier and planter to fortify a site best suited to potential Native allies. He sailed near the Severn River northward in the bay and set up on a network of islands off the Eastern Shore at the invitation of the Susquehannocks, surrounded by independent Algonquian groups on all sides.[30] By 1631, he had moved supplies and servants to territory contested between Eastern Shore Algonquians and Susquehannocks. "Not above a league and halfe distant from each other," the islands had safe docking points, and at least one nearby had reliable fresh water. Reconstructing the Virginia plantation atop a different topography, dozens of servants cleared vegetation, built palisades and homes, and stocked smaller but habitable Claiborne and Poplar Islands with hogs free to forage without becoming a nuisance to Claiborne or his crew.[31] At the core sat Kent Island, named after Claiborne's birthplace in England, the largest patch of land at over thirty square miles. Shaped like a fishhook and covered in discouraging marshland and shallows, defense-minded settlers built palisades and homes on the portions where "all along this necke there is not above 3 roode [rod] of water betwixt it and the maine land [the Eastern Shore], and at either end thereof about 3 foote deep when the tyde is out." Although potential invaders might worry about miring their watercraft in the sand, the proximity to the Eastern Shore was conducive to trade. The Susquehannocks could reach Kent Island in half a day from their main town at the head of the bay and make it back home in two days.[32] From Kent Fort, the English looked over the waters of the Kent Narrows and could see the tree line and cooking fires of Algonquian peoples of the Eastern Shore, who were more than likely unhappy with the English overtures to the Susquehannocks.

Claiborne's own mobility—his movement between Kent Island and politics and plantations on the James River—made it difficult for him to maintain surveillance and control over both the traders he employed and the forced labor that ran the fort on Kent Island. As he and other Virginians had done with Native captives in the past, Claiborne placed sailors, traders, and bonded laborers in positions as interlocutors with Native people and other traders, requiring their labor and skill for interpretation, security, and seamanship. Visiting Claiborne's fort at Kent Island, a Marylander learned of Susquehannock military tactics "from a Negroe which lived among them for to learne the language."[33] With water and diplomatic skills of their own, African and Native traders and unfree laborers stood to gain knowledge for their own safety and profit, as well as for Claiborne's. The islanders were cognizant of the precarious maritime and Native context in which they worked, and were responsible for safety in ships where "there wilbe sometimes att least 3 or 400 Indians about the Shallopp . . . with Axes, Tomahawkes and Bowes and Arrowes with them," or on smaller boats in which for safety they required "at least 6 or 7 men in each of them, else they are in danger to be cutt of by the Indians. . . . The Indians have served others soe."[34] While the Susquehannocks traded furs to the English, the English simultaneously purchased corn from their Algonquian neighbors, some probably to consume themselves but otherwise to sell to Virginians to the south.[35] Claiborne also withheld weapons and ammunition from servants, perhaps because he did not trust them but certainly because he did not want Native traders to take their munitions. He thus was forced to strike a balance between allowing unfree people's mobility that cultivated trade connections and knowledge of partners and enemies—trusting people like "a Negroe which lived among them"—and limiting access to resources that might encourage a threat to the trade venture from below. To keep the English outpost, a place created from extensive maritime connection, Claiborne attempted to enforce the colonial social caste system that limited the mobility of nonelites.

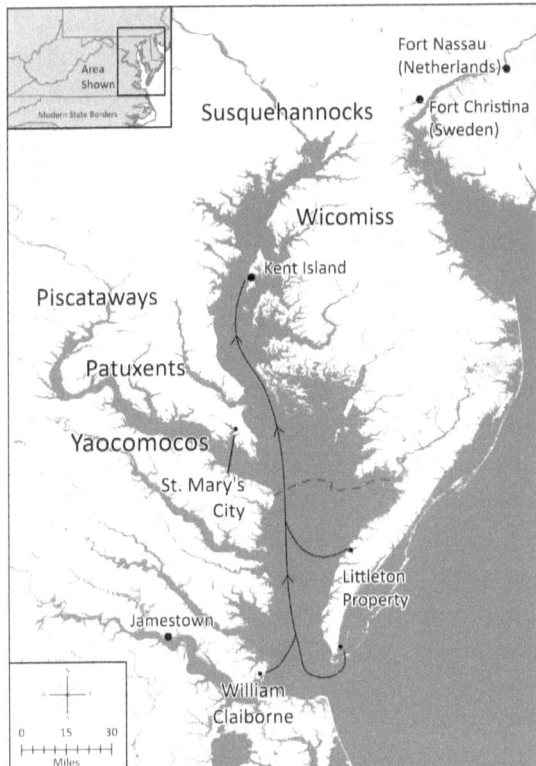

MAP 4. Conjectural trade route of Constantine Monohaten, c. 1644 (Stewart Scales and Gemma Wessels)

But this was no desert island. Kent Island was an immersive connecting point that provided unfree people with information as well as danger. Servants and interpreters deployed language and communication skills that defined the English presence on this portion of the Chesapeake. To hinder his potential recapture, for example, Fleet's escaped servant started a rumor among Native people that Fleet's trading commission was "only a copy" to call into question his right to trade.[36] On Kent Island, Claiborne's Native guide Constantine Monohaten sailed with other English traders and made contact with the Susquehannocks on Claiborne's behalf—and to Claiborne's irritation, contracted independently with other wealthy English traders to do the same on the Eastern Shore. In 1644, an argument erupted when a Mrs. Littleton, whose family had a sizable plantation and a trading outpost on the southeastern portion of the Eastern Shore, purportedly stopped another trader from sailing off with Monohaten to do Claiborne's business. When the problem reached court, the traders agreed that he had left the Eastern Shore after all but could not agree about who had sent him where.[37] While his travels no doubt also enriched himself, Monohaten's skills and travels connected moneyed planters with traders from Kent Island with Native trade networks beyond.

Traders and their partners did business in spaces where Native powers overlapped, and they relied on Native intelligence and communication to maintain their geographic foothold. Some Algonquians proximate to Kent Island, for example, resented that Claiborne's trade brought the Susquehannocks south so frequently. An unnamed Native group passed on to Claiborne's people advance notice of an imminent attack meant "to cut of the said Plantation" at Kent Island. Later confronted by several dozen Native people at the gates of the fort and trapped inside, the Englishmen had "cut severall Loope hooles on every side and end of the houses on the said Plantation . . . to shoot out att" and destroyed the element of surprise for the attackers. Low on ammunition, the Englishmen inside yelled to the people outside the palisade that they had been warned of their coming, "whereupon the said Indians imediately after theire treachery being discovered departed."[38] Although they survived the standoff, the encounter was a reminder that as traders accessed Native resources and places, their movements were ultimately circumscribed by Native peoples such as those who tipped off the English about the attack, with knowledge of local places and enmities.

As the loci of Native politics and exchange shifted from the Powhatan core to the fur-trading groups farther afield, Native networks guided the fate of traders and the knowledge they carried. Soldiers and traders were among the first to sail up the bay in search of connections that could enrich the colonists, and the post at Kent Island seemed a promising accommodation of northern, outsider Native traders. But English traders' mobility on the bay created increasingly apparent gaps in their claims to broad swaths of territory. They left discomfited Algonquian neighbors unhappy with the movement of longstanding enemies so close by. And their servants and Native trading partners who traveled with them gathered intelligence about the bay's inhabitants and maritime skills of their own. In the coming years, English attempts to grasp the trade in the northern Chesapeake would only underscore their own weaknesses, confusions, and divisions and reinforce Native mariners as masters of the bay.

Churning the Rumor Mill

Claiborne and other soldier-traders soon met a formidable English threat to their foothold in trade from the northern Chesapeake. As Marylanders settled on the Potomac in the 1630s, the flow of self-interested traders, and the intelligence and rumor they carried by water, undermined attempts to establish boundaries at every turn. Maryland and Virginia officials and traders, as neighbors to Algonquian groups like the Patuxents and trading partners with people like the Susquehannocks, were dependent on Native information in power plays against one another. Virginians, Marylanders, Algonquians, and others sought to control the movement of others inside of Maryland's chartered territory at Virginian-occupied Kent Island, all in waters traversed by Native people. This bit of ground reflected and magnified traders' and Native people's longstanding ambitions and insecurities. For the Susquehannocks, it was a node of regional trade. For some nearby Algonquians, it allowed Susquehannock raiders an insufferable foothold at the center of their bay. Both Maryland and Virginia traders forecasted danger and financial promise in sole occupation of the outpost. Maryland's governor, Leonard Calvert, saw that the line between Virginia and Maryland would remain imaginary if unpatrolled. With so much mutual suspicion and competition, Algonquian movement carrying carefully curated communication across the border—intelligence, rumors, threats, schemes, violence—both inflamed the fragmented nature of English colonial authority and provided Native leaders the means to create alliances and strike at enemies across borders. Maryland officials' insistence on stemming the expansion of Virginia's trade on Kent Island ignited a slow-burning border war that lasted over a century. Some Algonquians saw that the settlement of English Marylanders might give them diplomatic leverage with the Virginians and other Native people. Maryland's critical location on the northern Chesapeake, after all, could alter the flow of outsiders like the Susquehannocks and Virginians and change politics favorably for Algonquian nations. But Virginia's colonists also came ready to fight within Maryland's new borders, having learned that there was often profit in conflict.

Fears of Native and anti-Catholic enemies, and very real Virginian ill will, caused complications for the Marylanders on their arrival in 1634.[39] Maryland's first proprietor, Cecil Calvert, Baron Baltimore, had his finger on the pulse of investors in the fur trade, an eye on news from the colonies, and a recent decision from the Commissioners on Foreign Plantations against Virginia's northerly claims in his pocket. He commanded the Maryland colonists to skirt English lookouts at Jamestown and Point Comfort on their arrival to avoid trouble, and suggested they pick a place to settle that was "healthfull and fruitfull, next that it may be easily fortified, and thirdly that it may be convenient for trade both wth the English and savages."[40] Calvert and his brother, the new proprietary governor, Leonard Calvert, were deeply suspicious of the Virginians and Claiborne in particular, since he had lobbied against the colonization of Maryland and Marylanders' entrance into the fur trade.[41] Virginia's traders said they had legitimate claims to Maryland's piece of the bay not by right of occupation but by traffic, their movement across the bay for their own support and in support of the colony.[42] Further, Cecil Calvert also understood that his Catholic sympathies virtually guaranteed a degree of mistrust and hostility from Anglican Virginia and Protestant traders like Claiborne toward Maryland colonists, communicated in the language of maritime trade. Virginia governor John Harvey wrote in 1634 that some colonists "make it their familiar talke that they would rather knock their cattell on the heads then sell them to Maryland," rich words from settlers who only a few years before had relied on Native corn to ameliorate food insecurity.[43] Soldier-traders who had once searched for food by ship were now in a position to supply (or not) the Marylanders with livestock and supplies raised on land cleared of Algonquian farmland. Virginians' expressions of political and religious disdain, and their claims to Chesapeake waters by traffic, both stemmed from a generation of reliance on Native people and places.

The Virginians welcomed the Marylanders by spreading rumors to the Marylanders' new Algonquian neighbors, well calculated to cause diplomatic fractures in an already fraught environment. The Marylanders stopped in Virginia on their way up the bay against Lord Baltimore's orders, a mistake that gave Virginia mariners time to reach Algonquians to the north ahead of them. The Virginians raised the specter of a Spanish invasion, a rumor that resonated with Native and English people alike—and that would spread quickly among allied Native localities up the rivers. Soon, the lie spread from travelers to the most powerful Native leaders on the Potomac that "6 Spanish ships were a comeing to destroy them all." An additional European trade presence could be considered an opportunity by Native people; the rumor explicitly left little room for such hopes. The dangerous information spread along Native alliances and family networks. The werowance of the Patuxents heard from his cousin among the Yaocomocos that settlers were coming to disrupt their trade with the English, and the newcomers must be Spanish. Someone told the powerful Piscataways, to whom both the Patuxents and Yaocomocos probably turned for protection, to prepare for war and spread the word: "The king of Pascatoway had drawne together 500 bowmen, great fires were made by night over all the Country," a way in which Algonquians spread news quickly. Like that, they waited for the "Spanish" ships to arrive. While the standoff only created tension and a bad first impression, Maryland's Jesuit priest Father Andrew White blamed Claiborne; the Patuxent werowance maintained it was a misunderstanding, but that it began with Henry Fleet. Because it was rumor, White could never be certain.[44]

Overcoming this misunderstanding and probably a few more, the newcomers were forced to rely on Virginian mariners to help them plug into Native alliances. On the journey up the bay, the Marylanders' much larger ship caught up with "Henrie ffleet, and his 3 barkes, who" they now understood "had beene a firebrand to inflame the Indians against us." Fleet had arrived, he said, to trade, but perhaps seeing an opportunity to befriend newcomers along his trade routes, quickly jumped into the role of interpreter. He negotiated with Algonquian Yaocomocos on behalf of the Marylanders for the land to found their new home of St. Mary's City. In lieu of paying for the land, Maryland agreed to provide reinforcements against outsider Native enemies. The new alliance pitted the Marylanders against Claiborne, who traded with the Yaocomocos' enemies and probable outsiders in question, the Susquehannocks. Fleet's was a good bargain for the Yaocomocos and nearby people, who had watched the Susquehannocks grow more powerful and dangerous through the fur trade. To make the visit financially worthwhile, Fleet promptly violated the Marylanders' new sovereignty by trading "with out leave, and got that time above 200 skins" before sailing back to Virginia waters. Governor Calvert shrugged it off in view of the positive result, "as noble a seat as could be wished, and as good ground as I suppose is in all Europe."[45] As an interpreter, Fleet mapped for the Marylanders his powerful and carefully cultivated connections, held together through his journeys along the Potomac. But his transgression on the journey back foreshadowed Virginians' trouble with their new northern boundary.

Fear guided Maryland's new diplomatic relationships, and attempts to untangle rumors led to new insecurities. The alleged Spanish invasion led to a summit at a Patuxent town in June 1634 among Maryland and Virginia officials and Native leaders, with Maryland's new friend Henry Fleet interpreting. After the Patuxent werowance had retold the story about hearing about a Spanish invasion from his cousin among the Yaocomocos—which would implicate their English friend, Henry Fleet, as a possible source of the information—he intimated that he had also heard that the governor of Maryland was not a king but only a great man. In other words, proprietary governor Leonard Calvert's status did not mirror that of other werowances along the Potomac, trusted by tribal members to defend them, conduct diplomacy, make war, and direct trade. Revealing his understanding of the political order, the Patuxent werowance called Marylanders the "English at Yaocomoco" in reference to the people and place in which they had settled, rather than by a name that recognized Marylanders' sovereignty as purchasers of the land or even as distinct from English Virginians. Since the real "king" remained in England and would come up the bay later, the governor was a step below in authority among Algonquian elites and advisors who only influenced decision-making. Already concerned about the ability to control happenings within the new colony, this interpretation of the Calverts' leadership as conditional on Native and faraway English authority could invite further transgressions from Native people and Virginians.

Seizing the opportunity, Fleet once again proved his value as an interpreter: not only could he translate, but he could uncover the truth and the bad intentions of others. He pulled the werowance of the Patuxents aboard a ship to a meeting with Governors Calvert and Harvey in what must have been a cramped and jarring experience. The werowance at first refused to divulge the name of the person from whom he heard the "great man" rumor, despite Fleet's berating ("Noe body," "Nay, but it was some body") before conceding "John Tompkins did said soe."[46] Tompkins was a Maryland colonist, so the Virginians had not been the ones who had challenged the Maryland governor's authority after all. Against his hopes, Fleet's interrogation also cleared his rival Virginia trader from suspicion ("What said Captaine Clayborne to you?" "Nothing"). But keeping in view Claiborne's and Fleet's powerful alliances in the region, the werowance of the Patuxent provided the answer least likely to escalate tensions between the two governments' representatives aboard the ship with him.[47] No other person should have as much authority over Tompkins as Calvert. But as with the rumor of the "Spanish" ships, they could never know for sure who had called into question the Maryland governor's authority. Harvey had Claiborne arrested the following month anyway for "animating, practicing, and conspiring with the Indians to supplant and cut . . . off" the Marylanders.[48] In the long term, getting to the bottom of a single rumor did not increase the governors' control over how information moved and who spread it. If nothing else, it highlighted Marylanders' weakness relative to their Virginian and Native neighbors.

As interpreters and traders like Fleet demonstrated their utility to newcomers, Algonquian people reasserted the value of their knowledge not just of trade but of Virginians. Wannis, a tayac, or leader, of the Piscataways, pointed out in the 1634 conference with the Marylanders that "this gentleman of Yawacomico [St. Mary's City] did not knowe Captaine Fleete soe well as wee of Virginia becaus they were lately come." Wannis, with assent and cajoling from other gathered werowances and great men ("Let it alone." "Doe you tell it?" "I care not if you tell it") finally relented and shared a third rumor. Fleet had said that Paspahegh men were coming to kill Claiborne, that "it would bee in vaine for him to runne away any where, for that if hee go to the Isle of Kent the greate men can fetch him there." The Paspaheghs were once the closest neighbors of Jamestown far from Kent Island; it seemed more likely that Fleet manufactured a distant threat in an attempt to keep Claiborne at his home on the south Chesapeake and away from his trading post to the north. Wannis noted that he had kept his distance from Claiborne because Fleet had warned him of Claiborne's intentions toward the Piscataways. Fleet told Wannis not to board Claiborne's ship to trade, since Claiborne would take him captive and "tye his arms"—a story that might have had roots in Claiborne's captive-taking during the Anglo-Powhatan War, or in his engagement with unfree Native labor. Wannis's trading ally, the werowance of Patuxent, angrily corroborated Wannis's account of Fleet: "When they [the Marylanders] came to speake with Captaine Fleete, all the lyes would redound upon him and lye upon him as high as his necke, and at last breake his necke."[49] The great men and werowances emphasized the divisions they had perceived between Virginians and drove a wedge between the Marylanders and their Virginian interpreter. They also reinforced that knowledge about the rumors' origins lay in Native people's own networks.

The rumor that Calvert was no king proved true, and Maryland officials found they did not possess the power to control the movement of information or goods within their new bounds. Instead, their inability to patrol their borders produced more fear and anxious communication for all parties.

Virginian traders observed Dutch cloth and farming tools among Susquehannocks, and Virginians blamed Marylanders because they did nothing to stop European ships from the north from trading on the waters claimed by Maryland. Meanwhile, the Virginians complained, the Dutch and Swedes "furnished the Indians with powder, shot, and guns, to the great damage and danger of those [English] plantations."[50] Further, when his goods went unsold after an increase in investment in 1634 and 1635, Claiborne learned that the Susquehannocks desired Dutch cloth rather than finished coats and blankets, and their axes rather than hoes.[51] Maryland's lack of intelligence about movements across their boundaries, or lack of willingness to police them, damaged the English advantage in exchanges with their Native trading partners.

But that did not stop Marylanders like the gossiping John Tompkins from entering the fur trade almost immediately, giving groups like the Susquehannocks the chance to stoke competition between the two sets of English colonists as well as with the Dutch. The edge went to whichever trader could coordinate with backers and merchants from across the Atlantic to get products valued by Native communities, with high stakes for the security of the traders, new plantations, and Algonquian allies. When a Maryland fur trader boasted to a Virginian that he had saved the Virginian from an attack from a Native trader, the Virginian shot back, "not soe, And againe the Indians told me that it was by means of Capt Claybornes Cloth . . . it beinge better liked" than the Marylanders' goods.[52] Native people, who did the telling and the buying, remained in control of knowledge and exchange. Competition for goods and information along the bay demonstrated that Native trading partners and guides encouraged Europeans to violate their own boundaries while Native people dictated the terms of the trade.

At the local level, as they had during the Anglo-Powhatan Wars with soldier-traders, many Algonquians used these vague boundaries and the English desire for goods and information to establish advantageous diplomatic parameters. They treated Maryland and Virginia as two governments under the same king, which they were. In his interview, the Patuxent werowance introduced himself not as a friend of Virginia or Maryland but as "a lover of the English nation." He promised to bring any "idle fellowe of my people . . . which might perhaps kill" an Englishman to English authorities but did not clarify which authorities.[53] The ambiguity proved problematic for English officials attempting to keep authority in its appropriate geographical boundaries. In 1636, for example, Eastern Shore werowance Esmy Shichans traveled to the home of Virginian magistrate Obedience Robins to offer a hundred arms' length of roanoke, or wampum, for the murder of an Englishman. Using this negotiation tactic among leaders hoping to avoid violent retribution, Esmy Shichans approached through his headmen a representative of the Eastern Shore Virginians, an appropriate move toward the English settlers with whom he had decades of relationships. Robins refused to take it, since the place, time, circumstances, and victim of the murder were all entirely unclear: he had only heard rumors of a death at Kent Island ("how and where I could not tell"). But in storming out he left the Accawmacks' werowance in the same room with Virginian Daniel Cugley, who, vested with no particular authority, accepted the roanoke and other gifts for himself. Considering the problem solved, the werowance returned home. Robins was left to not only locate an unnamed dead man but reopen an issue considered already resolved by Esmy Shichans.[54] The predicament was a reminder that Native communication outpaced definite English intelligence about their own subjects, exacerbated in this case by Cugley's own differing motivations and also perhaps by the lack of communication between officials in Virginia and Maryland. Robins was in the dark, and Accawmack protocol prevailed.

The confusion between the web of county and colonial governments, and colonial usurpers of authority like Cugley, also provided opportunities unique to the disputed territory for Algonquian leaders to assert knowledge and control over diplomacy. In 1634, men from enemy Wicomiss and Susquehannock nations came to trade with Virginians at Kent Island at the same time that "one of the Susquehanocks did an Injury to a Wicomesse, whereat some [English] that saw it, did laugh."[55] The Wicomiss escalated the situation, killing five Susquehannocks, three Virginians, and some cattle, then absconding with trade goods belonging to both groups. The Wicomiss werowance sent messengers from the Wicomiss and Patuxents to the governor of Maryland, instead of Virginia, to offer restitution. Pouncing on a chance to assert authority over Claiborne's trading post, Calvert demanded that the werowance deliver the men responsible, though no Marylanders were present or would know who the culprits could be. The messenger refused on grounds that "you are heere strangers, and come into our Countrey, you should rather conforme your selves to the Customes of our Countrey, then impose yours upon us." Calvert's shot aimed at the Virginians backfired, and his assertion of Maryland's domain gave the Wicomiss a chance to deny not just Maryland but any sovereignty of English "strangers" at all.[56]

For Maryland officials, borders were central to maintaining authority and order, and the presence of Claiborne's ships and men on Kent Island—well within the bounds of Maryland provided by the charter—was the central irritation for the fledgling colony. Initially, the governor realized Maryland could profit from the Susquehannock trade and extended an olive branch to Claiborne by offering continued residence at Kent Island in exchange for acknowledgment of the Marylanders' authority.[57] Claiborne was unresponsive. Then suddenly, a fourth rumor, this one of a maritime attack, swirled again. Claiborne, it was said, encouraged Native friends to "supplant" Maryland before they "take their Country from them," perhaps recalling English understandings of Opechancanough's ambitions during the 1622 attack.[58] This time, Claiborne faced a verified witness, who said he heard Claiborne make a general violent threat against the Marylanders, when he had "publikely protested that if my lords plantation should surprize or take any of his boates, he would be revenged though he joined with the Indians in a canoa." In light of Claiborne's alliances, the Marylanders worried that the Susquehannocks would descend on St. Mary's City and further that the Virginians would supply the firearms to enable such an attack.[59] Algonquians might have feared the same, and Native rumors legitimated escalating mistrust of Claiborne and the Susquehannocks. Unknown Native people "confessed" a rumor that "the Indians had a purpose to have attempted it, had they not bene dissuaded by one Captayne Fleet [who] is now in good credit wth them."[60] Whoever they were, the informants made clear that among Native traders Claiborne's men (and by extension, the Susquehannock raiders) were the real threat. Calvert now had a tangible excuse to act.

Rumor of violence propelled the real violence that followed. Without enforced borders that modulated frenetic movement through the colony's waters, Marylanders sat uncomfortably vulnerable for months. To protect their interests, Claiborne's associates captured Maryland traders on their way up the bay to trade with the Susquehannocks in 1634 and 1635— including John Tompkins—and brought them back with their goods to Kent Island. Meanwhile, Claiborne's ships were seen on the western shore among St. Mary's City's immediate Native neighbors, a few miles away from the Marylanders' settlement itself. This was the intelligence that the

Marylanders needed. On the Patuxent River in April 1635, they confiscated Claiborne's largest ship, the *Long Taile,* and "bound his men and cast them into the hold besides beating and hurting them."[61] Among the justifications was another rumor, that Claiborne's commission to trade "was a false Coppie and grounded upon false information."[62] The Marylanders split the goods among themselves, confiscated the ship, and stranded Claiborne's crew on land "wthout any armes to defend themselves from the natives." The Virginians relied on Native mariners to bring them to safety by canoe. Claiborne's Virginian faction retaliated against their own Governor Harvey, who they deposed in part on grounds that he "betray[ed] theyr Forte into the hands of theyr enemies of Marylande."[63] The feared conspiracy never materialized, but Maryland pursued two Virginians who escaped alive, Thomas Smith and John Butler, on charges of treason as a reason to escalate violence. While the English mariners battled one another across Maryland's newly claimed territorial waters, the larger war was fought for access to Kent Island, a highly valued site located on the fringes of both colonies. Marylanders' successful challenge to Claiborne's commission and mobility on the bay demonstrated the tenuous nature of the Virginians' hold on the trade.

That the Susquehannocks helped legitimize the Virginia claim on waters north of the Potomac and continued to sail the Chesapeake provided impetus for Maryland to attack again with boats and rumors. In 1637, the Susquehannocks granted Palmer's Island to Claiborne, a position north of Kent Island and more convenient for their own position but even deeper in Maryland-claimed territory.[64] That same year, a dangerous fifth rumor made its way to St. Mary's City that at the urging of the wanted Virginian Thomas Smith, mentioned above, the Susquehannocks "intended in the spring following to make warre upon us at St. Maries pretending revenge for our assisting of our neighbors Indians against them two yeares before."[65] Perhaps the Susquehannocks considered the earlier attack on Claiborne as an attack on themselves, or maybe the rumor was just that. But under the cover of night, a group of thirty or forty men with Maryland's governor and interpreter Robert Evelyn landed on the south side of Kent Island and approached the fort. A defected Virginian servant from Claiborne's group of traders opened the gates. Over a hundred men on Kent Island were declared subjects of Maryland, and the Kent Islanders wanted by the Marylanders, Smith and Butler, were taken aboard the pinnace as prisoners. Smith and Butler were charged with treason, perhaps a warning to other traders with similar hopes beyond the bounds of Virginia.⁶⁶ Governor Calvert personally led a second attack to quell Virginian resistance to Maryland rule the following month, when Smith was drawn and hanged—at least in part over a rumor.⁶⁷

The Maryland governor and traders acted on rumors of a destabilizing and destructive Native force, and the results of their victories against a largely imagined enemy served to harden boundaries as Maryland tightened its control on the northern Chesapeake. The beneficiaries of the Virginians' loss of Kent Island were Maryland traders like newly arrived Kent Island resident Giles Brent.⁶⁸ The same year, Calvert lent Henry Fleet a servant and invested in his trade in furs, at least temporarily affirming Fleet's alliance to Maryland.⁶⁹ Finally, Claiborne's former servants benefited from the exchange in the ownership of their indentures. William Williamson, Philip West, and John Hopson served new Kent Island trader Robert Evelyn "as they had formerly done the said Claiborne" and were legally released after a year of service to the Marylanders, long before their indentures held by Claiborne would have expired.⁷⁰ The violent end to Virginia's early dominance in the fur trade taught elites and nonelites that crossing boundaries, particularly from Virginia to Maryland, could lead to individual profit and freedom.

In gaining Kent Island, Marylanders also gained a mobile and connected enemy in the Susquehannocks. The Susquehannocks continued to cross the bay and garner weapons from the Dutch and Swedes in exchange for furs, and in 1642 Marylanders declared war, ostensibly in part to respond to the deaths of Marylanders at Kent Island. The Marylanders mounted a campaign roundly destroyed by the Susquehannocks, and parties from both cycled through bouts of violence for a decade.⁷¹ Dislodging the Virginians from the island reinforced boundaries between colonies but only temporarily. Pirate and Parliamentarian Richard Ingle, an opportunistic tobacco merchant, invaded (Catholic) Maryland in 1645 on a craft splendidly named the *Reformation*. He was joined by "some revolters, protestants, assisted by 50 plunder[ing] Virginians" who stole cattle and booty from burning Catholic homes and plantations.⁷² Soon after, William Claiborne, accompanied by paid Virginian troops, allied with Ingle to retake the Susquehannock trading post at Kent Island he had lost a decade before, against the Virginia governor's wishes.⁷³ Ingle's politically and religiously motivated attack against the Catholic Marylanders triggered yet another rush of colonists who saw opportunity in Anglo-Native war and border instability until the Maryland governor reestablished control in 1647.[74] Meanwhile, soldier-traders on either side could not halt and in fact encouraged the Native movement across the water that the Marylanders had heard about in rumors. The bay's fur trade declined, and men like Maryland trader Giles Brent and Virginian traders William Claiborne and Henry Fleet turned their attention inland.

Trade Routes Become Escape Routes

The Virginians' retreat left northern Chesapeake residents with a host of problems. Having dipped into Native information networks and made Native enemies in their violent assertion of their borders, the Marylanders found that they could not control their claimed portion of the bay, and their failed attempts further undermined claims to authority. Instead, they experienced the same dependence and uncertainty as Virginians had. Gossip and anxiety about mobile Native people and the places that English settlers had not yet mapped and bounded highlighted power in the hands of Chesapeake Algonquians, who maintained access to knowledge unavailable to the English. Simultaneously, bonded labor, land grants, and a booming tobacco market turned the interest of Maryland and Virginia elites toward Native land and the Piedmont trade. The pursuit of both land and trade required the knowledge and goodwill of Algonquians. Native, nonelite, and traders' movements that disregarded the borders challenged notions that the Chesapeake's waters could serve as boundaries, and additional confusion caused by attempts to enforce the border indeed provided opportunities for information and people to move across successfully.

Elites now spent more time surveying, patenting, and exploring overland but that did not mean calm bay waters. Algonquians maintained connections with other Native nations and the Dutch, Marylanders, and Virginians, and orchestrated alliances and hospitality for newcomers along old networks and on their own terms. The rise of shore-hugging tobacco plantations along what newly arrived servants and enslaved Africans could see was an active network of Native travel routes contoured resistance to plantation regimes well after Claiborne's fall. Where plantations spread along Native waters on Native land, resistance spread as well. English people crossed into Maryland and New Netherland, taking advantage of poor communication between enslavers and planters across colonial boundaries, to escape the law or pursue wealth. Servants and troublemakers, informed by Native networks, appropriated them to find a way out of legal bondage by finding escape routes out of the colony. Information about what lay on the other side of the border developed alongside the border itself, reaffirming that Algonquians accommodated new nodes and sources of information. As their experiences at Kent Island showed, local diplomacy and information could have broad-reaching implications.

Escaping laborers, who were Chesapeake travelers and traders themselves, were informed by their knowledge of colonial politics and their involvement with Native trade. By the 1640s, New Netherland traders developed enduring ties with Dutch and English planters and traders on the Eastern Shore of Virginia and Maryland. At the same time, people running away from labor in the English colonies caused trouble in Dutch settlements along the Delaware and Hudson Rivers, lodging at the expense of settlers. These servants might steal from Dutch homes but also provided dissatisfied servants belonging to New Netherland with transportation and news beyond the colony.[75] Dutch and English servants moving beyond respective colonial boundaries could heighten the strain on relationships with Native people. In one instance in 1643, an unknown Englishman visited a Native town near New Netherland settlements, the inhabitants of which had been at odds with the Dutch for years. The man, perhaps a servant or a trader, was killed, prompting speculation of a large coordinated attack that would mirror Opechancanough and the Powhatans' assault on Virginian settlements.[76]

Settlers spotted and reported new escaped unfree people from Dutch and English colonies every day—young children, for example, who ran away to Native towns. Administrators were also up against escaped colonists boasting years of knowledge and experience with crossing boundaries. In response to a 1640 letter from Leonard Calvert brought by an Englishman, officials in New Netherland summoned to court an Englishman named Edward Griffins with the intention of returning him as a prisoner to Maryland. With the aid of a Dutch trader who frequented the Eastern Shore, however, Griffins verified that he had run away and actually served Captain William Claiborne, a Virginian. Griffins probably knew a little about the bay's people and how to navigate the Chesapeake from his time at one of the Virginians' outposts during the previous decade. While he had served Claiborne within the bounds of Maryland in the Anglo-Native trade, Griffins had "no master in Maryland." Claiborne's trading post, which in an earlier moment defied intercolonial borders, enabled Griffins to later travel to freedom and Maryland in the first place.[77]

Escaped people's destinations and modes of transport suggested that they shared knowledge from one another and from traders about transportation and the periphery of the colony. In 1640, for example, African and English laborers working in the southern fringe of the Virginia colony across the river from Jamestown grabbed guns and a ship and attempted an escape.[78] The man from whom they stole the arms and a vessel was William Pierce, appointed cape merchant in charge of the flow of commodities through the company's storehouses. Pierce accordingly kept himself apprised of all shipping interests in the bay including the Native and tobacco trades with the Dutch, to whose settlements the servants hoped to run. That same year, merchant Hugh Gwynn of Virginia's Middle Peninsula personally retrieved three of his servants from Maryland, and the Virginia General Court sentenced Gwynn's "Dutchman," "Scotsman," and "a negro named John Punch" to a dangerous thirty lashes apiece to set an example. (Additionally, John Punch was sentenced to a lifetime of enslavement, perhaps the first Virginia example of legalized slavery.)[79] Maryland's and New Netherland's perceived accessibility in the Chesapeake encouraged increasing numbers of Virginians to envision freedom elsewhere and abscond.

Unfree people in flight also played on political differences caused in part by the trading rifts, trusting that Maryland and Dutch trade rivals and Native people would shelter them. While those escaping Maryland—even the governor's own servant, in one case—fled to Virginia, the Jesuits reported that several Virginian servants sold themselves out of the colony and became good Catholics to the chagrin of Virginia planters. For their part, the Jesuits were pleased to purchase four more and bring them into the church. Charged with treason for carrying Maryland servants out of the colony to sell, Virginian Daniel Duffield reentered Virginia in 1644 familiar with the comings and goings of Maryland traders from his earlier work grinding corn for them on Virginia's Eastern Shore. Hiding out from Virginia authorities, he stole a canoe belonging to Native people and disembarked at the nearest Accawmack town but not quickly enough to avoid detection. Richard Hudson's dog tracked Duffield to the Marylanders' ships: "The said Duffeild told [Hudson] that hee would knock him in the head with his Axe, And this deponent seeing Duffield soe desperate told him that hee would shoote him, And the said Duffeild Asked this deponent saying wherefore will you hinder mee, And further [Hudson] saith That Lewis White did carry the said Duffeild on board the Maryland Vessell."[80]

Opportunities and knowledge of such opportunities grew as the trade across the Chesapeake and its tributaries in foodstuffs and people among colonies gained speed. Even as they farmed tobacco, servants and enslaved people watched for incoming ships with intensity and took note of nearby Native resources. Dutch officials noted in 1642 how ordinary the stream of escaping bonded people had become: "Many persons come here in New Netherland daily both from New England and Virginia who carry their passports under foot."[81] Knowledge of the space between Native towns and plantations, along waters that crossed borders, guided them.

Algonquians along the border conducted diplomacy with strangers carefully, with the knowledge that their conversations and trades might not remain local affairs. By the 1630s and 1640s, they drew on traders and other interlocutors as they would in other relationships, with sources of aid and information embedded in particular communities and places. As with a generation before, interactions with strangers remained fundamentally Algonquian, grafted atop intimately understood landscapes and habits of exchange at the core of network-building.

The experience of Colonel Henry Norwood, a member of the English Parliament shipwrecked on the Eastern Shore in 1649, provides a prime example of how Algonquians moved information among people of different languages, Native nations, and colonies.[82] The crew of the *Virginia Merchant* abandoned Norwood with some sick passengers during the night, and the survivors had no idea they lay stranded on Assateague, an island off the coast of Maryland. They cannibalized four passengers too sick to survive the cold nights and discharged firearms into the air hoping to attract attention. Native Assateague fishermen came in their canoes and found the survivors. Armed with knowledge from "*Mr.* [John] Smith's travels," Norwood instructed his fellow surviving castaways to offer gifts, to meet them "unarm'd," and to smile; they "hate to see a melancholy face."[83]

As they did for many immigrants to Virginia in the seventeenth century, these Eastern Shore Algonquians arrived prepared to orient Colonel Norwood to the Chesapeake through a long series of carefully curated, symbolic exchanges. After returning to their town to discuss the discovery and an appropriate response (the wait was long: "we thought our selves forgotten by them"), the next afternoon the same fishermen returned with dozens of people, entire families who wasted little time settling into familiar roles with the English newcomers. In Algonquian, Norwood and the families exchanged "many salutations" all around, and women dispensed generous portions of food. Assateague men recognized Norwood's gold and silver lace coat as expensive and addressed him as the party's leader.[84] The trade of food and clothing, objects so intimately tied to survival, accentuated the interdependency that Eastern Shore Algonquians carefully cultivated.

The Assateague people fed the stranded and grateful English but maintained careful control over where the newcomers went and what they saw. The Assateagues hoped to gain information about the English situation. Which colony or state was their "country"? How did they reach shore without a boat? Friendly but cautious, the families hid an extra canoe in the marsh and agreed to take the English to a nearby town, Kickotank, only after the English supplied satisfactory answers over several days. A werowance drew a map on the ground of the terrain for Norwood and sent a messenger to connect to another messenger south along the peninsula. These messengers took Norwood over the border from Maryland to Virginia and to a Native man named Jack, who had learned English through life in or near Eastern Shore plantations and from the man who either employed him or held him in bondage, Dutchman and trader Jenkin Price. In exchange for the Algonquians' help, Norwood left behind a pair of tweezers and his coat.[85] The Algonquians expected Jack and Price to translate to the werowance the circumstances of Norwood's visit and to take the exhausted Norwood back with him. Price was well known by both Native and English Eastern Shore residents and could be trusted to connect Norwood to authorities over fifty miles to the south. Jack translated through Price and guided the group overland through a network of swamps and small waterways, between Algonquian towns Norwood identified by smoke wafting over the trees. Moving between the homes of werowances at Algonquian towns, past one of the Littletons' properties where Monohaten might have stopped, and finally to Price's home, they paid a series of carefully curated visits despite the raw horror Norwood had just witnessed. Despite the unusual conditions surrounding Norwood's visit, Algonquians conducted diplomacy developed over the preceding generation, maintaining constant control over the visitors' experience. Perhaps the Native people were too accommodating and friendly for the castaways to notice that they were, to a degree, prisoners along a contested colonial border.

No English person was responsible for guiding them across English boundaries and terrain claimed by the English. While the border between

Maryland and Virginia had become more clearly mappable and definable through myriad conflicts between their respective colonists and with Native people, the border as experienced was dislocating for these English foreigners. English navigation along the coast did little to rectify that dislocation politically or geographically; Algonquian canoes instead followed routes familiar and habitual to their pilots, collecting and spreading information about the newcomers. Norwood was in the care of traders and Native people and was among the many who grafted new journeys onto old routes. The political reality of the border between Maryland and Virginia was decided not by Lord Baltimore or Governor Harvey or Governor Calvert but instead by those who crossed it: conspirators like Fleet, people on the run like Duffield or William Abram, and traders like the Susquehannocks.

Norwood also noticed changes on his journey from recognizably Algonquian territory into Virginia—more frequent English entertainments near "plantations that lay thicker together," and a friend appointed to a lucrative position commanding a fort across the bay.[86] Although Virginians now covered much more literal ground in their affairs, regularly trading, treating, and absconding to locations to the north, into the Piedmont interior and the Northern Neck, they had not yet dismantled Native dominance or nonelite resistance on the Chesapeake's waters. Although trader-planters gained control at the expense of Opechancanough and the Powhatans, on the Potomac and the Eastern Shore Algonquians thrived. Enforceable English borders proliferated and accrued wealth for men like Claiborne, but they were geographically confined to the plantations of the James River and Eastern Shore. News and goods still flowed between Native towns by road and on the water. Outsider Native people like the Susquehannocks, though strengthened by trade with the colonies, were not a new threat. Non-Native boundary-crossings were pushed, pulled, and even orchestrated by Native people—now overland as well as by sea but still along established routes. Native control over information highlighted how the bay and rivers could support diplomacy or resistance and reinforced English dependence on Native guidance.

— 5 —

Trade, Property, and the Meaning of Algonquian Places, 1650–1660

In the woods along the Virginia-Carolina border at Brewsters River, mid-seventeenth-century English travelers might have noted the gradual change to rockier, redder earth to the southwest, the shift in tree cover and hills, or drier air. The path parted at a pair of enormous trees and split into two semicircles, bowing away from itself symmetrically. Pyancha, an Appamattuck man, arrived at the parting and waited for a moment before clearing brush away to walk along the west side of the path. A Nottoway man, Oyeocker, arrived next and mirrored him along the path's east side. Virginian planters Abraham Wood and Edward Bland, who had traveled south from Fort Henry on the Appomattox River to explore and find Native trading partners, stalled behind them. They watched in mystification, "demanding the meaning of it." Pyancha refused to reply and left them behind, but Oyeocker "prepared himselfe in a most serious manner to require our attentions," according to Bland. He told a story Algonquians knew about a person also familiar to the English. Years before, when Opechancanough had visited the Chowanokes to the south with gifts, a lesser werowance "went to salute and embrace the King of Chawan, and stroaking of him after their usuall manner, he whipt a bow string about the King of Chawans neck, and strangled him." "In memorial of this," Bland continued, the friends of the Powhatans—in this case an Appamattuck man—follow the western trail, and the friends of the Chowanokes—a Nottoway—follow the eastern one.[1] The betrayal, memorialized at the spot by both people, caused the paths of the Nottoway and Appamattuck men to part ways when they encountered the tree. They came together again on the other side of the circular trunk, Opechancanough and enmities now behind them. Native and English travelers would have interpreted the meaning of the tree in light of the new dangers of the mid-seventeenth century and the interconnected Native networks surrounding them.

Wood's 1650 trek through the Piedmont mirrored for English traders an orientation away from William Claiborne's vision for Kent Island to the north. English planters and traders like him were increasingly caught up in local versions of much larger threats: political and religious divisions that crossed the Atlantic and the Maryland-Virginia border, misbehaving and runaway laborers, and violent conflicts with Native neighbors—all pushing boundaries from within and without. However, the Englishmen's decision to follow Oyeocker clockwise around the tree indicated that Native knowledge and politics still commanded European obeisance, and through their movement in a Native place they were thus folded into Native alliances, instabilities, and shared spaces. The English also would have noticed the change in reception from the Piedmont's Native people, who had met with unprecedented and destabilizing threats over the past generations. The trade in guns and the enslavement of Native people, which carried captives hundreds of miles from home to European colonies along the Atlantic, had fragmented chiefdoms and altered or destroyed life in Native towns. Fear and great care with information about the region's politics and resources prevailed. Native people who controlled the movement of traders inland at key river points, from the Nottoways to the Occaneechis along the Roanoke River, proved cautious in providing access to people who could be competitors or could be enslavers themselves.[2] These people, with trade connections on the coast, were culturally, politically, and linguistically distinct from Algonquians, but captive-taking and raiding still threatened violence to Algonquians living in fragmented chiefdoms and among English people, who considered them a buffer. For their leaders, inland politics and English interest in them heightened the need for clear boundaries and care for alliances. Algonquians and colonists thus understood how tenuous geographic placement made both vulnerable to political instability.

At the same time that Algonquians faced mobile threats from the Piedmont, planters faced threats from within. Tobacco production increased dramatically between 1640 and 1660; even though life spans were short for English colonists in the Chesapeake, Maryland and Virginia elites and small and middling planters had time enough to amass wealth.[3] Having profited from the Anglo-Native conflict and lucrative government positions of previous decades, a handful of men controlled a large proportion of the labor pool. The number of indentured servants from the British Isles only increased during this period, providing ordinary planters and elites alike with labor.[4] Enslaved or hired Native people, from nearby or from the interior, also labored on plantations, and Dutch and English merchants brought enslaved Africans to the Chesapeake's rivers. By the 1640s, traders and planters like William Claiborne and William Tucker, with land and connections to merchants, purchased increasing numbers of these Africans. Many people who survived the Middle Passage faced legal lifetime slavery, and if not, growing legal obstacles to release and upon release from servitude.[5] By the 1650s, Black people labored on almost all elites' plantations.[6] It was incumbent on enslavers to stop their chattel from accessing routes to freedom and to bring them back when they escaped. Resistance of nonelites, just like Native violence on the coast and in the interior, highlighted the threats of interconnectivity for elites and its promises for others.

Amid this frenetic movement, English and Algonquian leaders created new strategies. In 1641, the Virginia governor began encouraging exploration of the waterways that ran through Virginia, authorizing settlers to explore to the head of the Appomattox River.[7] A final war with the Powhatans in 1644, the decline of centralized Powhatan authority, and the ensuing spread of English settlement created new possibilities for planters through both local relationships with Algonquians and farther-reaching trade. English settlers spearheading these changes sought to understand and then control Native places for profit: first through conquest against the Powhatans, then diplomacy and trade in the Piedmont, and finally in claiming and cultivating land. A small group of traders reoriented established strategies—military campaigns, fortifications, exploration, patents—to set boundaries inland and funnel trade their way.

These changes, as demonstrated by the ritual at the tree, did not make places documented by English Virginians any less Native. As they had for decades, Algonquians allied with, surveilled, and policed their English neighbors to protect mobility and territory. Just as Claiborne had, Abraham Wood found that the presence and knowledge held by people like the Appamattucks were crucial to the pursuit of trade beyond English boundaries. However, as they asserted borders around plantations, and then traded beyond mapped boundaries south and west of the James River and into the Piedmont, settlers underscored their dependence on the mobility and connectivity of Native people across borders. They were never able to completely graft English territorial claims atop Native places convincingly enough. Even though in 1650, when Wood accompanied the two Native guides into the hinterlands, the Chowanokes and Powhatans were no longer the same polities they had been a generation before, a ritual performed on the landscape still memorialized historical shifts in power. When English people walked along older paths and through towns to seek trade connections, Native people and their landmarks shaped English knowledge. They also shaped their attempts to expand their boundaries as Native and settler conflict moved inland.

Fighting and Fearing War

Stretches of the shores along some of the rivers now occupied by Maryland and Virginia colonists looked like dry patches to people in canoes. There had once been homes, multiple fires, and the noise of families; now the distinctive shapes of men and cattle occasionally appeared through trees and near the water, visible through haze in the fields in the spring and summer.[8] Cattle and pigs created their own uneven, meandering paths through the woods beyond the English fences.[9] English homes ashore looked remarkably different from one another, especially to an Algonquian accustomed to bread loaf–shaped yahakans covered with mats: some clapboard-sided and others mud-walled, some rotting in place amid others under construction by new settlers.[10] Along the York and James Rivers, and to the north along the Potomac and Patuxent Rivers, English people planted small fields for food and larger ones for tobacco on cleared or stump-studded land.[11] Their tobacco met merchant ships at the nearest navigable water, rather than being hauled overland on Native roads that crossed plantations. Their seasons were organized around tobacco, and their everyday interactions were organized through neighboring plantations where laborers cultivated it.[12]

While it looked from the water like fewer people and less activity than before English settlement—and in some places, it was—it represented grand designs for English planters of Virginia and now Maryland.[13] Chesapeake land was worth relatively little to the English in the 1630s and 1640s; wealthy men carved out estates in prime trading and farming locations along the river, while for middling planters a patent of hundreds of acres was enormous when compared to an English farm, and tobacco still promised substantial profit.[14] By 1652, most of the land connected to the water was claimed by Englishmen; in some areas, elite Englishmen were the first to patent land, and their patents were often among the largest. This left the landlocked or inhospitable areas and small plots of land for Native people and colonists of fewer means.[15] To the north, Marylanders patented 37,000 acres of land by 1642, less than a decade after the initial voyage to the colony, but the few hundred settlers had only improved around three square miles in their five "hundreds" or governments around St. Mary's.[16] The ruling Calverts envisioned a feudal system of land tenure called "manors," plots of land of at least a thousand acres given to planters who brought over new immigrants to work it or who were friends of the colony. Giles Brent, for example, was provided with Kent Island Manor for his services in the fight against Claiborne. Sixteen private manors, the largest of which was twelve thousand acres belonging to the Jesuits, dominated patented land. Political instability and other pressures would all but kill this model, replaced by a private property model similar to that in Virginia.[17]

As elites began accumulating land, they faced threats to proliferating plantation and colonial borders from inside and out. With intelligence on English and European happenings in the Chesapeake and abroad, Opechancanough took advantage of religious and political divisions among English settlers to orchestrate a well-organized attack in 1644 on peripheral settlements. The use of English pinnaces and Native canoes to spread information and conduct diplomacy was critical to the cause and pursuit of the war over two years. Just like maritime trade in information and goods, the conflict spilled over colonial borders and beyond the reach of Virginia's authorities. The war between the English and the Powhatans resulted in large-scale demographic and political movement to the northwest following the ultimate defeat of Opechancanough's forces, and major investment in a fort system that would hold the new colonial boundaries along the rivers. As colonists moved into Algonquian districts and crowded the shorelines, Algonquians learned to negotiate with local elites and navigate English law and Anglo-Native politics.

With access to waterways and knowledge of other colonies, bonded laborers represented an inside threat to the English. English indentured servants, Native people, and Africans claimed as property entered broader geographic swaths of this world in increasing numbers and used waterways between plantations and colonies to escape beyond colonial boundaries. People who repeatedly fled and groups of servants involved in escape plots came before Maryland and Virginia courts in the 1640s, from plantations as far afield as Maryland's Kent Island and Virginia's outpost plantations on the south side of the James River. Some plots, one on the south side of the

James involving at least two separate plantations and a Black pilot of a stolen boat, revealed the formidable networking power and skills of young people who had only lived in the colony a few years.[18] Both Virginia and Maryland officials cracked down on escaped unfree people anew between 1640 and 1643, prescribing punishments like brandings and whippings and sentences of double the time lost, and requiring passes for passage out of the colony. Maryland punished abettors with a maximum of seven years' service.[19] By 1643, Virginian officials proposed sailing to Maryland to treat on the matter of returning one another's runaways; Maryland officials made the same overtures to the Dutch to the north. The tobacco economy and Native trade both relied on constant and predictable connections, undermining elite efforts to stamp out laborers' mobility.

Virginia's assembly recognized an additional threat posed by more than the loss of property to another colony: that servants and enslaved people could bolster Native power and vice versa. For example, as they had in the initial decade of colonization, unfree people could bring weapons and other goods to Native people in exchange for travel and assistance, an act the General Assembly made punishable by death.[20] English elites also no doubt recognized that their inability to control the movement of their servants and the goods they took to Native people could cause their Native neighbors to question their control. While patent records do not always correlate to a particular unfree person's location in a wealthy man's network of plantations, the starting points for a few of Virginia's escape plots in relation to Native settlement is suggestive: escaped Black man John Punch's enslaver, Hugh Gwynn, owned land on the Piankatank River near the Kiskiaks, patenting land near their town. Upstream from Gwynn's land was Dragon Run, crossed by Native roads running from settlements along the York and James.[21] Laborers might have moved between Native towns and English plantations illicitly or not, and might have even traded powder or shot for a trip across the river or food, but frightened planters had much more to lose sitting in an isolated plantation next to Native neighbors they did not trust. Certainly, elites worried about servants and enslaved laborers affecting the balance of power with Native people, and meted out harsh punishments accordingly.

While trying to hem their servants in, English leaders also noticed a rising tide of dangerous news from the north. They already knew that in New Netherland, Governor William Kieft's 1643 massacre of Native neighbors backfired when neighboring Algonquian peoples united to invade the tiny colony.²² Word was that it might spread: Dutch traders with Virginia ties reported that large groups of neighboring Native people threatened their borders, "giving rise to suspicion that they intended to start a general massacre, as they have boasted at times and heretofore has taken place in Virginia [in 1622] and elsewhere." At the same time, from prosecuting hog stealing to murdering their nearest neighbors' werowance, the English in Maryland pursued an intermittent war with the Susquehannocks, enemies of their Algonquian allies like the Piscataways.²³ In 1642, Maryland's leaders declared war and requested that the Virginians come north to take part in a joint expedition against the Susquehannocks. The Marylanders contended that along with burning Maryland homes and killing over a dozen people, the Susquehannocks also threatened Virginians. Susquehannocks had killed a fur trader working in both colonies, and the Algonquian Nanticokes, increasingly upset at Susquehannock occupation on the Eastern Shore, had also killed an Eastern Shore Virginian fur trader. Marylanders had proved willing to ally with Virginians for revenge in the past; the Virginians should return the favor. The movements of these traders across borders, and the resulting violence, necessitated that the colonies share the burden of policing borders, since, it seemed, Maryland could not do it alone. Indeed, the Susquehannocks bested the Maryland expedition against them the following year.²⁴

With tensions high, both English colonial governments attempted to halt the flow of guns as well as unfree people, punishing colonists who sold ammunition, weapons, or any other potentially dangerous trade items and entitling colonists to confiscate and keep guns found with a Native person.²⁵ However, English law did little to stop the movement of new weapons from the Dutch and Swedish colonies since the people who traded them were people on the move. When in 1643 Virginia planter John Nuttall testified about the death of Maryland sailor Roger Oliver at the hands of an unknown Native person wielding a Dutch knife, he demonstrated how maritime communications and trade irreparably entangled people from far-flung places through things and through escalating violence.²⁶

The flight of unfree people had a ripple effect, further undermining colonial authority by turning colonists against one another. The governor blamed "too much leniety" shown to previous escaped people, which he felt inspired others, "imbeasling the goods of theire said Maisters in hopes mistaken of the like favors shown to them as to others."²⁷ While servants continued to seek sanctuary with Native people or in neighboring colonies,

English elites also refused to respect English geographical boundaries. Virginian planter Edmund Plowden of Kecoughtan lost five servants to St. Mary's City in 1644, and when his call for Governor Calvert's assistance went unanswered, he sailed to Maryland and took three Marylanders and their boat and goods for himself.[28] These incidents went unpunished on the opposite side of the line and continued to weaken relations among colonial governments. Miscommunication and division among English people made the specter of pan-Native alliances all the more frightening. As one English commentator later asked, "Why should [Native people] scruple the cutting of [English] throats or driving them out from amongst them, who so little scruple the cutting each others throats?"[29]

Uncontrolled movement and conflicts among colonists compounded weaknesses obvious to their Native neighbors. If they were consistent in their resolution from decades before to control the trade in copper, Powhatans also sought to control the effects of these destabilizing relationships across the Chesapeake, which came along with rampant English settlement, within their bounds. The movement of weapons and non-Algonquian people to the north, and the English response to it, was especially disconcerting. The Susquehannocks were successfully moving south into English and Algonquian territories, and some Marylanders refused to serve in campaigns against attackers. Rumors meanwhile resurrected fears that Virginians would "doe mischife" with the Susquehannocks against the Marylanders.[30]

Algonquians also witnessed colonists struggle with English political divisions on Chesapeake ground. Foremost on every colonist's mind sat the English Civil War into which Ingle's and Claiborne's invasion of Maryland was folded, a struggle between loyalists to the crown and to the new parliament with Protestant sectarian overtones. Opechancanough "was by some English Informed, that all was under the Sword in England, in their Native Countrey, and such divisions in our Land; That now was his time or never, to roote out all the English."[31] A contemporary chronicler confirmed that trouble with Native people in 1644 "did divert a great mischief which was growing among us" over the new oath of allegiance to Oliver Cromwell. "If the Indians had but forborne a month longer," this observer continued with a touch of irony, "they had found us in such a combustion among our selves that they might with ease have cut of[f] every man if we had spent that little powder and shot we had among our selves." Timely intelligence of events from different corners of the English world, and the broader trend of violent and erratic behavior toward Native people and one another, likely informed Opechancanough's decision to attack.[32]

In April 1644, Opechancanough launched a coordinated assault on Virginian plantations and killed over four hundred settlers, beginning violence over land and settlement now known as the Third Anglo-Powhatan War. Recent settlement and English activity on Powhatan land became the Powhatans' specific geographic targets.[33] In the previous few years, the English had gained tracts of land from headrights for transporting immigrants, which turned into patents. These and earlier grants grew near the core of the remaining Powhatan chiefdom on the Pamunkey River, on the south side of the James River, and on the north side of the York River.[34] Opechancanough probably did not hope to root out all of the English but to reinstate a boundary of English plantations and behavior.[35] Twenty years later, one English chronicler was told that the Powhatans "assaulted, no persons, nor invaded any man, possessions or goods, that they knew had bought their lands of them, & convenanted with them and made good their convenants." Even if individual land deals did not factor into Opechancanough's rationale, some settlers and many Algonquians likely perceived a pattern of disregard for borders and saw Opechancanough and Powhatan leadership as asserting an intention to enforce borders.[36] While Opechancanough was planning, chronicler William Castell wrote, all of the Chesapeake would yield only three thousand Powhatan warriors total, and only a few hundred of these on the James River where most colonists lived and planted. Local understandings of borders established by Native districts—which waterways and land should remain in local chiefdoms' control and which were being crossed by the English—were therefore necessary for Algonquians to attack precisely.[37]

Opechancanough's strategies and allies in some ways mirrored his 1622 attack. The Chickahominies and former tributaries including the Weyanokes and Nansemonds—all who historically established towns on the south side of the James River—joined the fight. Like before, many Algonquian polities on the fringes of the Powhatans' orbit, on the Eastern Shore and Potomac, declined to participate. Opechancanough's force wrought extensive destruction, "executed so suddenly on all the Out-settlements."[38] The Powhatans attacked settlements farthest away from Jamestown and those on the York River near core Powhatan settlements.[39] Recognizing that "'twas impossible for him to destroy them at once, without an entire Conquest," the Powhatans again depended on the isolation of the English plantations to harass inhabitants with little risk.[40] By "killing all their Cattell [and] destroying in the nights, all their Corne Fields," the Powhatans drew on the experience of a previous war of attrition.[41]

Because of demographic growth among the English, Powhatans' attack destroyed a smaller percentage of settlements, cattle, and people than before. But like in 1622, the attack sowed disorder and discontent. The lack of foodstuffs compelled the Virginia Assembly to pass a 1645 law against hoarding and "ingrossing" corn to sell for extortionate prices.[42] The Powhatans surely knew that war would create opportunities for servants and enslaved laborers to run for Native towns or the borders, and the Anglo-Powhatan treaty signed at the end of the war demanding the return of runaway servants and enslaved people proves they were right.[43] On one of the Wormeley plantations along the York River, Black laborers rioted in 1644 as English militia conducted military campaigns against the Chickahominy and Pamunkey to the northwest.[44] The Powhatans were correct in their assumption that the Virginians would run low on ammunition and predictable shipments of supplies, and with few Virginian exports during the war, merchants took their wares north to Maryland instead. The colony's secretary Richard Kemp wrote to the governor while campaigning against the Chickahominies in 1645 that his troops came down to a single barrel of powder. If not for a last-minute delivery of shot, one Englishman recalled, "wee must have againe disbanded," implying that at least some commanders were marching until a lack of powder and ammunition forced them to retire. "The people cryed oute loud for marches," Kemp said, and the shortage of shot "was not by them considered."[45] Fear, economic concerns, and a dearth of supplies put planters and officials at odds with each other. Planters wanted to destroy Powhatan power and resume the business of planting tobacco, but the war underscored the costs and vulnerabilities of running plantations on claimed Native land.

The Powhatan attack and the war in England provided opportunities for elites to once again transgress their own borders. During Maryland's longstanding conflict with the Susquehannocks, members of the General Assembly in Maryland disagreed about how to resolve tensions with Native people.[46] Ingle, in power after overthrowing Maryland's established government, was familiar as a tobacco trader with the plantations and planters of both Virginia and Maryland. Amid both Susquehannock and Powhatan incursions, Claiborne used Virginian troops to grab Kent Island back from the Marylanders to reopen trade with the Susquehannocks.[47] The rebels looted Catholic estates and imprisoned Jesuit leaders. They also incited Maryland's Protestant servants to rebel against elite Catholics who held their indentures. Colonial official Thomas Cornwallis, who had an armed face-off with Claiborne at Kent Island not even a decade before, sued Ingle for damages after Ingle incited Cornwallis's servants to steal cattle, burn fences, and kill pigs. Other servants chose to fight for Ingle directly or help him capture sailing vessels on the bay.[48] Not until after the Anglo-Powhatan War in 1647 did the Calverts resume control of the government; Ingle was executed in 1653.[49] Occurring at an opportune and distracting moment of Anglo-Native relations, Ingle's and the Virginians' attack to the north further laid bare religious and class fissures at the expense of English authority.

After their initial attack on the Virginians, the Algonquians mounted no sustained campaigns, allowing the English to organize responses through local governments. While the 1622 attack led to ten years of sporadic raids and violence, a new governor and his council hoped to quickly end the conflict and strategically reinforce settlement boundaries to avoid future incursions. To contain the conflict, young and educated Governor William Berkeley and the assembly drew on the colony's county governments to extract soldiers, money, and supplies for the war from the colonists themselves. Small groups of armed men burned Native cornfields while palisaded homes protected two or three families together to avoid the isolation and vulnerability of distant plantations.[50] After the initial attack, authorized commanders from the counties on the south side of the James took supplies from colonial inhabitants and pursued Native people onto the "frontiers." Men north of the James, in contrast, were tasked with holding the narrow neck of the peninsula at Middle Plantation, through which ran access between English plantations and forested areas controlled by Native people. Wounded men and horses, lost property, and stolen vessels (and officers' salaries) were accounted for by the local courts, which now levied taxes on householders in whatever amount "they conceive reasonable."[51] Servants and others could be impressed to fight by the county councils of war. To better support this costly militia, all Black men and women were deemed tithable, a key moment in the development of racialized slavery over the course of the century.[52] Property owners and enslavers from the new counties on the south side of the James thus invested labor as well as financial resources to hold new borders and move toward the violent transformation of Native landscapes to the south and west.

To destroy the Pamunkey leadership, the English used intelligence of Native people's movement to infringe on their domains. After the initial assault in 1644, Opechancanough retreated up the Pamunkey River. Surrounded by wooded swamps and streams on the winding river, the Powhatans occupied a prime spot for defense, and the swamps established a barrier between the Algonquians and outsiders.[53] The English noticed and decided to build nearby. On the Pamunkey River just a year later in 1645, carpenters and laborers set to work building Fort Royal. Trader William Claiborne led an attack coordinated between English boats and foot soldiers on the Pamunkey River, and English forces also took aim at the "kings owne house" in 1645, sacking Powhatan religious structures and burning Opechancanough's fortifications. Captain Ralph Wormeley, who ventured up the Chickahominy River, "brought in one prisoner by the locke to the great joy of the Armye, and was of great Consequence to them in guiding them to their townes and Corne feildes."[54] The English military strategy once again relied on Native knowledge, here forcibly taken from captives, in tandem with building and surveilling nearby Native strongholds.

The death of Opechancanough marked the end of fighting. By 1646, recognizing "the almost impossibility of a further revenge" against an enemy "lurking up & downe the woods in small numbers," the General Assembly and governor agreed to send interpreter Henry Fleet by boat to Opechancanough for peace talks.[55] Receiving intelligence, perhaps from Fleet, of the werowance's location, Governor Berkeley himself met him with mounted troops from the county militias, and "surprised and took him Prisoner."[56] At almost a century old, Opechancanough was shot in the back by an Englishman at Jamestown, the capital of a polity that harnessed communication networks Opechancanough himself had helped build and master.[57]

The treaty of 1646 between the English and Powhatans ended the Powhatan chiefdom as it had existed before, and it put in place barriers between English and Native people, forcing acknowledgment of the ways they had been and continued to be intertwined. The English declared the Powhatans, or more specifically the Pamunkey and their allies, to be tributaries of the colony, subject to the crown in exchange for protection of their land and people.[58] The treaty also authorized Virginia's governor to approve the Native leaders in the future. The Powhatans' defeat meant that the treaty shored up the power of land- and labor-rich officials, who wanted to both reinforce boundaries around land and labor and open access to trade in the Piedmont. Opechancanough's successor, Necotowance, was to return "all such negroes and guns as are yet remaining" with him and any that might come his way in the future, emphasizing the English designation of Africans as property. The English also realized how mobile enslaved and indentured laborers had become, and how political divisions encouraged them to use it at opportune moments. Stipulations about the return of any Native prisoners and servants that "shall hereafter run away" anticipated that Native and African captives and European indentured servants would escape from the English in the coming years. As tributaries to the English, Chesapeake Algonquians were to physically pursue planters' interests through woods and fields.

The results of the war further sapped Algonquians' power in the Chesapeake by pushing them apart from one another. The treaty established that the area between the York and James Rivers from the Atlantic Coast west to the falls belonged to the English. The Pamunkey seat of power remained on the Pamunkey River but surrounded by English settlements. The new boundary was east of the core of the Powhatan chiefdom and its farthest reaches: the falls had been the boundary between Algonquians and non-Algonquians beyond for hundreds of years. The English would push the new line with them as they settled beyond these boundaries.[59] The 1646 treaty was an attempt to confine Native people north of the York River. Within a short while, the countryside along the Rappahannock River was opened to patents and settlements. Borders between individual plantations and Native towns proliferated north of the York River.

For Algonquians in the Chesapeake most affected by the county militia campaigns and English settlement, the war caused unprecedented migrations that pulled Algonquians into new alliances. After their defeat, the Nansemonds in the southern Chesapeake split in two, one group leaving for Blackwater Swamp to the southwest and another staying within the Virginia colony's orbit.[60] Some Indigenous people subsequently relocated away from English plantations to the inhospitable (for English people) Great Dismal Swamp southeast of the colony, where after around 1660 archaeology shows they were joined by escaped servants and enslaved people turned maroons.[61] The Weyanokes had moved south during the war and killed messengers from the Powhatans who came to retrieve them, and fell in with Piedmont Native people instead.[62] Other Native people consolidated resources and governments, if not identities: Wicomocos and Chicacoans, for example, were granted fifty acres of land per adult man together through a Northern Neck patent in the 1650s, under the Wicomocos' name.[63] Displacement forced on Algonquians the difficult work of constructing and reconstructing alliances and boundaries based on local conditions.

A second, more ominous migration of Indigenous people—through captivity and slavery—helped the English balance the financial cost of the war. Members of tributary nations were supposedly protected from slavery, but hostile or outsider people were not; individuals remained bound to English plantations with ambiguous origins and legal status.[64] Ostensibly hostile Native people over the age of eleven were shipped to the "Western Island," probably what is now Tangier Island in the middle of the Chesapeake Bay.[65] In 1650, Thomas Wilkinson, who patented newly opened land on the Potomac River, listed four "transported" Native people in the land book as his headrights, their origins unknown.[66] Elites like Edward Hill used shipping connections to sell Indigenous captives in Maryland. Ordinary planters who had access to the Piedmont trade like Thomas Smallcomb and Sackford Brewster, a fellow explorer alongside Abraham Wood, sold Indigenous people overland to elite planters like Governor Berkeley.[67] Although Native people worked as bonded laborers on English plantations consistently through the seventeenth century, the trade in captives made future wars with Native people seem increasingly opportune to Virginia's colonists.[68] The sale of unfree people could help pay for wars after the fact and hasten the depopulation and destabilization of Native towns and polities. English and some Native people continued the practice of slaving after the war; in 1652, the assembly put in place laws to restrict colonists from selling Native children entrusted to their care and to stop Native people from buying or stealing the children of other families or nations.[69] Planters and soldiers ultimately profited from scattering their enemies into the wind through violence, labor, and boundaries around their settlements.

New treaty relationships and laws shaped Anglo-Native relationships for Native people living proximate to settlers. In Virginia, Berkeley's energetic governance heralded further transformation of the Native landscape through the proliferation of new counties encouraging settlement and ambitious officeholders.[70] More subtle changes, like ordering the construction of bridges and fining colonists who stole canoes from one another, promised to change the way people and goods moved across the water.[71] In lieu of using Powhatan's necklace as a passport for the English coming into Powhatan places, the new peace treaty stipulated that Necotowance's men would use an English object—a matchcoat or badge of "striped stuff"—to deliver messages into English territory. Necotowance agreed to travel to Jamestown to pay tribute and promised that his messengers would repair to Fort Henry on the Appomattox River to trade or communicate with the English.[72] These new rules threatened to curtail free, safe movement through the Algonquians' former domains, and placed both chance encounters and formal diplomatic visits in English spaces and on English terms.

However, the 1646 treaty was largely unenforceable from the perspective of Pamunkey leadership, which had lost its battle over mobility of people and goods in the Chesapeake. Necotowance's power over Algonquian districts and intelligence was diluted by the scattering of people and proliferation of local relationships, and he found it difficult to control Algonquian movement as head of a decentralized and decreasing number of towns and people. Berkeley was even forced to hire bodyguards to protect against assassination attempts perpetrated by Algonquians who continued the war against the English despite the peace treaty. Referencing more mundane trespasses, Necotowance complained, "My countrymen tell me I am a liar when I tell them the English will kill you if you goe into their bounds." One of the same militia captains who had fought with Claiborne for Kent Island "made him no liar when lately he killed three Indians without badge encroaching."[73] Other accounts corroborate that English planters actively patrolled their plantations' boundaries, killing Native trespassers and revealing the violence implicit in protection of private property.[74]

For neighboring Algonquians, the hope that the English might be (even violently) incorporated into the Powhatans' landscape died with Opechancanough, and new dangers emerged as planters settled on the shores near Native towns. But despite new rules, werowances and Algonquian men and women had independent bargaining power in local and colony-wide contexts. Necotowance relayed to Governor Berkeley information about non-Powhatan peoples to the south and west: Native knowledge and diplomatic skills—and those of traders' servants—would prove necessary for the development of a second and hopefully more lucrative fur trade.

With the ability to corral money and labor to mount the war, and captives and land to turn a profit, the English won the capacity to define boundaries to their own ends. Opechancanough, aware of the politically disadvantageous moment for the English in 1644 and the ongoing labor and land disputes, demonstrated to the English the threat that internal divisions posed from the outside. Control of goods and information would become more crucial for elites, and harder to obtain, as isolated settlements spiraled outward from the shores of the James River. From eight thousand colonists in 1640, the number of English swelled to fourteen thousand by 1653.[75] Growth after 1653 intensified to the north of Jamestown, especially near the Potomac River, where travelers noted "the commodiousnesse, and pleasantnesse of the soyle much inhabited" by Native peoples.[76] The end of fighting in 1646 signified the beginning of new disputes and negotiations over land, which would also provide access to new connections in the Piedmont and potential profit for would-be settlers. To protect English-claimed land, the English placed a burgeoning number of physical and legal boundaries between themselves and Native people.

Displacing and Policing Native People

The rapid river currents, pooling and snaking past rock outcroppings, looked and sounded different from the Chesapeake, which lay to the northeast. Voices speaking a Siouan language matched the rolling water. Other Native people, fellow Siouan-speakers, had come south to the river, over wooded hills, along the old road, to trade beads and copper for deerskins. They would return north with skins to English forts. The hosts here started a giant fire to feed their visitors, the Occaneechis, with familiar foods—corn, fish, game, and foraged greens—and with new sweet flavors, watermelon and peaches. Here between the coast and the mountains, palisades protected towns with few or no guns for defense—both visitors and hosts understood the differences in power created by their disparate geographic and political connections to European settlement. The Occaneechis carried guns and hatchets from the Europeans, a worrying sight in the hands of anyone but trading partners. People in the Piedmont remained always on the lookout for enemies thus equipped, no doubt searching for loot and captives.[77]

Military victories, forts, and draconian legal boundaries on the coast had paved the way for the English to more confidently pursue trade into the interior. After the war ended in 1646, however, Algonquians familiar with the Native world beyond the Chesapeake directed English trade and reconnaissance along precontact land routes like those in the Piedmont. They developed personal networks with growing numbers of English people interested in trade, gathering intelligence about political and economic turmoil in the Piedmont. Native interlocutors were intentionally selective with the intelligence they offered to Virginian traders, who it was understood sought trade in firearms and enslaved Native people through networks controlled by powerful nations. Encounters like Abraham Wood's 1650 expedition demonstrate how Native movements continued to facilitate or thwart the English presence in the trade, and how together Indigenous and English traders reinterpreted and reconfigured Native routes and their uses.

In this context, the English series of forts built right after the 1644 offensive were checkpoints intended to aid the English in monitoring the movements of the Algonquians and outsiders by land or water. Protestants William Claiborne, Richard Ingle, and Nathaniel Pope restored St. Mary's Fort during the rebellion; after Calvert regained control, the Marylanders relied on St. Inigoes Fort down St. Mary's River to halt traffic in and out of the colony.[78] In Virginia, Fort Royal on the York River, closest to the Pamunkeys' seat, was the first in a series of forts during this period. Forts and palisades signaled political divisions and tension but, as at James Fort, served as gathering spots for settlers and Native people, official points of access between Native and English domains, and a place of trade.[79]

Ultimately, the forts assisted elites in accruing land, labor, and geographic situations at cost to taxpayers. Roger Marshall, a county militia captain who led a charge against the Pamunkeys during the final Anglo-Powhatan War, was rewarded for his service with control of Fort Royal.[80] In exchange for over three thousand acres of land, Marshall was tasked with building and maintaining the necessary structures and ten men on the premises for three years.[81] To halt Indigenous fishing and agriculture on the Appomattox River in 1646, the General Assembly ordered Fort Henry built and staffed with forty-five paid soldiers. Also in exchange for land, Thomas Rolfe, son of John Rolfe and Pocahontas, built Fort James on the Chickahominy River to cut off Native access to plantations on the Lower Peninsula and to displace Native towns.[82] While a few were active for only four or five years, the forts were intended to disrupt Powhatan patterns of sustenance and communication, and remained part of the public levy for the war for years afterward and a centerpiece of political conflict.

Other householders no doubt saw that county- and colony-level appointees both directed and profited from boundary-making and trading forts, with the forts' connections to Native places and routes to the interior obvious. The fall line and the paths to reach it had remained Native even in English records. The land sale of Fort Royal on the south side of the York

River mentions that it was also called "Ricahock," the Rickahock path ran to the Chickahominy Fort, showing the two forts to be connected by the same route. Nearby, the Pamunkey fort, Asiskewincke, stood by the fresh water on the same side of the York River and was home to the Pamunkey werowance and Necotowance's successor Totopotomoi.[83] The fort system reinforced the reorientation from water to land and promised access to Algonquian overland routes leading to non-Algonquian people.

As nodes of connection, however, the combination of Native and English fortifications changed opportunities for enterprising Native people and colonists alike. As at earlier forts like Kent Island, forts proved places to exchange guns, skins, and Native people. The new Virginian forts sat on the fall line splitting the Chesapeake basin from the Piedmont, the point at which English ships could advance no farther upriver. Beyond the forts, archaeology at midcentury Native towns located to the south and west of the James River falls reveals that non-Algonquian people built "trading towns" where women processed skins to trade.[84] The English began trading and pushing boundaries in accessible places for the Powhatans' neighbors, and many Native people responded by orienting their settlements toward the English trade. Forts and trade routes facilitated new connections that altered daily life.[85]

Men with the fortune to sit at the shifting geographical borders between Native and English territories at the right time used the reorientation of settlement inland to advance their own positions. In 1652, after ten years of tension and fighting, Marylanders negotiated a new treaty with the Susquehannocks. The Susquehannocks ceded land on the Eastern Shore that had historically belonged to Algonquians and reaffirmed that while any English person could settle on Palmer's Island, Kent Island and its fort belonged to their friend William Claiborne. Of course, Maryland officials and Maryland planters who already held land at Kent Island maintained their claims. But the Virginian Eastern Shore's wealthiest planter, Edmund Scarborough, immediately sought to claim thousands of acres on Maryland's side of the line, raising men and supplies to invade the settlements of neighboring Algonquians on the grounds of supposed Native hostility toward the Virginians. Meanwhile, he claimed trading rights on Palmer's Island, gifted to Claiborne by the Susquehannocks but within Maryland territory, for himself. At the same time, Algonquians angry with Susquehannock and English incursions from Maryland and Virginia harassed Kent Islanders with weapons they acquired from Dutch and English ships, pushing free colonists to consider a move to the mainland.[86] Algonquians shaped politics at the border as they held their own boundaries, but the true victors in these conflicts were increasingly officials and wealthy men who could leverage the tension of unclear borders to redirect resources. Of course, their actions, like Scarborough's, bred more rumors and violence.

In Algonquian territory, no one understood these strategies better than established traders, who continued to benefit further from land grabs upriver. In 1653, the General Assembly gave three men with extensive contact with Native peoples—Henry Fleet, William Claiborne, and Abraham Wood—the exclusive privilege of both trading and patenting land "in places where no English ever have bin and discovered."[87] Fresh from forging maritime connections for the Marylanders, Fleet found himself once again at the center of diplomatic negotiations and at the head of a company of troops in both Chesapeake colonies. First, he had been instructed by Maryland officials to sue for a peace on their behalf with the Susquehannocks in 1644 before visiting with the Powhatans in 1646. Moving among a myriad of different polities and languages, Fleet negotiated handsome levy-funded salaries, land grants, and trade avenues for himself on both sides of the Potomac, and license to build a fort on the Rappahannock.[88] A lifelong interpreter and trader, Fleet had proved himself, if sometimes untrustworthy, capable in a myriad of delicate diplomatic situations. William Claiborne had lost the outpost at Kent Island to Maryland once again and, like Fleet, played a critical role in the campaigns against the Powhatans that had opened new lands to settlement. Abraham Wood bought and controlled Virginia's outpost at Fort Henry on the Appomattox River, the treaty-defined point of contact between English people and Algonquians and what would become a central node of the trade to the interior. He began life in Virginia as an indentured servant, under future governor Samuel Mathews. Mathews introduced Wood into the Anglo-Native trade as it began to flourish in the 1620s.[89] After the war with Opechancanough accelerated the building of forts, Wood capitalized on the flow of Native goods and communications rerouted through his plantation.[90] Because he was raised into the Native trade by an Englishman, Wood joined the privileged ranks of men like Fleet and Claiborne. Both a planter and trader, he invested in expeditions beyond the colony as a means to patent land and establish trade connections.

Planters and traders like Wood needed assistance navigating wetlands and overland routes between rivers, in what was often a frightening new geography. The southern Chesapeake and hillier areas west proved a physical and navigational challenge for colonists unfamiliar with them. Many fordable spots along the rivers were connected by Native roads and, in the Piedmont, controlled by nations including the Nottoways, Weyanokes, and Occaneechis, comprising what traders found to be a long, circuitous, social journey.[91] But neither could Europeans venture alone; Anglican minister James Blair later wrote that a guide was necessary to enter the nebulous area between Carolina and Virginia because "there is no possibility for a stranger to find his road in that country, for if he once goes astray (it being such a desert country) it is a great hazard if he ever finds his road again."[92] French traveler Francis Louis Michel "returned alone through the wilderness and lost my way, because, when I reached a path, I thought it was the way, but it was only used by the game. After several hours it suddenly ended, which dumbfounded me." The southern Chesapeake's riverine environment proved an inconvenience, but colonists were even more concerned with the disorienting, impassible swamps, neither navigable water nor navigable land. The proximity of swamps made Englishmen and -women, promotional literature writer Samuel Wilson admitted, "subject to Agues, as those who are so seated in England."[93] By the 1660s, county officials on the Middle Peninsula were ordered to build a bridge if possible over the "dangerous" swamps near the Rappahannock River, perhaps referring to the thirty-five-mile-long Dragon Swamp running between the counties.[94] Wet, frightening, incomprehensible: the interior seemed unknowable and hostile for English settlers in particular, underscoring their relative lack of power and understanding of a Native landscape juxtaposed with cleared fields.

For the English, the alien routes to trade with powerful groups like the Occaneechis and the Tuscaroras relied on proximate Algonquian tributaries. Fleet and Claiborne patented huge swaths of land on the modern-day North Carolina–Virginia border and along the roads of the interior trade, but Wood used his connections to a neighboring Algonquian polity, the Appamattucks, to plan his expedition south and west in 1650.[95] A core group of the Powhatan chiefdom in the sixteenth and early seventeenth centuries, the Appamattucks had provided access to distant and valuable goods for Powhatan via preexisting trade routes that ran through their towns. After they began appropriating Appamattuck land at the confluence of the Appomattox and James Rivers by 1619, the English damaged or destroyed most of their towns in 1623 during the Anglo-Powhatan War.[96] Appamattuck residents moved west of Fort Henry sometime after 1623 and gained Wood as a new neighbor when the fort became his in 1646.[97] They took their trade connections with them as they moved. In 1650, Nottoway guide Pyancha and Appamattuck guide Oyeocker agreed to lead Wood's men along these old routes. Pyancha and Oyeocker led them to several points on the fall line for at least sixty miles, past Fort Henry on the Appomattox River, down the Blackwater River and then the Roanoke River, through trading sites controlled by the Nottoway and Meherrin.[98] Wood's local relationships granted him access to paths in what was for him distant and foreign land.

Guides Oyeocker and Pyancha were suited for the work because they understood the politics and language to the south, and Native enmities and anxieties that existed even before regional instability accelerated movement. Pyancha took the travelers a hundred miles south along paths and across rivers to the major towns belonging to the Nottoway and Meherrin, a diplomatic effort to make the colonists' presence known to the leaders in these territories. There, a Nottoway king named Chounterounte discouraged the travelers from proceeding, citing the weather but probably hoping to avoid an alliance between the Tuscaroras and the English on their way toward them. Pyancha received intelligence about a forthcoming Meherrin attack from "a woman that was his Sweet-heart" living in Meherrin town. When a Meherrin man claiming to be a werowance presented himself, Pyancha turned him away to avoid violence or misinformation. By pulling on his geographically wide-ranging kinship and knowledge, he steered the group toward safety.[99]

At every turn, Wood saw European movement along Native routes that potentially subverted his own ambitions and his exclusive right to trade. The Nottoways reported that a different Virginian from near Fort Henry had come to town with "bells, and other petty truck," a potential competitor and one originating at his back door. What kind of intelligence was this trader delivering about the English, and what new friends or enemies was he making? And how did he get here? Meanwhile, Native people also relayed news of another non-Native outsider trading among the Tuscarora; a European trader had beaten Wood to this potential market, perhaps by another path entirely. Wood wrote a note in "English, Latine, Spanish,

French, and Dutch" to deliver to the Tuscarora town where the European man was reported and asked the Tuscarora headman to visit his party at the Meherrin town.[100] (The Dutch had indeed been told by their Native allies about cheap furs in southwest Virginia two years before the Wood expedition.[101]) The Tuscarora headman never came, and Wood and his party concluded their trip with some uncertainty about the future of diplomacy and trade to the south and west.

Staking tentative claims, the members of the Wood expedition confronted the Native presence everywhere, creating new place-names that reflected continued use by Native people. Wood's fellow traveler Edward Bland named a patch of woods "Farmers Chase" when his servant Robert Farmer chased Nottoway women and children into the woods, his "hallow" misinterpreted as a sign of aggression.[102] Native history and behavior as recorded in English travel accounts simultaneously affirmed English rights to name and claim Indigenous land and reaffirmed continued Native activity on and knowledge of that land. While guiding the English travelers, Oyeocker paused to reflect at "a place of severall great heapes of bones" and told Wood and his companions "that at this place Appachancano [Opechancanough] one morning with 400. men treacherously slew 240. of the [Nottoway] River Indians in revenge of three great men slaine by them." Intrigued by the story, together the colonists named the ossuary Golgotha, referencing the place in Jerusalem where Jesus was crucified and more generally a site of suffering, sacrifice, and burial.[103] Grafting Christian meaning atop a Nottoway landmark was, of course, colonization at work. But Bland neither remembered the place's Native name nor replaced it with another self-referential marker of the expedition's progress, like "Blandina." Instead, Bland acknowledged his surroundings as imbued with shared Anglo and Native history and gravity. Both the English and Nottoways, after all, had lost great numbers to Opechancanough, whose defeat had made their travel possible.

Excursions like Wood's were crucial to the expansion and legitimacy of the Virginia colony: claiming new territory, gathering intelligence on rival European powers, and searching for trade. Just like settlement along the rivers, exploration overland would not have been possible without bounded private property and the accrual of wealth on coastal Algonquian land. For Wood, these were also crucial for the accumulation of personal profit and political clout in the colony. But English traders moved through this uncharted territory unsure of their place and dependent on their hosts and their places for survival. Exploration in the Piedmont further demonstrated dependence on extended Indigenous networks, crossing linguistic and political lines. It also underscored the integral part that Native people played in Chesapeake politics and competing spatial visions, even after the defeat of the Powhatan chiefdom.

English Surveying Meets Native Land

Although Maryland and Virginia governments disallowed most direct land sales from Native polities to English settlers by the 1650s, the same cast of characters, elites profiting from plantation labor in tandem with the Anglo-Native trade, enriched themselves with geographically and politically well-situated land. Traveling from their forts, symbols of English ascendancy, into a diverse and indecipherable landscape, English explorers depended on Indigenous knowledge to claim ownership of Native places. These processes were reflected in the proliferation of not only forts but also land patents and surveys along the banks of major rivers. The science of marking and surveying land developed on both sides of the Atlantic, much like in trading, and Virginian private property was defined more by the riverine geography of the Chesapeake and local Native landmarks than by math.

In the Chesapeake, the inconsistent nature of surveying and granting property promised problems for the future. Methods employed during the "cartographic revolution" in late sixteenth-century Europe were inexact, with different understandings of common units of measurement like the acre, and with different instruments included in kits of surveyor's tools. Surveyors required a clear line of sight and the ability to draw chains across fields, difficult in some of Virginia's woods and more so in swamps. Even the most mathematical, impartial surveyor still marked a line by shaving the bark from trees that might be cut the following year or with stakes that might rot away. Property lines of those who claimed shoreline often ran from the water inland one mile, leading to overlap when someone else's property ran inland by one mile from the opposite direction. A set of patents issued in the 1650s and 1660s in Caroline County had this issue when multiple patents overlapped at odd angles dictated by the waterways bounding them in, which was resolved only with another survey in the 1730s.[104] Analysis of one Maryland parish demonstrates patterns of overlap in planters' mapped boundaries, promising future conflicts among their descendants as they sought unambivalent and exclusive ownership of their land.[105]

Community considerations further complicated these logistical problems: on the British Isles, property boundaries relied more on community consensus and history developed over generations, and surveyed maps failed to upend this system into the eighteenth century.[106] In early modern England, neighbors shared understandings of the landmarks and collectively ascribed responsibility for land to those who occupied it.[107] Practices like "beating the bounds," in which community members walked the bounds of a parish together during the Easter season, reinforced collective understandings of property boundaries, often defined by natural markers like stones and creeks, and held in the heads of longstanding parishioners. The process of bounding local spaces situated the average Englishman as a player in local and regional conflicts. When parishioners of neighboring churches found that they disagreed about boundaries, ensuing verbal and physical fights reminded them of the stakes of local identity.[108] Unlike in the orderly towns of New England, the dispersed nature of Virginia plantations—not to mention a demographic lack of older, knowledgeable residents—meant that fewer English people walked, shared boundaries, and created community consensus on location.

The lack of established English spaces and the claims made through the headright system created a need to bound and map land in the Chesapeake. In 1623 and again in 1631, the General Assembly ordered that every "private planter's devident" be surveyed to avoid future boundary disputes. Maryland followed suit with laws setting the responsibilities and compensation for surveyors in the 1630s and 1640s, appointing a counterpart to Virginia's William Claiborne, their first surveyor general, a friend of the Calverts, in 1641.[109] Surveys were time-consuming and expensive, however, and by 1644 the Virginia General Assembly regulated costs and required planters to pay for surveyors' travel.[110]

In a return to custom, English people used landmarks as boundaries recognizable to both Native and English people: along with lines of marked trees or rocks, the creeks and forts and highways that were actual hallmarks of connectivity also served as boundaries. English settlers and Algonquians both might have recognized the establishment of land tenure as a process defined by familiarity with and occupation of local places, with frames of reference shared by people regardless of social status.[111] The land book had few formal place-names beyond forts and creeks named for Algonquian or English neighbors. Places "commonly knowne or called by the name," with meanings that only local residents would understand, served as points of reference. "The Indian Snares" and "the Nutt tree neck," for example, reference knowledge of everyday work taking place nearby.[112] Ephemeral markers of Native settlement—a cabin at the head of a creek, or more frequently a patch of earth Native women let lie fallow, "an Indian cleerefield"—also served as boundary markers, with the hope that Native people would permanently abandon the area, opening it to settlement.[113] Alongside terms used by nearby English residents for Native places, surveyors often used Algonquian names. Some entries used English and Algonquian names side by side ("a Creek called by the Indians Amburcomico, now [the plantation] Gargaphia"), indicating that the Native and English cultural meanings overlapped even as places shifted to private property.[114] Some landmarks functioned the same as during Algonquian land tenure: from 1623 the waterways themselves, the connecting ties in the Native Chesapeake from the James River and its tributaries outward, were among the earliest and most common boundary markers that also divided Powhatan districts.

When it came to surveying, however, landholders often found the Chesapeake landscape Native, formidable, and difficult to parse. Without a community history of English bounds, landholders relied on an unreliable landscape of marked trees, a problem when they all blew down in a hurricane, for example.[115] The dense vegetation and waterlogged ground that marked unfarmable "wastelands" compounded the problematic borders between Algonquians and English. Algonquians and English farmers had in common their disinterest in clearing or draining the pocosins, an Algonquian word for a type of wetland, for agriculture. For the English the pocosins (or poquosons) were culturally foreign and physically impenetrable. While surveyors' lines snapped the Indigenous landscape into smaller and smaller pieces, pocosins remained indomitable. An English settler could turn "the Indian Road" into "the Ferry Road" or "the Horse Path" by altering its use, but a pocosin was unusable and would always be a pocosin. The pocosin's unchanging nature made it a perfect boundary. No one wanted their property line to run directly through a pocosin; even Abraham Wood's extensive land grants near the Appomattox River explicitly included the adjoining swamps. Fathers most often gifted pocosins to an heir as a single unit, keeping them intact legally as well as physically. "The

Pocosin" simply became "Hoskins Pocosin" or remained anonymous but especially horrible: "a terrible myery Pocosin" or "my Great Pocosin."[116] As with other named places, or places "formerly called" by their Native names, the title "my Great Pocosin" brought together assertions of private property atop definably Native places.

Wastelands also encouraged movement and trespass, promoting conflict and concern for private property and the mobility of people in bondage.[117] In addition to traversing through marshes as they had for decades, Native people relied on plant and animal life in marshes for foodstuffs, particularly when corn yields were disappointing or harvests disrupted. Settlers then let loose their pigs into the pocosins to forage for themselves, precisely because the practice provided a physical barrier between pigs and productive land they might destroy.[118] Since wetlands were poor property markers—and because pigs are notorious trespassers—English and Native people, sometimes together, took the opportunity and risk of liberating such hogs from swamps and woods. A Northampton County planter walking along the "middle swamp" heard a scream from within, only to find a nearby resident had killed a hog, cut off the marked ears identifying the owner, and threw them into the fire.[119] To the north, a freeman, two English servants, and a Native man together stole an unmarked (or perhaps similarly earless) hog. Lancaster County planters David Fox and John Carter, both with claims to prime land on the often very marshy but navigable Corotoman River, took to court several servants who took hogs from their plantations. At least one of them was a captured unfree person who had also attempted escape, adding years to their indenture.[120] Simultaneously, the Rappahannocks nearby agreed in a Lancaster County treaty to both let the hogs live and turn in anyone else who appropriated planters' cattle and swine, an acknowledgment that they or other nearby nations might have ignored English conventions surrounding feral swine in the past. For the English elites who turned in servants to court, hog stealing was a threat to control over multiple forms of property—labor, real estate, and chattel—and was tied to concerns over servant mobility. When a Mrs. Burdett in Accomack County faced not only her servants' refusal to work but rumors that her servants had killed and roasted a hog, she told the undersheriff who came to investigate, "I am affrayd they [the servants, not the hogs] willl overrunn mee."[121] The landscape itself often undermined authority and attempts at marking property, lending itself to illicit, often communal activity and theft of property occurring at the fringes of the surveyed plantation.

Patent holders and planters deployed the status that came with land ownership itself to impose their own ordered plantation visions. Property ownership and the independence it seemed to convey demonstrated the political authority and social prowess of ambitious planters and the landed gentry.[122] Elite landowners (and often surveyors) were, of course, well represented in the General Assembly, Governor's Council, and county governments. As the number of patents and settlers at a distance from Jamestown increased, Virginia county officials gained more power to contour the everyday lives of their neighbors, in charge of maintenance of roads, procuring arms and ammunition for defense, and judgments for transgressions like running away. In Virginia, all were substantial landowners, claiming from five hundred to fifteen thousand acres, and so were invested in carefully guarding their own claims to land and trade networks.[123] Within the office of surveyor, landowners could direct paths and property lines to their own ends, like when highway surveyor John Biggs in Lower Norfolk cleared only a piece of the main road that ran through his own land.[124] With new assets vulnerable to a variety of Native and non-Native outsiders, landholders had a stake in the expansion of the colony. Fleet and Wood further leveraged their authority as traders and explorers when they served together as representatives in the General Assembly from their respective counties in 1652, two years after Wood's expedition with Oyeocker and Pyancha. They convinced that assembly to backtrack on previous legislation promoting southern and westward exploration and instead grant Claiborne, Fleet, and Wood first pickings in both trade and land.[125] Just as landholding at well-placed locations provided entrée to the trade, well-placed trade provided opportunities to expand claims to property. The accumulation of power through trade, land ownership, and political office was mutually reinforcing.

Elites sought to extend control further through surveying lands, a process which buried Native landmarks and history under property boundaries that gave the patent holder greater clout in colonial politics. Even the scientific process of surveying relied on Native reference points, and increasingly English references to earlier Native reference points, in surveyors' attempts to make the landscape more English. The imperfect nature of surveying, and the indomitability of the landscape itself, meant that Native resources, places, and the meaning behind them remained in the Anglo-Native Chesapeake. Native and unfree people maintained and created literal space for resistance, connection, and sustenance.

Amid thousand-acre land grants and thousand-mile journeys, Native people like Oyeocker and Pyancha oriented themselves, the English, and outsider Native people through extensive and violent networks embedded in local places. The process of creating real estate and transforming those places through exploration, trade, and surveying would not ultimately be possible without Native people and their ties to one another. The expanded fort-building, trading, and surveying that followed the final Anglo-Powhatan War tested but did not break the meaning of Algonquian spaces. When confronted with spaces and routes impossible to exploit, or forced to orient themselves through Native places and people, settlers acknowledged that some places remained Native.

Yet the final Anglo-Powhatan War reoriented Anglo-Native ties irreparably. Concerned with controlling their bounded labor and plantation bounds, English elites patrolled their overland borders with increasing violence. Native nations, although still connected with one another across the region, negotiated with nervous and ambitious planters often on their own, at a local level. But the same Native people who were dispossessed also maintained power and connection through their political and social ties to other Native people along the Piedmont's rivers.

At the same time, marking dividing lines, both physically and on maps, proliferated social and political divisions among the English. Elites who surveyed and traded, and who held huge amounts of land, separated themselves through their immense wealth from other English people and the people of color they held in bondage. Their wealth was based on diminishing Native control of land and trade along the water, pulling asunder the Native riverine landscape. Native connectivity, however, continued to promise opportunities for mobility and escape, and other chances to undermine English authority proliferated alongside the expansion of plantations and trade into the Piedmont.

— 6 —

Neighbors, Local Authority, and Local Violence, 1660–1666

On a hot September day in 1661, officials met a gruesome scene at Richard White's tobacco plantation on the south bank of the curving Rappahannock River. They were joined by "a grat man" named George of the Nansemonds (not to be confused with people along the James River of the same name). The Nansemonds had built their town across the river from White by 1654.[1] George was a potential witness to the death of "two Englishmen lately murthered" at the house of Richard White. As the impaneled jury recounted,

> We went to the said plantacon and viewed the bodies & found the body of Jo[?] cruelly massacred in the house of the aforesaid White . . . his scull splitt on the forehead . . . his Skull beaten in the side of his head over the eye. Moreover neer the door of the said house we found the body of Thomas White Sonn of the aforesaid Richard . . . striped naket with his skull beaten in over the Eye. Also we found the skull of Daniel Pignell Servant to the said Richard White beaten in the side of the head with an ax as we conceive by the bigness of the hole in the skull. Also we found that part of the body of the said Pignell was carried away with Varment but the hind quarters from the towes we found dragged in a Swamp.[2]

The three men—according to the report—had been surprised by multiple assailants wielding axes and clubs. The members of the White household had all been in or near the house rather than dispersed across the plantation working. This attack, like others perpetuated during mealtimes or at night when people congregated predictably, evoked the English vulnerability during the Anglo-Powhatan Wars decades before.³ All signs pointed to Native perpetrators, and there was a fourth man present who could confirm officials' fears: "an English Servant of the said Whites named John Evens that escaped out of the house at that time when the murther was committed." "We do all agree in our Verdict that it was the Indians," the jury concluded.⁴

With people from farther afield like the Susquehannocks using local roads, members of the inquest were unsure of who among "the Indians" to blame. The evidence suggested a local conflict rather than a random killing since only Thomas White, the son of Richard and the only man with direct ties of ownership to the plantation, had been singled out for a humiliating disrobing. English people complained about the "Northern Indians" and nearby Algonquian nations like the Doegs and Rappahannocks, but the small settlements of Nansemonds and their neighbors, the Nanzaticos, were most proximate. Therefore, they almost certainly knew the White family well enough to differentiate Thomas, a freeman, from his father's servants. And with increasing numbers of land patents and scuffles over livestock and boundaries with patent holders, Native people certainly had reason enough to lash out. However, the suspicious settlers were forced to rely on the Nansemonds for intelligence about the attackers' identities and whereabouts. For his part, George was quick to place the blame elsewhere, since "he found the footing of divers Indians going from the said Plantacon."⁵ Evidence only George could see convinced officials to look down the road instead of across the river.

Everyday trade in goods, days in court, paddling or sailing along shared waterways, and shocking bloodshed all defined what it meant to be neighbors in the 1660s Chesapeake. As land claims multiplied on the Northern Neck and Eastern Shore, individuals learned each other's movements, formed new ways of communicating, and developed local relationships that directly influenced broader colonial diplomacy. In part through these relationships Algonquian leaders preserved the centrality of rivers and Native roads, and the ability of Native and English people to move freely across the Chesapeake, after over five decades of colonizers' attempts to curtail mobility. Although brisk immigration and changes in the landscape provided undeniable visible evidence of a shift toward English control of the Chesapeake region, the authority of English elites over the areas in and around their patents remained contested. The boundaries of land patents in the west overreached planters' abilities to securely settle the land, while their Algonquian neighbors continued to use it as before. However, some English elites who received large land grants in this part of Virginia consolidated power over their neighborhoods and developed outsized influence on these relationships. They harnessed fear of a Native threat and developing tensions between local and colonial governments to thwart Native assertions of sovereignty and demands for justice. As a consequence, leaders like George were forced to find solutions largely without the help of Governor William Berkeley or the colony-level leadership.

Algonquians saw shifting behavioral patterns in English settlements across the Chesapeake; escalating violence in Virginia was reflected in and inseparable from the situation in Maryland. Elites in both colonies jockeyed for control over their shared border, and Algonquians and leaders in the Maryland and Virginia colonies hardened boundaries between Algonquian and English lands during the 1660s. The harassment of settlers in Algonquian towns, and the role of Algonquian neighbors in rumored or real attacks and as a "buffer" between outsider Native people and the colony, encouraged negotiations. During the 1650s and onward, the Marylanders allotted some land to Native people through the archaic manor system. Originally drawing elements from the feudal system in which Catholic lords governed land and tenants, the manor system was later deployed to allot a certain acreage per Native person under a white Maryland caretaker, who hypothetically could serve as an interpreter and preside over disputes among "tenants." To the south, Virginians protected Native land on the Eastern Shore and had granted the Weyanokes, Pamunkeys, and Kiskiaks five thousand acres apiece on the York and James Rivers, provided a patent to the Pamunkeys, and allocated fifty acres per adult man per tributary nation.[6] In 1662, Berkeley promised to burn the homes of squatters on Native land, and the assembly ordered "fixed" bounds surveyed around Native towns.[7] A few years later, the assembly discouraged Native people living near southside plantations from coming north into southern Virginia by making trespass into the colony a capital offense.[8] Both Marylanders and Virginians enacted a three-mile buffer around Native towns to discourage conflict (which colonists ignored) when Native people complained of encroachments. After the request of Native leaders, the province of Maryland affirmed fishing and hunting rights and prescribed punishment for murders perpetrated by settlers in the Treaty of Amity signed by twelve Algonquian nations in 1666. It also required Native people coming into English territory to follow specific rules: to yell out loud at three hundred paces, to approach without face and body paint, and to lay down weapons first. Further, in both colonies the English attempted to control what Native people did inside of Native bounds to better shore up their own: in Maryland, Native people were forbidden from hosting or making agreements with outsiders, or hosting bonded laborers or others avoiding the law, regulations mirrored in Virginian local treaties of the time.[9] These stipulations, as in Virginia, probably reflected "transgressions" that Native people continued to commit throughout the second half of the seventeenth century either as individuals or as nations, and reflected English elite anxieties about their inability to control the movements of any of these people.[10] Algonquians were not just a buffer between "Northern Indians" and the English but were responsible to some degree for safe and lawful movement between Native and English territories.

As outsider Native nations raided and local conflicts between Algonquians and settlers simmered, Algonquians living near English plantations engineered new boundaries and strategies. They surely understood the danger of their separation from one another as violence increased but also saw promise of material gain in trading skins, food, and other goods. They sought to stay connected to one another, to spearhead trade and diplomacy with English colonists and other Native people, and to stay near crucial riverine resources. In everyday life, through the practices of fishing, foraging, and traveling along thin roads and through wetlands, English-bounded places remained Native. At important places, as archaeologists have demonstrated through evidence of visits and site use after English colonization and destruction, displacement from town sites and foraging spots did not mean abandonment.[11] Political alliances between Native people, affirmations of friendship and territory alongside local English elites, and strategically deployed violence could sustain connection to or steer conflict away from home. As in the case of George, Native movement created a patchwork of efforts to execute a vision for the Chesapeake that remained connected by Native places and networks.

The problem for English and Native leaders, which would lead again to the outbreak of warfare, ultimately proved to be the Algonquian world's interconnectedness. Local conflicts and bargains hardly ever stayed local, and no one could halt the uneven, rippling effects of a dispute or curb increasingly frenetic movement across hard-won boundaries. From the 1660s for decades onward, local courts called on Algonquian neighbors, like the

Nansemonds and the Nanzaticos, for their knowledge of and action against outsider incursions and attacks originating in Algonquian towns to make sense of trespassing and to aid in legitimizing colonial borders.[12] Openly and subversively, planters, servants, and traders were drawn into the lucrative and lawless process of border-crossing into Native territory or through Native channels. Both Native and colony-level attempts to monitor border-crossing, contain county elites' power, and stymy the rising tide of violence failed. Elites appropriated routes and networks, attempting to eradicate perceived threats to their power.

English Infrastructure and Native Mobility

The Chesapeake in the 1660s looked very different in some areas than it had a generation or two before. English land claims, demographic stabilization, and the tobacco economy left a visual mark on the landscape, and the cultivation and sale of tobacco and livestock on plantations brought a new daily and seasonal rhythm. A regular trade in enslaved Africans began in the 1650s and 1660s in Virginia, and Africans worked alongside white indentured servants primarily along the James and York Rivers. While more land was cleared every year, the possibility of freed people owning the land became increasingly tenuous as the land itself became a valuable investment.[13] English people claimed between 80 and 90 percent of the available land in some of the newest counties in Virginia by the early 1660s, leaving few opportunities for newly freed and formerly indentured servants, and newly arriving European immigrants, even if they could afford it.[14] Following treaties with the Susquehannocks, Nanticokes, and Assateagues in 1661, the fastest growth of Maryland settlements moved from along the Potomac River and lower western shore to the Eastern Shore and Baltimore County.[15] Maryland planters, like those in Virginia, who could afford to purchase large numbers of indentures for arriving servants and enslaved laborers amassed them on their plantations, and by the end of the decade the ability to buy servants and hold local office—markers of power and advancement—became limited.[16] Claims stretched northwest along both banks of the Potomac, across the Eastern Shore, and via Virginian emigrants into the far southern Chesapeake and North Carolina where around five hundred new settlers and small numbers of enslaved laborers settled.[17] While smaller plantations with a limited number of laborers punctuated the landscape in recently settled areas, Algonquians saw the rise of wealthy landholders with a growing number of fields who claimed even the land beyond them.

The English population of the Chesapeake expanded precipitously, bolstering changes in the landscape. In Virginia, the English numbers in 1662 reached 25,000, and an increasing number of people lived long enough to see freedom from indentured servitude and begin their own households.[18] During the 1660s, Maryland's English population experienced rapid immigration and the population more than doubled from six thousand in 1663 to twelve or thirteen thousand in 1671. Fewer Europeans crossed the Atlantic as indentured servants, coinciding with an economic depression that pushed planters to plant maximum amounts of tobacco in response to low prices.[19] By the 1670s, Africans comprised the majority of the labor force on the plantations of elites, numbering 2,600 individuals in Virginia by 1685; corresponding changes in law during the 1660s had made it more difficult for them to pursue freedom legally—for example, through Christian baptism.[20] Native laborers, some from nearby Algonquian towns and others taken captive and enslaved or placed in servitude from as far afield as Spanish Florida, worked alongside Africans.[21] The rising English, servant, and enslaved populations generated new demands on the Chesapeake's soil, and demand for more land pressed the property, county, and colonial boundaries already in place.

Many Native people were for the first time meeting English people as neighbors, rather than more distant trading partners, and strategizing in a local context how to maintain an environment that promoted mobility and subsistence. The population and number of tributary Algonquian towns overall demonstrated marked decline and consolidation. The 1669 census counted 605 Native fighting men on the western shore, compared to an estimate of 2,600 on the eve of Opechancanough's 1644 attack.[22] The towns of the 1650s and 1660s employed a range of strategies for settlement and attitudes toward English trade. Archaeology along the Potomac River shows that residents in some towns, situated on creeks navigable by canoe for trade, remained in loaf-shaped homes, hunted wildlife indigenous to the Chesapeake (even when English pigs might make easy prey), and manufactured goods requiring considerable learning and skill, like shell beads and lithic projectile points. Some artisans produced goods for the English to purchase, like pots made with recognizably English feet or handles; others made new projectile points out of English brass and glass for their own use.

Algonquians living in towns situated between English settlements and outsider Native movements cut brass sheets traded from the English into decorative triangles, perhaps for trade along their routes to the north and west to non-Algonquian people.[23] English materials were channeled along Native routes and shaped into Native objects, and reinforced Native people's place along those trade lines.

Because English people occupied and traveled the patents they claimed unevenly, areas of the Rappahannock and Potomac Rivers would have looked more familiar to George of the Nansemonds than laws and patents suggested. By 1660, Lancaster and, to the west, Old Rappahannock Counties straddled the Rappahannock River, where people including the Portobacco, Morattico, Totuskey, Rappahannock, Nanzatico, Wicomico, Mattaponi, and Nansemond contended with county officials, often in both counties. To the north, resident Doegs, Mattawomans, Wicomocos, and Patawomecks traded and conducted diplomacy with many of their Native neighbors to the immediate south and new landholders in Westmoreland and Northumberland Counties along Virginia's side of the Potomac River. Around a quarter of men lived with people like the Nanzaticos, in towns composed of multiple nations created in response to colonial displacement.[24] Here, Native people adapted to colonial disruptions and contoured life for themselves and new settlers.

English attempts at dominance over the landscape were marked by impermanence. In the 1660s, for example, Maryland still had no towns beyond St. Mary's, at which the colonial government was only just beginning to fund public buildings.[25] A 1662 "act for building a towne" attempted to bring planning and urban living to Jamestown, but almost all people beyond Jamestown lived in modest housing. The wooden structures fell into disrepair and needed replacement after twenty years, exposing as fragile the image of stability planners hoped to convey.[26] During the 1660s, the founding of Stafford County to the far northwest and Middlesex County on the Middle Peninsula encouraged further settlement. However, elite landowners who bought tens of thousands of acres to the north of Jamestown repeatedly filed for extensions to settle them, while elsewhere, less wealthy settlers like those in southside Virginia fought to make smaller parcels productive year after year.[27] Some men like George Nicholls and Matthew Wilcox, with their four thousand acres in Old Rappahannock County, a large, now-gone county encompassing the head of the Rappahannock River, acquired more than they could ever hope to develop in a lifetime.[28] In 1668, one mariner from Plymouth, Thomas Shepheard, requested 119 headrights for settlers brought from Britain on three of his ships. Shepheard lived in England and almost certainly never saw his six thousand acres even if they were patented.[29] Although the General Assembly made provisions to reassign "Deserted Lands" after three years of inactivity, the law only applied if anyone noticed.[30] In 1671, a thousand-acre plot bordering Algonquian fields on Moratico Creek in Old Rappahannock County was granted again after its previous two holders never settled there; the original grant date was 1 January 1660.[31] Fewer colonists claiming large tracts of land, unevenly placed, meant that Native lands and resources remained intact for longer than the patents or county maps might suggest.

English ways of settling and using land may have looked familiar to Algonquian observers. To save labor, planters initially turned already cleared "Indian fields" into English tobacco fields rather than cut through forest. In 1668, for example, Thomas Cooper deeded a thousand acres to Thomas Goodrich that "formerly & lately the Matapony Indians did Inhabite."[32] Farther downriver on the Totuskey Creek on the south side of the "freshes," where the salty bay water gave way to incoming fresh water, John Hull bought "both . . . Townes" of the Totuskeys and Morraticos, which included both forested and cleared surrounds, sometime before 1667; when he resold some of that land years later, it was still mentioned as a "town."[33] Christ Church Parish on the Rappahannock River built its "Mother Church" in the middle of the "Small Indian Field next to ye head of Capt. Brocas his ground."[34] English repurposing of vacated tracts in the northern Chesapeake depended on previous Native settlement practices, as it had since the English first settled.

The mix of Indigenous and English landscapes extended to a network of roads and trails, routes that connected neighbors and distant places alike. In fact, archaeologists' research into land patents suggests that Native roads increase the precision and accuracy of land patents, perhaps because these roads provided access to the surveyors themselves.[35] Between settlements like Middle Plantation and their surrounding agricultural landscapes, "horse paths" built atop the local Native network of trails served as the connectors between small communities.[36] Native bridges were used again and again. The same "Indian" bridge over "Whitsapenny Creek" on the south side of the Pungoteague on the Eastern Shore was referenced in three separate patents dating between 1654 and 1661. Once appropriated, roads situated between creeks connected the plantations of elites, like the "Indyan path" that ran past the Lee family's Gloucester County home; of course, these roads often ran from plantation homes to or past Native towns.[37] Tobacco also transformed the use of rivers east of the falls, where big planters controlled private landings to which less wealthy planters could request access.[38] Just as the English built profitable plantations in already cleared fields or floodplains that would have appealed to Native farmers, they also used the Native roads in between plantations to emphasize their power and reach.

Attempts to maintain colony-controlled and taxpayer-funded roads were often threatened by planters' interpretations of their own boundaries and their shirked responsibility for roads as shared space. There were regulations for maintaining trails and roads for the sake of the "dispatch of business," but authorities found that property boundaries obstructed connectivity. Planters fenced their boundaries with little concern over whether someone could pass through their land or maintained no discernible overland route to their plantation at all.[39] The care of roads funded by public levies was left to respective county officials, who did little to coordinate improvement of overland travel. Legal efforts to remediate the "King's Roads" and ferries were met with apathy on the part of property owners, especially the wealthiest whose plantations and boats sat on navigable waters. Northampton County planter William Greening complained that he could not visit the other side of Hungars Creek because, despite the county court's payment to "certain undertakers" to remedy the situation, "there is but a rotten stick or 2 left for a bridge, the same being a high road way, and necessary passage for travelers, so that either the passenger must be constrained to go 3 or 4 miles about, or adventure both health and life in going over."[40] Pleas for aid like this one were shot down by fellow settlers, sometimes provoking hostility at perceived violations against private property. Planter Thomas Gregg built a fence across a freshly cleared road in Stafford County, presumably to mark his property line and discourage trespassing people and animals; his neighbor Robert Alexander helpfully placed a different fence blocking "the old way so that it is not passable for strangers in the night," so there was no obvious way forward at all.[41] English efforts at mastery over the land notwithstanding, the process of expanding and maintaining road systems that crossed the Native Chesapeake was at odds with enthusiasm for marking private boundaries.

The network of waterways and smaller, local paths therefore continued to provide reliable ways to move. Even when the English developed a ferry system, complete with fares and a schedule, the way down to the dock in Middlesex County's case was "by the Indian Road now called the Ferry Road."[42] As Jamestown officials pressured county officials to build centralized infrastructure, at the local level planters were content to simply use what came before. That "Indian paths" consistently facilitated connection and orientation speaks to the permanency of Indigenous landscape features in English life. They continued to provide transportation and direction to Indigenous peoples as well as settlers along the same boundaries and roads. The path to and away from Richard White's land, for example, was also likely the path that hemmed in the plantations of Thomas Bryant and Thomas Maddison, his nearest neighbors, but it was first and continued to be "the path that leadeth to Chickasony" for Native people.[43] For Algonquians and colonists going about their daily business, a vernacular developed around notched trees, local landmarks, and nonvisual cues that emphasized continuity, keeping travelers on the path. Most colonists, after all, did not have maps depicting an aerial distinction between empire and its fringe. The roads both demarcated boundaries and encouraged defiance of them, allowing anyone to move away from surveillance and control on the plantation and connect with roads out of the colony.

In an environment where English officials and planters were insecure in their authority, the mix of Algonquian and English land claims and haphazard land and resource use forced reciprocity, new communication channels, and political ties. The rise of large-scale plantation agriculture deepened the contradictory need to facilitate connections while controlling labor, as servants and increasing numbers of enslaved Africans moved from the plantation with news and hogsheads of tobacco. English people relied on Indigenous knowledge and trade, using connected Native landscapes even while attempting to enforce new boundaries.

Diplomats and Neighbors

Francis Louis Michel of Switzerland met an emissary from an unknown Algonquian nation at a celebration in Jamestown:

> A Frenchman and I were astonished . . . that two of them could speak English. One of them looked at us and said in poor English, whether we thought that if they had been taught like we, they could not learn a thing just as well as we. I asked him, where he had learned to speak

English, he answered, they were not so stupid, because they had to come every year, they could hear us speak and learnt it that way.[44]

Certainly no one familiar with the Chesapeake would have made the same mistake. The Europeans' inadvertent insult also underscores that Native people found opportunities at gatherings and legal proceedings to surveil English political shifts and movements that might affect them. Their growing body of knowledge and ability to communicate in both Indigenous and English places forced colonists to contend with them as people who understood English and Native worlds brought together in the courtroom and on the path.

Meanwhile, broader trends in local politics and geography influenced changes in Indigenous landscapes. Census records demonstrate that Native polities that interacted with one another often merged governments or lands, sometimes granted shared land by the English or joining voluntarily to pool resources. In southern Maryland and northern Virginia, the Native lands below the falls were isolated on peninsulas and among English neighbors, forming a "checkerboard pattern," in anthropologists' words, with English parcels.[45] Clement Herbert, for instance, patented four hundred acres on a point on the opposite side of the Rappahannock River from "Nansemond & Nanzatiquou Town," sharing the same waterfront; others patented on the same shore in between Native towns.[46] County officials claimed some control over mobility through forested areas. Representatives from Old Rappahannock County and the Mattaponi nation met and decided that "our Indians may have Freed & Liberty" to hunt and forage "without Englishmens Clear fenced ground . . . providing our Indians not committing any Trespass [against] their Stocks."[47] The Virginia Assembly also instructed men in Gloucester and Lancaster Counties to "assigne . . . sch places and bounds to hunt in as may be convenient, both for the inhabitants and the Indians."[48]

It was also at the local level that Algonquians and English landowners settled disputes and learned about one another through diplomatic visits. As they would with other Native people, Algonquian men and women accommodated exchanges of all types with the English as part of maintaining neighborly relationships. At least some Algonquians simultaneously maintained tribal identities and lived on land claimed by settlers. At the town of Portobacco, an area claimed by landowner and councilman Ralph Wormeley, people lived autonomously across the Rappahannock from the residences of him and his servants. Wormeley used the water as a natural barrier between his crops and his hogs, which he left on the Native side of the river. When French Huguenot immigrant Durand de Dauphine visited the plantation in 1685, three Portobacco men brought tobacco pipes and pots full of corn, supplied by Portobacco women who hung back. Wormeley himself received a separate gift of deerskins. When he and his visitor later left for the next county over, the same men reappeared to see them off. Their hospitality kept them diplomatically connected to the land's other occupants and the movement atop it, and gave them important visual information about the comings and goings of outsiders.[49]

Algonquians shaped neighborly relationships in their towns to facilitate exchange. They continued to host non-Native people, particularly servants, on the day of rest "to the disquiet of the Heathen, but certainly to the great Scandall of the Christian Religion."[50] A visiting scholar of England's Royal Society reported that planters habitually visited Native towns seeking medical treatment for enslaved Africans, for which they paid.[51] Visits adopted the seasonality of both Algonquian subsistence and trading practices and the tobacco cycle: Algonquian men traded in fish during fish runs and deer meat during the busy seasons when planters had no time or labor to spare for the task. Planters illegally traded firearms to Native people for this purpose.[52] Once meat sold locally, Native people could then sell dressed hides into the regional deerskin trade.[53] Archaeology demonstrates that at the Hallowes Plantation on the Potomac River in the 1650s and 1660s, former Kent Island trader John Hallowes traded in both butchered deer and tobacco pipes at his fortified home adjacent to a Native road or path leading to the Matchotic town in the 1660s.[54] Tobacco, and the wealth it produced, contoured continued English dependence on their Algonquian neighbors.

Algonquian men's marksmanship and skill with nets meant that they found a market for deer and fish in middling and elite Anglo households, while women's cuisine found a place in English hearths. The assembly reaffirmed the right of Native people to gather fish, oysters, and tuckahoe from the waterways in 1662.[55] Refuting claims that masters starved their Chesapeake servants with a meatless diet, former Maryland servant George Alsop wrote in a promotional tract that he ate plenty of meat as a servant because Native men brought many months' worth of venison directly to their table.[56] Planter John Hammond pointed out that for daily subsistence, "the rivers afford innumerable sortes of choyce fish," and that planters could hire "the

Natives, who for a small matter will undertake it."⁵⁷ One visiting clergyman in Virginia noted that the English who had fresh meat beyond the slaughtering season sold and distributed it to those who did not, a display of excess as well as magnanimity.⁵⁸ Algonquians almost certainly manufactured and sold some watercraft colonists required to fish for themselves, shaping dugout canoes from logs with both fire and metal tools.⁵⁹ Indigenous technologies expanded both diet and mobility for English households.

Sustenance for servants, or lack thereof, also revolved around Native proximity. While Alsop might have enjoyed better, traveler Thomas Reade journaled that the planters "live well themselves but keep their Servts. to hard dyet of Homine." He also marked the servants' food, water, and even habits of procuring it as Native, writing, "Indian corn is their great food, and water their drink, wch they Call up in the Sabbath day Succhanna, wch is the Indian name for watr."⁶⁰ Other writers confirm the servants they met did not eat bread at all, and that "Homine" or hominy—an Algonquian corn cake made by women for meals or to pack for travel—was a food relegated to servants.⁶¹ In 1661, when York County officials questioned servants about a potential escape plot, the servants' central dissatisfaction focused on their diet, "that they had nothing but corn and water." William Clutton, a newcomer to Virginia arrested for "mutinous and seditious words tending to tumultuous and dangerous behavior of several servants," told a neighboring planter in front of the servants that "the servant ought to have pone [an unleavened cornbread], hominy, and meat two times a week."⁶² Foods made by enslaved people and servants with Native techniques, or hunted and processed by Native people, deepened caste divides and at least in some cases contributed to nonelites' common hardship justifying resistance.

One shared object that facilitated the trade in wild game, the firearm, bridged the geographic gap between plantations and towns with an auditory signal understood by Native and non-Native people. Despite laws that prohibited Native people from owning firearms, they were necessary for Native inclusion in the markets for meat and furs. People within a radius of several miles heard the discharge of a weapon in solitary shots, volleys and patterns, or calls and responses, and the residents of Algonquian towns and English plantations were aware of each other's goings-on because everyone integrated the report of musket fire into their lives. One trader who witnessed the funeral of a Waxhaw child remembered, "When they began to throw in the Earth an Indian fired five Gunns over him."⁶³ In comparison, this was a practice so common among the English that the assembly specifically excepted "marriages and ffuneralls" from their ban on recreational shooting in 1656.[64] Both English and Algonquians stalked deer, geese, raccoons, and even grackles in the woods with firearms, or found company in barking dogs on seasonal or extended hunting trips.[65] Chesapeake residents understood that these sounds were constant reminders of their combined presence.

Beyond usual affairs, Algonquians shaped the development of Chesapeake society through their labor and trade routes, as southern Virginia settlers brought increasing numbers of enslaved captives into the colonies through trade with outsider Native people in the Piedmont. Native people, particularly young children, appear in inventories across Virginia during this period, in some cases explicitly "as slaves."[66] Others worked as servants, but the line could be blurry. On the Eastern Shore, for example, Accawmacks, perhaps to facilitate relationships with planters and traders or perhaps under duress, placed youth into Virginian homes to work at tanneries and plantations and inside households. During the 1660s and the 1670s, the number of Native laborers on the Eastern Shore increased, and young Native people served as apprentices or as servants, perhaps while their families lived nearby.[67] Such arrangements allowed Algonquian and English leaders to keep an eye on each other through economic partnership, but delicate boundaries could be easily crossed.[68] On Kent Island in Maryland, one Native father retrieved his child and took additional goods from a planter who had been using the child as a servant. The planter, of course, complained that he had an agreement with the father, but the child and goods seem not to have returned.[69] Perhaps the planter treated the boy poorly or, as suggested by the stolen goods, the planter did not provide sufficient goods to the family for the boy's labor. Either way, in risking violence by transgressing into plantation boundaries, the Native man prioritized his son over the bonds of any agreement he had with the planter.

Colonial borders also complicated the movement of Native captives and highlighted abuse of a poorly regulated or often outright illicit trade. A group of Virginian planters living across the Potomac from the Patuxents—who had diplomatic relationships with Maryland—kidnapped two women and stole ninety deerskins. Other Algonquians to the south and on the Eastern Shore—who had diplomatic relationships with Virginia—had been hostile with the Patuxents since before the English arrived. The kidnapping and theft invited the wrath of the Patuxent-allied Marylanders (into whose borders the Virginians crossed or whose trade the Virginians intercepted), the

Patuxents, and allied Algonquians and Virginians on the Northern Neck. Rather than create an intercolonial and international incident, the Virginian Northumberland County court ordered the planters to pay restitution to the Patuxent leadership.[70] The planters might have been frustrated that a crime committed against allies of another colony was punished, even if the punishment was light, but the incident reaffirmed the power of the local courts to conduct diplomacy in tense times.

Native knowledge about their English neighbors' movements, accumulated in a variety of ways, informed their strategies when disputes arose. English settlers who stretched past their bounds or broke the peace often met with correction at the hands of their Algonquian neighbors, in some combination of retributive violence and court proceedings. Werowances and male elites were frequent visitors to county courts. In Stafford County, for instance, an unnamed Native man was hunting game for an Englishman named John Simpson when he was shot in the back near a hunting cabin. After he had been missing for over a week, another Native man found him, recognized him, and reported his death directly to Simpson. He showed Simpson "horse or Mare footings" and "a small twigg about ye thickness of a mans figure . . . that the shott [that] killed the Indian did cutt" after the ball had exited his chest. Like George on Richard White's plantation, this man delineated the crime scene for the English by making meaningful the evidence around him. Another Englishman, August Knighton, came forward the same day with a matching piece of circumstantial evidence: Thomas Norman, a carpenter and landholder, had stopped by Knighton's house after a suspiciously fruitful hunting trip, four deer slung over the back of his horse. But it was the nearby Mattawoman werowance Chequeton who had the final word. Not only had Norman been "angry wth them" in the past, but he was the only English person nearby known to hunt game on horseback—it may have been his horse that left "footings" behind. Chequeton's war captain chimed in that "it was an Englishman that killed him for if it had been an Indian hee would have Tommahawked him & Cutt a Lock of Hayre & flesh together from his head."[71] The court reached a compromise verdict: Norman was found innocent but compensation of some kind—which apparently was what the Mattawomans sought—was paid out, acceptable Algonquian justice. The Mattawomans not only knew where and how their neighbors hunted, lived, and traveled daily, but watched out for their own when they came into contact with the English. That Chequeton said Norman had been angry with "them" meant that the unknown murder victim was probably a Mattawoman or perhaps a Native person living with the Mattawomans. Although the dead man did not receive English justice, by insisting the killer was not one of them, the Mattawomans protected their living from accusations. Entrance into English political machinations would not be necessary if the English had not adopted the same hunting grounds as the Mattawomans and other groups in the first place. The English who coopted Native travel routes now encountered Native surveillance of their habits and routines, and so were held accountable.

The county courts did not replace Algonquian ideas about justice and instead became another possible route for Algonquians seeking solutions in boundary disputes. Simultaneously, werowances unhesitatingly demonstrated their displeasure at late payments and broken agreements. During one spectacular incident in 1664, the werowance and great men of Great Matomkin, a town on the Eastern Shore, visited their neighbor, John Dye, who may have occupied the land he purchased from the Algonquians before it was patented or may have not yet paid for it. One great man tried to take Dye's axe, some held him on the ground "by the haire of the head, and put Durt in his mouth & eares," while the rest disassembled his house. Once the structure lay in pieces, at the werowance's cue they left with no further violence to person or property.[72] The tactile symbolism of the suffocating dirt and the fallen house indicate the Matomkins' anger that Dye had claimed the ground and presumed to settle on it without meeting an agreement. Controlling the type and extent of punishment empowered headmen to take English ideas about property into their own hands.

A map of Virginia's English settlements or a planter's property survey might provide quantifiable evidence of Virginia's growth and success, but Native people who attended court, let alone passed non-Native people on the road or visited English plantations, were aware of the gap between ownership as declared by individuals and county courts, and how the landscape remained the same beyond. Once contested, these claims only undermined the authority of Virginian elites and their legal system, even as some Algonquians sought protection from the governor or local courts. English assertions of power presented an opening to all Algonquians, making it possible to simultaneously flout English authority and invest in its trappings through testimony and land deals. Even as English settlers replaced Algonquian women's fallow fields with rows of tobacco, Indigenous knowledge of Native and plantation landscapes remained central to daily life.

Finding Excuses for Expansion

By the 1660s, local elites thrived on plantations formed on top of the Native landscape and sought to expand their land claims further. Using fear of Native outsiders, wealthy landholders—here, planter and justice Moore Fauntleroy on the Rappahannock, surveyor Edmund Scarborough on the Eastern Shore, and surveyor John Catlett along the Potomac—flouted both colony and county systems of justice and upended relationships with Native people. Their rumors of attacks and other plots, justifying violence and border transgressions against Native people and their land, were met by Native assertions of their own histories as responsible neighbors. Rappahannock and Patawomeck werowances responded with appeals to the colonial government's power over these county officials and elites. Although many of these relationships founded on Indigenous knowledge and landscapes endured, others were reshaped to a stronger English advantage through Native servitude and slavery, Anglo-Native violence, and land claims on Native soil. Patrolling the borders for perceived or conjured threats on the other side, local elites found ways to change boundaries in their favor.

The deaths of Thomas White and Daniel Pignell along the Rappahannock River were an early contribution to a reign of rumors and confusion in Virginia's northern border counties. For the English elites, fear of unknown Native assailants and servant revolts encouraged policing of borders. Meanwhile, Algonquians rightly feared capture and harassment from outsiders like the Haudenosaunees and Susquehannocks. Tensions over land use and ownership agreements made between planters and werowances in county courts quickly spilled over county lines and reached Jamestown. In 1662, the assembly cited the rise in conflict from corrupt interpreters, intimidation, and malicious rumors when prohibiting the further sale of Indigenous land and vacating dubious claims.[73] But just as before, colonists moved onto land they argued had been "deserted" by Native people; Algonquian leaders' demands for payment for land in county court demonstrated that colonists or their livestock moved onto Native land anyway.[74] When the governor or assembly sided with Native people over squatters or fraudsters, distrust and irritation brewed over a seeming Native, improper alliance.[75] Land-hungry planters founds new ways in addition to these strategies to challenge Native people's occupation. The resulting conflicts, which started as small-scale disputes among neighbors, broke through the customary methods of problem-solving in local courts, on paper, and through the everyday interactions that reinforced mutual dependency. Ultimately, expensive wars justified on the grounds of profitable Native enslavement and imperative colonial security were engineered to clear the landscape of Native residents and make way for plantation agriculture.

While they saw their Native neighbors inside the colony every day, colonists had long feared Native threats that entered Virginia from beyond its borders. When the Susquehannocks to the north pulled Maryland colonists into their war with Haudenosaunee rivals, no badges or checkpoints could stop them from raiding south of the Potomac and then returning to safety in Maryland—while both Maryland and Virginia traders sold them weapons.[76] English pamphlets discussed at length the scenes of Susquehannocks' (real or exaggerated) executions of their war captives and (real or exaggerated) subjection by force of other Indigenous polities, resurrecting the specter of an intertribal alliance against Virginians that had so terrified settlers right before Opechancanough's last large assault in 1644.[77] The Susquehannocks' Haudenosaunee enemies also ventured south from the Great Lakes region in search of new territory for the fur trade, another factor beyond English control or surveillance. Less than six months after the attack on the White plantation, Governor William Berkeley's committee on Indian affairs recommended closing the border to "Marylanders, English and Indian" to halt the flow of "Susquehannock and other northern Indians, in considerable numbers frequently com[ing] to the heads of our rivers, whereby plain paths will soone be made which may prove of dangerous consequence."[78]

Policing the border was becoming more expensive during an economic downturn and sustained outside pressure from Indigenous people. Instead, men like trader Abraham Wood, with a financial interest in shutting down illicit trade and cutting out Maryland traders, took responsibility for ensuring that no outsider Native traders came south for "trucking, tradeing, bartering or dealing" with the English or tributary Algonquians.[79] The Maryland governor also cut the general trade in furs, issuing licenses only to specific individuals starting in 1663. In response to murders committed by strangers wielding bows that same year, Maryland rangers deployed to secure the heads of the rivers with permission to kill or capture Native people who did not defer peaceably to the scouts.[80] By 1667 Berkeley reported that the Virginians were "now building five smal forts for the securing of shipps and that at James Towne is almost finisht two in James River one in the Yorke one in Rappahannock and one in Patomeck a great charge for this poore country."[81] That "great charge" meant taxes that would become a rallying cry for rebellion in the following decade.

Attempts to build fortifications raised the specter of violence and resistance from a different angle. Enslavers raised concerns "about theyr negros being commanded to work att ye fortificacons," either because of the proximity of escape or because of labor lost in the field.[82] Commitment to tobacco cultivation and increasing dependence on African labor also deepened costs and consternations. In Berkeley's words, "Wee leave at our backs as Many Servants besides Negroes as there are freemen to defend the Shoare and on all our Fronteirs, the Indians, Both which gives men fearfull apprehentions of the dainger they Leave their Estates and Famelies in" while on a march against Native enemies.[83] Early chronicler John Oldmixon wrote that in the 1660s, the Virginians could muster a force of six or seven thousand men—and would leave twice as many at home to guard the plantations and servants.[84] Berkeley saw the expenses of stopping unfree people from escaping and Native people from coming into the colony as interrelated, writing, "Wee begin to make provisions for these our people fly to Maryland, and by this meanes heighten our publick charges; and weaken our defence against our perpetuall Enemies the Indians."[85] In 1663 the Virginia Assembly reconfigured its "ineffectual" laws concerning the retrieval of escaping unfree people; the threats from the periphery and plantation were mutually reinforcing.[86]

During this period of heightened tensions, wealthy Virginian landowners exploited the fears of other elites, made sharper by the absence of Indigenous culprits to bring to court after a raid. In 1662, Moore Fauntleroy decided to resolve longstanding tensions with his Rappahannock neighbors by arresting them. Local officeholders arraigned the Rappahannock great men and new werowance, Wachiopa, for refusing to pay tribute to Governor Berkeley. Such a breach of etiquette on the part of the Rappahannocks would have been a dangerous and foolhardy threat to the tributary relationship. The Rappahannocks insisted that they had not only paid the tribute but also paid Fauntleroy a ransom for the return of their werowance and great men on their arrest. It was Fauntleroy who had not paid for land he bought from the Rappahannocks. Colony officials sided with the Rappahannocks. Fauntleroy was barred from holding office, and his unpaid claims to Rappahannocks' land made void. The Rappahannocks used their trip to Jamestown to complain also about the damage to their crops wreaked by Fauntleroy's hogs, and Fauntleroy was then ordered to hire a hog-keeper until his servants could erect a fence.[87] County-level officials like Fauntleroy were in a unique position to deliberately miscommunicate with officials at Jamestown, misconstruing threats, making false charges against Native leaders to discredit claims of mistreatment, and making arrests that advertised their usefulness in restoring order. Native leaders could nevertheless undermine elites' false claims and document their own lists of planter transgressions when colony officials examined cases closely.

The illusion of restored order had the opposite to the intended effect, however, breeding suspicion and mistrust of county officials in Jamestown. The same month Moore Fauntleroy arrested Wachiopa, Gerrard Fowke and former Kent Island trader Giles Brent issued a warrant for the arrest of Patawomeck werowance Wahunganoche, whose people were then living near Potomac Creek along the southern crook of the Potomac River, to answer accusations of murder. Like Wachiopa, Wahunganoche turned the tables and convinced officials at Jamestown that Brent and Fowke had repeatedly harassed the Patawomecks. Most damning of all, Wahunganoche testified that he had delivered the actual murderer (of unknown national origin) to Fowke personally, and that Fowke had allowed him to escape. This was precisely the type of border policing that colonial officials intended tributary Native people to do, and it was being undermined by county-level officials. Brent, Fowke, and others accused by Wahunganoche of harassment were ordered to pay the Patawomecks restitution in the form of roanoke and matchcoats, currency and a mantle made of cloth both crucial to Anglo-Native trade. Brent was forced to pay court costs, and Fowke was hit with fines amounting to 25,000 pounds of tobacco.[88] Fowke's punishment reflected the real danger he unleashed on his neighbors while manufacturing a fictional one.

For the seriousness of Fowke's and Brent's crimes, the governor and council escalated from simply barring individuals from office. They dissolved Westmoreland County, from which Brent and Fowke had issued their illegal warrants. Dissolving Westmoreland and reverting land and offices back to Northumberland County was a clear display of colonial over county authority. The move had serious implications for Englishmen using local offices to climb the social ladder. Westmoreland County's elites fought back, using allied members on the commission to reaffirm that "the countyes shall bee two distinct countyes and their bounds to remaine as they were."[89] They then appointed as justices elites like John Washington, Isaac Allerton, and, incredibly, Gerrard Fowke himself. The following year, Fowke represented Westmoreland County in the General Assembly, and he and the county remained legitimate at the colony level.[90] Fowke was the latest in a line of settlers who transgressed and helped redefine boundaries at the expense of both the colony and Native people without much loss of political power, encouraging neither respect for nor faith in colonial authority.

Despite the uncertainty about who was to blame, Governor Berkeley had all but predicted the deaths at the White plantation. Earlier in 1661, he acknowledged frequent and insistent complaints from "Indians of Rappahannock River" concerning vague "unnecessary injurys" but threw responsibility to the county authorities and landholders, writing, "I know not at this distance what judgment to make. . . . I beseech you to be careful of this."[91] Only after the murders did the Governor's Council focus their attention on the dealings of local elites with neighboring Native leaders. It seems Berkeley saw the two as connected; immediately after his commission barred from office men who had harassed nearby Rappahannocks and Patawomecks, he paid Richard White ten thousand pounds of tobacco from the public levy for the loss of his son.[92]

Meanwhile, elite aggressors altered political dynamics on the Eastern Shore as well, where longstanding friendly relations and isolation from Anglo-Native warfare to the west had created more trusting relationships between Algonquians and colonists. Eastern Shore Algonquians, longtime allies of the English, had been relatively successful in fending off extralegal attacks. Perhaps in response to planter aggression against their northern neighbors, Algonquians on Virginia's side of the border asked Berkeley directly for protection against encroachment in 1660. Because "the English seat [is] so neare them," they endured "much damage in their corne," probably from wandering livestock. The governor authorized a reservation on a neck of land facing the Atlantic to be surveyed to exist in perpetuity, with "no power to alienate it."[93] For other Algonquians and the colonies themselves, however, nebulous borders exploitable by planters looking for additional land and trade on the bay escalated tensions. Edmund Scarborough, one of the wealthiest planters and colonial officials in Virginia, yoked English fear and outright vigilantism at the border in a meshing of the fur traders' and planters' spatial visions: to remove Native people from land, harness their labor, and widen access to trade on the bay.

By the 1650s, Scarborough held a seat in the Virginia Assembly, considerable power in local courts, title to thousands of acres of land, and dozens of enslaved Africans, indentured Europeans, and more Native laborers than anyone else on the Eastern Shore.[94] Governor Charles Calvert asked his assistance in granting Maryland land to Quakers expelled from Virginia, while Governor Berkeley made Scarborough surveyor general of Virginia like William Claiborne had been. Both asked for his assistance in negotiating the boundary between Virginia and Maryland on the Eastern Shore. In 1668, as surveyor he would assist in creating a new boundary, the Calvert-Scarborough line between Virginia and Maryland, ceding land to the Virginia side where he held more sway.[95] Interested in Palmer's Island, Scarborough may have hoped to expand trade with the Susquehannocks or the Dutch in the northern part of the bay and within Maryland bounds. An alliance with the Susquehannocks, however, would put him at odds with surrounding Algonquians, with whom relationships remained uneasy.[96] But as a local leader and merchant himself, he could harness manpower, ships, weapons, and ammunition, and he used his access to these resources to intimidate and neutralize neighboring Native people, along with other colonists.

Scarborough almost certainly recognized the dual promise of acquiring Indigenous land and labor through attacks on Native people at the Maryland-Virginia border, and he used anxieties about Native conspiracies just over the border to attempt to rally support for these campaigns. In 1659, he wrote to the governor of Maryland that in ten days he would destroy the Assateagues' settlements; the Marylanders should join in a venture representing their common interest. His plan included stationing a garrison that would stop Eastern Shore Algonquians from seeking allies for aid or assistance and starving out the Assateagues who might try to rebuild or search for sustenance. He hoped to eventually do the same to the Nanticokes and Wicomiss, also Algonquians at the border, but in the meantime would intimidate them with a campaign destroying a neighboring nation. The Maryland governor's response was brief: Why? What had the Assateagues done to warrant a costly and dangerous campaign, in another colony? Struggling simultaneously with the Dutch colonies over their shared bounds and with Native violence in new settlements along the Potomac, Calvert exercised caution with his contested Eastern Shore boundary.[97] But the Marylanders' assent did not matter, and Scarborough and colonists from the Virginians' Eastern Shore, with the Virginian governor's authority, marched against the

Assateagues anyway. Although little else is known about how they survived the attack, the Assateagues remained on the Eastern Shore. Presumably Scarborough and his garrison took loot, but they passed the costs of the campaign to taxpayers across the colony—who voiced their ire.[98] As past traders and planters had done, Scarborough deployed rumor and resources to undermine established English boundaries when it suited him while other settlers and Native people faced the consequences.

Rather than gain power during the consolidation of counties like Fowke and Fauntleroy, Edmund Scarborough used his power as a surveyor to manipulate new boundaries. In 1663, Scarborough divided Accomack and Northampton Counties on the Eastern Shore along their present bounds, allocating two-thirds of Virginia's Eastern Shore to less populous new Accomack County, appointing himself sheriff, and building himself a fort on his Accomack County plantation.[99] Like Berkeley, Scarborough saw economic downturn, servant plots, political infighting, and fear of Native attack as interrelated threats to elite control.' He was often at odds with other merchants and neighboring planters.[100] He had previously faced resistance on his plantations from servants who threatened him with death, burned down a barn, assaulted him with words and farm implements, and attempted escape to the Dutch.[101] Given an order from the assembly to redraw the border with Maryland, he chose to seize the opportunity by gaining more land for Eastern Shore Virginians. To publicly justify his plan, he exploited growing anxiety reflecting his own experiences with nonelite people, choosing enemies he shared with the governor: runaway servants and dissenters who crossed the border out of the colony.

Unlike the smaller-scale battles instigated by Fowke and Fauntleroy, in October 1663 Scarborough traveled with forty horsemen, some again from the western shore, alongside watercraft with planters seeking escaped bonded laborers, to disputed territory between Maryland and Virginia. They were backed by the assembly with the intention of claiming land for Virginia and Accomack County thirty miles beyond the disputed boundary at Watkins Point.[102] The battle was one-sided because it was fought not between Maryland and Virginia but between powerful and relatively marginalized Virginians over formalized boundaries. Many of Maryland's newcomers were actually Virginians who, upon receiving freedom from servitude or searching for new land, migrated north to Maryland; others were expelled Virginian Quakers for whom Scarborough had drawn bounds in an agreement with Maryland.[103] Among the settlers who lived there, the boundary line Scarborough was surveying was certain: everyone with whom he spoke knew himself to be in Maryland. According to a proclamation issued by Charles Calvert, Scarborough was indeed "many miles into this province to the Terror of the people . . . there by him long before seated by vertue of a Comission from this governmt."[104] Moreover, the settlers were in Maryland explicitly to be beyond Virginia.

As he had before, Scarborough called on his authority as surveyor and soldier to change physical boundaries to suit his own interests. The first man Scarborough encountered was Quaker Stephen Horsey, a former burgess and local official on the Eastern Shore who probably knew Scarborough's high-handedness from his previous time as a Virginian.[105] According to Scarborough's report to the Virginia governor, Scarborough promised to arrest Horsey, who continued to claim his home sat in Maryland, for "Contempt & Rebellion." Horsey shrugged that if he obliged Scarborough, "The Governor of Maryland will Come soe soone as you are gone and Hang me & them at our doares." Scarborough arrested the Maryland official anyway and "sett the broad arrow on the doore," or scored arrows onto Horsey's door, a traditional boundary marker stamped on ships, goods, and property meant for the crown to claim Horsey's home for the king, an absurd interaction between two Englishmen. Scarborough then stopped in to check on two Quakers and former Virginians, local officials Thomas Price and George Johnson, the latter of whom Scarborough called a "proteus of heresy."[106] More indignant and verbose than Horsey, they refused to assist Scarborough. The Virginians arrested them and before moving onto the next house. (The owner of this house, Henry Boston, asked that Scarborough come back another day.) Amazingly, Scarborough coerced the Maryland commissioners into recording the land of the new Marylanders as part of Virginia, and the commissioners "agreed to" appoint new officials for the county. He told Berkeley that news of his invasion by horse and boat had not reached and terrified nearby Native people; the English "had undoubtedly bin cutt of[f], therefore desired course to be taken therein which accordingly was done."[107]

Writing to the Maryland governor after being placed under arrest by Scarborough, planter John Elzey referenced the residents' unique place on the border to plead for help. He wrote that the Marylanders were trapped between two sea monsters, Native people who claimed "wee are Lyars, & tht our greate Men care not for us," and the Virginians.[108] The Maryland governor saw a familiar, mutually reinforcing set of Native and Virginian threats to his legitimacy and demanded justice from Scarborough, citing his attempts to alter the intercolonial boundary as well as his naked violence. The two governors agreed that people on either side of the line should live peacefully until colonial leadership could settle their differences.[109] In the aftermath, the Virginia assembly determined that "the unnecessary feares of the Indians by Some perticular persons hath put the Country to an excessive charge" and ordered planters along each of the four major rivers to pool financial resources for their own defense rather than pulling, as Scarborough and past planters had done, on the colony's resources.[110] It would not be the last time Scarborough, still powerful and ambitious, would cross boundaries with violence in mind.

Like Fowke and Fauntleroy, Scarborough thwarted an imaginary enemy, this one a bizarre combination of servants, religious dissidents, and a Native threat waiting in the shadows. For Scarborough, all personified the threat to elite control: Native people and "the English their residing and other vagrant & ingaged persons . . . without law and government."[111] Scarborough did not name specific Native nations as potential aggressors. Instead, Native people's place on the geographical fringes that they shared with "Runawaies" and religious dissidents served as enough justification for their demise. Scarborough called landholders to arms by identifying diverse threats as a cohesive political unit. As a surveyor, Scarborough could restore order, annihilating the threat by adjusting boundaries and then enforcing them.

Although the werowances across Virginia were sometimes successful in calling out blatant corruption and receiving restitution in Jamestown, the conflict with elites created insecurities among English leaders about the tributary Native people's real loyalties. As tensions rose along the Potomac, the General Assembly became concerned that the Patawomecks might drift away from their relationship with the colony to the east and toward groups less friendly to the English to the north and west, like the Doegs. The English had offered very little protection, and alliances with nearby groups also facing possible depredations from outsider nations who might take their people captive made sense. These fears began to alter demands on Native people. In 1663, the assembly imposed new laws governing only Algonquians on the Northern Neck, ordering that they turn over the children of werowances as security for good behavior and pursue "foreign" Native raiders who committed crimes against the English. The law also singled out Wahunganoche specifically, prohibiting him from holding council with the

Doegs or any other groups without consent from the officers of the militia. Wahunganoche was also to pursue the Doegs, who migrated between both Maryland and Virginia, to punish murders that traders insisted they had committed. In justifying and proposing enforcement for these laws, the English drew from the Algonquian communication networks that ran through these borders. Pushing tributary werowances to police English boundaries on their behalf only increased both the dependence and suspicion that beleaguered colonists already felt.[112]

These tensions negatively affected the already strained relationship with the Patawomecks along the Potomac. In 1664, not only did nearby servants plot "to arme them selves with their masters armes," but according to surveyor (and Richard White's coroner) John Catlett, "the King of Potomeck" was hatching a plot to "extirpate" all the English people from the northern Chesapeake.[113] He and other settlers from Rappahannock and Westmoreland Counties petitioned for Governor Berkeley's aid in suppressing attacks from "the Northern Indians," who they felt might be coordinating a plot to destroy the English. Not receiving an immediate response, the planters pretended ignorance of any Patawomeck "plot." They lied to the Patawomecks, plotting to destroy them in actuality but for the moment agreeing to aid them in destroying the Rickahockians, a non-Algonquian outsider group who the Patawomecks insisted were the actual threat.[114] Catlett suspected that the Patawomecks had guessed the Englishmen's lie but that they remained cool because "they [the Patawomecks] had so cunningly wrought their business." In other words, Catlett repeated a rumor that the Patawomecks were plotting an attack and that they knew about a preemptive English plot, and he positioned himself to fend off criticism as only searching for an opportunity to preempt a Patawomeck attack. Through an orchestrated effort across Patawomeck territory, Catlett and others captured nine "chief conplotters as wee supposed," stole weapons from others, and brought the Patawomecks to Jamestown to be tried for a murder.[115] Rumors about Native attacks had once again led to an escalation of violence.

"But to ye astonishment of all that knew any thing of the certainty of this affaire," all nine men were dismissed and sent home with a reward, surely a slap in the face to the elites who had risked their reputations on the murder charge. Why had the Patawomecks not met the county elites' conception of justice this time? In a tangled ball of lies, it is difficult to tell politics from paranoia, and no Patawomeck "plot of extirpation" was mentioned beyond

Catlett's account. He was quick to blame some "private Interest," perhaps referring to traders among the Patawomecks allied with the governor. Regardless of the exact reason, the series of debacles in northern Virginia over the previous few years had been a breach of trust between the colonial and county governments, and officials at Jamestown knew what to expect.[116] According to Catlett's own account, the Patawomecks were a human barrier between the English and hostile groups like the Doegs, and much larger groups like the Haudenosaunee—and their friendship with the English was much more consistent. Regardless of whether the plot was true, the geographic and political placement of the Patawomecks was for the moment too important to the colony to give in to surveyors and landholders.

Native efforts at diplomacy would yield fewer positive results over the rest of the decade as their own fears about both northern Indigenous nations and English landholders were realized. On his way home from Governor Berkeley's acquittal in 1664, Wahunganoche died.[117] The following year, the assembly used funds from "the sale of the king of Potomacks land" to fund a fort project to the south.[118] The colony declared war on and enslaved many of the remaining Patawomecks and some Doegs in 1666, once again using the murders of colonists as justification, and Susquehannocks took Patawomecks captive as well. John Catlett patented five hundred acres in 1666 that included the "Doeggs cleare ground," while Catlett and John Washington moved on to other nations and made claims to Nanzatico town.[119] Documentation regarding Fowke's property that same year mentioned no Native occupation and no specific western boundaries at all. "All the land comonly called by the name of Machapungo formerly enjoyed by the King of Potomack" was in Fowke family hands, the exact boundaries disputed for decades.[120] Proximity to Indigenous settlements ultimately facilitated land grabs and expensive, destabilizing violence by a tiny group of troublemaking elites, even as friendship and exchange had made for years of neighborliness. Finally, despite pursuing mutually beneficial trade and neighborliness, redress through the court system, and diplomatic relationships with English officials, the Patawomecks and other groups in northern Virginia were not immune to English warfare, enslavement, and removal. Their removal meant shoring up colonial and property boundaries that served planters and encouraged the spread of slavery.

The promise of profit through the policing of borders sometimes brought county and colonial officials together against nearby Native polities. In response to supposed Doeg raids in 1666, Catlett and three other planters wrote a missive to Jamestown proposing to pool the military resources of the northwestern counties: "Wee doubt not wth assistance of Almighty God by the strength of our Northerne parts utterly to destroy and eradicate wth out Further Incouragment then the spoyles of our Enymies."[121] Berkeley agreed that the wholesale destruction of the Doegs, who had traveled between Virginia and Maryland and had no colony-acknowledged land, was necessary to avoid their alliance with other Native people. "It may be done without Charge" since through the enslavement of survivors, "the Women and Children will Defray itt." Berkeley hoped to convince young colonists not overtly involved in the previous arrests and murders to fight "for their share of the booty."[122] To incentivize vigilante violence, elites could capitalize on another, more insidious tendency to fear "that there was a combination of all the Indians in these parts" justified a war for enslavement on all Native people within and without English boundaries.[123] Berkeley's decision chipped away at the custom in some localities of the movement of Native youth to English households and was another step toward legitimizing the growing trade in enslaved Indigenous people.

However, decisions like this also had unforeseen and long-term results for internal politics. On the surface, Berkeley's plan seemed chillingly pragmatic. But upholding alliances with leaders like Wahunganoche at the expense of planters, failing to punish planters for vigilante violence, and opening the door for profitable enslavement campaigns, while contradictory, all could turn colonists away from local neighborly relationships and colony-wide diplomacy. As Catlett angrily wrote after the Virginia government's decision to support Wahunganoche, planters with Indigenous neighbors were less likely to trust the colony leadership again: "I believe wee of the northern parts fronters to the Indians shall not be so forward as wee have been for publique redress of o[u]r wrongs."[124]

While Scarborough's campaigns to move Virginia's border seemed like conflicts apart from day-to-day life for Native people, elites' unmediated violence precipitated breakdowns of Anglo-Native customs on both sides of the bay. Scarborough's final and most violent attack on Native people on the northern fringes of Virginia's Eastern Shore in 1670 finally led to his arrest. Berkeley's warrant, issued several conflicts too late, speaks for itself: "Col. Edmund Scarburgh hath contrary to my order and the Peace long since established between us & the Indians unjustly & most Treacherously oppressed them by Murthering Whipping & burning them, By taking their children by forcing from them who are their Parents & many other waies to the apparent hazard of the said Peace established."[125] The struggle to subjugate Indigenous people with brutal force and to take their children revealed the tie between fear of Anglo-Native war and English desire for land and labor. It was one thing for the English to absorb Native neighbors' children as servants and Indigenous captives from faraway nations; it was another to enslave a neighbor's children despite established relationships and formal diplomatic and legal ties that protected them.

Scarborough had violated colony-level diplomatic ties and the colonial boundaries that, as surveyor general, he was supposed to create and legitimize. When Berkeley ordered him remanded without bail and brought to Jamestown, somehow Scarborough simply refused to be arrested—he informed the marshal he was headed that way anyway—and escorted himself to James City to take his seat in the House of Burgesses. Only then was he stripped of his office. What followed was a political coup of sorts following the strategy of Westmoreland County's dissolution: the assembly reunified the counties and Northampton residents to the south of Scarborough's seat dominated the new administration.[126] But planters and traders saw over decades what wealth might be gained, and problems eliminated, by amalgamating strategies of raiding, trading, surveying, and planting. Their actions challenged the permanence of colonial borders (that they themselves drew) and encouraged vigilantism against marginalized colonists and Virginia's Native allies at nebulous boundary lines. Simultaneously, Indigenous people on both sides of the English colonial border observed the malleable and selective nature of English law and Anglo-Native diplomatic relations as the men who had destabilized their diplomatic ties went unpunished.

Throughout the 1660s, local relationships between Native leaders and their English neighbors facilitated communication and shaped broader changes in labor patterns and landscapes. Local relationships enabled mobility on the part of Native people, inside and outside of tributary and manorial systems designed to bound them in. Using knowledge of their neighbors and English boundary-making, Algonquian leaders navigated regional crises with connection to one another and boundaries in mind. Complicated machinations like Scarborough's campaigns and reactive, opportunistic murders in the woods were foremost reactions to Algonquian spatial visions that made room for mobility. Manufactured or otherwise, incidences of violence and retribution were caused by fear, ultimately stemming from rumors serving elite power grabs or from lack of English knowledge of outsider Native movements. Few besides elites like Scarborough benefited from the broad and untenable reach of colonial boundaries into Native land. But during these decades, Native people along the Rappahannock and Potomac Rivers and on the Eastern Shore maintained access to the connective tissue of roads and waterways facilitating trade and diplomacy across the region.

Directly and indirectly, Native places and mobility threatened growing plantation and labor systems. The English and Native people alike understood that the burden of policing movement inside and outside of property, county, and colonial boundaries was inextricably tied to trade, servitude and slavery, and they realized the limits of Jamestown officials in managing peripheral issues. A handful of elites valued Native land and bodies more than Native knowledge and diplomatic skill, using the limitations and fears endemic to areas shared by Native and English people to break established diplomatic ties and change the nature of border landscapes through violent displacement. However, they could not change the nature of Native landscapes, border violence, and diplomacy, even locally, without lasting consequences.

─ 7 ─
Rebelling by the Bay, 1670–1680

Over the course of a year, a group of at least thirteen unfree people from neighboring plantations on Virginia's Eastern Shore planned a voyage to the north. The conditions for indentured servants drove them to action. Newly arrived servant Isaac Medcalfe remarked that "he never saw any people kept so in the country before, and if he had so long to serve here as some of us had, he would hang himself before he would serve it."[1] Inspired by word of an escape from Pocomoke in recent years, he relayed the success to other servants, who shared this story at hearths from plantation to plantation on the Eastern Shore's bay-bordering coast between Deep and Nandua Creeks. They reported back that, if they planned an escape, servants at each plantation in between the two creeks would come with them. According to Medcalfe, a mutual agreement was made among the men to "to knock the person on the head who should first reveal it," deepening commitment to the plot and one another.[2]

Women like Mary Warren also committed to helping the escapees and worked at cross-purposes with planters and the conspirators. Mary herself had no intention to sail, but she prepared regardless. Over several weeks, she made extra amounts of cheese and butter, stashed flour and cloth, and stole the storehouse keys from the planter's bedchambers. The foodstuffs and clothing made longer journeys possible and could help thwart recapture. That the co-conspirators hoarded fourteen cheeses and other food probably prepared by women suggests that they relied on broad networks of women as well as the men who spread the plot.[3] While storing away provisions, the conspirators and their compatriots stole goods valued at an astounding 13,260 pounds of tobacco. The greater the value of the goods they

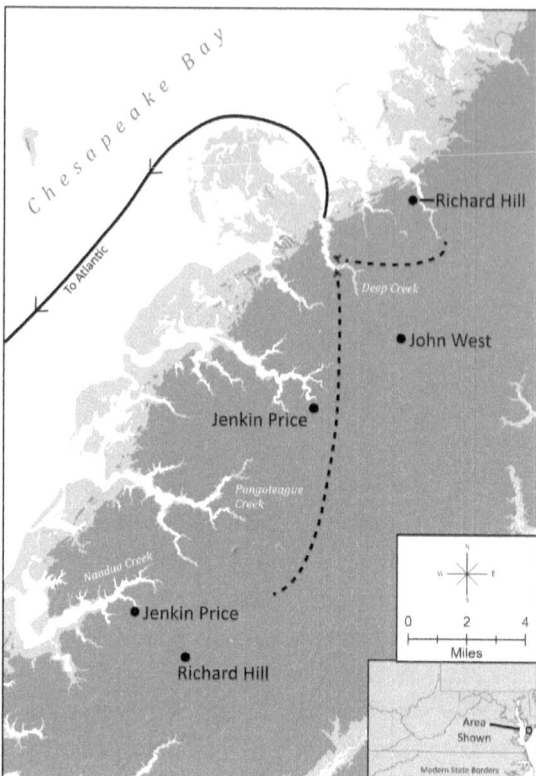

MAP 5. Conjectural servant routes and locations along Nandua Creek from a servant plot, c. 1670 (Stewart Scales and Gemma Wessels)

stole, the greater their chance of success, but also the greater the stakes. Lost goods directly translated to time added to an indenture by the court if they were caught. They probably noted the changes occurring at the assembly, which added a bounty on escaped people at a thousand pounds of tobacco. This encouraged planters to seek redress against servants in court even if they inflicted corporal punishment at home, which would sink captured escapees further into servitude and debt.[4]

An opportune moment for the servants came when one planter traveled to James City and left a sailing boat behind in the creek. Coordinating the perfect time to flee required intimate knowledge of the political and social calendars, as well as the storehouses, of Virginia's elites. The crew met up, loaded the vessel, and tried to exit Deep Creek toward the bay, but the wind blew too hard and forced them back to shore. Soon, however, word leaked out about the attempt as planters noticed missing goods, and the conspirators meanwhile tried to control intelligence about the incident.

When interrogated, servant John Carter blamed nameless thieves from somewhere beyond the plantation: "Was it not well turned?" he bragged about his deception. "Let [me] alone for a scurvy trick any time."[5] Despite the seriousness of their conspiracy, the servants hid evidence rather than turn on one another because escape still seemed within their reach.

Members of the group then hatched a new plan "to be loose again" for Christmas. They could steal Dutch trader Jenkin Price's boat, which he used in the Native trade. Thomas Watts suggested they sail to Venice, presumably Italy, "and there they would live." Their hopes hung on the focal point of any water-based escape plan, a pilot to navigate to freedom in other colonies through broader, unfamiliar waters. If a pilot in a larger vessel met their little boat propelled by stolen sails or homemade oars, they could get to Maryland or maybe beyond. Visitors, perhaps sailors, from beyond the Eastern Shore had promised they could take them away when they returned. According to one servant, the pilot who agreed to take them was a "Black James that came down with Cornelius a Dutchman's wife."[6] "Black James" is difficult to identify; the lack of last name suggests he was not an Englishman. The murky reference to Black James and to wherever he "came down" from, simultaneously obscure but central to the plot, reflected expansive Atlantic trade that brought servants to Virginia and helped them plan to leave it.

The Christmas plot was ultimately aborted while county court officials deposed those suspected of involvement. Before long, indentured servants began to implicate one another in some aspect of the plot. Medcalfe, accused by his co-conspirators as the instigator and leader, protested his innocence and blamed the influence of his fellow servants. He lived past the trial but may have stayed a servant for longer as punishment: the man who held his indenture, Robert Pitt, died in 1670 before Medcalfe was freed.[7]

Beyond the boat belonging to the Price family, Dutch fur traders who dealt with Native people, the conspirators and county officials mentioned no Native people or places in court. Yet the plantations where the conspiring took place were founded on the Chesapeake's river systems and on Native networks. Algonquians continued to live in towns near Nandua Creek, a parcel of which a werowance had granted to Jenkin Price not even two decades before.[8] The co-conspirators met in the woods that Algonquians used for hunting and foraging, and no doubt traveled roads and paths through the woods between creeks. Medcalfe and his network of allies echoed Algonquian spatial visions as they evolved to sustain trade and connection across colonial boundaries in nearby Native towns and across the bay.

The past and continued presence of Native people laid the foundation for connection across smaller waterways by road and bridge, for those wooded and brushy spaces between plantations that sustained life for Algonquians. It channeled resistance for nonelites in settler society along old routes that crossed colonial boundaries with information and people. Ordinary Native people, werowances, and traders became part of this conversation about the shores beyond plantation boundaries. As in William Abram's escape plot featuring a language book and bolt of cloth two generations earlier, Native connections helped to define the world and its possibilities beyond the Chesapeake for people bound to plantations. Servants, enslaved laborers, and other nonelites relied on one another's information and skill sets necessary for trading and settling, from piloting to cheese-making, and developed understandings of the Chesapeake rooted in the interconnected maritime world of the Algonquians.

Elites understood as much. Medcalfe and his fellow servants had correctly sensed opportunities for freedom fading in the early 1670s. As more African and Indigenous people were forced onto plantations as laborers, since the 1660s the assembly had attempted to crush cross-cultural interactions that made elaborate escape attempts possible and made special demands of the "neighboring Indians" who independently negotiated with servants. Just months after the servants' trial in September 1672, Virginia's General Assembly passed "An Act for the Apprehension and Suppression of Runaways, Negroes and Slaves," which underscored a distinctly racial component to the body of laws against bonded laborers who absconded. Because "many negroes have lately beene, and now are out in rebellion in sundry parts of this country," and "Indians or servants should happen to fly forth and joyne with them," the assembly legalized the wounding or murder of "runaways either negro, mulatto, Indian slave or servants, resisting." Promising rewards, the assembly once again required "neighboring Indians . . . to seize and apprehend all runawayes whatsoever that shall happen to come amongst them."[9] As they surveyed their lands claims, paying special attention to the gaps in the boundaries between plantation and Native domains, elites saw the danger of alliances across race and nation. They understood the porousness of their own borders because they themselves had pushed and bent them for their own profit. But in ordering Native leaders to return their human property, elites admitted the limits of their own power to retrieve and control unfree people.

As planters claimed more property—in the form of more land and labor—across the transformation of the Algonquian landscapes, they erected boundaries to protect those gains. Increased investment in African labor, bought through elites' Atlantic shipping networks, heightened the stakes surrounding rebellion and mobility.[10] Motivated nonelites like Medcalfe transgressed boundaries or sought to tear them down completely, and in doing so undermined planters' claims to authority over labor and boundaries in the Chesapeake. Between the 1660s and 1670s, Virginia's and Maryland's county and colony officials faced incursions and loss from foreign and domestic enemies. The Dutch, Susquehannocks, and Haudenosaunees appeared as ominous threats beyond their borders, while servants, enslaved people, and rebels they knew intimately pushed and flouted boundaries from within. Their boundaries—mapped lines between the colonies and Native nations, between landowners and counties, or between people—showed signs of failure and made these threats mutually reinforcing. Illicit movements across colonial borders such as indentured and enslaved people's escape plots and Bacon's Rebellion highlight the limits of official control. They also demonstrated the persistence of Algonquian visions of connectivity, and how unfree people and others who tapped into those networks fueled breakdowns in colonial authority and reach.

Reactions to these pressures demonstrated settlers' continued dependence on Algonquians and the connectivity they preserved. Servants and enslaved people plotted routes to freedom, ran away, escaped recapture, and committed violence based directly and indirectly on evolving knowledge of the Algonquian Chesapeake and the localized ways in which the English had come to traverse them. Where Native connections had afforded Virginia elites their trade, land, and plunder, nonelites appropriated the same connections to escape or improve their own lives. Reliance did not mean alliance: many servants might have hated or feared their Native neighbors, but they still moved with an awareness of the usefulness of their presence.[11] Although planters crushed these plots, the lengthening boundaries of the colony remained perpetually porous, particularly for Native people contesting English boundaries and enforcing their own. Over decades, Native movements and boundaries subverted English systems of labor control, boundaries, and claims to those boundaries' legitimacy. Further, planter violence and illicit movement in response to Native people's borders and landscapes had wide-ranging effects across the colony and the Native Chesapeake, fueling participation in Bacon's Rebellion on the part of a broad range of people embroiled in boundary conflicts.

Nathaniel Bacon and other rebels also exploited knowledge of the surrounding Native world and anxieties about keeping it at bay. Many of the rebels held goals similar to those of local English leaders in years past—to chip away at Algonquian occupation in the Chesapeake and grab hold of lucrative trade opportunities, plunder, and captives beyond English boundaries for themselves and friends. Desire, anger, and fear blurred together. Native attacks and rumors of them underscored the wastefulness of public levies for "the building of forts back in the woods upon severall great mens Lands, under pretence of securitie for us against the Indians which we perceiving and verrie well knowing that ther pretence was noe securitie for us."[12] Besides, depredations on English plantations continued unabated since "the Indians quickly found out where about these Mouse traps were sett, and for what purpose, and so resalved to keepe out of there danger."[13] Surrounded by rhetoric both of trade in captives and of dangerous Indigenous foes, planters feared and desired connections to Native people. Their desires complicated the fear of losing through those Anglo-Native networks valuable laborers already held in bondage who could run away from plantations. Alleged Native boundary-crossing and rumors of Native violence helped spark both unfree people's resistance and planters' rebellions, and Native trade routes spread it. This ultimately resulted in a crisis in colonial authority and destruction of many of the networks among Native and English people. Algonquian landscapes, and Algonquian people who shaped and guided English settlement and movement in preceding generations and into the 1670s, shaped this moment almost silently.

Previous generations of scholars of the early Chesapeake blamed Nathaniel Bacon, a newcomer, and his rebellion in 1676 for damaging the influence of Native people in the Piedmont and on the coast.[14] Yet the traders and planters who preceded him were the ones who, having once sought Native partners in exchange, then chose to use longstanding Native networks in order to destroy them. Bacon was not an outlier; if we put Bacon in the context of Edmund Scarborough's invasions of Maryland on the Eastern Shore, or planter violence against the Patawomecks in northern Virginia, his rebellion seems timeworn. As Virginia transitioned toward permanent social stratification and furthered claims to Native land, structural and military violence became crucial to maintaining expansion. Men like William Claiborne and Scarborough taught the next generation of elites to ask for neither permission nor forgiveness when it came to crossing boundaries, to start conflict in contested territory, and to challenge known borders, particularly Native ones, for greater profit from land and goods. In sum, successful planters demanded not only land but uniformity of a landscape with borders that worked solely for them; control of labor was predicated upon control of land. Only through brutality at the fringes could planters consolidate power on their own plantations.

Closing the Borders

In the years preceding Bacon's Rebellion, mapped boundaries nominally protected portions of Algonquians' land.[15] During the 1660s and 1670s, the colonial governments of both Virginia and Maryland ordered land surveys and the eviction of squatters, and reaffirmed ownership of tracts earlier set aside for some Native groups. Tributary people in Virginia were forbidden from selling their land; Maryland used treaties to guarantee land rights to neighboring Algonquians. Virginians surveyed the Nansemonds' land in the southern Chesapeake region in 1663 and legitimized Native possession of the Pamunkeys' and Kiskiaks' land on the Middle Peninsula, and in 1669 Maryland set aside reservation land for the Choptanks. The Gingaskins' land on the Eastern Shore was reaffirmed in 1660 and 1674.[16]

However, these legislative actions were also threatening to Native sovereignty and served English landholders. Colonial law governing tributary Native behavior revolved around these explicit boundaries. In Virginia, militiamen laid out the bounds at the falls of the rivers, and patrols looked for Native people who did not "keep their direct pathes."[17] Simultaneously, Virginia's House of Burgesses promised pieces of some of the same land they affirmed as belonging to Algonquians, now surveyed, to elite planters like John Catlett and John Washington upon the "abandonment" of the land.[18] Paternalistic legal clauses that purportedly offered Indigenous nations protection were nominal, and "abandonment" might mean removal forced by violence, harassment, or the search for sustenance. Forced to sustain themselves by moving farther and farther inland and up the Chesapeake's peninsulas along tributary streams, Native people who found their boundaries violated petitioned the governmental officials of Virginia and Maryland for protection from encroachment.[19]

Algonquians' role as a living boundary between the English and outsider Native people disrupted their everyday lives as the Haudenosaunees and Susquehannocks came down Algonquian paths from beyond the heads of the rivers to raid.[20] Native concerns about outsiders were reflected in the Articles of Peace and Amity between Maryland and eleven Native nations signed in 1666, in which Piscataways and nearby Algonquians received the promise of land and "a place to which the Indians of the aforesaid Nacons shall bring their wives & children to be secured from danger of any foreign Indians."[21] The frequency of the raids discouraged seasonal dispersal for hunting and foraging, and many Algonquians returned to the tactic of palisading their towns.[22] Other groups like the Doegs, formally within Maryland's bounds, may have permanently moved into northern Virginia to escape the press between "foreign Indians" moving in from the north on one side and on the other Maryland's settlers. The move across the border then put them into conflict with Virginians.[23] Displacement during this period meant more than just starting over elsewhere; it also meant loss of local knowledge and resources. Archaeology at sites occupied by the Piscataway in Maryland, for example, demonstrates that established ceramic-making practices were left behind as women struggled to find new sources for good clay while setting up housing and agricultural lands from scratch. In some cases, the marginal places where they removed lacked good soil and clay altogether, a complaint echoed where foraging places were too small and fields barren.[24] The regional rise in violence forced communities into unfamiliar places, and made familiar places feel dangerous.

As pressure from English neighbors increased on Algonquians, so did pressure from outsiders. Virginia's western fringe had a history of conflict with relatively unknown (to the English) Native people. The Rickahockians, who some scholars believe to be the Westo or Eries, nations who enslaved people from other Native nations for trade to colonizers, had made incursions against the Pamunkey at the fall line in the 1650s and among the Patawomecks in the 1660s.[25] However, much of the violence through the last quarter of the seventeenth century was a product of Haudenosaunee-Susquehannock conflict to the north and west, and of the trade in enslaved Native captives to the south and in the mountains.[26] Like the 1661 murder at the Richard White plantation in Old Rappahannock County, the number of Native attacks from the north and west rose at the heads of the major tributaries to the bay during the 1660s, following the treaty between Maryland and enemies of the Haudenosaunees, the Susquehannocks. In response to Haudenosaunee raids, Marylanders had provided the Susquehannocks with arms and ammunition, and the Susquehannocks had met with the Marylanders' allies, the Piscataways, to negotiate a truce.[27] In 1675, the Susquehannocks suffered a major defeat at the hands of the Haudenosaunees, and Lord Baltimore invited the Susquehannocks to live inside of Maryland's bounds. Algonquians along the Potomac and in the northern Chesapeake had despised generations of Susquehannock raiders, and some—like the Piscataways, who were largely independent of their allies in Maryland's government—openly declared their desire for war.[28] The Algonquians and settlers watched uncomfortably as the Susquehannocks built fortifications on Piscataway Creek just over the Potomac River from Virginia.[29] Patrolling and fortifying against Native attacks proved expensive for Maryland, and new tensions rose not only over the flaring of old tensions but also over the expense to planters.[30] The question of the cost of the border would affect Anglo-Native politics in both colonies.

English colony officials attempted to share the burden with tributary Native people by controlling their networks. Presuming that members of offending Native nations like the Doegs would come to trade among tributary Algonquians, for example, the Virginia House of Burgesses insisted that any visitors be imprisoned and brought to the English. Relying on Algonquian networks and diplomacy beyond the Chesapeake, people of tributary nations were to "joyne and pursue" the Doegs into other nations' territories, or any other place where "intelligence" indicated the Doegs might be.[31] Likewise, as depredations multiplied against plantations with no recourse, the assembly ordered Native people living near a deadly raid to "use all their care and diligence in finding the doers and actors." But the law came with a more serious mandate as well, that in order to maintain English control over diplomacy over tributary nations, "Indians shall not have the power within themselves to elect or constitute their owne Werowance." Instead, the governor would choose a "chiefe commander . . . in whose fidelity they may finde the greatest cause to repose a confidence" to better defend the colony.[32] By 1663, Virginia law had prohibited the werowance of the Patawomecks from treating directly with "foreign Indians" without the presence of militia officers; Algonquian signers of Maryland's Treaty of Amity agreed to not entertain outsider Native people. Colonists inserted themselves into established practices of treaty-making and communicating among Native nations to better control intelligence networks, justifying further intervention and codifying suspicions of tributary Algonquians.

Along with neighboring Native people, local officials and colony fortifications at the English colonies' borders did not inspire confidence in planters. County leaders had often made self-interested land grabs, affecting diplomacy across the colony. This went hand in hand with a lack of confidence in the scarcity of military supplies and lasting political conflict over fortifications. In some counties, militia captains were accused after Bacon's Rebellion of unwarranted fines on soldiers and unaccounted colony funds meant for local defense.[33] With military action against Native people on the Eastern Shore, in the northwestern counties, and along the James River in living memory, planters no doubt saw an Anglo-Native war as a looming expense.[34] Adding to their ire, Henry Norwood wrote, many Virginians saw the forts as only "great mens new plantations" funded by taxpayers, a form of favoritism found on the colony's fringes alongside license for the Anglo-Native trade.[35] Fortifications remained expensive to maintain and impossible to staff and supply, while planters relied on their own taxable, often rare, and expensive arms and ammunition.

At the local and colony levels, leaders struggled to effectively position resources and manpower. In Virginia, to meet outsider Native threats more quickly, local officials in Henrico County, a growing center of the Piedmont trade in skins and furs at the falls, and Charles City County restructured their militias; in 1673, Governor Berkeley raised taxes to arm them. Both acts increased the control of local landholders over border patrols.[36] In 1673, Berkeley declared the earlier York River fort indefensible, and in 1674 issued a warrant for the arrest of men who had accepted payment for repair of Jamestown's fortifications but had not followed through.[37] Archaeology shows that planters began to palisade their own plantations as they had in earlier decades, although perhaps as much concerned about violence from other colonists that rose in the 1670s as Native violence.[38] Virginians had little trust in a broken border system that officeholders and contractors so easily made work for themselves.

During the 1670s, conflict between the Dutch and English compounded fears and brought violence within Maryland's and Virginia's bounds. Long annoyed about a border dispute with the Dutch over Delaware Bay, Maryland officials issued an edict declaring a Dutch settlement at the mouth of the bay as within the bounds and under the authority of Maryland.

Marylanders successfully invaded and occupied the Dutch-claimed territory in late 1673 during the larger Anglo-Dutch War, but they had cause to fear a backlash from Dutch-allied Native people.[39] Early in the year, the Dutch had challenged Virginia's coastal fort system as well. The Dutch sailed into the bay and up the James River in pursuit of dozens of merchant vessels loaded with tobacco, capturing as many as they could and torching the rest with their contents. It had been only six years since Berkeley had last attempted to mount a futile defense as the Dutch captured twenty ships and plundered the coast.[40] Beyond forcing planters to sell tobacco to English ships for lower prices than they would get from the Dutch, war so close to plantations also caused fear of unrest: What would happen should planters leave their homes to patrol either the fall line for Native intruders or the sea for European ones? Berkeley wondered, what would stop the "single freemen (whose labour Will hardly maintaine them)" from defecting to the Dutch at the first opportunity? He saw the breaches in western and eastern borders by different nations as connected by its waters, allowing for both trade and violence: "all that Land which now bares the name of Virginia be Reduced to little more then sixty Miles in breadth towards the Sea, Yet that Small Tract is intersected by Soe many Vast Rivers as makes more Miles to Defend them."[41]

With the English at war with the Dutch and facing Susquehannock and Haudenosaunee raids in the northern reaches of the colony, Berkeley sought to raise funds to expand the fort system that had long defined Jamestown and its surroundings.[42] His plan grew from maintaining five forts along the core rivers harboring the English—two on the James, and one each on the York, Rappahannock, and Potomac—to ten. The English would garrison forts along every major waterway, along tributaries of the James—Nansemond, Pamunkey, Mattaponi, Appomattox—and along the Blackwater to the south and the Pocomoke on the Eastern Shore. Some of the forts sat or would sit on lands of wealthy, longstanding traders William Claiborne, Abraham Wood, and prosperous planter and trader William Byrd, where Native people could trade or bring outsider Native captives in exchange for bounties.[43] With the exception of the fort on the Eastern Shore, each fort required men to garrison them and stores of food, medical supplies, and ammunition. Perhaps most ambitiously, Berkeley's proposals for more forts would reinstall the power of border defense in the colony's government rather than with local officials who had proven untrustworthy.[44]

Facing declining tobacco profits and multiplying threats to their borders, officeholders passed the pressures of economic stagnation and rising violence on to the rest of their communities. County and colony taxes, which paid for the assembly to convene, for border defense, and for a buyout of a Northern Neck grantee, hit nonelites and small planters hardest. Evidence of discontent bubbled up during this period: in 1663, Gloucester County servants plotted a seizure of arms and an escape, and in 1674 middling householders at Lawne's Creek in southside Virginia refused to pay taxes.[45] While local elites speculated with patents, non-landholding men were denied suffrage in 1670, a moment when it became particularly difficult to acquire land and when suffrage meant success and manhood for Englishmen.[46] Frustration mounted with governor-appointed county and parish officials who levied unfair taxes and had little accountability to county residents.[47] After 1660, upwardly mobile planters found themselves increasingly cut off from county office and the Native trade as county populations grew. In Maryland, for example, freed servants found it difficult to reach even small public offices like sheriff.[48] In 1675, Berkeley clamped down further on the already restricted trade inland to the Piedmont, making it difficult for Virginians to acquire licenses to trade without his permission.[49] Opportunities shriveled quickly. Algonquian possession of valuable land and the expensive fort and militia systems both drew boundaries benefiting some elites and drew other Chesapeake planters' ire.

Plotting as Servants and as Natives

Amid economic and social constriction, planters persisted in legislating against the illicit movement of servants and enslaved people in the Chesapeake colonies. "The greatest part of our rude multitude," sighed wealthy Virginian planter Nicholas Spencer to Maryland's Philip Calvert, "have served an apprenticeship to the art of escape."[50] Servants learned the network of plantations and Native towns, the people who lived there, and the goods they stored, to mitigate servitude or escape to freedom. Like in colonial diplomatic and defensive undertakings, Chesapeake Algonquians, their networks, and their domains remained at the center of servant plots to better their lots and anxious planter plots to keep their labor force inside of plantation boundaries.

As middling planters and free people of few means saw opportunities for mobility sunset, the everyday experiences of servitude and slavery also changed, hardened, and separated from free society. Most elites from county-level officials up had purchased Africans by the 1670s, marking a key shift toward a separate and permanently enslaved class of laborers. The material experience of labor and resources differed markedly between free and bonded people on the plantation. Some Chesapeake elites lived in brick dwellings built in high style, where the planter family dined from imported wares. Increasingly, their servants and enslaved laborers lived at a distance, perhaps in a separate structure, eating and smoking from cheaper, local wares, at death buried in plots separate from planter families. Longtime servitude also affected physical health.[51] Beyond early death and chronic illness, analysis of skeletal remains at Patuxent Point, occupied between the 1650s and 1680s, shows evidence of anemia and stunted growth from malnutrition and injuries from heavy lifting and constant kneeling.[52] But as growing numbers of enslaved laborers and indentured servants lived a separate existence from free people, they formed relationships with one another across plantations. For example, an archaeological study of tobacco pipes smoked by laborers and made locally near James City shows that they shared designs and decorations with people of like status at neighboring plantations and often farther afield, suggesting cultural and economic exchange apart from planters.[53] While the growing number of people at the bottom felt the squeeze disproportionately, through mobility they found resources and networks among people who shared many of the same experiences.

Laws around servant movement and escape reflected planter anxieties, resulting in repeated attempts to bind servants and enslaved people to plantations. In 1671, Marylanders passed a law worsening the punishments for escaped laborers and people sheltering them. It was an acknowledgment that the previous 1650 and 1662 laws had been largely ineffectual, particularly in encouraging people to capture servants and enslaved people on the move.[54] Escape across English bounds and up the Chesapeake, at a time when planters felt under siege by their neighboring colonies, undermined claims to authority over English domains beyond just their laborers. For example, in 1663 Berkeley vented about all of it together: "Maryland being a destructive Government from us hath hindred the growth, wealth, and Reputation of this Colony, more then both the Massacres [by Native people], by entertaining of our Run-away Servants, and not complying with us in those designes, which were for the Advancement of both our Interests & Trade."[55] The feelings across the border were mutual, and

Maryland legislators passed similarly severe laws to discourage their own servants from absconding into Virginia.[56] Berkeley wrote to as far away as the English governor of New York to ask for the return of an escaped person from Surry County in southern Virginia, so that "runaway Roges may perceave ther is no protection for them in your government." Treaties that Algonquians signed with landowners and with the governor had since 1646 demanded the return of escaped laborers and others running from authorities who, in the words of an Old Rappahannock County agreement, "usually throngs themselves amongst us the Indians for harbour or to be pillotted unto remote parts."[57] Of course, the Virginian governor could not force New Yorkers, Marylanders, or Algonquians to comply.

Instead, the governor and assembly recognized that upholding an image of peace and order to Native people and the rest of the Atlantic seaboard's colonies started at the local level. Both Maryland's and Virginia's laws were designed to tether servants and enslaved people to the plantation—anyone more than ten miles away would be assumed a fugitive.[58] By 1670 bonded laborers could be whipped for piloting a boat and boarding another, and by 1672, shortly after Medcalfe's plot was discovered, they could be maimed or, if Black or Native, killed for resisting capture.[59] New practices informed locals of captured and punished people within and beyond their communities such as hair chopped around the ears. Escaped people caught counties or colonies away endured lashings at the whipping posts of each county between where they were discovered and their home plantations.[60] The assembly asserted authority over the movement of people of low status through the execution of these punishments, and marked racial order between unfree people through differences in how these laws were written and executed.

Alongside laws and court cases that lengthened bondage for sexual transgressions or enslaved Native war captives for life, the series of runaway laws passed in the 1660s and 1670s were designed to make capture and the indenture itself more lucrative for free people and planters. In 1670, Virginian planters had complained that the cost to reach court was prohibitive: "Divers Servants Running away into Maryland are there deteyned and not suffered to bee fetcht away without paying for them a greater Summe then the Servant is worth." Furthermore, captors intentionally overestimated the distance they traveled to return a servant, driving up costs.[61] Community policing of escaped people initially relied on raising "hue and cry," common practice in England that obligated all able-bodied males who heard the shouted alarm spread from town to town to join in the search for a criminal. By the 1650s, however, "huy and cries after runaway servants hath been much neglected to the great damage and loss of the inhabitants of this colloney," planters attested.[62] The Virginia Assembly added financial penalties and incentives: fines for settlers who entertained escaped people and rewards for people (and matchcoats for Native people) who returned them.[63] Specifically concerned about servants who absconded to the Dutch plantations along the Delaware River in a time of Anglo-Dutch tension, in 1663 the Virginia Assembly assumed the pursuit of escaped people as a public responsibility.[64] In 1669, they authorized county courts to sell servants after their original indenture was complete to recover the costs of their retrieval and lost time.[65] Planters continued to complain of the costs of pursuit for decades, and the law regarding restitution was amended several times, suggesting it never fully worked as intended. The increasingly complicated and severe body of law demonstrates that escapes continued, with occasional assistance from sympathetic householders, and that the greater the distance gained by the escapees, the lesser likelihood of pursuit and capture.

Servants' actions also undermined intercolonial borders and the reach of local authorities. Sheriffs, usually elite white men, and constables, low-ranking white officials appointed by county justices to keep order, were placed in charge of capturing and punishing people who escaped. If escapees then escaped again from sheriffs or constables, these officials were responsible for the cost.[66] On the Eastern Shore, Native bonded laborers John the Bowlmaker and Jack of Morocco grabbed the constable "by the hair of the head and drew blood from him" when he attempted their arrest.[67] In York County, a fisherman on the York River pulled his boat ashore and glimpsed two Black men on the run, leading to their capture by a constable and captivity in his home. The constable awoke the next morning to find his clothes, his canoe, and the men missing, their temporary capture having replenished their supplies.[68] For free colonists ready to ignore the hue and cry and to view local officeholders in terms of their own onerous taxes, the airing of incidents like these in court demonstrated the undignified, wasteful, and ineffective actions of local officials.[69]

Even with increasingly stringent legal restrictions, escaped unfree people were still able to flout local authorities' jurisdictions. For their part, servants and enslaved people developed knowledge of the expansive network of plantations alongside their understandings of the Chesapeake landscape, and they may have previously had or developed the skills necessary to sail or row in English or Native watercraft. In 1674, on the Eastern Shore, "A Negro Woman commonly called Pendall took with her sonne a Negro youth, and in company with other Negroes stole a boate" and navigated across the bay. Pendall and her child journeyed to Thomas Goodrich's plantation in Old Rappahannock County, where she worked for a year.[70] Edmund Scarborough's daughter Tabitha Browne, who claimed Pendall and her son as property, could only send repeated letters across the bay asking Goodrich for their return, but "Col. Goodrich made slight thereof scornefully throwing the same [letters] from him." While it is unclear how Pendall came to stay on Thomas Goodrich's plantation, or the nature of their racialized and gendered power dynamic, Pendall and her co-conspirators' skills as mariners played on the geographical and political distance between the two plantations—the bay and rivers became important connectors and dividers for those with the skills to interpret a new landscape. Looking beyond the plantation to escape or at least soften the impact of slavery, servants and enslaved people built far-reaching networks of places, perhaps places they had never been, mirroring those of Algonquians. Unfree people then used those networks to move beyond plantation boundaries and the reach of the law. And perhaps in Pendall's and Goodrich's case, escaped people exploited planters' disregard for one another's private property and plantation boundaries as well.

Pulling together understandings of local plantations, Native towns, and the networks in between, servants cultivated intelligence and trade. For English planters, servants' illicit exchange of information and household goods further undermined their authority, and losing control of either goods or information could be expensive. On the Eastern Shore, planter William Jones's Native and English servants ran away frequently, and in 1665 he accused a local tanner, formerly his servant, of encouraging unfree people to run away. The tanner had told the Native servants that Jones wanted "to send them to the Barbadoes," a fate that all involved probably knew had befallen another Eastern Shore Native person as punishment for theft only a year before.[71] Unfree people who heard this found what would be a deeply frightening threat credible—the tanner was Jones's former servant, after all—and they used their understandings of local resources to act on it by escaping.

Considering trade, non-Native servants also brought together understandings of Native and English household resources: near the Maryland border in 1671, servant Andrew Price stole arms, powder and shot, and fishing gear—but no food—from the house of the man who held his indenture and ran away. When he was caught thirteen days later, "there was one gun brought back again," a sign he had traded either with other planters or Native people.[72] The planter who held Price in bondage had settled land on the Pocomoke River adjacent to Edmund Scarborough, who had made the Virginians there few friends through his decades-long harassment of Native people and nonelites on the border.[73] Those people might be uninterested in capturing Price even for compensation, particularly if trade in arms and ammunition was involved in an encounter. Virginia elites' attempts to clear the intercolonial border of threats, and strengthen their claims to the land, created a climate for resistance and connection for others.

Overseers and planters also often struggled to keep bonded laborers on their plantations, particularly when Native towns proved a draw. In 1652, a white servant of one household on the Eastern Shore beat a Native servant belonging to another household, the latter of whom ran away to a nearby Native town presumably for safety and recovery. Unable to stop the beating that led to the escape, overseer Hugh Baker was ordered to retrieve the Native servant and, instead of the white servant or his household, Baker was responsible for court fines.[74] In the same county in 1651, overseer Farmer Jones fell into conflict with his employer as he struggled to keep a Dutch boy from escaping to a nearby Algonquian town, claiming that the boy "was not fit to do any work in the ground" anyway.[75] In each case, neither Native people nor the servant was held responsible, precluding of course physical confrontation beyond the public eye. Instead, the onus rested with the overseers, who had no direct relationship with the leaders of Eastern Shore towns, to find the servants themselves and control their mobility. The proximity of unfree people and Algonquian towns complicated the task of curbing escape. Whatever their tributary status might dictate, Algonquians remained conspicuously absent from these instances as abettors or captive-takers.

In addition to providing a destination, Native people could provide networks, hospitality, and directions to escaped servants and enslaved people. More than anyone, Native unfree people understood the power of both the networks among Native towns and the intercolonial borders that frustrated the reach of men who held them in bondage. In the 1660s and 1670s, for example, Eastern Shore Algonquians continued to send children and young people to plantations in a system controlled nominally by county officials. (Although supposedly consensual, in light of Scarborough's recent campaign against neighboring Algonquians at the border, and witnesses who described Virginians' stealing "children by forcing from them who are their Parents," there are clear indications of the enslavement of Native children.[76]) A werowance from the Matomkins named Amongos used his location near the Maryland-Virginia border, however, to facilitate the movement of Native unfree people, maintaining diplomacy with English planters while continuing to shelter children.[77] Amongos and the Matomkins did not always provide shelter, returning for example a Nanticoke man, a person from another nation, to planter John West and signing an agreement to help negotiate with other Native people for the delivery of a Native man wanted for murder in Maryland.[78] In so doing Amongos emphasized his knowledge of the place and of other Native people's mobility both to the English and other Native people.

In other cases, however, Amongos did provide aid to escaped Native people and English justice. In one incident, an Eastern Shore man named Winsewack escaped repeatedly into Maryland, gone for a total of twenty-two months between 1667 and 1675; the punishment for escape that long would probably have been almost four years in additional labor. As an indentured servant at the plantation of county clerk Robert Hutchinson, Winsewack had lived near the Matomkins on the south side of the Matomkin Creek. After nineteen months, Amongos somehow convinced Winsewack to return to servitude. However, in his time on Hutchinson's plantation, Winsewack cultivated connections to Native people at other plantations by a broad horse path running by Hutchinson's land. He subsequently ran away with two other Native boys kept in bondage at one of Edmund Scarborough's nearby plantations.[79] Amongos harbored all three in 1670, for which he was jailed but otherwise unharmed. When Winsewack escaped again from Hutchinson, he absconded to the Nanticokes rather than to the Matomkins. But in a feat of networking and intelligence gathering, in 1675 a Matomkin man named Dick Shoes tracked him down across the border to Maryland and transported him back to Virginia, as Amongos had, to collect a reward for his capture.[80] Winsewack was returned to servitude for an additional three years. However, his escape demonstrated shared knowledge and connections unique to the politics of the Matomkin community, tying him to fellow Matomkins like Dick Shoes even as he traveled beyond Virginia's bounds.

Why would a Native leader like Amongos capture some Native people, harbor others, and capture and harbor the same person at different times? Kinship ties now invisible to us perhaps played a role. Capturing and harboring, particularly when those actions crossed borders, were both demonstrations of power and knowledge that enslavers could not replicate. Further, these actions might be corrective of injustices, from an Algonquian and English perspective, endemic to the indenture and enslavement of Native people. For example, four Native people among many other servants came to county court to ask for freedom after Scarborough's death in 1672. Each said that they had served past the times of their indentures, implying that Scarborough had overstepped legal bounds to exploit their labor and the nebulous legal status of many Native captives and laborers in the colony.[81] In sheltering two boys from Scarborough's plantation, Amongos may have been calling Native people back to enforce an agreement. Or as other Algonquians had done in previous generations, Amongos could have simply withdrawn the boys to diplomatically express displeasure at the English leaders' behavior toward Native people or mistreatment of servants—or maybe the boys were protected by Amongos as a family member.

As nonelite understandings of the Chesapeake's waterways, locales, and opportunities deepened, Native places served as markets for goods and information exactly because they were beyond the control of elites. Legislation punishing escaped people and their abettors failed to suppress the growing networks of bonded laborers and the strategies they developed among plantations and Native towns. Servants and enslaved people without kinship ties to Native people certainly brought goods and intelligence from English homes to Native towns, and perhaps labor and skills that made them valuable. Servants' knowledge of the Chesapeake landscape made capture an onerous, prohibitively expensive, time-consuming, and repeat venture for planters. Evidence of the presence and role of Native people in servant and enslaved plots and strategies is often indirect. It is crucial, however, to understanding the shape of bonded laborers' experiences and its role in the everyday interactions of Anglo-Native diplomacy. Servitude did not always change a Native person's place in Algonquian kinship networks and in inter-Native and Anglo-Native diplomacy, with potential familial and leaders' support shaping the strategies they employed and the success of their ventures. Native unfree people were still very much a part of the Algonquian world, even if their everyday experiences were different than if they lived in a Native town with kin. They contributed to a repeating pattern of resistance, which encouraged Native and non-Native unfree people to look beyond colonial Virginia's legal, social, and geographical boundaries using Chesapeake Algonquian landscapes as conduits.

Cutting the Knot

Amid Anglo-Native conflicts and servant escapes, Bacon's Rebellion began with realized fears about the porous nature of the colonial border. In 1675, a group of Doegs stole some pigs from planter Thomas Mathews as a replacement for an overdue payment for trade goods. The Doegs took the pigs by boat across the Potomac River and the Virginia border to Maryland, where Virginia planters pursued and killed members of the Doeg group. Some survived the encounter and returned to kill one of Mathews's servants with a hatchet.[82] Unlike raids farther to the west, this incursion hit English elites close to home. In retaliation, traders and planters Giles Brent and George Mason chased the Doegs across the Potomac again, ambushed a group of Native people, and killed them. They were Susquehannocks, not Doegs, however, and this misstep by the English inaugurated the Susquehannock War, years of raids and captivity for Algonquian people and their English neighbors across the Chesapeake.[83]

This initial encounter and the following violence in the Susquehannock War and Bacon's Rebellion nested conflicts among factions of servants, enslaved people, loyalists, rebels, freeholders, and people simply trying to stay out of the way in Virginia. It further ignited longtime concerns about social mobility, and the Native presence across the Chesapeake. During Bacon's Rebellion in 1676, an army of rebels against Governor Berkeley careened along the water routes and paths that tied Virginians to surrounding Native and non-Native communities. In a rejection of trade relationships, diplomacy, and the colony's system of border defense, Nathaniel Bacon's army of a few hundred colonists went up to the falls of the James River and down paths well known to traders to the Roanoke River. From May to September, they attacked the trading post of the Occaneechi and nearby Susquehannock forces to the west of Virginia, returned to east of the fall line and chased the Pamunkey into the Dragon Swamp north of the York River, and eventually set fire to Jamestown itself. They looted plantations and enslaved the Native people they encountered outright, while forming a political faction that exposed a range of colonists' longstanding grievances. Before and after the death of their titular leader, they fought for control of the arteries of the Chesapeake with the ships of the governor's loyalists on their tails.

The conglomeration of people who took part in the rebellion undermined the authority of Berkeley's colonial government in part by using trade routes to defy borders raised around them—around personal property and English plantations, and between Native people and settlers. Bacon's Rebellion was the result of a long series of simmering tensions: between Algonquians and outside Native enemies, planters and bonded laborers, county and colonial governments, and ultimately competing visions of how geographical and social boundaries might unite or divide disparate groups. One of the central contradictions of their rebellion, the destruction of Native places and connections accomplished through the use of Native places and connection, fueled by the food, plunder, knowledge, and now fear of Indigenous people, also fit the irony of many seventeenth-century battles over boundaries. On landscapes interconnected by Native people, in Bacon's words, "I adventured to cutt ye knott."[84]

In response to violence, landholders took control over the pursuit of Native people and bent the rules and bounds of the colonial government just as they had done previously. Nathaniel Bacon, who had taken part in the Piedmont trade with prosperous planter William Byrd I, sought a commission from Berkeley to go to war after his servant was killed in a raid, likely conducted by the Susquehannocks.[85] In the ensuing months, fear of Native reprisals grew until Berkeley commissioned Potomac planters John Washington and Isaac Allerton to "expel the enemy if they make further attempts upon them." Washington and Allerton caught up with Native men "who had ye Cloathes of such as had bin a little before murdered upon there backs" and sailed directly into Maryland to "demand satisfaction."[86] A parley at the Susquehannock fort among Susquehannock leaders, Maryland militia, and Washington's and Allerton's men ended with the murder of five Susquehannock leaders. The Virginians and Marylanders blamed each other for the injustice as well as for the subsequent six-week English siege on the Susquehannock fort. Archaeologists discovered graves of forty-two Susquehannocks, their deaths perhaps the result of starvation, inside of the structure dating to this period of occupation.[87]

In defying Maryland's boundaries in their pursuit and attack, Virginians opened the door for the Susquehannocks to make the same transgressions in return. Leaving behind everything except arms in late 1675, the Susquehannocks broke from the fort in the night and headed south, threatening to kill, in the words of one Susquehannock leader, "10 for one of the Verginians; such being the disperportion betwene his grate Men Murther'd, and those, by his command, slane." The commentator chided the Virginians as "so eager in there groundless quarill, as to persew the chase into anothers dominions." In February 1676, the Susquehannocks nonetheless requested a renewal of their alliance with the colony, dating back to their trading relationship at Kent Island with Claiborne. Berkeley rejected the offer, plunging Virginians further into fear of Susquehannock incursions unchecked by the colony's border system.[88]

Although continuous warfare had weakened them considerably, Susquehannock transgressions into English fields and houses underscored the ineffectiveness of English "hyred ships, sloups and planted great guns" defending Virginians.[89] To the north, the Susquehannocks' old enemies, the Piscataways, promised to keep their Maryland allies safe.[90] But in Virginia, wielding and stealing the implements that built the plantation landscape, the Susquehannocks "toke their spades and armes, and made themselves there with stronger and stronger."[91] Rumors of attacks and alliances swirled that "a very considerable bodie of them are come downe upon James River, within fifty or sixty miles of the plantations, where they lye hovering over us." Conspiracy theories resurfaced, and Virginians awaited attacks from Susquehannocks and tributary Native people closer to home. As Berkeley noted, "Not being able to guesse where the Storme will fall, for that all Indians as well our neer Neighbours as those more remote, giving us dayly suspitions that it is not any private grudge, but a generall Combination of all [Native nations] from New-England hither."[92] That was not the case, however, and in early 1676 the Susquehannocks resettled at the Roanoke River a few days' journey south and west of Virginians and their Algonquian neighbors. They would not stay there long.[93]

Participants in the conflict were not confined by colonial boundaries, and Native movement along western routes far from the eyes of Virginians was especially anxiety-inducing. English governors from New England to Virginia passed frantic letters containing rumors about the curious timing of their respective wars and skirmishes with Native people. Maryland and Virginia governors were particularly concerned about the possibilities that the Susquehannock War, Virginian attacks against Native allies, or a conflict between New England colonists and Algonquian nations to the north in Metacom's War might reach past colonial bounds. Berkeley decided in February 1676, before the rebellion had begun, that the "infection of the Indians in New-England has dilated it selfe to the [Marylanders] and the Northern parts of Virginia."[94] Later, rumors swirled that Bacon rushed messengers to Carolina, Maryland, and even New England to persuade colonists "with large remonstrances and reasons for his taking arms."[95] Some in Maryland blamed "the French (who is believed hath a great hand in the late New England Indian warr and burning Boston)."[96] Virginia's assembly blamed the governments of Carolina and Maryland for failing to send reinforcements to Berkeley.[97] In addition to letting traitors through, Maryland and Carolina habitually failed to police their borders: "Our Servants and Slaves Runn away thither upon any fault Committed, Sullen humo'r & disgust of theires . . . Indians that are soe mortally enimyes to us, are in peace and amity with them, and upon all injuries offer'd us retreate."[98] Although only meant to pass blame, the sentiment was correct: shared borders meant that crumbling colonial authority in one colony could soon affect its neighbor's authority. The Virginians feared for a future with constantly contested boundaries and constant threats generated from instability beyond them.

Nathaniel Bacon was a young and well-connected newcomer to the colony and situation and his entrance into Chesapeake politics was informed by his geographic and social place inside of it. From his plantation called Curles in Henrico County, he could access the road between Coastal Plains people and the Piedmont trade nearby, upon which settlers (and fort commanders) like Abraham Wood had, with the help of Algonquians, built wealth from exchanges in furs and captives from the interior. Bacon learned from colony elites like William Byrd, men who had made Henrico County the center of the trade in enslaved Native captives for the colony. Both Byrd and Bacon claimed ownership of Native people themselves who, unlike the escaped people on the Eastern Shore and other Algonquians, were mostly young children traded by captors from outside the colony to English traders. In conflicts occurring in the interior, some women might be adopted by victors and few men made it out of captivity alive. Many were traded for weapons to men allied with Governor Berkeley who, by the 1670s, had a monopoly on the Native trade.[99] Unlike coastal Algonquians who might be enslaved or bonded on plantations near their families, Native children from the Piedmont lacked family networks nearby, even if they recognized elements of a southeastern landscape. This source of Native labor looked promising to small landholders and traders alike, and Bacon had seen firsthand the wealth stored at the fort of the Occaneechis dozens of miles to the southwest, the entrepôt for goods moving through the

Piedmont between the English and Native people for decades. He may have also been aware that the Occaneechis attempted to intercept their own enemies farther inland on their way to visit English traders like Abraham Wood.[100] When unknown Native assailants killed Bacon's servant at his outlying plantation on the falls of the James River, they may have been familiar with the site as a trading post and an important Native-controlled connective node in the interior trade.[101]

In March 1676, Bacon gathered militiamen from Charles City and his home county of Henrico and demanded sanction from Berkeley in the form of a written commission to fight the Susquehannocks in retaliation. Failing that, he led his followers toward the Susquehannocks' new home in the Piedmont to attack. Bacon's rise to popularity tapped the long and personal histories of planter and trader violence that had plagued Algonquians for generations. Similar to elites like Edmund Scarborough, Bacon had already attempted to bully his Native neighbors, earning Governor Berkeley's censure for imprisoning an Appamattucks man for stealing (someone else's) corn stores in 1675. Bacon understood the usefulness of fears of Native attacks among the English population in Virginia; "reports and alarumes," he acknowledged to Berkeley, may have been "raised or fomented by private interests."[102] Although Bacon was a relative newcomer to the colony, he understood that rumors about and pursuit of nearby Native people could rally followers and resources to his cause, as Edmund Scarborough, John Catlett, and other Potomac planters had attempted the decade before.

As colonists took sides, they were informed by the fear and violence they experienced in their personal experiences of Virginians' conflicts with Native people. In petitions to England, a young colonist recalled the parents he lost in Opechancanough's 1644 attack and an older colonist referenced his loyalty to the colony through his service "under Sir William Berkeley against the Great Indian Emperor Appochaukonaugh, when he received several wounds."[103] For those who remembered the Anglo-Powhatan Wars, some scenes would look familiar: families waiting behind "Pallisadoes and redoubts," where "no Man Stirrd out of Door unarm'd."[104] John Godfrey of Old Rappahannock County wrote in his 1676 will, "Wee have a faire Election to be destroyed by ye Heathen, & no more then our deserts for it is Just with God to cutt us of[f] for our Sinns & Wickedness that is daily enacted among us."[105] Another colony leader advised royal authorities to move against Native raiders as Berkeley had against Opechancanough, through seasonal burnings and corn raids and fortifying groups of families in the line of fire.¹⁰⁶ Still others remained convinced that their Algonquian neighbors, rather than the outsider Susquehannocks, were to blame; the governor was just not yet "rightley informed."¹⁰⁷ The local relationships, understandings, and enmities cultivated among English and Native people across generations spilled over into a colony-wide movement that only underscored the fragility of settlement at the border.

As the rebellion spread from the Northern Neck down to the south side of the James River, local leaders pushed their Algonquian neighbors to "go against the Indians" without a hint of irony. Northumberland County officials ordered that Native men meet at the fairgrounds at the beat of the drum on the same day as white volunteers, although they recognized they could only rely on "such of them may be drawn out."¹⁰⁸ Others were threatened if they chose not to aid the rebels.¹⁰⁹ Among those who joined the rebellion was Edward Gunstocker, a Nanzatico man who had lived among the English and served county elites in past disputes with Native people. "Now designed upon an Expedition with the English against my Countrymen the Indians," Gunstocker took up arms after news of Jamestown's destruction spread, while Bacon's forces cruised along Native roads through woods surrounding English settlements with Native guides, looking for Native people to capture or destroy.¹¹⁰ However, the decision of many Native people to steer clear of the English during the rebellion demonstrated that they ultimately upheld their own interests and those of other Algonquians. Perhaps for some Native people like Gunstocker the rebellion called forth previous obligations and relationships with local planters, reinforcing rather than severing their roles as go-betweens and diplomatic allies. But those numbers were very small; only ten Native guides joined Bacon on his expedition into the Piedmont.

Bacon's march into the Piedmont in May 1676 made sense considering his prior experience as a trader: unlike many of his followers, he was familiar with the path to the Occaneechi town where licensed settlers traded. He understood the politics and protocols. He led 211 men beyond Virginia's farthest forts on foot to the Occaneechis' fort along the Dan and Roanoke Rivers. Far past Abraham Wood's Fort Henry on the Appomattox River, they were now in eastern Siouan territories, and as men turned back their number was half of what it had been days before. They ran low on provisions after their last stop among the Nottoways and Meherrins, but the Occaneechis' fort was a nerve center for Native intelligence and goods. Bacon had traveled days to reach the sustenance and intelligence promised by such a site. The Occaneechi chief Persecles, an ally of the English traders, agreed to replenish English provisions and, equally critically, informed Bacon that the enemy he was after—the Susquehannocks—were camped nearby on the Roanoke River. Would the English like them captured?[111]

English accounts of what occurred afterward differ—either as evidence of Persecles's or Bacon's betrayal. The Occaneechis brought the Susquehannocks into the fort to put them to death for the English, but soon a disagreement erupted between the colonists and their allies over either prisoners or provisions. It ended with the fort aflame, with men, women, and children—Occaneechis and Susquehannocks alike—inside. According to some accounts, forty or fifty Native allies lay dead, including Persecles, and his daughter was among the women and children Bacon and his men "disposed of" into slavery.[112] With plunder and a "victory" won by harnessing and then betraying Native alliances and communication lines, Bacon turned back to Jamestown to face Governor Berkeley.

After the violent encounter with the Occaneechis, Bacon's ranks swelled as he moved eastward toward another confrontation with the governor. The goods and labor of Chesapeake Algonquians, to which many of Bacon's men had grown accustomed, were the targets of Bacon's forces along the way. Bacon confronted trader Abraham Wood at Fort Henry, a central site for Native trade and then the place to find an Appamattuck man named Jack Nessom. A former servant of Wood's, Nessom had guided an English expedition to the mountains only a few years before, like Appamattucks guide Pyancha had done for Wood in 1650.[113] Bacon accused Nessom of murder and demanded that Wood turn him over; Wood refused, and Bacon's men forcibly took captive Nessom and his family and marched them to the county jail.[114] While the context of Bacon's accusation against Nessom is unclear, he chose to attack an Algonquian who traveled along similar routes as the Virginians' trading parties. Bacon and his men probably believed that his status as guide at a prominent trading center had helped him avoid English justice.[115] While the Occaneechis had loot Bacon wanted, Algonquians' intimacy with the English, Bacon's allies argued, made them a danger.

After his battle with the Occaneechis, Bacon returned to meet with the governor at Jamestown, only to be captured and brought inside the gates as a prisoner rather than military leader.[116] After Bacon's capture and brief arrest for marching against the Native people without a commission, he was reinstated to the council before Berkeley expelled him again. The newly elected assembly, however, imposed reforms including restrictions on the tax collecting, fees, and reelection of local and colonial authorities, from sheriffs to surveyors to county justices to the governor, and reinstated the right of freemen to vote—all measures popular with Bacon's followers. In anticipation of the cost of a war with the Susquehannocks, the assembly halted the building of forts, ordered the forts' garrisons to actively pursue Native people, and claimed "abandoned" Algonquian lands for the public rather than private grants. (All of these laws would be immediately repealed after the rebellion but placated many of Bacon's followers for the time being.)[117] In the meantime, Bacon gathered hundreds of men to confront the governor at Jamestown, received a commission to make war on Native people, and commenced confiscating supplies from settlers. Now that Bacon had left, Berkeley declared Bacon a rebel once again, and with Bacon in pursuit Berkeley fled to the Eastern Shore.[118]

Although they survived as a nation, Bacon found no more Susquehannocks to fight and instead repeatedly turned to seeking Pamunkey settlements and loot to rally exhausted troops. These followers were eager to defeat Natives; Bacon was not picky which. He "seized two Indians, a man & a Boy, who then did & always had lived in peace & friendship amongst the English, these he bound to trees, & wth much Horror & cruelty put to Death, wthout examining their crime," Philip Ludwell, a council member loyal to Berkeley, wrote nervously. Former Native friends "are not our worst enemies, having had a ffrequent and free intercourse amongst us these 20 odd years, & well knowing our Plantacons and manner of Living," he lamented.[119] Bacon's men also looted English goods, mats, hides, and wampum from a Pamunkey town. The English perpetrated gruesome public executions and captured other Pamunkeys to be sold into slavery.[120]

For Algonquians, residing too near roads and waterways became a heavier liability than a benefit, and they transitioned quickly to a strategy of isolation. As colonists evacuated the most isolated plantations and moved toward the bay and denser English populations to avoid outsider attacks, Native people moved inland to the wetlands that had long befuddled surveyors and planters. In the Middle Peninsula's Dragon Swamp, along roads that crisscrossed high points between Mattaponi and Pamunkey land to the Rappahannock River peoples and beyond, Algonquians from multiple groups gathered and built cabins. In the swamps, they kept their families together and stored the trade goods the rebels were after. Knowledge of the routes through the wetlands and the foliage allowed for defense. Men easily spied any invaders, and their families left few sights and sounds to indicate their presence.[121] Wetlands provided resources and safety for Algonquians when places beyond proved too dangerous.

The pursued Algonquians recognized that unlike along the well-traveled trading path to the Piedmont, the rebels were out of their depth in the Dragon Swamp, woods, and wide marshes. They moved to temporary locations in the wetlands and subsisted, as Powhatan himself had promised John Smith they would: "What can you get by warre, when we can hide our provisions and fly to the woods? Whereby you must famish by wronging us your friends."[122] The rebel's Native guides found Native homes first and were met with a defensive volley of shot. The Pamunkey leader ordered that the men not discharge their firearms in the direction of the English, hoping to deescalate the conflict while the families ran into the swamp. A Pamunkey woman was captured beyond the camp and led the men off course from the hideout of Cockacoeske, the Pamunkey werowansqua, or female hereditary chief, for which Bacon ordered her execution. Cockacoeske stayed in a camp in a pocosin that eluded Bacon's Native guides and mired Bacon's soldiers in the swamp. The English took trade goods, furs, and food, as well as captives. Finally discovered and forced to leave her temporary encampment to the pillagers, the werowansqua avoided capture for two weeks living in the woods with a child.[123] The wetlands sustained them and unknown others. Elsewhere, as at the end of the rebellion in northern Virginia, Native people sought sanctuary in English homes and the intercession of specific English leaders, leaning on the relationships they had developed with nearby landholders with some success. Nicholas Spencer, a loyalist and official who scattered rebels in Westmoreland County, helped his neighbors the Nanzaticos, who "notwithstanding their strong desire to peace, and endeavours for it, had bin destroyed by our wild headed rabble, if I had not interposed, and restrained them, to their dissatisfaction."[124]

Individuals like Spencer across the Chesapeake had chosen sides based on their own identities and situations, switched sides, or chosen neutrality until opportunity or coercion presented itself. While numbers are incomplete given the counties' few remaining records, a third of the documented men identified as part of Bacon's army were from the fringe of the colony—Stafford, Rappahannock, New Kent, Charles City, and Henrico Counties—indicating a personal and financial interest in patrolling the borders of the colony.[125] Some of these men, from Edmund Scarborough's son Charles to trader William Byrd, knew that there was loot and enslaved labor to be taken from organized attacks against Native people who had access to goods from beyond Virginia. Additionally, perhaps as many as two-thirds of the rebels were nonelites, including enslaved people and servants, and may have had freedom or Indigenous land in mind.[126] Contrary to allusions to the "rabble," elites and middling farmers, not just the desperate and uneducated poor, were well represented in this spree of looting and violence against Native people.[127] Bonded laborers had joined "upon the Invitation and encouragement of Libertie," and later, "distrest of their hoped for liberty," refused to surrender. Their presence may have pushed elites with their own bonded laborers away from the rebel side. An observer noted that Bacon invited unfree laborers to join the army but never promised more: "He hath not taken that Corse yet of proclaiming freedome to Servants, & when he doth, I verily believe itt wil in a short time ruine him, since by itt he will make all masters his Enimies." If they were free and without Native land to take, where would they go? "To live a life of wood Kerns" was the answer, referencing the phrase for an Irish vagabond, "which is the best they can propose to themselves."[128] Both Berkeley and the armed servants saw their participation in the rebellion as yet another escape attempt—a plot with Chesapeake landscapes and Algonquian people as resources, made by people escaping colonial boundaries inside of which they could hope for no status or freedom.

Conflict along the main waterways—attempts on the part of loyalists and rebels to halt the mobility of the other—helped dictate the pursuit of loot, the control of government, and the settlement of land. Governor Berkeley allied with several captains and seafaring merchants who used their craft to pursue capture and halt the movement of the rebels. Berkeley escaped by ship twice, in July and September 1676, to regroup with loyalists on the Eastern Shore and to avoid Bacon's armies encroaching on Jamestown. Mariners allied with Bacon pursued the loyalists on the Eastern Shore, where Berkeley's allies captured their ships and brought them into the loyalists' service in September.[129] Robert Morris's ship, the *Young Prince*, traveled the James for the governor for four months starting in September, gathering intelligence, moving supplies, and collecting information from and about the rebels. His sailors launched coordinated attacks on the south side of the James, besieging Bacon's fortifications and capturing Bacon's followers. Morris also noticed that Bacon's forces captured and plundered vessels and used them to control the shorelines. Men in one of Bacon's sloops harassed the crew of the *Young Prince* before disappearing into a tributary creek, and Morris spotted Bacon's spies in another ship from the York River. Encounters aboard the *Young Prince* also spotlighted servants' travels during the rebellion: at the mouth of the James, Morris captured four bonded laborers who had escaped with a boat belonging to Henry Chicheley, carrying a chest full of clothes and three guns. They had traveled from Chicheley's plantation on the Rappahannock River to join the fight far to the south, evidence of the spread of intelligence and continued movement among nonelites even during political chaos.[130]

Bacon died of disease after burning Jamestown in October 1676, though bitter fighting continued between loyalists and multiple small armies composed of Africans, servants, middling farmers, and several elites. In southern Virginia, rebel forces on Chippokes Creek, an area of dense settlement in Surry County, were easily reduced by men aboard loyalist Nicholas Prynne's boat, precisely because the settlement clustered along navigable waterways.[131] In 1677, the mariners came for the enslaved people and servants holding out with their ammunition and supplies at West Point to negotiate their surrender. Servants and enslaved people escaped and led a fight for the separate cause of freedom, some armed and holding a strategic point up the York River with "armes, Colours, Ammunition, &c."[132] Rebels surrendered when told in a parley that they might have freedom at the governor's discretion—only to be returned to the men who held them in bondage downriver. One hundred Africans did not trust the authorities and refused to lay down arms, instead threatening to kill the captain after the other rebels had agreed to the terms.[133]

After the rebellion ended in 1677, longstanding dissatisfaction with how county and colonial leaders dealt with Anglo-Native diplomacy remained.[134] There was no one Anglo-Native relationship but many different relationships, and negotiations developed over generations with multiple visions for the future of the Chesapeake. English king's commissioners Herbert Jeffreys, John Berry, and Francis Moryson, sent with a thousand troops to restore order, collected county and individual grievances sent by middling and elite planters. The reports often mentioned high levies and corruption but contradicted one another when it came to relations with Native people based on their location. Complainants from the centers of the trade in enslaved Indigenous people in Henrico County, for example, asked that war captives be enslaved and that the wars against Native people continue, a circumstance from which they would profit through their geographic proximity to trade connections. Isle of Wight County landholders on the southern Virginia border were exposed to raids and the taxes that came with attempts to prevent them. Although their Native neighbors had little to do with the rebellion, they still asked that "ther may be a continuall warr with the Indians that we may have once have done with them."[135] Men from James City County suggested a peace be reached with all neighboring Native people and a return to mapped "bounds ... between us and them."[136] Meanwhile, in the northwest, Old Rappahannock County men asked for immediate peace with Native people and in strong words that every county pitch in to cover the costs of past and future wars: "O[u]r neighbor Counties are soe narrow hearted & close fisted as to think it none of their duty to assist us in destroying the blood thirsty Indians, but would willingly leave us to fight the battles of the Republique."[137] Westmoreland County authors agreed with their Rappahannock neighbors but asked that a specific tribe, the Doegs, be annihilated for revenge killings which had occurred in that area of the colony before the rebellion.[138] Lancaster County also asked that trade with Native people be completely halted and that the colony declare war on Indigenous people living next door in Northumberland County.[139] With the exception of planters and traders aspiring to enslave Native people, each set of men had in mind not Native people in general but those nearby with whom they dealt every day. With local geography and relations in mind, they wrote to defend their livelihoods instead of the colony.

Regardless of location, many county grievances and petitions highlighted the self-interested nature of elite participation in Anglo-Native conflicts and its costs to landholders. In words from the Lower Norfolk County grievances, "Wee humbly desire to know what is done wth our money." In an effort to avoid levies altogether, planters in Nansemond made the unreasonable request that "no P[er]son bee paid or allowed for any reall or prtended services."[140] Many blamed the actions of landed elites—who wreaked havoc by bending colonial, county, and private property boundaries— for their losses in the first place. Northampton County's landholders reminded the commissioners that "our county som yeares since was contrary to our expectation divided into two Counties to our great Detriment and Loss notwithstanding ye great advantage of Colonel Scarborough," and they asked for their land back from Accomack County.[141] Old Rappahannock County men examined the very beginning of the rebellion, in which Virginian militia leaders followed Susquehannock hunters over the border and into Maryland where they were killed. They suggested the officials "would be pleased to examine & Know by what Authority Coll George Mason &

Major George Brent went over into Maryland & Killed severall of the Indians there wch wee suppose was the Originall cause of the murthers Comitted in o[u]r Country."[142] The Charles City County grievances and several testimonies and petitions skewered Edward Hill, a "most notorious coward and insolent turbulent fellow." Hill was accused by tenants and fellow elites alike of calling out the militia for a week to plunder, rather than protect, the county and of attempting to sell governor's pardons to men who attacked Native people under Bacon. In one spectacular case, Hill purportedly imprisoned a man as a rebel at his plantation, where the imprisoned man saw evidence his own home had been raided, as Hill's servants walked past in the new stockings he had left at home.[143] Hill then issued a grievance of his own against the Charles City County grievances. But the rebellion eroded the authority of local elites and demonstrated to other colonists that planters with enormous tracts of land like Hill were willing to take advantage of others' and their own boundary transgressions, and the chaos that resulted. The battle was far from over, and Native efforts in defense of their polities, lands, and families would continue in both new and old ways.

By February 1677, Governor Berkeley had called a new assembly, justified the hanging of several rebels to the commissioners, appropriated goods from the estates of condemned rebels, and squabbled with the king's commissioners before he left for England to plead his case to King Charles II.[144] Asked to explain the rebellion to royal officials, commissioners investigating its causes reflected on many of the issues long on the minds of colonial officials, among them the nature of settlements and boundaries. Harder boundaries around Native nations and a new agreement were a priority, as the officials sought to restore land and possessions to longtime allies like Cockacoeske and the Pamunkeys. Harder limits on the English seemed necessary as well to address a series of problems. English settlers, the commissioners lamented, lived in small households "at great Distances" from one another. The men who operated the forts at great taxpayer expense stayed inside for their own protection when there was trouble and would not come out when people were killed nearby. And elite engrossing of land, the "apparent cause of the struggling of the people, and enlarging and widening of the Bounds," was foolish, "in noe wise able to defend." The commissioners recommended a land tax to discourage elites from hoarding undeveloped land, an idea of Berkeley's from previous decades. The king did not immediately follow up with this suggestion.[145]

Between escape plots, outsider Native violence, and Bacon's Rebellion, Chesapeake residents witnessed the breakdown of every kind of boundary in the 1670s: the plantation could not keep in laborers; the forts could not keep Native people out, nor surveil the Native people who came to trade; and county officials could not defend and adjudicate without corruption and waste.

Imposing expansive and extralegal property, county, and colonial borders, elites had reached too far. Borders during these tumultuous years only served to undermine the goal of ensuring ownership and control, crossed often enough to delegitimize claims to authority inside of them. Native networks and connectivity, as well as their own boundaries and occupation of the Chesapeake, undermined systems of labor and land control upon which Virginians placed their authority. Planter vigilantes, often not held accountable in the past, sought to capitalize on the situation in the name of restoring order. All this, along with the rise in numbers of enslaved Africans and the stagnation of profits to be made from tobacco, made the situation for Virginia landowners tenuous even as the rebellion folded.

In 1677, the commissioners approached Native leaders, including the Pamunkeys, Weyanokes, Nansemonds, and Nottoways, about a new peace agreement, encouraging the Virginia Assembly to "understand there own Security and Interest and make peace." Still more Native nations joined the agreement in 1680. Each Native nation had been affected differently by the violence of the previous years: in trade lines severed, family killed, goods stolen and destroyed.[146] In the aftermath of Bacon's Rebellion, colonial officials took back control of Anglo-Native relations from the counties, enabling the assembly to better regulate movement of enslaved and indentured people and Algonquians into and out of Virginia's borders.[147] The Articles of Peace, also called the Treaty of Middle Plantation, in 1677 once again drew lines, requiring patents for Native lands, reaffirming Native rights to water access, and requiring three miles between English and Native settlements. As part of their tributary status, Native people were to escort outsider Indigenous people—and escaped people—into the colony. Meanwhile, the General Assembly reaffirmed earlier laws that made neighboring Native people responsible for pursuing Native outsiders who attacked plantations and revised but kept alive the fort system under planters and traders like William Byrd I.[148] As enslavement of Native people and Africans grew in Virginia, a new, harder boundary required enforcement in the places between the colony and the Native-dominated West.

Cockacoeske sought to centralize control over Native movements and boundaries at the same time. The colony seized traitors' estates and redistributed their goods, including Native people enslaved in Bacon's Rebellion; petitioning the new colonial government, Cockacoeske extricated all but five captives, including a woman returned at the colony's expense from the island of Bermuda in 1682.[149] She then secured the return of land stolen from the Pamunkey in the rebellion, as well as fishing and hunting rights.[150] Her relationship with Virginia gave her new bargaining power and facilitated her ambition to pull other Algonquians again into the Pamunkey orbit, to make them "of the same mind and affection to His Majesty as herself."[151] The werowansqua negotiated through the Treaty of Middle Plantation to reestablish the Pamunkeys' historical authority over some nations formerly part of the Powhatan chiefdom, which would be "(as she desired) under her subjection, as anciently they had beene." She also pointed out to the English the ways her interest in controlling Native diplomacy and mobility intersected with theirs, like when the Chickahominy promised but failed to mobilize warriors on behalf of the English, or in one case refused to return a woman to English settlements.[152] Using shared Powhatan history and an understanding of English desires and vulnerabilities, her efforts were backed by consolidated English authority also invested in restraining Native mobility.

For Indigenous people, the conclusion of Bacon's Rebellion accelerated changes already in motion in the wider Native world and Algonquians' struggle to hold power in the Chesapeake. Algonquians' knowledge of the interior proved crucial in the dire times that followed. While the Occaneechi maintained their island, the weakening of these longtime middlemen in the fur trade and trade in enslaved people not only left them vulnerable to attack but encouraged increasing violence in and migration through the Piedmont.[153] English traders exploited the chaos with enthusiasm, increasing the number of Native women and children in the colony as bonded laborers, and then as victims of a trade in Native captives codified in law in 1682.[154] In the following years, the Susquehannocks came back to raid Virginian plantations and surrounding Algonquian towns that were tributary to the colony. The situation only worsened when the Susquehannocks joined the Haudenosaunees and the movements of these "Northern Indians" proved difficult to track or predict.

In 1690, Stafford County officials in northwestern Virginia captured a group of Native people, among them the werowance of the Doegs, who had raided in Virginia at the beginning and at the conclusion of Bacon's Rebellion. When asked "by what means he being a stranger came here," the werowance explained he was not a stranger at all. Native people—likely the Haudenosaunees—captured him from his home with the Nanzaticos near the Potomac River in 1676 or 1677.[155] He remained their adopted kinsman for thirteen years and then, in 1689, left to plant corn on Nottoway land to the south of the colony. He left before the year's harvest—perhaps the Nottoway themselves had moved towns—and arrived back home intending to live among the Nanzaticos, who had a friendship with the Doegs.[156] On familiar land with familiar people, he had inherited the place of or been chosen as werowance. His complex identity and his well-traveled past demonstrated the adaptation to mobile and settled lifeways required of displaced Algonquian people, who remained invested in the places they were forced to leave behind.[157]

The Doeg werowance made sense of his own history by connecting one place and one's role there to the next, in the Haudenosaunee north, the Nottoway south, and the Virginia courtroom. His testimony to county officials reinforced that people and conflicts over space crossed permeable property, county, and colony lines. It was the failure of such borders, after all, that drew him away from home in the first place. Algonquian people maintained a sophisticated grasp on English conceptions of boundaries as they evolved or were destroyed. During Bacon's Rebellion, rebels and loyalists all blamed outsider Native groups for the rumors and fear that gripped the colony, but Native people and English planters understood that many threats to supposedly sovereign borders—Bacon, escaped laborers, county and colony officials—breached the walls from the inside.

— EPILOGUE —
Native History at Dividing Lines

In 1683, a mother and her two children, a boy and a girl, escaped enslavement through the Chickahominy Swamp in New Kent County. The Virginia General Assembly had legalized the trade in enslaved Native captives just the previous year. Marched by traders to coastal Virginia and sold, they ran away only four days after arriving at the plantation of Daniel Crafford. To escape Virginia's trade in Native women and children, they first had to pass through its heart, back up the James River and into Henrico County. They crossed the James to the mouth of the Appomattox River, and from there found the home of Henry Batts, Henrico explorer and trader. He welcomed them to his plantation, only to separate the boy from his family and sell him into slavery to a planter named Peter Proby. Proby lived back down the James River in Warwick County, even farther away from the boy's mother and sister than Crafford's plantation had been. Days later, desperate and bearing the marks of Proby's abuse, the boy ran away from that planter and circled back to Crafford's plantation. Initially inclined to send him back to Proby, Crafford changed his mind at the sight of the boy's body and went with him to Warwick Court instead, proving the boy to be his, and not Proby's, property. Upon return to Crafford's plantation, the subject of the property dispute did not wait long to retrace the escape route he took with his mother and sister and returned to the Batts plantation on the Appomattox River. There, he reunited with his family. This time, Henry Batts refused to return him. Crafford sued for the return of the family, and it is here where the record of the case ends.[1]

This family was almost certainly not Algonquian, and they had no connection to the Chesapeake territories they traversed. But their story, and that of the boy in particular, demonstrates how the routes appropriated by planters and traders claiming ownership over bonded laborers and their property also connected those who subverted that ownership. Maps of the region in the seventeenth and early eighteenth centuries, from surveys of land to soundings along the river, tell stories of English expansion and knowledge of places throughout the Coastal Plain and into the Piedmont. As the trade in Native captives grew in Virginia during this decade, however, the routes between expanding plantations and the Piedmont to the south, and to the Haudenosaunees to the north, brought not just enslaved women and children but also more threats of violence to residents. Algonquian hunters feared meeting outsider Native people in the woods during the 1670s and 1680s, and garrisons of settler "Rangers" patrolled the heads of the rivers to stop outsiders from accessing the Chesapeake.[2] But this family's particular quest to leave Virginia, and to do so intact as a family, demonstrates that the emerging structures of the trade could still be resisted: this family's journey involved a literal backtracking and a vision for their own future beyond Virginia.

Slavery had changed the Native geography of the Chesapeake, but resistance to servitude and slavery in English labor regimes was also continuously shaped by Native landscapes. Since the first decade of English colonization, escaping unfree people had undermined English authority using Native routes, walking away from James Fort or sailing upriver to trade. By the 1640s and 1650s, English traders and their servants and enslaved people habitually tapped into the broad-reaching networks of the northern Chesapeake and into the Piedmont, from whence this family came. Their escape paths traversed the James River through Algonquian districts once at the heart of the Powhatan chiefdom. As in 1683, earlier travels revealed how the familiar coastline and the farthest reaches of English knowledge were connected in lucrative but often uncontrollable ways, ultimately undermining planters' authority over labor. As servants and enslaved people moved from water to land, and planted tobacco at a distance from one another, the vast network of Native routes and towns among English holdings only became that much more important.

In response, planters attempted to sever networks and control the movement of enslaved laborers. In addition to defining plantation boundaries and rules governing movement, Maryland and Virginia officials ordered and violently enforced martial and legal boundaries that were increasingly based on race. Moreover, Anglo-Native treaties repeatedly implicated Native complicity in plantation regimes, dictating the return of escaped laborers and specifically Black unfree people who sought shelter with them. The mobility of bonded laborers over Native land led in part to the codification of draconian punishments for people who attempted escape meted out at James Fort during Sir Thomas Dale's years as deputy governor, the step in evolution of permanent enslavement in the case of John Punch in the 1640s, and additional sentences to service and corporal punishment passed by the General Assembly in the 1660s and 1670s. Elite attempts to harness and control that mobility, especially in the interior—as in the case of Bacon's attack on the Occaneechis—caused the destabilization that brought this family to the coast. In an iconic historical moment, the popular uprising demonstrated that shifting attempts to control movement across proliferating English boundaries were failures. By the 1680s, colonial authorities not only legally codified the enslavement of Native people traded from outside of the colony, but doubled down on punishing resistance of enslaved people, reflecting their reliance on enslaved Africans.[3] Yet, as this family's story demonstrates, resistance to detention continued along the same routes—and knowledge of Native networks, even distant, shaped hopes for the future.

Inside the Chesapeake colonies, Algonquian people reimagined a geography surrounded by planters and a future of working with colonial governments. In 1686, Algonquian leaders from the Eastern Shore traveled across the peninsula, traversed the bay, and sailed up the river to St. Mary's with interpreters and ten deerskins in tow. Pocomoke and Assateague leaders sought an audience with the Council of Maryland to negotiate for the removal of their English neighbors. The Assateague werowance accused Englishman Edward Hammond of grave robbing: a werowance and another Native person living among the English had seen Hammond with skins and strings of roanoke buried with a deceased werowance and wished to revoke their consent to his living nearby. The planter had violated propriety and the importance of the werowance's grave, and so the Assateagues sought to legally push him off their ground. Despite the gravity of this crime for the Assateagues, the council judged this revocation "unreasonable," even if a grave robbery had happened. The council's dismissal undermined established diplomatic relations and the value of the Assateagues to upholding boundaries against hostile neighbors.

After the Assateagues had spoken, the Pocomokes presented a separate set of concerns about the encroachment of the English. They framed their protest in terms of the history of their locality and its resources. Their first complaint, among several, was of other planters' encroachment onto the town of Askiminokonson in Maryland. They explained to the council how Algonquian people came to be at Askiminokonson in the first place: five chiefdoms had joined together, driven from one settlement to another by English encroachment. But the soil where the Pocomokes were seated was "worn out," and they wished to cross to the land on the opposite side of the creek. Virginian Charles Scarborough, a former participant in Bacon's Rebellion and the son of planter Edmund Scarborough, had seated where Pocomoke women needed to plant the next year's crops, within the bounds of Maryland. Multiple planters had settled within their bounds and built bridges across the head of the Pocomoke River, allowing cattle to cross into and destroy Native fields. They had also denied Native people hunting rights, and even attempted to steal valuable furs resulting from their hunts. The Pocomoke werowance also engaged the English on terms they privileged, pointing to their own trade, "labor," and "improvements." On this basis the Pocomoke won an order from the council for the planters to install swinging gates on the bridges. This did not address their original concern, that the boundaries of their current town ensconced "barren and good for nothing" land. The Pocomokes had asked for land returned from two planters to sustain themselves after a long history of displacement; the council replied, while presenting the Pocomokes' new survey, that their land was already taken. The werowances left, unhappy at the selective enforcement of boundaries.[4]

This local story on the fringes of the Chesapeake illuminates wider Native efforts to reconfigure English settlement near and within their bounds to preserve peace and sustenance across the Chesapeake. As English elites' settlements expanded, they made new efforts to control the movement of people through their domains: evolving policies and settlement patterns broadly excluded non-Christian Native people, and new geographic boundaries threatened local relationships among English and Native Chesapeake residents.[5] Harnessing local networks at the turn of the seventeenth century, Algonquian chiefdoms inside and surrounding Wahunsenacawh's domain upheld their own territories as they conducted trade, diplomacy, and everyday travel as neighbors. English colonizers initially found themselves folded into Native friendships and grudges, and knowledge about Native places and relationships were necessary for survival in the first decades of the seventeenth century. Indeed, settlers found that local places and in particular local waters were at the core of Algonquian identities. English plantations' threats to these places were met with denial and violence, as in the large-scale Powhatan assaults of 1622 and 1644. As traders moved north on the bay and west into the Piedmont at midcentury, local Native boundaries, alliances, and action to protect them—on Kent Island or Brewsters River, for example—shaped the fate of competing spatial visions for the Chesapeake.

Historical alliances and enmities among Native people could shut down a fur-trading empire to the north for the Marylander traders, or keep hopes alive for an easy route to the interior for Abraham Wood. Indeed, continued assertions of dominion and influence, as with the Pocomokes' insistence that their burial places deserved respect, spoke to the constant innovation of Algonquian leadership to maintain those claims and networks despite displacement and political realignments. And in response to outsider Native and English transgressions, they made new claims and justifications.

As elite planters gathered enslaved labor, land claims, and offices in the colonial administration, they made increasingly powerful challenges to Native boundaries. Even as they legally maneuvered to enforce boundaries and govern the movement of their servants and enslaved laborers, by the 1660s and 1670s planters ignored the established boundaries, asserted by both Native and English people, surrounding Native places. As they had during the northern Chesapeake fur trade, elites used rumors and threats of violence disseminated along Native and English networks to justify attacks on and displacement from Native lands. Attacks like Edmund Scarborough's foray into Maryland, and the rebels' march through Pamunkey territory in 1676 undermined the larger colonial project by bringing the reach of authority of Maryland and Virginia authorities into question. Meanwhile, the destruction and violation of Native places, and destabilization, most benefitted only a few men.

Through the retelling of their own histories of displacement and migration accrued over the course of the seventeenth century, Native people sought to enact their own spatial visions. At a Nottoway town along the broad, swampy floodplains and braided creeks feeding into the Nottoway River, Virginian officials Nathaniel Harrison and Philip Ludwell prepared to record history as told by three Weyanoke women. By 1710, they had been collecting testimonies for years from colonists and Meherrin, Nottoway, and Nansemond peoples about seventeenth-century regional instabilities and the Weyanokes' resistance to annihilation. Betty, Mary, and Jenny Pearce told their story, "heard from theyr fathers & the old people of theyr Nation." Occupying one of the most populous of the Powhatan chiefdom's districts at the turn of the seventeenth century, the Weyanokes were pushed south from their seat on the north side of the James "for fear of ye resentment of ye English" during the 1644 contest between the Powhatan under Opechancanough and Virginian colonists.[6] They settled temporarily along the Roanoke River in the Piedmont with the permission of the Tuscaroras and took over the fallow fields of previous Native occupants. But relationships with neighbors spoiled over only a few years: the Weyanokes built defensive fortifications, relied on tuckahoe in nearby wetlands for subsistence, and quickly depleted their stocks of wild plants when they were unable to grow corn due to fear of attack.[7] In 1660, the neighboring Nansemonds attacked the Weyanokes, pushing them north again. They made a tentative return south to escape English harassment, only to be attacked by the Tuscaroras for the intrusion. Nansemond man Great Peter added to the women's story that the English "fetched them up again."[8] Finally in 1676, continued Great Peter, "when Bacon disturbed the Indians," they moved back south of the Blackwater River. By the turn of the eighteenth century, the Weyanokes were "almost wasted," according to planter and chronicler Robert Beverley, whittled down in the grind between fickle English alliances and aggression from other Native people. Ludwell found Mary, Betty, and Jenny Pearce living with the Nottoways.[9]

The Virginia officials had come because Native history was once again at the center of a colonial boundary dispute. This time, they used Native accounts of possession and displacement to draw the line between modern-day North Carolina and Virginia. By the 1650s, settlers had left Virginia and begun settling in Albemarle Sound in northeastern North Carolina. The contest between the two colonies began over vague language in the Carolina Charter of 1663, which declared that Virginia ended and Carolina began "upon a strait westerly line to Wyonoak creek . . . and so west, in a direct line, as far as the South-Seas."[10] The Carolinians argued that the surveyors had simply misnamed the Nottoway River, thus pushing the North Carolina border twenty miles north into Virginia.[11] The Virginians placed hope in a rumor that the aforementioned creek actually referred to a temporary Weyanoke settlement on Wycacon Creek.[12] The

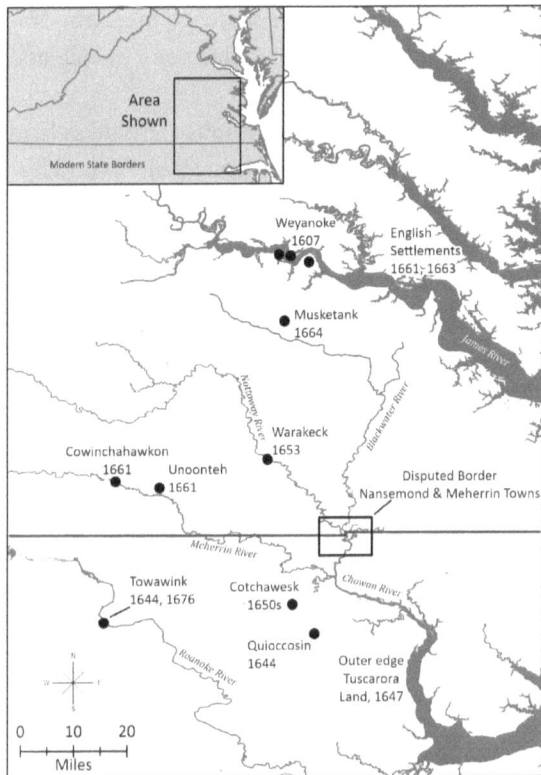

MAP 6. Conjectural migration routes of the Weyanokes, 1644–1710 (Stewart Scales and Gemma Wessels)

original Virginian surveyors thought Weyanoke Creek a permanent fixture of the Carolina landscape, but the Weyanokes not only moved seasonally like other Algonquians but had resettled no fewer than ten times. Moreover, to contemporary Native inhabitants who knew the history, Weyanoke Creek was likely no longer Weyanoke Creek after the Weyanoke left. Once again, Native occupation and movement across arbitrary English borders, especially those defined by waterways central to movement, confounded colonial officials.

As they had during the seventeenth century, officials on both sides saw a permanent boundary through this Native place as a prerequisite for expansion west. Carolinians had much to gain: traders sought to edge out their Virginian counterparts; planters sought to edge out Virginian planters' potential land claims.[13] Meanwhile, Alexander Spotswood, who became lieutenant governor of Virginia in 1710, saw value in gaining a sliver of land with no western boundary, envisioning that "a very profitable Trade might be established with forreign Nations of Indians."[14] With similar ambitions, the Virginian and North Carolinian commissioners searched in nearby Native towns and plantations for the oldest available Indigenous people and settlers who could provide decades-old evidence.

Pushed by the "pretending incroachment" of ambitious Carolinian land speculators, Native people in the disputed territory threw their lot and testimony in with the Virginians, a fateful decision that defined the shape of North Carolina and Virginia and fueled class-based enmity between the colonies.[15] Native interpretations and omissions emphasized a century of history with Virginians strategically told through the local story of the Weyanoke struggles. Although the English pushed the Weyanoke south away from plantations on the James River no fewer than three times, this conflict was never mentioned to the commissioners, nor did the Weyanoke women discuss how the English had jailed their werowance for debt in 1660.[16] Testimony uniformly referenced the Third Anglo-Powhatan War in terms of "appachachanough's massacre" or the time "before Appachancanaugh Was taken," omitting any part that the Nansemonds and Weyanokes had played in the violence, as well as the violence the English had inflicted on them.[17] Native people smoothed over past enmities with Virginians to strengthen the Virginians' case for their own perceived benefit.

Off the record, Native people deployed rumors, reinforcing the increasingly common narrative of Carolinians as liars and general lowlifes. Great Peter confided that the North Carolinians, in their travels through the Nansemonds' town, became angry at the depositions that Native people chose to give and "urged him very much to drink." Great Peter had replied "he would tell him the truth but if that would not please him he would not tell him a lye." Another Nansemond man named Robin Tucker swore that a Carolinian attempted to bribe him, "persuading him to deny that ye Wyanokes had lived on Wycacon Creek & promised him a bottle of powder & 1000 Shot to doe it."[18] In this case, because Native histories were at the center of the dispute, everyday abuse and attempts at coercion on the part of colonists suddenly took on new import and discredited the Carolinians' case.[19] Ludwell concluded that North Carolina's witnesses "are all verry Ignorant men & most of them men of ill fame that have run away from Virginia."[20]

Governor Spotswood pushed aside the search for the dividing line less than a year later when another set of Virginians came south, this time to prevent the Meherrins, Nottoways, and Nansemonds from joining the Tuscaroras in a bloody war against North and South Carolina, a conflict that united the North Carolinians and Virginians against Native people and territory blocking English expansion of their plantations. In 1728, a compromise between Virginian and North Carolinian surveyors decided the dividing line.[21] But the Weyanokes' story of migration through all of the major events rocking seventeenth-century settler society—conflict with colonists, Opechancanough's military campaigns, Bacon's Rebellion—is one of survival through knowledge of the landscape and connection to other Native people. Into the eighteenth century, these factors largely defined regional politics, emanating from boundary lines.

Native people understood colonial surveying and English boundary-marking to be hallmarks of dispossession. After all, scheming elites like John Catlett and Edmund Scarborough were surveyors as well as planters. The older Weyanoke and Nottoway people had witnessed the evolution and variety of ways that colonists had marked their boundaries, and the ways in which those bounds crumbled or proved unstable. Palisades along the James River and forts at the falls had come and gone before midcentury, while in the 1660s and 1670s planters on the western fringes of Virginia's and Maryland's land claims still feared neighboring Algonquians and foreign Native raiders. By 1710, the commissioners' quest for a correct answer leading to a definitive boundary probably seemed arbitrary.

As was the case during previous spats among colonists, Native knowledge of the Chesapeake's history was powerful. The region's history, as Native people told it—the stories of their movements during bouts of intense violence found throughout this book—are foremost about the places where they lived and the other Native people to whom they were connected. Into the eighteenth century, even displaced and reduced in numbers, Algonquians and their places influenced how people experienced the Chesapeake Bay and its surrounds. Native people used rumor, mobilized English rhetoric surrounding boundaries and ownership, and exploited divisions among English factions—strategies honed in earlier conflicts—to curate English borders. They understood that English officials and surveyors on either side of the border would also fall into certain patterns of behavior, exploiting Native places for plantation land and trade routes even as they squabbled over colonial control. At Weyanoke Creek and at every boundary where English people relied on Native presence or knowledge, Native history and strategy remains visible in official testimony and mapped boundaries, not to mention how quickly those boundaries were contested and overrun by nonelites and Native people. Native knowledge of Virginia's waterways and roadways could still become a weapon when paired with knowledge of English divisions and desires.

Narratives of dispossession and English maps of Native American land along the Atlantic seaboard in the seventeenth and eighteenth centuries do not account for the variety and porousness of English and Native boundaries. Instead, mapped boundaries offered opportunities for Native people and others looking to subvert colonial authority. Despite their attempts to segregate themselves legally and geographically from Algonquians, early colonists constructed entangled histories and landscapes that perpetually acknowledged the Native past and contemporary presence. Native people's insistence that they remain in the Chesapeake and stay connected to one another undermined the expensive encroachments of local elites and their attempts to impose inequality by limiting mobility of oppressed and enslaved people. The higher the investment in bonded labor and valuable land, the more fiercely elites protected their own boundaries and pushed others, and the more authority they lost when nonelites and Native people violated them. Their maps, as men like Philip Ludwell could testify, always had questions attached, answered by careful and self-protective Native men and women who stewarded a place.[22] Because plantations and resistance grew atop centuries of Native-made places and movements, Native people maintained power in the Chesapeake, a place never totally bounded or bound.

~ NOTES ~

INTRODUCTION

1. Darrin Lowery, *Archaeological Survey of the Chesapeake Bay Shorelines Associated with Accomack County and Northampton County, Virginia* (Portsmouth: Virginia Department of Historic Resources, 2001), 1:23.
2. Walter I. Priest III, Sharon Dewing, and Gene M. Silberhorn, "Richmond County Marsh Inventory, Special Reports in Applied Marine Science and Ocean Engineering No. 306" (Williamsburg: Virginia Institute of Marine Science, College of William and Mary, 1990), 52–56; Scott M. Strickland et al., *Defining the Rappahannock Indigenous Cultural Landscape* (St. Mary's City: St. Mary's College of Maryland, 2016), 86.
3. Martin D. Gallivan et al., *The Werowocomoco (44GL32) Research Project: Background and 2003 Archaeological Field Season Results* (Richmond: Virginia Department of Historic Resources, 2006), 37.
4. Stephen C. Potter, *Commoners, Tribute, and Chiefs: The Development of Algonquian Culture in the Potomac River Valley* (Charlottesville: University Press of Virginia, 1994), 3. Potter placed the migration of Algonquian people into the Chesapeake at either 100–200 or 700–900 CE. Martin Gallivan suggests a date range that starts several hundred years earlier in *The Powhatan Landscape: An Archaeological History of the Algonquian Chesapeake* (Gainesville: University Press of Florida, 2016), 73.
5. Philip L. Barbour, "The Earliest Reconnaissance of the Chesapeake Bay Area: Captain John Smith's Map and Indian Vocabulary," *Virginia Magazine of History and Biography* 79, no. 3 (1971): 286, 296.
6. Alejandra Dubcovsky argues that southeastern Native communication networks were crucial to forming colonies and conflict in *Informed Power*. Jacob F. Lee's *Masters of the Middle Waters* focuses on local social networks and alliances founded in kinship facilitated by the midcontinent river system, which by its nature crossed borders and undermined fragile imperial

authority. While this work focuses on how rivers served to spread violence and disjuncture more so than alliance, it builds on a central source of tension Lee points out that waterways linked people who sought to colonize and those who sought to halt colonization. Dubcovsky, *Informed Power: Communication in the Early American South* (Cambridge, MA: Belknap Press of Harvard University Press, 2016); Lee, *Masters of the Middle Waters: Indian Nations and Colonial Ambitions along the Mississippi* (Cambridge, MA: Belknap Press of Harvard University Press, 2019), 3, 8. In its discussion of the expansionist strategies of the Powhatan chiefdom, this study echoes Matthew R. Bahar's point that Native people belonging to some Native polities were aggressive and creative in their political transformation of the coastline at the expense of the English. Bahar, *Storm of the Sea: Indians and Empires in the Atlantic's Age of Sail* (New York: Oxford University Press, 2019), 11–12. See also Cynthia Van Zandt, *Brothers among Nations: The Pursuit of Intercultural Alliances in Early America, 1580–1660* (New York: Oxford University Press, 2008). For map 1, see "Virginia" (Kraus Map), c. 1610, Harry Ransom Center, University of Texas Austin, https://hrc.contentdm.oclc.org/digital/collection/p15878coll9/id/9/.

7. Martin Gallivan, "Powhatan's Werowocomoco: Constructing Place, Polity, and Personhood in the Chesapeake, CE 1200–CE 1609," *American Anthropologist* 109, no. 1 (2007): 86. For similar processes in the Northeast, see Katherine Grandjean, *American Passage: The Communications Frontier in Early New England* (Cambridge, MA: Harvard University Press, 2015), 140.

8. Dubcovsky, *Informed Power*, 4. Archaeologists like Martin Gallivan and Stephen Potter and anthropologist Helen Rountree have examined precolonial Native landscapes and how diverse Algonquian groups harnessed them to trade, to influence one another, to spread news, and to incorporate newcomers in ways that informed local responses to English boundary lines. Indigenous cultural landscapes studies, particularly in the Chesapeake, demonstrate how Native people engaged in "place-making" in everyday acts from farming to feasting. See Alex J. Flick and Julia A. King, "'We Can Fly No Farther': Colonialism and Displacement among the Piscataway of Southern Maryland," in *The Archaeology of Removal in North America*, ed. Terrance Weik (Gainesville: University Press of Florida, 2019), 21. See also Gallivan, *Powhatan Landscape*; Stephen Potter, "Early English Effects on Virginia Algonquian Exchange and Tribute in the Tidewater Potomac," in *Powhatan's Mantle: Indians in the Colonial Southeast*, ed. Gregory Waselkov, Peter H. Wood, and Tom Hatley (Lincoln: University of Nebraska Press, 2006), 215–41; and Helen C. Rountree, *Pocahontas's*

People: The Powhatan Indians of Virginia through Four Centuries (Norman: University of Oklahoma Press, 1990).

9. Following the work of Lisa Brooks in *Our Beloved Kin* about northeastern nations and Michael Witgen's *An Infinity of Nations,* the following chapters take as given that Native knowledge of the landscape and movement thrived well past attempts to colonize, or past the deaths or defeats of major leaders. Brooks, *Our Beloved Kin: A New History of King Philip's War* (New Haven, CT: Yale University Press, 2018); Michael Witgen, *An Infinity of Nations: How the Native New World Shaped Early North America* (Philadelphia: University of Pennsylvania Press, 2012). April Hatfield demonstrated in *Atlantic Virginia* how Native trade routes and other spaces worked in tandem with ocean navigation to inform English understandings of North American political geographies. Scholars like Philip Levy point out that Native roads and paths informed travel customs and strategies across the southeast during the colonial period, and others like James Rice and Kristalyn Shefveland have added that the formation of Virginia's settlement, politics, trade, and the accrual of wealth and status on the part of the first families of Virginia were built on Native diplomacy and trade. Levy, *Fellow Travelers: Indians and Europeans Contesting the Early American Trail* (Gainesville: University Press of Florida, 2007); Rice, *Nature and History in the Potomac Country: From Hunter-Gatherers to the Age of Jefferson* (Baltimore: Johns Hopkins University Press, 2009), 255; Shefveland, *Anglo-Native Virginia: Trade, Conversion, and Indian Slavery in the Old Dominion, 1646–1722* (Athens: University of Georgia Press, 2016); April Hatfield, *Atlantic Virginia: Intercolonial Relations in the Seventeenth Century* (Philadelphia: University of Pennsylvania Press, 2007), 24. Also see April Hatfield, "Spanish Colonization Literature, Powhatan Geographies, and English Perceptions of Tsenacommacah/Virginia," *Journal of Southern History* 69, no. 2 (2003): 245–82. For local border negotiations, see Alan K. Henrikson, "Facing across Borders: The Diplomacy of Bon Voisinage," *International Political Science Review* 21, no. 2 (2000): 121–47, and Brooks, *Our Beloved Kin.*

10. See Kevin Dawson, *Undercurrents of Power: Aquatic Culture in the African Diaspora* (Philadelphia: University of Pennsylvania Press, 2018), 2.

11. Allan Greer outlines frameworks for a broad range of Indigenous and European conceptions of property and territory in *Property and Dispossession: Natives, Empires and Land in Early Modern North America* (Cambridge: Cambridge University Press, 2018), 10, 18–19. See also Étienne Balibar, *Politics and the Other Scene* (New York: Verso, 2002), 75, and James Wesley Scott, "Borders, Border Studies and EU Enlargement," in

The Ashgate Research Companion to Border Studies, ed. Doris Wastl-Walter (New York: Routledge, 2011), 133. Readers will not find the word "frontier" very often in this book. As many historians have noted, the term is fraught and value-laden for readers familiar with and directly affected by narratives of westward colonial and US expansion central to US identity. Despite the work of historians emphasizing Native power and fluidity and opportunity on the frontier, the term evokes for our students images of violence, rugged white adventurers, and, on a map, a hard and constantly westward-moving line between Europeans and Indigenous people. Many colonial officials would have liked their superiors and constituents to believe that there was, in fact, a drawable line between English and Native people. Most importantly for our students and for the public, however, that image changes very little regardless of time and space. I have argued elsewhere that the nineteenth-century image of the seventeenth-century Virginia Cavalier, for example, is only Daniel Boone in pantaloons. In this particular study, the term "frontier" is geographically unspecific as well. For example, where is the line between English and Powhatan people in 1622 versus in 1623, after the Powhatan attack? What do we make of Eastern Shore Algonquians who could not be "driven west"? See Jessica Taylor, "Bully! Said Bacon: Seventeenth-Century History, Nineteenth-Century Masculinity, and Literature about Bacon's Rebellion," *Virginia Magazine of History and Biography* 130, no. 1 (2022): 2–37.

12. Philip Levy, "'A New Look at an Old Wall': Indians, Englishmen, Landscape, and the 1634 Palisade at Middle Plantation," *Virginia Magazine of History and Biography* 112, no. 3 (2004): 229.

13. Peter Sahlins noted that unlike precise national borders of modern nation-states, early modern European monarchs defined borders through their jurisdiction over the subjects inside of them, a concept that, when considered in terms of influence rather than total authority, applies in some respects to the Powhatan chiefdom. Sahlins, *Boundaries: The Making of France and Spain in the Pyrenees* (Oakland: University of California Press, 1991), 8.

14. Balibar, *Politics and the Other Scene*, 78.

15. Pekka Hämäläinen and Samuel Truett, "On Borderlands," *Journal of American History* 98, no. 2 (September 2011): 359. Hämäläinen and Truett argue here and elsewhere that a push past local or microhistory is necessary to create new conceptual frameworks rather than "punch holes" in the master narrative.

16. Histories of colonial Virginia demonstrate that Native labor and politics, but also English interest in Native land, played a key role in the origins of southern plantation systems and racial categories. Edmund S. Morgan's

classic *American Slavery, American Freedom* charted the slow shift toward African slavery through planters' efforts to exterminate Algonquians and usurp their land, then to be worked by English servants and enslaved Africans. After the land formally or violently changed hands, however, Native people largely disappeared from the story. Morgan pointed to the aftermath of one particularly seminal event in seventeenth-century Chesapeake history—Bacon's Rebellion, featuring marches against Native people—as the moment that elite "engrossers" of their land, fearing an underclass united against them, worked "to separate dangerous free whites from dangerous slave blacks by a screen of racial contempt." Morgan, *American Slavery, American Freedom: The Ordeal of Colonial Virginia*, 2nd ed. (1975; New York: Norton, 2003), 328. Kathleen M. Brown added in *Good Wives, Nasty Wenches, and Anxious Patriarchs* that lack of traditional markers of English manhood like landholding, wives, and legal freedom led to unrest, the result being reinforced race and gender hierarchies. Brown, *Good Wives, Nasty Wenches, and Anxious Patriarchs: Gender, Race, and Power in Colonial Virginia* (Chapel Hill: University of North Carolina Press, 1996), 139–40. But as the history of race unfurls, narratives like Bacon's Rebellion and the following ascendancy of the plantation system often crowd out ongoing Native histories beyond large-scale acts of violence or treaty-making, even as the histories of Native lands and plantations remain tied together. Additionally, Anthony Parent's *Foul Means* asserts that an elite group of seventeenth- and eighteenth-century planters consciously grabbed Native land and substituted enslaved Africans for white servants, particularly through the headright system that gave them fifty acres of land for every African imported. I heartily agree that a small group of men acted antisocially and in their own interests—and I discuss some of those same men, like William Claiborne, Edward Hill, and John Washington. However, I emphasize that, as they ratcheted up bills for the forts on the fall line and militia gatherings against the Native people they displaced, these men actively acted against the interests of the colony as they forced its boundaries outward. Parent, *Foul Means: The Formation of a Slave Society in Virginia, 1690–1740* (Chapel Hill: University of North Carolina Press, 2003).

17. Most recently, Matthew Kruer's study of the Susquehannocks, *Time of Anarchy*, demonstrates how Native people, even those operating from a place of weakened political and martial power, inflamed conflicts in multiple North American colonies with brittle colonial structures. He also emphasizes that local arrangements often determined power dynamics among elites, their lessers, and Native people more so than colony government.

Kruer, *Time of Anarchy: Indigenous Power and the Crisis of Colonialism in Early America* (Cambridge, MA: Harvard University Press, 2021). Paul Musselwhite describes the variety of political-economic visions apparent in seventeenth-century Chesapeake plantation structures in "Naming Plantations: Toponyms and the Construction of the Plantation System in the English Atlantic," *Journal of Social History* 54, no. 3 (Spring 2021): 741–74.

18. Sahlins, *Boundaries*, 8; Karen Kupperman, *The Jamestown Project* (Cambridge, MA: Belknap Press of Harvard University Press, 2009), 43; Juliana Barr and Edward Countryman, "Introduction: Maps and Spaces, Paths to Connect, and Lines to Divide," in *Contested Spaces of Early America*, ed. Juliana Barr and Edward Countryman (Philadelphia: University of Pennsylvania Press, 2014), 4–8; Ethan Schmidt, *The Divided Dominion: Social Conflict and Indian Hatred in Early Virginia* (Boulder: University Press of Colorado, 2014). On the "many sides" to Anglo-Native conflict, see chapter 3 of this book and James D. Rice, "'These Doubtfull Times, between Us and the Indians': Indigenous Politics and the Jamestown Colony in 1619," in *Virginia 1619: Slavery and Freedom in the Making of English America*, ed. Paul Musselwhite, Peter C. Mancall, and James Horn (Chapel Hill: University of North Carolina Press, 2019), 215–35.

19. After English settlers violently asserted still-developing conceptualizations, and messy execution, of surveying and local government, Native people debated the meaning of land ownership and strategized ways to assert territoriality in new colonial contexts. Literature about "indigenous cartographies" emphasizes functional and mutually enforcing records of territory and history. As Allan Greer and Ian Saxine have demonstrated, Native individuals and groups incorporated the implications of land titles and chains of ownership as they asserted their own conceptions of space. Greer, *Property and Dispossession*; Saxine, *Properties of Empire: Indians, Colonists, and Land Speculators on the New England Frontier* (New York: NYU Press, 2019); Andy Doolen, "Claiming Indigenous Space: John Dunn Hunter and the Fredonian Rebellion," *Early American Literature* 53, no. 3 (2018): 689; Juliana Barr, "Geographies of Power: Mapping Indian Borders in the 'Borderlands' of the Early Southwest," *William and Mary Quarterly*, 3rd series, 68, no. 1 (January 2011): 8.

20. Stephanie Camp, *Closer to Freedom: Enslaved Women and Everyday Resistance in the Plantation South* (Chapel Hill: University of North Carolina Press, 2004), xviii. Daniel O. Sayer's archaeological study of marronage in the Great Dismal Swamp on the border between Virginia and North Carolina also explores how self-emancipated Africans built societies in the

interior of the swamp by taking advantage of the plantation system's "spatial and socio-economic blind spots and margins." Sayers, *A Desolate Place for a Defiant People: The Archaeology of Maroons, Indigenous Americans, and Enslaved Laborers in the Great Dismal Swamp* (Gainesville: University Press of Florida, 2014), 2–3; Rinaldo Walcott, "The Black Aquatic," *liquid blackness* 5, no. 1 (2021): 63–73.
21. Tiffany Lethabo King, *The Black Shoals: Offshore Formations of Black and Native Studies* (Durham, NC: Duke University Press, 2019); Justin P. Dunnavant, "Have Confidence in the Sea: Maritime Maroons and Fugitive Geographies," *Antipode* 53, no. 3 (2021): 884–905.
22. James D. Rice's "Bacon's Rebellion in Indian Country" and Matthew Kruer's "Bloody Minds and Peoples Undone" demonstrate that the actions of Native people, not just their land or presence on the periphery, explain key turning points in Virginia history. Rice, "Bacon's Rebellion in Indian Country," *Journal of American History* 101, no. 3 (December 2014): 726–50; Kruer, "Bloody Minds and Peoples Undone: Emotion, Family, and Political Order in the Susquehannock-Virginia War," *William and Mary Quarterly*, 3rd series, 74, no. 3 (July 2017): 401–36. See also James D. Rice, *Tales from a Revolution: Bacon's Rebellion and the Transformation of Early America* (New York: Oxford University Press, 2012). From a Chesapeake Native point of view, the turbulence and drama prior to the Treaty of Middle Plantation were no historical watershed and did little to resolve preexisting tensions over land and violence. My work is a response to Rice's and Kruer's calls to move the focus away from Jamestown, using literal movement between places and both well-trodden and overlooked conflicts over borders of all types.

1. THE MOVING PEOPLE AND PLACES OF THE POWHATAN CHIEFDOM

1. Helen C. Rountree, *Pocahontas, Powhatan, Opechancanough: Three Indian Lives Changed by Jamestown* (Charlottesville: University of Virginia Press, 2005), 12; William Strachey, "The Historie of Travell into Virginia Britania," in *Captain John Smith: Writings with Other Narratives of Roanoke, Jamestown, and the First English Settlement of America*, ed. James Horn (New York: Library of America, 2007), 1053.
2. See Greer, *Property and Dispossession*, 306–8.
3. See especially James D. Rice, "War and Politics: Powhatan Expansionism and the Problem of Native American Warfare," *William and Mary Quarterly*, 3rd series, 77, no. 1 (January 2020): 3–32. For more on Powhatan warfare, see Frederic Gleach, *Powhatan's World and Colonial Virginia: A Conflict of Cultures* (Lincoln: University of Nebraska Press, 1997);

Margaret Holmes Williamson, *Powhatan Lords of Life and Death: Command and Consent in Seventeenth-Century Virginia* (Lincoln: University of Nebraska Press, 2003); and J. Frederick Fausz, "An 'Abundance of Blood Shed on Both Sides': England's First Indian War, 1609–1614," *Virginia Magazine of History and Biography* 98, no. 1 (January 1990): 3–56.

4. This vignette is derived from the archaeological assemblage associated with the Hatch site, which was occupied at least until 1450. Leverette B. Gregory, "The Hatch Site: A Preliminary Report (Prince George County, Virginia)," *Archaeological Society of Virginia* 34, no. 4 (1979): 239; Douglas Makin, "Zone-Decorated Pots at the Hatch Site (44PG51): A Late Woodland Manifestation of an Ancient Tradition," MA thesis, College of William and Mary, 2019, http://dx.doi.org/10.21220/s2-mcpc-s920. I owe a great debt to the burgeoning field of landscape archaeology, and in particular the collaborative and systematic study of Indigenous cultural landscapes across the Chesapeake. These archaeologists explore colonial-era sources for ethnographic information, primarily surrounding watersheds, to examine economic and social practices as evidence of "place-making" and "acts of dwelling." My work builds on these archaeologists' central point that the meaning of particular places and community identities are constructed at specific historical moments based on environmental resource use. Flick and King, "'We Can Fly No Farther,'" 21. Also note that Algonquians in the Chesapeake observed five seasons, so these are approximations here.

5. Gallivan, *Powhatan Landscape*, 93.

6. Madeleine Gunter Bassett, Christopher M. Stevenson, and Laure Dussubleux, "Re-Examining the Trade Network in Late Woodland Virginia (900–1600 CE): An LA-ICP-MS Analysis of Copper Artifacts," *Journal of Archaeological Science* 27, no. 2 (2019): 10; Helen C. Rountree and E. Randolph Turner III, *Before and after Jamestown: Virginia's Powhatans and Their Predecessors* (Gainesville: University Press of Florida, 2002), 26.

7. Helen C. Rountree, *The Powhatan Indians of Virginia: Their Traditional Culture* (Norman: University of Oklahoma Press, 1989), 56–57.

8. Scott M. Strickland, Julia M. King, and Martha McCartney, *Defining the Greater York River Indigenous Cultural Landscape* (St. Mary's City: St. Mary's College of Maryland, 2019), 24–25.

9. Strickland, King, and McCartney, *Defining the Greater York River Indigenous Cultural Landscape*, 110. See also E. Randolph Turner III, "An Archaeological and Ethnohistorical Study on the Evolution of Rank Societies in the Virginia Coastal Plain," PhD diss., Pennsylvania State University, 1976.

10. Gallivan, *Powhatan Landscape*, 76.

11. Strickland, King, and McCartney, *Defining the Greater York River Indigenous Cultural Landscape*, 26.
12. Gallivan, *The Powhatan Landscape*, 132–33.
13. Although this was true on the York River, archaeologists also note a dispersal of settlement around the same time on the Potomac River, between 900 and 1300 CE. See Potter, *Commoners, Tribute, and Chiefs*, 142.
14. Helen C. Rountree and E. Randolph Turner III, "On the Fringe of the Southeast: The Powhatan Paramount Chiefdom of Virginia," in *The Forgotten Centuries: Indians and Europeans in the American South, 1521–1704*, ed. Carmen Chaves Chesser and Charles M. Hudson (Athens: University of Georgia Press, 1994), 362.
15. Strickland, King, and McCartney, *Defining the Greater York River Indigenous Cultural Landscape*, 31.
16. Martin Gallivan, *James River Chiefdoms: The Rise of Social Inequality in the Chesapeake* (Lincoln: University of Nebraska Press, 2003), 154, 171.
17. Potter, *Commoners, Tribute, and Chiefs*, 16–17.
18. Gallivan, *James River Chiefdoms*, 174. As chiefdoms on the James River rose "through their association with palisade construction, elite mortuary ritual, and communal feasting, certain towns in the Chesapeake became places of chiefly authority." Gallivan, "Powhatan's Werowocomoco," 87.
19. "Virginia" (Kraus Map), c. 1610.
20. Barbour, "The Earliest Reconnaissance of the Chesapeake Bay Area," 287; William Wallace Tooker, "Meaning of Some Indian Names in Virginia," *William and Mary Quarterly*, 3rd series, 14, no. 1 (July 1905): 63. Edward Ragan discusses the importance of place-names in "Where the Water Ebbs and Flows: Place and Self among the Rappahannock People," PhD diss., Syracuse University, 2005. The author thanks Ragan for his crucial suggestion of incorporating Keith Basso's *Wisdom Sits in Places: Landscape and Language among the Western Apache* (Albuquerque: University of New Mexico Press, 1996), esp. 34, one of the first studies to tie "knowledge of place" with "knowledge of the self" and community.
21. "A Letter from Mr. John Clayton Rector of Crofton at Wakefield in Yorkshire, to the Royal Society, May 12, 1688. Giving an Account of Several Observables in Virginia, and in His Voyage Thither, More Particularly Concerning the Air," in *Tracts and Other Papers Relating Principally to the Origin, Settlement, and Progress of the Colonies in North America*, ed. Peter Force (Washington, DC: Clerk's Office of the District Court of Columbia, 1836–46), 3:11.
22. Arthur Barlowe, "The First Voyage to Roanoke. 1584. The First Voyage Made to the Coasts of America, with Two Barks, Wherein Were Captains

M. Philip Amadas and M. Arthur Barlowe, Who Discovered Part of the Countrey Now Called Virginia, Anno 1584. Written by One of the Said Captaines, and Sent to Sir Walter Ralegh, Knight, at Whose Charge and Direction, the Said Voyage Was Set Forth," in *Old South Leaflets No. 92* (Boston: Directors of the Old South Work, 1898), 3; John Smith, "The Generall Historie of Virginia, New-England, and the Summer Isles" (1624), in *The Complete Works of Captain John Smith, 1580–1631*, ed. Philip L. Barbour (Chapel Hill: University of North Carolina Press, 1986), 2:117.

23. Helen Hornbeck Tanner, "The Land and Water Communication Systems of the Southeastern Indians," in Waselkov, Wood, and Hatley, eds., *Powhatan's Mantle*, 27–28; C. G. Holland, "The Kiskiak/Chiskiak Path," *Archaeological Society of Virginia Quarterly Bulletin* 39, no. 3 (September 1984): 171.

24. George Percy, "Observations Gathered Out of a Discourse of the Plantation of the Southerne Colonie in Virginia by the English, 1606," in Horn, ed., *Captain John Smith*, 928–29; John Smith, "A True Relation of Such Occurrences and Accidents of Noate as Hath Hapned in Virginia" (1608), in Barbour, ed., *Complete Works of Captain John Smith*, 1:73.

25. Clarence W. Alvord and Lee Bidgood, *The First Explorations of the Trans-Allegheny Region by the Virginians, 1650–1674* (Cleveland: Arthur H. Clark, 1912), 209–26; Alan Vance Briceland, *Westward from Virginia: The Exploration of the Virginia-Carolina Border* (Charlottesville: University Press of Virginia, 1987), 169.

26. Smith, "The Generall Historie," 2:155.

27. Henry Spelman, *Relation of Virginia* (London: Chiswick Press, 1872), 43–46. The werowance of the Patawomecks is never named in this account.

28. Stephen Warren, *The Worlds the Shawnees Made: Migration and Violence in Early America* (Chapel Hill: University of North Carolina Press, 2014), 81.

29. Gleach, *Powhatan's World and Colonial Virginia*, 52.

30. Helen Rountree, "Powhatan Indian Women: The People Captain John Smith Barely Saw," *Ethnohistory* 45, no. 1 (Winter 1998): 11–13.

31. E. Randolph Turner III, "An Intertribal Deer Exploitation Buffer Zone for the Virginia Coastal Plain-Piedmont Regions," *Archaeological Society of Virginia Quarterly Bulletin* 32, no. 3 (1978): 42–48.

32. Spelman, *Relation of Virginia*, 54–55. Contrasting the English experience of warfare in "open fields," captive Henry Spelman referred to the ground for a battle between Algonquians and northern Native people as "ther place," perhaps a reference to consciously chosen or familiar "marish ground full of Reede."

33. Smith, "The Generall Historie," 2:118.

34. Rountree and Turner, *Before and after Jamestown*, 34; Strickland, King, and McCartney, *Defining the Greater York River Indigenous Cultural Landscape*, 78; John Smith, "A Map of Virginia. With a Description of the Countrey, the Commodities, People, Government and Religion" (1612), in Barbour, ed., *Complete Works of Captain John Smith*, 1:171.
35. Williamson, *Powhatan Lords of Life and Death*, 189–90.
36. Gallivan, *The Powhatan Landscape*, 213. Potter, *Commoners, Tribute, and Chiefs*, 154.
37. Strachey, "The Historie of Travell into Virginia Britania," 1042.
38. See Daniel K. Richter, "Tsenacommacah and the Atlantic World," in *The Atlantic World and Virginia, 1550–1624*, ed. Peter C. Mancall (Chapel Hill: University of North Carolina Press, 2007), 29–65.
39. Smith, "The Generall Historie," 2:127.
40. Potter, "Early English Effects on Virginia Algonquian Exchange and Tribute in the Tidewater Potomac," 215.
41. Jeffrey L. Hantman, *Monacan Millennium: A Collaborative Archaeology and History of a Virginia Indian People* (Charlottesville: University of Virginia Press, 2018), 77–107.
42. Emporer of Piscataway, Memorandum, n.d., in *Archives of Maryland*, ed. William Hand Browne et al. (Baltimore: Maryland Historical Society, 1883–1937), 3:402–3; Scott Strickland, Virginia R. Busby, and Julia A. King, "Indigenous Cultural Landscapes Study for the Nanjemoy and Mattawoman Creek Watersheds," St. Mary's College of Maryland, November 2015, 15–17. See also Paul Cissna, "The Piscataway Indians of Southern Maryland: An Ethnohistory from Pre-European Contact to the Present," PhD diss., American University, 1986.
43. Rountree and Turner, *Before and after Jamestown*, 363; Jeffrey L. Hantman and Debra L. Gold argue that this territoriality continues into the colonial period across the mid-Atlantic region in "The Woodland in the Middle Atlantic," in *The Woodland Southeast*, ed. David G. Anderson and Robert C. Mainfort (Tuscaloosa: University of Alabama Press, 2002), 275.
44. Vincas P. Steponaitis, "Contrasting Patterns of Mississippian Development," in *Chiefdoms: Power, Economy, and Ideology*, ed. Timothy K. Earle (Cambridge: Cambridge University Press, 1991), 202–3. Steponaitis also noted declines in long-term exchange in his study area in modern-day Mississippi and Alabama sites called Moundville and Pocahontas around the beginning of the sixteenth century corresponding with the decline in those chiefdoms, a disruption that would have been noticed by trading partners.
45. Dennis B. Blanton, "Drought as a Factor in the Jamestown Colony, 1607–1612," *Historical Archaeology* 34, no. 4 (2000): 76; Clifford M. Lewis

and Albert J. Loomie, *The Spanish Jesuit Mission in Virginia* (Chapel Hill: University of North Carolina Press, 1953), 46, 62–63.

46. There is some debate about the effects of disease on Algonquians in the Coastal Plain. Wahunsenacawh told John Smith that he had seen the death of his people three times, which some historians have interpreted as a reference to epidemics. But Helen Rountree contended that this was a reference to his age. The famine in the Chesapeake was mentioned by Jesuit missionary Luis de Quiros in a 1570 letter. See Potter, *Commoners, Tribute, and Chiefs,* 166, and Rountree, *Pocahontas's People,* 25.

47. Although their origin is unclear, the Massawomecks were also a major outside force in the late sixteenth century. James F. Pendergast, "The Massawomeck: Raiders and Traders into the Chesapeake Bay in the Seventeenth Century," *Transactions of the American Philosophical Society* 81, no. 2 (1991): 6, 37.

48. John Smith's 1612 map suggests that they came from a large body of water, leading historians to postulate that they arrived annually from the Great Lakes region. See Wayne E. Clark and Helen C. Rountree, "The Powhatans and the Maryland Mainland," in *Powhatan Foreign Relations, 1500–1722,* ed. Helen C. Rountree (Charlottesville: University Press of Virginia, 1993), 112–35.

49. Rice, *Nature and History,* 49.

50. Potter, *Commoners, Tribute, and Chiefs,* 160; Rice, *Nature and History,* 52–56; Don Pedro de Zúñiga, Map of Virginia, before September 15, 1608, Archivo General de Simancas, Valladolid, Spain. Similarly, when the Powhatans captured John Smith in 1607, they made a special trip overland across the Middle Peninsula to the Rappahannock peoples, who had heard that Smith was a European man responsible for the deaths of some Rappahannocks three years prior. Rather than meting out judgment himself, Wahunsenacawh demonstrated both respect for the Rappahannocks' sovereignty and the power to bring them desired information and a captive. Kupperman, *Jamestown Project,* 106–7.

51. Rountree, *Pocahontas, Powhatan, Opechancanough,* 45.

52. Strachey, "The Historie of Travell into Virginia Britania," 1053.

53. On Indigenous territoriality, see Pekka Hämäläinen, "The Shapes of Power: Indians, Europeans, and North American Worlds from the Seventeenth to the Nineteenth Century," in Barr and Countryman, eds., *Contested Spaces of Early America,* 35.

54. Tanner, "The Land and Water Communication Systems of the Southeastern Indians," 28; Smith, "A Map of Virginia," 1:174.

55. See Joshua A. Piker, "White and Clean and Contested: Creek Towns and Trading Paths in the Aftermath of the Seven Years' War," *Ethnohistory* 50, no. 2 (Spring 2003): 321.
56. Rountree, *Pocahontas, Powhatan, Opechancanough*, 43.
57. Helen C. Rountree and Thomas E. Davidson, *Eastern Shore Indians of Virginia and Maryland* (Charlottesville: University of Virginia Press, 1997), 9–14, 45. John Pory wrote in 1621 that the Eastern Shore Algonquians farmed more intensely than did western shore people and held a store of about six months' worth of corn. Quoted in Rountree and Davidson, *Eastern Shore Indians of Virginia and Maryland*, 16.
58. Strachey, "The Historie of Travell into Virginia Britania," 1076.
59. Smith, "The Generall Historie," 2:122.
60. Helen Rountree, "The Powhatans and Other Woodland Indians as Travelers," in Rountree, ed., *Powhatan Foreign Relations*, 81; E. Randolph Turner III, "Native American Protohistoric Interactions in the Powhatan Core Area," in Rountree, ed., *Powhatan Foreign Relations*, 81.
61. Ethan A. Schmidt, "The Right to Violence: Customary Rights, Moral Economy, and Ethnic Conflict in Seventeenth-Century Virginia," PhD diss., University of Kansas, 2007, 97.
62. Lewis R. Binford, "An Ethnohistory of the Nottoway, Meherrin and Weanock Indians of Southeastern Virginia," *Ethnohistory* 14, nos. 3–4 (Summer–Autumn 1967): 137. Helen C. Rountree evaluated and agreed with his conclusions about the early period in "The Termination and Dispersal of the Nottoway Indians of Virginia," *Virginia Magazine of History and Biography* 95, no. 2 (April 1987): 193–214.
63. Smith, "The Generall Historie," 2:119. The Powhatans told the English that the Monacan were "very barbarous" and came "downe at the fall of the leafe and invaded his Countrye." The quote about invasion is from Navirans's interview in Gabriel Archer, "A Relatyon of the Discovery of Our River," in Horn, ed., *Captain John Smith*, 940.
64. Potter, *Commoners, Tribute, and Chiefs*, 158.
65. Gallivan, *James River Chiefdoms*. See appendix A for site summaries.
66. Richter, "Tsenacommacah and the Atlantic World," 38–39; Jeffrey L. Hantman, "Between Powhatan and Quirank: Reconstructing Monacan Culture and History in the Context of Jamestown," *American Anthropologist*, new series, 92, no. 3 (1990): 685.
67. Hantman, *Monacan Millennium*, 115–22.
68. Smith, "The Generall Historie," 2:175–76.
69. Rountree and Davidson, *Eastern Shore Indians of Virginia and Maryland*, 45.

70. Potter, *Commoners, Tribute, and Chiefs*, 164.
71. As April Hatfield has noted, "Because Powhatan's geographical position allowed him to exercise control over the exchange of copper and shell beads between the coastal and mountain regions, it provided economic advantages that likely enabled him to create Tsenacommacah." Hatfield, *Atlantic Virginia*, 14–15.
72. Gregory Waselkov counted and discussed six early maps of the southern United States in his chapter "Indian Maps of the Colonial Southeast," in Waselkov, Wood, and Hatley, eds., *Powhatan's Mantle*, 435–502.
73. Historians and archaeologists disagree about the importance of the animals and the significance of the number of circles, since Strachey only listed twenty-four greater and lesser werowances in his description of the Powhatan chiefdom. Waselkov, "Indian Maps," 457.
74. Williamson, *Powhatan Lords of Life and Death*, 247.

2. WATCHING CAREFULLY IN THE BAY

1. Strachey, "The Historie of Travell into Virginia Britania," 1082–83.
2. Ralph Hamor, "A True Discourse of the Present State of Virginia, and the Successe of the Affaires There Till the 18 of June 1614," in Horn, ed., *Captain John Smith*, 1121.
3. Smith, "The Generall Historie," 2:243.
4. Ibid., 2:243; Hamor, "A True Discourse of the Present State of Virginia," 1121.
5. Smith, "The Generall Historie," 2:243. See also Camilla Townsend, *Pocahontas and the Powhatan Dilemma: An American Portrait* (New York: Hill and Wang, 2004), 100–106.
6. Jean B. Russo and J. Elliott Russo, *Planting an Empire: The Early Chesapeake in British North America* (Baltimore: Johns Hopkins University Press, 2012), 30.
7. Laura Benton, *The Search for Sovereignty: Law and Geography in European Empires, 1400–1900* (Cambridge: Cambridge University Press, 2010), 57–59. In her chapter "Treacherous Places," Benton envisions European possession of land in the New World through "corridors" of control. In this particular case, however, the Powhatans' well-being and political authority were also vested in maintaining control of the river system, and during this period the English never came close to control over the waterways. The term "nodes," as they are represented on this chapter's map, might be a more appropriate characterization.
8. Kupperman, *Jamestown Project*, 43. Kupperman's argument in the *Jamestown Project* that the initial years of English colonization in the Chesapeake

involved the accumulation of knowledge about Native people and the landscape is crucial to this work, as is her earlier grounding in the reality that Native people "set the agenda for encounters" and that the English documented Native people as precisely as possible as Native people guarded that knowledge. Karen Ordahl Kupperman, *Indians and English: Facing Off in Early America* (Ithaca, NY: Cornell University Press, 2000), 14, 79, 86. This chapter builds on Kupperman's work, particularly the emphasis on diverse visions for the future in *Indians and English,* to emphasize dissonance between individuals from disparate classes of English colonists and individuals from different Algonquians as a central factor driving movement around the bay. It also echoes James D. Rice's conclusions about the year 1619, "There were never 'two sides' to the story but rather multiple sides with competing agendas and alternative strategies for navigating such 'doubtfull times.'" Rice, "'These Doubtfull Times,'" 216. While this work concerns encounters in the Chesapeake, English people and Algonquians learned about each other in contexts beyond the Chesapeake and communicated that information to their leaders. See Jace Weaver, *The Red Atlantic: American Indigenes and the Making of the Modern World* (Chapel Hill: University of North Carolina Press, 2017), chapter 3, and Alden T. Vaughan, *Transatlantic Encounters: American Indians in Britain, 1500–1776* (Cambridge: Cambridge University Press, 2006).

9. As in the previous chapter, and James Rice's "War and Politics," much longer and geographically broader geopolitical contexts and insecurities drew the English and Algonquians into conflict with one another. Ken MacMillan explains the role of mapping Native places to prove "effective occupation" and a "symbiotic relationship" with Native people in the larger struggle of the English crown to ensure broader European recognition of English claims to the North American content in *Sovereignty and Possession in the English New World: The Legal Foundations of Empire, 1576–1640* (Cambridge: Cambridge University Press, 2006), 169. Daniel K. Richter expresses how climate change created similar collapses of large polities in Europe and North America during the centuries preceding contact, and how during contact both Europeans and Native people saw themselves as connected both locally and continentally, in Richter, *Before the Revolution: America's Ancient Pasts* (Cambridge, MA: Belknap Press of Harvard University Press, 2013).

10. Fausz, "An 'Abundance of Blood Shed on Both Sides,'" 18. Fausz argued that the titular timeframe was marked by high-stakes, sustained warfare over the threat that English leadership's hostility toward Native people and appropriation of their food stores posed to Powhatan sovereignty. I

do not dispute the term "First Anglo-Powhatan War" or Fausz's argument that better leadership and appropriation of Native corn gave colonists an edge, but I do argue here that a focus on "Anglo" and "Native" sides of a war obscures the importance of the actions of people beyond Powhatan and English leadership in escalating tensions.

11. See Schmidt, "The Right to Violence," chapter 4, and Seth Mallios, *The Deadly Politics of Giving: Exchange and Violence at Ajacan, Roanoke, and Jamestown* (Tuscaloosa: University of Alabama Press, 2006), chapter 5.
12. Karen Ordahl Kupperman, *Jamestown Project*, 8. James Horn, *Adapting to a New World: English Society in the Seventeenth-Century Chesapeake* (Chapel Hill: University of North Carolina Press, 1994), 2.
13. For more on Roanoke, see Karen Ordahl Kupperman, *Roanoke: The Abandoned Colony,* 2nd ed. (1984; Lanham, MD: Rowman and Littlefield, 2007), and James Horn, *A Kingdom Strange: The Brief and Tragic History of the Lost Colony of Roanoke* (New York: Basic Books, 2010).
14. Smith, "The Generall Historie," 2:138; Percy, "Observations Gathered Out of a Discourse," 924.
15. Smith, "The Generall Historie," 2:102.
16. George Percy, "Observations by Master George Percy" (1607), in *Narratives of Early Virginia, 1606-1625,* ed. Lyon Gardiner Tyler (New York: Charles Scribners Sons, 1907), 19.
17. See Barbour, ed., *Complete Works of Captain John Smith,* vol. 1, and Kupperman, *Jamestown Project.*
18. Hatfield, "Spanish Colonization Literature," 246.
19. Benton, *The Search for Sovereignty,* 42; Hatfield, "Spanish Colonization Literature," 246–48; Hatfield, *Atlantic Virginia,* 3; Richter, *Before the Revolution,* 111. See also Peter C. Mancall, *Hakluyt's Promise: An Elizabethan's Obsession for an English America* (New Haven, CT: Yale University Press, 2010). For more on the Spanish and English exchange of ideas and intelligence, see J. H. Elliott, *Empires of the Atlantic World: Britain and Spain in America, 1492–1830* (New Haven, CT: Yale University Press, 2007), and Greer, *Property and Dispossession,* 282, 320.
20. Virginia Council, "Instruccons Orders and Constitucons to Sir Thomas Gates Knight Governor of Virginia," May 1609, in *The Records of the Virginia Company of London,* ed. Susan Myra Kingsbury (Washington, DC: Government Printing Office, 1906–35), 3:19.
21. Ibid., 3:16.
22. James Horn, "The Conquest of Eden: Possession and Dominion in Early Virginia," in *Envisioning an English Empire: Jamestown and the Making of the North Atlantic World,* ed. Robert Appelbaum and John Wood Sweet

(Philadelphia: University of Pennsylvania Press, 2005), 33; Lisa Blansett, "John Smith Maps Virginia: Knowledge, Rhetoric, and Politics," in Appelbaum and Sweet, eds., *Envisioning an English Empire*, 78; Lesley B. Cormack, *Charting an Empire: Geography at the English Universities, 1580–1620* (Chicago: University of Chicago Press, 1997).

23. John Speed, *The Theatre of the Empire of Great Britaine: Presenting an Exact Geography of the Kingdomes of England, Scotland, Ireland* (London: William Hall, 1611), 139–40.

24. J. H. Andrews, *The Queen's Last Map-Maker: Richard Bartlett in Ireland, 1600–1603* (Dublin: Geography Publications, 2008), 9; Sir John Davies to the Earl of Salisbury, August 24, 1609, in *Cecil Papers in Hatfield House*, ed. G. Dyyfnallt Owen (London: Her Majesty's Stationary Office, 1970), 21:113–24.

25. Blansett, "John Smith Maps Virginia," 71; Smith, "A Map of Virginia," 1:174.

26. John Smith, "The Proceedings of the English Colonie in Virginia" (1606–12), in Barbour, ed., *Complete Works of Captain John Smith*, 1:215; Smith, "A True Relation of Such Occurrences and Accidents of Noate," 1:57. For more on spatial relations between Powhatan people, see Williamson, *Powhatan Lords of Life and Death*.

27. Michael Jarvis and Jeroen van Driel, "The Vingboons Chart of the James River, circa 1617," *William and Mary Quarterly*, 3rd series, 54, no. 2 (April 1997): 377–94. Thanks to Martha McCartney for the correction on the date of the Vingboons chart.

28. John Woodlife's 1637 renewal of his father's 1620 patent refers to "the Territorie of great Weyanoake neare the head land . . . W. upon the place where the pale rann." John Woodlife, 24 August 1637 patent, Land Office Patents Reel 1, No. 1, 467, Library of Virginia, Richmond. Please note that all patents before 1683 are transcripts of originals.

29. The Rickahock is mentioned primarily as a path, rather than a single place, running east–west in seventeenth-century land records. The Trucking Point is referenced at the mouth of a tributary leading to "old Pasbye Hayes" [Paspahegh], making it a likely point of contact between the English and their early allies. See Thomas Ellis, 24 August 1637 patent, Land Office Patents Reel 1, No. 1, 469. For an example of the Rickahock path, see Daniel Parke and Robert Bourne, 25 November 1658 patent, Land Office Patents Reel 4, No. 4, 334.

30. Robert Tindall, "Chart of King James River, Virginia, and the Entrance of Chesapeake Bay, drawn by Robert Tindall of Virginia," 1608, Western Manuscripts, Cotton MS, Augustus I, 46, British Library, London.

31. Don Pedro de Zúñiga, Map of Virginia. Jarvis and von Driel, 388.
32. Smith, "A True Relation of Such Occurrences and Accidents of Noate," 1:49.
33. Eric Klingelhofer, "Tudor Overseas Fortifications: A Review and Typology," in *First Forts: Essays on the Archaeology of Proto-Colonial Fortifications*, ed. Eric Klingelhofer (Leiden: Brill, 2010), 69.
34. Michael A. Palmer, *Command at Sea: Naval Command and Control since the Sixteenth Century* (Cambridge, MA: Harvard University Press, 2005), 38.
35. Klingelhofer, "Tudor Overseas Fortifications," 72.
36. For the Irish wars in an American context, see Eric Hinderaker and Peter C. Mancall, *At the Edge of Empire: The Backcountry in British North America* (Baltimore: Johns Hopkins University Press, 2003). Hinderaker and Mancall consider the forcible occupation of Ireland in the sixteenth century to be the first Western fringe and colony for the English. Archaeologist Audrey Horning considers interactions between Irish tenants and English colonizers alongside Powhatans and English colonizers in *Ireland in the Virginian Sea: Colonialism in the British Atlantic* (Chapel Hill: University of North Carolina Press, 2013).
37. Mancall, *Hakluyt's Promise*, 92, 183; Richard Hakluyt, *Divers Voyages Touching the Discoverie of America, and the Ilands Adjacent unto the Same, Made First of All by Our Englishmen, and Afterward by the Frenchmen and Britons* (London: Thomas Woodcocke, 1582); Richard Hakluyt, *The Principall Navigations, Voiages, and Discoveries of the English Nation* (London: George Bishop and Ralph Newberie, 1589).
38. Smith, "Generall Historie," 2:102.
39. Ibid., 2:165–66.
40. Smith, "A Map of Virginia," 1:146.
41. Archer, "A Relatyon of the Discovery of Our River," 936.
42. Ibid., 943.
43. Virginia Council, "Instruccons Orders and Constitucons to Sir Thomas Gates Knight Governor of Virginia," 3:16.
44. Archer, "A Relatyon of the Discovery of Our River," 936, 948; Rountree, *Pocahontas, Powhatan, Opechancanough*, 58–61.
45. James H. Merrell, "Cultural Continuity among the Piscataway Indians of Colonial Maryland," *William and Mary Quarterly*, 3rd series, 36, no. 4 (October 1979): 553; Rice, *Nature and History*, 73; Smith, "The Generall Historie," 2:141.
46. Rountree, *Pocahontas, Powhatan, Opechancanough*, 45, 111.
47. Hamor, "A True Discourse of the Present State of Virginia," 1151; Spelman, *Relation of Virginia*, 22, 26.

48. Daniel K. Richter comments extensively on the decline of the trade in prestige goods and the increase of dependence on European materials over time in *Facing East from Indian Country: A Native History of Early America* (Cambridge, MA: Harvard University Press, 2001), 39–62, and *Before the Revolution*, 114–26.
49. Michael B. Barber and Eugene B. Barfield, "Native Americans on the Virginia Frontier in the Seventeenth Century: Archaeological Investigations along the Interior Roanoke River Drainage," in *Diversity and Accommodation: Essays on the Cultural Composition of the Virginia Frontier*, ed. Michael J. Puglisi (Knoxville: University of Tennessee Press, 1997), 138.
50. In recent decades, archaeology at Jamestown Fort has shown that some disparaging rumors were actually true, including evidence of cannibalism. For historical perspectives on mortality and failure in the first few years of Jamestown, see Carville Earle's original environmental history "Environment, Disease, and Mortality in Early Virginia," in *The Chesapeake in the Seventeenth Century: Essays on Anglo-American Society*, ed. Thad W. Tate and David L. Ammerman (Chapel Hill: University of North Carolina Press, 1979), 95–125. Kupperman, *Jamestown Project*, and James Horn, *A Land as God Made It: Jamestown and the Birth of America* (New York: Basic Books, 2007), provide complementary accounts of the social, intellectual, and religious trends undergirding English expansion and the play-by-play of politics inside the company, respectively. Archaeologists of the Jamestown Rediscovery Project, who wrote many of the field reports referenced in this chapter, have also released their findings about the consumption of fellow colonists during the Starving Time in William Kelso et al., *Jane: Starvation, Cannibalism, and Endurance at Jamestown* (Williamsburg, VA: Colonial Williamsburg Foundation, 2013).
51. Blanton, "Drought as a Factor in the Jamestown Colony," 76.
52. Kupperman, *Pocahontas and the English Boys*, 3.
53. Gallivan, *James River Chiefdoms*. Working with both archaeologists and historians, anthropologist Helen Rountree engaged living history and comparative ethnography as well as more traditional ethnohistorical approaches to reconstruct the lives of Powhatan women. Rountree, "Powhatan Indian Women," 1–29. Increasingly other archaeologists have undertaken the pursuit of peoples marginalized by even the archaeological record, including those defined by long-distance migrations like the Susquehannock and the Shawnee. See Warren, *The Worlds the Shawnees Made*, and Martin Gallivan, "The Archaeology of Native Societies in the Chesapeake: New Investigations and Interpretations," *Journal of Archaeological Research* 19, no. 3 (September 2011): 281.

54. See Michael Leroy Oberg, *The Head in Edward Nugent's Hand: Roanoke's Forgotten Indians* (Philadelphia: University of Pennsylvania Press, 2010), and Helen C. Rountree, *Manteo's World: Native American Life in Carolina's Sound Country before and after the Lost Colony* (Chapel Hill: University of North Carolina Press, 2021).
55. Pendergast, "The Massawomeck," 13; Virginia Council, "Instruccons Orders and Constitucons to Sir Thomas Gates Knight Governor of Virginia," 3:19; Strachey, "The Historie of Travell into Virginia Britania," 1088.
56. John Smith and Gabriel Archer quoted in Kupperman, *Indians and English*, 60; Henry Spelman quoted in Rountree, "Powhatan Indian Women," 11.
57. Howard A. MacCord Sr., "The Indian Point Site, Stafford County, Virginia," *Archaeological Society of Virginia Quarterly Bulletin* 46, no. 3 (1991): 117–40.
58. Gregory, "The Hatch Site," 239–50.
59. Sir Thomas Dale, Report from Virginia, 25 May 1611, Papers of Robert Rich, Earl of Warwick (1607–24), MSS 9202, Albert and Shirley Small Special Collections Library, University of Virginia, Charlottesville.
60. Hamor, "A True Discourse of the Present State of Virginia," 1146.
61. Sir Thomas Dale, Report from Virginia, 25 May 1611, Papers of Robert Rich, Earl of Warwick.
62. Virginia Bernhard, "'Men, Women, and Children' at Jamestown: Population and Gender in Early Virginia, 1607–1610," *The Journal of Southern History* 58, no. 4 (November 1992): 606; Mallios, *The Deadly Politics of Giving*, 5; Martin H. Quitt, "Trade and Acculturation at Jamestown, 1607–1609: The Limits of Understanding," *William and Mary Quarterly*, 3rd series, 52, no. 2 (1995): 233, 244.
63. Horning, *Ireland in the Virginian Sea*, 298–301.
64. William M. Kelso and Beverly Straube, eds., *2000–2006 Interim Report on the APVA Excavations at Jamestown, Virginia* (Richmond: Association for the Preservation of Virginia Antiquities, 2008), 4, 7–8, 23, 47. Also see Rountree, "Powhatan Indian Women," 1–29.
65. Archaeological evidence also suggests that Englishmen and particularly Algonquian women sustained selective contact for almost a generation. Simple-stamped pottery, made and carried by Algonquian women, was not only found in James Fort features dating to the earliest years of settlement but also on outlying plantations as late as the second quarter of the seventeenth century. Luke J. Pecoraro and David M. Givens, "'Like to Perish from Want of Succor or Reliefe': The Provisioning of 17th-Century Virginia during Times of Change," *Post-Medieval Archaeology* 40, no. 2 (2006): 4; Rountree, *Pocahontas, Powhatan, Opechancanough*, 107.

66. Richter, *Before the Revolution*, 127.
67. William Strachey quoted in Alfred Cave, *Lethal Encounters: Englishmen and Indians in Colonial Virginia* (New York: Praeger, 2011), 82.
68. Smith, "The Proceedings of the English Colonie in Virginia," 1:215; Edmund Morgan, "The Labor Problem at Jamestown, 1607–1618," *American Historical Review* 76, no. 3 (June 1971): 606.
69. Smith, "The Proceedings of the English Colonie in Virginia," 1:215.
70. Ibid., 1:264.
71. Ibid., 1:240.
72. Percy, "Observations Gathered Out of a Discourse," 1100; Smith, "The Proceedings of the English Colonie in Virginia," 1:265.
73. Smith, "The Proceedings of the English Colonie in Virginia," 1:263, 265.
74. Smith, "The Proceedings of the English Colonie in Virginia," 1:250–56, 256 (quotation).
75. Smith, "A Map of Virginia," 1:150.
76. Thomas Harriot, *Narrative of the First Plantation of Virginia* (London: Bernard Quaritch, 1893), 36.
77. Smith, "The Generall Historie," 2:156.
78. Hamor, "A True Discourse of the Present State of Virginia," 1147. The centuries-long practice of bringing Native peoples to European courts is well documented. See Camilla Townsend, "Mutual Appraisals: The Shifting Paradigms of the English, Spanish, and Powhatans in Tsenacomoco, 1560–1622," in *Early Modern Virginia: Reconsidering the Old Dominion*, ed. Douglas Bradburn and John C. Coombs (Charlottesville: University of Virginia Press, 2011). On Namontack specifically, see the passage on the "Pocahontas Contingent" in Vaughan, *Transatlantic Encounters*, 46–52.
79. Smith, "The Generall Historie," 2:187. See also Alden T. Vaughan, "Namontack's Itinerant Life and Mysterious Death: Sources and Speculations," *Virginia Magazine of History and Biography* 126, no. 2 (2018): 170–209.
80. See also James H. Merrell, *Into the American Woods: Negotiators on the Pennsylvania Frontier* (New York: Norton, 1999); Kupperman, *Pocahontas and the English Boys*; and Celine Carayon, *Eloquence Embodied: Nonverbal Communication among French and Indigenous Peoples in the Americas* (Chapel Hill: University of North Carolina Press, 2019).
81. Kupperman, *Jamestown Project*, 234; Smith, "The Generall Historie," 2:193.
82. Spelman, *Relation of Virginia*, 16. Spelman also claimed that Smith was returned to England over this conflict because he had conspired with Wahunsenacawh to kill West, an idea that closely correlated in timing to

an attempt on West's men as they went upriver to trade in Smith's own account. Smith, "The Generall Historie," 2:232.
83. Spelman, *Relation of Virginia*, 11, 16–17; Rice, "War and Politics," 17.
84. Spelman, *Relation of Virginia*, 21–22. See also Karen Kupperman, *Pocahontas and the English Boys* (New York: NYU Press, 2019).
85. E. M. Rose, "Lord Delaware, First Governor of Virginia, 'the Poorest Baron of This Kingdom,'" *Virginia Magazine of History and Biography* 128, no. 3 (2020): 238, 253; Smith, "A True Relation of Such Occurrences and Accidents of Noate," 1:79; E. Randolph Turner III, Dumpling Island Archaeological Site, National Register of Historic Places No. 98000046 (1997), Suffolk, Virginia.
86. George Percy, "Trewe Relation," in Horn, ed., *Captain John Smith*, 1095.
87. Rountree, *Pocahontas, Powhatan, Opechancanough*, 145–49.
88. Strachey, "The Historie of Travell into Virginia Britania," 1051.
89. Percy, "Trewe Relation," 1102.
90. Kelso and Straube, eds., *2000–2006 Interim Report*, 32.
91. Smith quoted in Kupperman, *Jamestown Project*, 230.
92. William Strachey, "A True Reportory," in Horn, ed., *Captain John Smith*, 1020.
93. Strachey, "The Historie of Travell into Virginia Britania," 1046.
94. Rose, "Lord Delaware, First Governor of Virginia," 235; Percy, "Trewe Relation," 1104.
95. Lord de la Warr, "A Short Relation," in Horn, ed., *Captain John Smith*, 1171.
96. Kelso and Straube, eds., *2000–2006 Interim Report*, 22.
97. John Chamberlain to Sir Dudley Carleton, 9 July 1612, in *Calendar of State Papers, Colonial, America and West Indies, 1574–1739*, ed. W. Noel Sainsbury and J. W. Fortescue (London: Her Majesty's Stationary Office, 1860–96), 1:13–14.
98. Edward Maria Wingfield, "A Discourse of Virginia," in Horn, ed., *Captain John Smith*, 952–53.
99. Percy, "Trewe Relation," 1106.
100. Ibid., 1100.
101. Strachey, "A True Reportory," 1032.
102. "The Humble Petition of Captayne John Martyn Esq and Captayne Robert Haswell wth Many Others," in Kingsbury, ed., *Records of the Virginia Company*, 2:40–41.
103. Kupperman, *Jamestown Project*, 257.
104. Gleach, *Powhatan's World and Colonial Virginia*, 128.
105. Strachey, "The Historie of Travell into Virginia Britania," 1029.
106. Percy, "Trewe Relation," 1109–12; Fausz, "An 'Abundance of Blood Shed on Both Sides,'" 6, 32.

107. Williamson, *Powhatan Lords of Life and Death*, 39; Jarvis and van Driel, "The Vingboons Chart," 386.
108. Percy, "Trewe Relation," 1112.
109. Percy, "Trewe Relation," 1113; Sir Thomas Dale, Report from Virginia, 25 May 1611, Papers of Robert Rich, Earl of Warwick. See also William Kelso, Beverly Straube, and Daniel Schmidt, eds., *2007–2010 Interim Report on the Preservation Virginia Excavations at Jamestown, Virginia* (Richmond: Preservation Virginia, 2012), 41.
110. Sir Thomas Dale to D.M., 18 June 1614, in Hamor, "A True Discourse of the Present State of Virginia," 1157.
111. Ibid., 1158, 1121.
112. Ibid., 1129.
113. Strachey, "The Historie of Travell into Virginia Britania," 1043–44.
114. Hamor, "A True Discourse of the Present State of Virginia," 1128.
115. Sir Thomas Dale to D.M., 18 June 1614, in Hamor, "A True Discourse of the Present State of Virginia," 1160.
116. Horn, "The Conquest of Eden," 37.
117. Hamor, "A True Discourse of the Present State of Virginia," 1146.
118. Ibid., 1146–52.
119. Rountree, *Pocahontas, Powhatan, Opechancanough*, 166.
120. John Rolfe, "A True Relation of the State of Virginia," in Horn, ed., *Captain John Smith*, 1180.
121. Hamor, "A True Discourse of the Present State of Virginia," 1148.
122. William M. Kelso and Beverly Straube, *1999 Interim Report on the APVA Excavations at Jamestown, Virginia* (Richmond: Association for the Preservation of Virginia Antiquities, 2000), 29–30.
123. Pecoraro and Givens, "'Like to Perish from Want of Succor or Reliefe,'" 5.
124. Ibid., 5; David Hackett Fischer and James C. Kelly, *Bound Away: Virginia and the Westward Movement* (Charlottesville: University Press of Virginia, 2000), 27.
125. John Pory to Sir Dudley Carleton, 1619, in Tyler, ed., *Narratives of Early Virginia*, 284–85.
126. Robert Gray, *A Good Speed to Virginia* (London: Felix Kyngston, 1609); John Pory to Sir Dudley Carleton, 30 September 1619, in Tyler, ed., *Narratives of Early Virginia*, 283–84; Sir Thomas Dale, Report from Virginia, 25 May 1611, Papers of Robert Rich, Earl of Warwick.
127. Lorena Walsh, *Motives of Honor, Pleasure, and Profit: Plantation Management in the Colonial Chesapeake, 1607–1763* (Chapel Hill: University of North Carolina Press, 2010), 30–43, 111–12.

128. Brent Tarter, *Grandees of Government: The Origins and Persistence of Undemocratic Politics in Virginia* (Charlottesville: University of Virginia Press, 2013), 19, 27.
129. Philip D. Morgan, "Virginia Slavery in Atlantic Context, 1550 to 1650," in Musselwhite, Mancall, and Horn, eds., *Virginia 1619*, 86.
130. Kupperman, *Jamestown Project*, 277.
131. George Sandys to John Ferrar, 5 March 1623, Papers of Robert Rich, Earl of Warwick.
132. "The Letter to the Last Quarter Court Signed by the Lords," 16 February 1619, in Kingsbury, ed., *Records of the Virginia Company*, 1:311.
133. William Capps to John Ferrar, 31 March 1623, Papers of Robert Rich, Earl of Warwick.

3. NEW BORDERS, NEW CONNECTIONS, NEW FRACTURES

1. Edward Waterhouse, *A Declaration of the State of the Colony and Affaires in Virginia* (London: G. Eld, 1622), 8; Keith Pluymers, "Atlantic Iron: Wood Scarcity and the Political Ecology of Early English Expansion," *William and Mary Quarterly*, 3rd series, 73, no. 3 (July 2016), 414; Thomas F. Higgins III, "Falling Creek Ironworks Archaeological Site (44CF7)," National Register of Historic Places, Virginia Department of Historic Resources, 1995. Ironworkers hailed from Sussex, Warwickshire, and Staffordshire; it is unclear how many were alive and working in 1622. Citing recent ground-penetrating radar studies, Pluymers is uncertain about whether the furnace actually produced anything before it was demolished. "Atlantic Iron" also details how English gentry violated acceptable use of common rights and privileges to illegally erect ironworks for their own profit, an interesting parallel to planters' inappropriate use of resources on Indigenous land beyond their fields and homes (404–6).
2. In "Escape from Tsenacommacah," James D. Rice reminds historians to look beyond the "Powhacentric worldview" and at the numerous other people in the Chesapeake "who had the power to make things happen in seventeenth-century Virginia." This chapter examines the Powhatans' decisions from both the perspective of non-Powhatan Algonquians along the bay and from the perspective of Powhatans who had local as well as larger geopolitical concerns in mind. Rice, "Escape from Tsenacommacah: Chesapeake Algonquians and the Powhatan Menace," in Mancall, ed., *The Atlantic World and Virginia*, 101, 139. For map 3, see John Smith and William Hole, *Virginia* (London, 1624), Library of Congress Geography and Map Division, Washington, DC, https://www.loc.gov/item/99446115/; Rountree, *Pocahontas, Powhatan, Opechancanough*, 188; Charles E. Hatch Jr., *The First*

Seventeen Years in Virginia, 1607–1624 (Charlottesville: University Press of Virginia, 1957), 32–33; and "Here Following Is Set Downe a True List of the Names of All Those That Were Massacred by the Treachery of the Savages in Virginia," in Kingsbury, ed., *Records of the Virginia Company*, 3:564–71.
3. Rountree, *Pocahontas, Powhatan, Opechancanough*, 189.
4. Archaeology of the Virginia Chesapeake has long established the variety of settlement layouts and patterns, even inside of particular hundreds. See Ivor Noel Hume, *Martin's Hundred* (Charlottesville: University Press of Virginia, 1991); Horning, *Ireland in the Virginian Sea*, 165–66, 88; Charles Thomas Hodges, "Forts of the Chieftains: A Study of Vernacular, Classical, and Renaissance Influence on Defensible Town and Villa Plans in 17th-Century Virginia," MA thesis, College of William and Mary, 2003, 392–97; Andrew C. Edwards, "Archaeology of a Seventeenth-Century Houselot at Martin's Hundred, Virginia. 44JC647 (Carter's Grove Site CG-8)" (Williamsburg, VA: Colonial Williamsburg Foundation Library Research Report Series 1702, 2004), 70.
5. Seth Mallios and Shane Emmett, "Demand, Supply, and Elasticity in the Copper Trade at Early Jamestown," *Journal of the Jamestown Rediscovery Center* 2 (2004): 3; Rolfe, "A True Relation of the State of Virginia," 1178.
6. Rountree, *Pocahontas, Powhatan, Opechancanough*, 129.
7. Rountree, *Pocahontas's People*, 69.
8. William Keith, *The History of the British Plantations in America, Part I* (London: S. Richardson, 1738), 136–37.
9. Cave, *Lethal Encounters*, 113.
10. Kupperman, *Jamestown Project*, 272.
11. Strachey, "The Historie of Travell into Virginia Britania," 1049.
12. Robert Bolling, "The Indians of Southern Virginia, 1650–1711: Depositions in the Virginia and North Carolina Boundary Case," *Virginia Magazine of History and Biography* 7, no. 4 (1900): 350.
13. Nicholas M. Luccketti, Beverly A. Straube, and Edward A. Chappell, *Archaeology at Arlington: Excavations at the Ancestral Custis Plantation, Northampton County, Virginia* (Richmond: Association for the Preservation of Virginia Antiquities, 1999), 5; Joseph Douglas Deal III, "Race and Class in Colonial Virginia: Indians, Englishmen, and Africans in the Eastern Shore during the Seventeenth Century," PhD diss., University of Rochester, 1981, 11; Kupperman, *Pocahontas and the English Boys*, 156–57.
14. Smith, "The Generall Historie," 2:290.
15. John Pory quoted in James R. Perry, *The Formation of a Society on Virginia's Eastern Shore, 1615–1655* (Chapel Hill: University of North Carolina Press, 1990), 21.

16. Smith, "The Generall Historie," 2:290, 298. J. Frederick Fausz also discusses the role of interpreters in this critical period in "Middlemen in Peace and War: Virginia's Earliest Indian Interpreters, 1608–1632," *Virginia Magazine of History and Biography* 95, no. 1 (January 1987): 56–57.
17. Charles E. Hatch Jr., "The Great Road: Earliest Highway Used and Developed by the English at Jamestown," *Virginia Magazine of History and Biography* 57, no. 1 (January 1949): 14; Paul Musselwhite, "Private Plantation: The Political Economy of Land in Early Virginia," in Musselwhite, Mancall, and Horn, eds., *Virginia 1619*, 161.
18. Walsh, *Motives of Honor, Pleasure, and Profit*, 30, 38–39; Virginia Company, "Instruction to George Yeardley," 18 November 1618, in Kingsbury, ed., *Records of the Virginia Company*, 3:100–101; James Horn and Paul Musselwhite, "Introduction," in Musselwhite, Mancall, and Horn, eds., *Virginia 1619*, 11.
19. H. R. McIlwaine, *Journals of the House of Burgesses of Virginia, 1619–1658/9* (Richmond: Virginia State Library, 1915), 23–25; Alison Bell, "White Ethnogenesis and Gradual Capitalism: Perspectives from Colonial Archaeological Sites in the Chesapeake," *American Anthropologist* 107, no. 3 (September 2005): 450. See also Cary Carson et al., "Impermanent Architecture in the Southern American Colonies," *Winterthur Portfolio* 16 (1982): 135–92, and Seth Mallios, *At the Edge of the Precipice: Frontier Ventures, Jamestown's Hinterland, and the Archaeology of 44JC802* (Richmond: Association for the Preservation of Virginia Antiquities, 2000), 30.
20. Audrey Horning notes that while archaeological sites such as Jordan's Journey and Flowerdew Hundred revealed assemblages of trade goods like copper and beads meant for Native people, Martin's Hundred, settled around the same time, did not. Horning, *Ireland in the Virginian Sea*, 165.
21. The brick feature may date to 1612. Bell, "White Ethnogenesis and Gradual Capitalism," 446; James Deetz, *Flowerdew Hundred: The Archaeology of a Virginia Plantation, 1619–1684* (Charlottesville: University Press of Virginia, 1995), 32.
22. Michael J. Braddick, *State Formation in Early Modern England, c. 1550–1700* (Cambridge: Cambridge University Press, 2000), 34–36.
23. See Paul Musselwhite's discussion of the use of boroughs in the Atlantic world in *Urban Dreams, Rural Commonwealth: The Rise of Plantation Society in the Chesapeake* (Chapel Hill: University of North Carolina Press, 2018), 37–48; Walsh, *Motives of Honor, Pleasure, and Profit*, 28–39.
24. Rice, "'These Doubtfull Times,'" 226; Sarah E. McCartney, "A Blueprint for the Colony: The Virginia Company Charters and the Role of Religion at Jamestown," MA thesis, College of William and Mary, 2010.

25. Edmund Morgan, "The First American Boom: Virginia 1618 to 1630," *William and Mary Quarterly*, 3rd series, 28, no. 2 (April 1971): 183.
26. "A Court Held at Mr Ferrars Howse," 21 July 1619, Kingsbury, ed., *Records of the Virginia Company*, 1:249–50; Hatch, *The First Seventeen Years in Virginia*, 38–49, 66–67.
27. Walsh, *Motives of Honor, Pleasure, and Profit*, 111.
28. Warren M. Billings, *A Little Parliament: The Virginia General Assembly in the Seventeenth Century* (Richmond: Library of Virginia, 2004), part 1.
29. Treasurer and Company, "Letter to the Governor and Council in Virginia," 25 July 1621, in Kingsbury, ed., *Records of the Virginia Company*, 3:490.
30. "Instructions to Governor Yeardley, 1618," *Virginia Magazine of History and Biography* 2, no. 2 (October 1894): 165; Martha W. McCartney, *Virginia Immigrants and Adventurers, 1607–1635: A Biographical Dictionary* (Baltimore: Genealogical Publishing, 2007), 73.
31. See also Warren M. Billings, "The Growth of Political Institutions in Virginia, 1634–1676," *William and Mary Quarterly*, 3rd series, 31, no. 2 (1974): 225.
32. "The Letter to the Last Quarter Court Signed by the Lords," 16 February 1619, in Kingsbury, ed., *Records of the Virginia Company*, 1:311.
33. Rice, "'These Doubtfull Times,'" 215; Tarter, *Grandees of Government*, 19.
34. McIlwaine, *Journals of the House of Burgesses of Virginia, 1619–1658/9*, 10–13.
35. Ibid., 10; Seth Mallios, *Archaeological Excavations at 44JC568, the Reverend Richard Buck Site* (Richmond: Association for the Preservation of Virginia Antiquities, 2000), 62. Other archaeologists have posited that by the second quarter of the seventeenth century, deer was a luxury meat acquired from professional hunters. Henry Miller, "An Archaeological Perspective on the Evolution of Diet in the Colonial Chesapeake, 1620–1745," in *Colonial Chesapeake Society*, ed. Lois Green Carr, Philip D. Morgan, and Jean B. Russo (Chapel Hill: University of North Carolina Press, 1988), 183–87, 192.
36. William Weldon to Sir Edwin Sandys, 6 March 1619/20, in Kingsbury, ed., *Records of the Virginia Company*, 3:264; John Pory, "A Reporte of the Manner of Proceeding in the General Assembly Convened at James City," July–August 1619, in Kingsbury, ed., *Records of the Virginia Company*, 3:165.
37. McIlwaine, *Journals of the House of Burgesses of Virginia, 1619–1658/9*, 12–13.
38. Walsh, *Motives of Honor, Pleasure, and Profit*, 40.
39. Alderman Johnson, "Declaration of the State of the Colonie in the 12 years of Sr Thomas Smiths Government," April 1623, in Tyler, ed., *Narratives*

of Early Virginia, 412–18; Warren M. Billings, "The Law of Servants and Slaves in Seventeenth-Century Virginia," *Virginia Magazine of History and Biography* 99, no. 1 (1991): 48–50.

40. McIlwaine, *Journals of the House of Burgesses of Virginia, 1619–1658/9*, 11; Pory, "A Reporte of the Manner of Proceeding in the General Assembly Convened at James City," 3:167; Billings, "The Law of Servants and Slaves in Seventeenth-Century Virginia," 50.
41. "Quarter Courte Helde for Virginia," 15 November 1620, in Kingsbury, ed., *Records of the Virginia Company*, 2:427, 485, 496; Kupperman, *Jamestown Project*, 273.
42. John Rolfe to Edwin Sandys, January 1619/20, in Kingsbury, ed., *Records of the Virginia Company*, 3:242.
43. "Quarter Courte Helde for Virginia," 16 February 1619, in Kingsbury, ed., *Records of the Virginia Company*, 1:310.
44. Kupperman, *Jamestown Project*, 304.
45. George Yeardley to Sir Henry Peyton, 18 November 1610, in Kingsbury, ed., *Records of the Virginia Company*, 3:30.
46. Rebecca Seib and Helen C. Rountree, *Indians of Southern Maryland* (Baltimore: Maryland Historical Society, 2014), 63; Robert C. Johnson, ed., "The Indian Massacre of 1622: Some Correspondence of the Reverend Joseph Mead," *Virginia Magazine of History and Biography* 71, no. 4 (October 1963): 408–10.
47. For more on this shift, see Potter, "Early English Effects on Virginia Algonquian Exchange and Tribute in the Tidewater Potomac," 215–42.
48. Smith, "The Generall Historie," 2:295.
49. Rountree, *Pocahontas's People*, 74.
50. English actions preceding the attack and the development of the Second Anglo-Powhatan War are thoroughly covered in Gleach, *Powhatan's World and Colonial Virginia*, 123–73; Alden T. Vaughan, "'Expulsion of the Salvages': English Policy and the Virginia Massacre of 1622," *William and Mary Quarterly*, 3rd series, 35, no. 1 (January 1978): 57–84; and J. Frederick Fausz, "The 'Barbarous Massacre' Reconsidered: The Powhatan Uprising of 1622 and the Historians," *Explorations in Ethnic Studies* 1, no. 1 (1978): 16–36.
51. Smith, "The Generall Historie," 2:144. Because the servants sought out George Thorpe and did so overland, it makes sense that Morgan would have been located on the north side of the James either in Charles City, where Thorpe was a magistrate, or in the College Lands, where Thorpe was in charge of tenant labor. They needed a boat to reach the governor, who was reported to be six or seven miles away, consistent with

Governor Yeardley's lands at Flowerdew Hundred on the south side of the James River.
52. Council in Virginia, "Letter to Virginia Company of London," 20 January 1622/3, in Kingsbury, ed., *Records of the Virginia Company*, 4:11; Smith, "The Generall Historie," 2:144.
53. This attack is not usually considered a maritime event. In the background of Theodor de Bry's now-famous woodcut of the "Massacre at Jamestown, Virginia," Algonquian men stab and cudgel colonists at their breakfast table, but the coming danger waits in the background, in dugout canoes making their way toward the shore. Thedor de Bry, "De magna clade, quam Angli anno 1622. 22. Martiij in virginia acceperunt," 1634, engraving, John Carter Brown Library, Newport, RI, jcb.lunaimaging.com.
54. Waterhouse, *A Declaration of the State of the Colony and Affaires in Virginia*, 14.
55. Robert Beverley, *History and Present State of Virginia* (London: R. Parker, 1705), 40–41.
56. Johnson, ed., "The Indian Massacre of 1622," 409.
57. Peter Arundell to William Canning, April 1623, Papers of Robert Rich, Earl of Warwick.
58. Christopher Bishop to Peter Woodal, "Notes Taken Out of the Lres, Wch Came from Virginia in the Abigail and Were Del. the Comrs. in June 1623," Papers of Robert Rich, Earl of Warwick; Governor and Council of Virginia to the Earl of Southampton, 3 April 1623, in Sainsbury and Fortescue, eds., *Calendar of State Papers, Colonial*, 1:41–42.
59. Treasurer and Council for Virginia, "Letter to Governor and Council in Virginia," 1 August 1622, in Kingsbury, ed., *Records of the Virginia Company*, 3:670. McCartney, *Virginia Immigrants and Adventurers*, 54–69.
60. "An Abstract of the Lres Receaved from Virginia Conducing to the Discovery of the State of the Colony in or about April 1623," Papers of Robert Rich, Earl of Warwick; Christopher Davison to John Ferrar, 14 April 1623, in Kingsbury, ed., *Records of the Virginia Company*, 4:115.
61. George Sandys to Sir Miles Sandys, 30 March 1623, Papers of Robert Rich, Earl of Warwick.
62. George Sandys to Sir Samuel Sandys, 30 March 1623, Papers of Robert Rich, Earl of Warwick.
63. John Harvey, "From the Attestations of Divers Sufficient and Understanding Sea Men," April–June 1623, Papers of Robert Rich, Earl of Warwick.
64. Richard Frethorne to parents, 20 March 1623; Richard Frethorne to Robert Bateleman, 5 March 1622, Papers of Robert Rich, Earl of Warwick.

65. "An Abstract of the Lres Receaved from Virginia Conducing to the Discovery of the State of the Colony in or about April 1623," Papers of Robert Rich, Earl of Warwick.
66. Rice, *Nature and History*, 91; McIlwaine, *Journals of the House of Burgesses of Virginia, 1619–1658/9*, 23.
67. William Capps to Dr. Thomas Winston, March or April 1623, in Kingsbury, ed., *Records of the Virginia Company*, 4:38; Fischer and Kelly, *Bound Away*, 26–28.
68. Treasurer and Council for Virginia to Governor and Council in Virginia, 1 August 1622, in Kingsbury, ed., *Records of the Virginia Company*, 3:670.
69. Waterhouse, *A Declaration of the State of the Colony and Affaires in Virginia*, 18.
70. William Bullock, *Virginia Impartially Examined* (London: John Hammond, 1649), 12.
71. Smith, "The Generall Historie," 2:294.
72. Stephen R. Potter and Gregory A. Waselkov, "Whereby We Shall Enjoy Their Cultivated Places," in *Historical Archaeology of the Chesapeake*, ed. Paul A. Shackel and Barbara J. Little (Washington, DC: Smithsonian, 1994), 31.
73. George Sandys to Sir Miles Sandys, 30 March 1623, Papers of Robert Rich, Earl of Warwick.
74. John Martin, "The Manner Howe to Bringe the Indians into Subjection," 15 December 1622, in Kingsbury, ed., *Records of the Virginia Company*, 3:706–7.
75. Waterhouse, *A Declaration of the State of the Colony and Affaires in Virginia*, 11.
76. Treasurer and the Council for Virginia, "Letter to Governor and Council in Virginia," 1 August 1622, in Kingsbury, ed., *Records of the Virginia Company*, 3:672.
77. Council in Virginia, "Letter to the Virginia Company of London," April 1622, in Kingsbury, ed., *Records of the Virginia Company*, 3:612.
78. McIlwaine, *Journals of the House of Burgesses of Virginia, 1619–1658/9*, 24; McCartney, *Virginia Immigrants and Adventurers*, 35, 53.
79. Hodges, "Forts of the Chieftains," 93–94; *The Statutes at Large; Being a Collection of All the Laws in Virginia, from the Session of the Legislature, in the Year 1619*, ed. William Waller Hening (New York: R. and W. and G. Bartow, 1819), 1:127.
80. John Martin, "The Manner Howe to Bringe the Indians into Subjection," 15 December 1622, in Kingsbury, ed., *Records of the Virginia Company of London*, 3:708.

81. John Harvey to Sir Nathaniel Rich, 24 April 1624, Paper of Robert Rich, Earl of Warwick.
82. On seasonal movements, see Rice, *Nature and History*, 41–43.
83. John Martin, "The Manner Howe to Bringe the Indians into Subjection," 15 December 1622, in Kingsbury, ed., *Records of the Virginia Company of London*, 3:704.
84. John Harvey to Sir Nathaniel Rich, 24 April 1624, Paper of Robert Rich, Earl of Warwick.
85. Kupperman, *The Jamestown Project*, 322.
86. Peter Arundell to William Canning, April 1623, Paper of Robert Rich, Earl of Warwick.
87. Ibid.; Fausz, "Middlemen in Peace and War," 57.
88. Rountree, *Pocahontas, Powhatan, Opechancanough*, 217–21.
89. "Answere to the Propositions Made by the Right Honorable the Lord Chichester for the Better Selling of the Plantation of Virginia," August–September 1623, Papers of Robert Rich, Earl of Warwick.
90. Council in Virginia, "Letter to the Virginia Company of London," April 1622, in Kingsbury, ed., *Records of the Virginia Company*, 3:611–13.
91. Waterhouse, *A Declaration of the State of the Colony and Affaires in Virginia*, 22.
92. Christopher Bishop to John Woodall, "Notes Taken Out of the Lres, Wch Came from Virginia in the Abigail and Were Del. the Comrs. in June 1623," Papers of Robert Rich, Earl of Warwick.
93. Governor and Council of Virginia to the Earl of Southampton, 3 April 1623, in Sainsbury and Fortescue, eds., *Calendar of State Papers, Colonial*, 1:41–42.
94. Kupperman, *Jamestown Project*, 316–21.
95. Richard Frethorne to Robert Bateman, 5 March 1622; Frethorne to parents, March–April 1623, Papers of Robert Rich, Earl of Warwick.
96. Peter Arundell to William Canning, 15 April 1623, Papers of Robert Rich, Earl of Warwick.
97. H. R. McIlwaine, ed., *Minutes of the Council and General Court of Colonial Virginia*, 2nd ed. (Richmond: Virginia State Library, 1979), 198.
98. Francis Wyatt to John Ferrar, 7 April 1623, in Sainsbury and Fortescue, eds., *Calendar of State Papers, Colonial*, 1:41–45; Martha W. McCartney, *Virginia Immigrants and Adventurers*, 35.
99. Hening, ed., *Statutes at Large*, 1:128; Francis Wyatt and Council of Virginia to Henry Earl of Southampton, 2 December 1624, in Sainsbury and Fortescue, eds., *Calendar of State Papers, Colonial*, 1:70.
100. Rountree, *Pocahontas, Powhatan, Opechancanough*, 222.

101. Rice, *Nature and History*, 91.
102. Council in Virginia, "Letter to the Virginia Company of London," April 1622, in Kingsbury, ed., *Records of the Virginia Company*, 3:614.
103. Francis Wyatt and Council of Virginia to the Lords Commissioners for the Affairs of Virginia, 3 January 1626, in Sainsbury and Fortescue, eds., *Calendar of State Papers, Colonial*, 1:77.
104. Fausz, "Middlemen in Peace and War," 59.
105. George Sandys to Sir Samuel Sandys, 30 March 1623, Papers of Robert Rich, Earl of Warwick.
106. Potter, "Early English Effects on Virginia Algonquian Exchange and Tribute in the Tidewater Potomac," 224.
107. Smith, "The Generall Historie," 2:308.
108. Rice, *Nature and History*, 89.
109. Governor and Council to the Virginia Company, 30 January 1624, Colonial Office (CO) 1/3, no. 1, State Papers (SP) 14/156:134, Colonial State Papers, National Archives, London, UK; Peter Arundell to William Canning, April 1623, Papers of Robert Rich, Earl of Warwick; Governor of Virginia, "Commission to Captain Ralph Hamor," 23 October 1622, in Kingsbury, ed., *Records of the Virginia Company*, 3:696.
110. Peter Arundell to William Canning, 15 April 1623, Papers of Robert Rich, Earl of Warwick; Smith, "The Generall Historie," 2:296–97. If the men were the same who killed Spelman, whose death is referenced in the same letter but not explicitly connected to this event, they may have been Piscataways, according to anthropologist Helen Rountree, or Anacostians/Nacotchtanks according to interpreter Henry Fleet, quoted in Seib and Rountree, *Indians of Southern Maryland*, 64.
111. Governor and Council of Virginia to the Virginia Company, James City, 30 January 1624, CO 1/3, no. 1, SP 14/156:134; Rice, *Nature and History*, 87–88.
112. Hening, ed., *Statutes at Large*, 1:167. As April Hatfield suggests in *Atlantic Virginia*, the Accawmacks as an Algonquian people may have played roles as go-betweens on established Native trade routes for fur traders trading with larger groups, in this case the Susquehannocks. Hatfield, *Atlantic Virginia*, 24. Although the Accawmacks may have traded furs to the English as well, anthropologists argue that consistently, larger groups like the Susquehannocks tended to dominate over smaller groups like the Accawmacks in the European fur trade. For the Accawmacks' part, the presence of mats and pots in English homes suggests a trade in food as well as in land. Potter, *Commoners, Tribute, and Chiefs*, 198–99.
113. Rountree and Davidson, *Eastern Shore Indians of Virginia and Maryland*, 54.

114. Luccketti, Straube, and Chappell, *Archaeology at Arlington*, 14. Luccketti, Straube, and Chappell also reported that artifacts associated with martial occupation, namely gun flints, were contained in early period deposits associated with a slot trench.
115. Susie M. Ames, ed., *County Court Records of Accomack-Northampton, Virginia, 1640–1645* (Charlottesville: University Press of Virginia, 1973), 97, 181; Beverley Fleet, ed., *Virginia Colonial Abstracts Accomacke County, 1637–1640* (Baltimore: Genealogical Publishing, 1961), 100.
116. "Buildings Records: 1624/5 Muster Databases," Virtual Jamestown, Virtual jamestown.org. See also Morgan, "Virginia Slavery in Atlantic Context," 85–107.
117. Thomas Utye, 3 November 1624 patent, Land Office Patents Reel 1, No. 1, 14; Thomas Flint, 20 February 1626 patent, Land Office Patents Reel 1, No. 1, 77.
118. John Leyden, 2 December 1628 patent, Land Office Patents Reel 1, No. 1, 69.
119. John Moone/Moore, 6 March 1633 patent, Land Office Patents Reel 1, No. 1, 127. Francis and Bridget Fowler and Bridges Freeman held land along the Chickahominy River by 1632. Bridges Freeman, 1 June 1635 patent, Land Office Patents Reel 1, No. 1, 331. Martha W. McCartney, "Last Refuge: Tribal Preserves in Eastern Virginia," in Dennis B. Blanton and Julia A. King, eds., *Indian and European Contact in Context: The Mid-Atlantic Region* (Gainesville: University Press of Florida, 2004), 222–43.
120. Hening, ed., *Statutes at Large*, 1:141, 152–53.
121. Ibid., 1:191.
122. John Daly Burk, *The History of Virginia from Its First Settlement to the Present Day* (Petersburg, VA: Dickson and Pescud, 1804), 2:37.
123. Hening, ed., *Statutes of Virginia*, 1:141; Fischer and Kelly, *Bound Away*, 41. See also Virginia DeJohn Anderson, *Creatures of Empire: How Domestic Animals Transformed Early America* (New York: Oxford University Press, 2004), and Anderson, "Animals into the Wilderness: The Development of Livestock Husbandry in the Seventeenth-Century Chesapeake," *William and Mary Quarterly*, 3rd series, 59, no. 2 (2002): 377–408.
124. Captain Mathews to Sir John Wolstenholme, 25 May 1625, in Browne et al., eds., *Archives of Maryland*, 3:34.
125. Morgan, *American Slavery, American Freedom*, 136.
126. William Berkeley, "A Discourse and View of Virginia, 1661/2," in *The Papers of Sir William Berkeley, 1605–1677*, ed. Warren Billings and Maria Kimberly (Richmond: Virginia State Library, 2007), 162; Philip Levy, "Middle Plantation's Changing Landscape: Persistence, Continuity, and

the Building of Community" in Bradburn and Coombs, ed., *Early Modern Virginia: Reconsidering the Old Dominion*, 188.
127. "Grant to John Chew, 6 August 1637," in *York County, Virginia Records, 1665–1672*, ed. Benjamin B. Weisiger (Athens, GA: Iberian Publishing, 1995), 112. For more on the palisade, see Levy, "'A New Look at an Old Wall,'" 226–65.
128. Hening, ed., *Statutes of Virginia*, 1:224; Billings, "The Growth of Political Institutions in Virginia," 228–30.
129. "Proceedings of the Virginia Assembly," 1619, in Kingsbury, ed., *Records of the Virginia Company*, 3:161; Hening, ed., *Statutes at Large*, 1:224, 228.
130. Pecoraro and Givens, "'Like to Perish from Want of Succor or Reliefe,'" 7. Edwards writes of an early Martin's Hundred home that lower-class households routinely "made do" with locally made utilitarian wares. Edwards, "Archaeology of a Seventeenth-Century Houselot at Martin's Hundred," 57.
131. Rountree, *Pocahontas, Powhatan, Opechancanough*, 223.
132. Mallios, *Archaeological Excavations at 44JC568*, 62. Cow and pig remains, in contrast, showed evidence of onsite processing.
133. Mallios, *At the Edge of the Precipice*, 58, 63.

4. SAILORS AND RUMORS IN THE BAY

1. Vocabularies featuring common Native phrases and words for trade goods have been documented among European mariners and in published accounts about North and South America. See Laura J. Murray, "Vocabularies of Native American Languages: A Literary and Historical Approach to an Elusive Genre," *American Quarterly* 53, no. 4 (December 2001): 590–624.
2. Susie M. Ames, ed., *County Court Records of Accomack-Northampton, Virginia, 1632–1640* (Washington, DC: American Historical Association, 1954), 120. The Dutch were not obligated to return bonded laborers to Virginia until the "Articles of Amity" were passed in 1660. See Warren Billings, *Sir William Berkeley and the Forging of Colonial Virginia* (Baton Rouge: Louisiana State University Press, 2004), 121.
3. Matthew Bahar's work about the Wabanaki and New England demonstrates how movement by water connected peoples competing for resources, presenting an opportunity for Native leaders with expansionist policies to counterbalance European leaders, who needed Native allies where their authority was uncertain (everywhere). The 1630s Chesapeake provides an interesting counterpoint—where Native leaders intended to remain moored in a particular locality on the water while profiting from trade, information shared with English settlers tended toward removing

destabilizing influences (soldier-traders, the Susquehannocks) rather than destabilizing colonial projects. Bahar, *Storm of the Sea*, 3–5.

4. As Christian Koot writes, "Many colonists imagined the Chesapeake to be a unified whole," and the promise of Native trade and war facilitated that thinking. Colonists and Native people remained easily accessible to one another through the Chesapeake, whether they liked that or not. Koot, *A Biography of a Map in Motion: Augustine Herrman's Chesapeake* (New York: NYU Press, 2018), 6. In Alejandra Dubcovsky's study of the southeast, communication networks show "the link among peoples who share no consensus of the physical or political boundaries of their worlds," a dangerous liaison for colonists with tenuous claims to territory. Dubcovsky, *Informed Power*, 6. Dubcovsky's emphasis on the tension between local and imperial power, and how communication created conflict as colonists created new local spaces for themselves, also illuminates how traders and people on the run in the Chesapeake understood the geographical limits of legal slavery, servitude, and boundaries. It seemed and sometimes proved possible to slip through the cracks between and inside of localities strung together through broad knowledge supplied by mariners. The orientation of Native, Dutch, and English people toward shared waters thus gives us insight into how localities remain informed, regardless of status, and part of the larger Chesapeake world.

5. Katherine A. Grandjean identifies two key parallels in New England that also began in the 1630s: first, consistent fear that drove violence and fear of Native reprisal for decades after the Pequot War, and second, the power of rumor and mobility along Native roads to undermine English authority. While Native people were not just reacting to plantation expansion and desire for trade—and in fact, as this chapter demonstrates, came up with their own strategies to thwart certain individuals with those ambitions—I choose to highlight safety and stability as ongoing motives for Native people in the mid- and northern Chesapeake because a similar pattern of dislocation and violence had evolved since at least the reign of Wahunsenacawh. Illicit movement of people and information undermined boundaries and therefore the colonial project in the Chesapeake due to the connectivity of the landscape itself. The English did make conquest on the "communications frontier" in the Chesapeake as they did to the North, and indeed profited from it, but neither Marylanders nor Virginians had any ability (and in some cases, desire) to control or bound movement except through punishment and violence. See Grandjean, "The Long Wake of the Pequot War," *Early American Studies* 9, no. 2 (Spring 2011): 379–411; and Grandjean, *American Passage*.

6. McIlwaine, ed., *Minutes of the Council and General Court of Colonial Virginia*, 147.
7. Henry Fleet, "A Briefe Journal of a Voyage Made in the Barque Warwick to Virginia and Other Pts of the Continent of America Anno 1631," MS 688, ff. 517r–522v, Lambeth Palace Library, London; Van Zandt, *Brothers among Nations*, 123; Walsh, *Motives of Honor, Pleasure, and Profit*, 87; Kruer, *Time of Anarchy*, 24–28.
8. Russo and Russo, *Planting an Empire*, 45. According to Andrew Ferris, English people in New England wrote of and acted on their suspicions of Native conspiracies in New England, due to Natives' political differences from the English and their lack of understanding of those differences. As in Virginia, a lack of knowledge and the "invisibility" of the Native threat against English colonies sustained these narratives of conspiracy. See Andrew Ferris, "'Vile and Clamorous Reports' from New England: The Specter of Indigenous Conspiracy in Early Plymouth," *Early American Literature* 54, no. 2 (2019): 381–412.
9. See Gregory Evans Dowd's discussion of the sociology and historiography behind rumors in *Groundless: Rumors, Legends, and Hoaxes on the Early American Frontier* (Baltimore: Johns Hopkins University Press, 2015), 1–14. Dowd demonstrates that rumor as well as verified information provided action points and justifications for violence for colonists as well as Native people. Further, Dowd points out that much of what colonists wrote about Native people was hearsay at best; as in Katherine Grandjean's work, it also reflected fear of justified reprisal and, in the Chesapeake, further highlights proximity of Native people and their access to English colonists largely beyond English understanding.
10. Katherine Grandjean's historical actors are often informed or driven by rumors of incoming violence, and the seventeenth-century "English conquest of the communications frontier," like here, is never completed. Grandjean, *American Passage*, 12.
11. Claiborne's venture on Kent Island has been extensively discussed elsewhere, starting with J. Frederick Fausz's work. Fausz tied English traders and their infighting to Native politics during the conflict at Kent Island in "Merging and Emerging Worlds." Like this study, Fausz's research situated the values and strategies of elite English traders inside of the feed fights of the Second Anglo-Powhatan War and the pull of the Susquehannock trade. Fausz, "Merging and Emerging Worlds: Anglo-Indian Interest Groups and the Development of the Seventeenth-Century Chesapeake," in Carr, Morgan, and Russo, eds., *Colonial Chesapeake Society*, 47–98. Fausz also recounted the dangers of the initial years of Maryland

in light of the fur trade and Virginian hostility toward the new colony, and how Native people determined the rhythm and diplomacy of the Chesapeake trade, in "Present at the 'Creation': The Chesapeake World That Greeted the Maryland Colonists," *Maryland Historical Magazine* 79, no. 1 (1984): 7–20. The trade at Kent Island is covered in comparison to other English trading ventures in Cynthia Van Zandt's *Brothers among Nations*. Van Zandt covers the large geographic range of the Susquehannocks' alliance with the Hurons and negotiations with the French and Dutch traders as well. She argues that competition between Europeans and between English people, rather than the breakdown of the Virginian-Susquehannock alliance, ended Claiborne's venture; I qualify that slightly to argue that soldier-traders well versed in exploiting cross-cultural alliances and tensions leveraged a much more local geographic range to gain an edge in the broad-ranging intercolonial trade. Francis Jennings underscored the Susquehannocks' influence over the movement of people in the northern Chesapeake through violence and trade in "Glory, Death, and Transfiguration: The Susquehannock Indians in the Seventeenth Century," *Proceedings of the American Philosophical Society* 112, no. 1 (1968): 15–53. James Rice's discussion of Native politics at the time of the founding of Maryland, and his argument in *Nature and History* that English traders' visions of a "fur-trading preserve" in the north Chesapeake gave way to "dreams of wealth from tobacco production," are not the focus of this chapter but inform the central Anglo-Algonquian reorientation away from water occurring during this time period (97, 92). Lorena Walsh identifies the management of Kent Island as a continuation of the particular plantation model of the Company period, in line with Claiborne's actions as a soldier and leader who took action largely independent of Jamestown's colonial authorities—despite the fact that he was also a colonial authority. Walsh, *Motives of Honor, Pleasure, and Profit*, 76.

12. This idea is informed by histories found elsewhere in the Native studies field. Native people traveling via canoe or pinnace, as historian Joshua Reid states in his study of the Makah people, were empowered "to participate in global networks of exchange, to resist assimilation, and to retain greater autonomy." Reid, *The Sea Is My Country: The Maritime World of the Makahs, an Indigenous Borderlands People* (New Haven, CT: Yale University Press, 2016), 3–4.

13. Rice, *Nature and History*, 87; McIlwaine, ed., *Minutes of the Council and General Court of Colonial Virginia*, 30.

14. Seib and Rountree, *Indians of Southern Maryland*, 25–26.

15. Rice, *Nature and History*, 92–93; Pendergast, "The Massawomeck," 19.

16. Seib and Rountree, *Indians of Southern Maryland*, 52.
17. Rice, *Nature and History*, 92–96.
18. Henry Fleet, "A Briefe Journal of a Voyage Made in the Barque Warwick to Virginia and Other Pts of the Continent of America Anno 1631," MS 688, ff. 517r–522v, Lambeth Palace Library, London.
19. Pieter Hovens, "The Netherlands," *American Indian Quarterly* 17, no. 1 (Spring 1993): 242–44.
20. Victor Enthoven and Willem Klooster, "Contours of Virginia-Dutch Trade in the Long Seventeenth Century," in Bradburn and Coombs, eds., *Early Modern Virginia*, 97.
21. Rice, *Nature and History*, 102.
22. Commission to William Tucker, 23 December 1621, in "Documents of Sir Francis Wyatt, Governor, 1621–1626," *William and Mary Quarterly*, 2nd series, 7, no. 1 (January 1927): 42; Commission to Ralph Hamor, 23 October 1622, in "Documents of Sir Francis Wyatt, Governor, 1621–1626," *William and Mary Quarterly*, 2nd series, 7, no. 3 (July 1927): 204.
23. Fleet, "A Briefe Journal of a Voyage Made in the Barque Warwick."
24. Horn, *A Land as God Made It*, 271.
25. "Extracts of all the Titles and Estates of Land, sent Home by Sir Francis Wyatt," May 1625, Kingsbury, ed., *Records of the Virginia Company of London*, 4:558–59; Strachey, "A True Reportory," 1029.
26. "Governor Sir Francis Wyatt and Council of Virginia to Privy Council," 17 May 1626, in Sainsbury and Fortescue, eds., *Calendar of State Papers, Colonial*, 1:80–81.
27. Fausz, "Present at the 'Creation,'" 11.
28. "Proceedings of the Council of Maryland, 1667–1687/8," in Browne et al., eds., *Archives of Maryland*, 5:159–60.
29. "Commission Signed by John Pott, Governor and Captain General of Virginia," in Sainsbury and Fortescue, eds., *Calendar of State Papers, Colonial*, 10:29.
30. Ames, ed., *County Court Records of Accomack-Northampton, Virginia, 1632–1640*, 34. Claiborne's settlement at Kent Island coincided with the collapse of the tobacco boom in 1630 and the corresponding rise in beaver prices. Fausz, "Merging and Emerging Worlds," 61; Kruer, *Time of Anarchy*, 25.
31. Cyprian Thorowgood, "A Relation of a Voyage Made by Mr. Cyprian Thorowgood to the Head of the Baye," in George E. Gifford Jr. and Marion Tinling, "A Relation of a Voyage to the Head of the Bay," *The Historian* 20, no. 3 (May 1958): 349. Walsh reports that the Kent Island plantation had between eighteen and forty-nine workers, hired and bound, between 1631 and 1636. Walsh, *Motives of Honor, Pleasure, and Profit*, 44.

32. Thorowgood, "Relation of a Voyage Made by Mr. Cyprian Thorowgood to the Head of the Baye," 349.
33. Ibid., 350.
34. William Claiborne, "Petition of Colonel William Claiborne, a Poor Old Servant of Your Majesty's Father and Grandfather, to King Charles II," in Browne et al., eds., *Archives of Maryland*, 5:192–94.
35. Walsh, *Motives of Honor, Pleasure, and Profit*, 77–79. Claiborne also had patented land and connections to squatters on the Eastern Shore, which may explain how he acquired corn from nearby people to trade. Van Zandt, *Brothers among Nations*, 126.
36. Fleet, "A Briefe Journal of a Voyage Made in the Barque Warwick."
37. Perry, *The Formation of a Society on Virginia's Eastern Shore*, 49; Ames, ed., *County Court Records of Accomack-Northampton, Virginia, 1640–1645*, 377–85; William Clayborne [Claiborne], 3 June 1624 land grant, Land Office Patents Reel 1, No. 1, 41.
38. Claiborne, "Petition of Colonel William Claiborne," 5:200.
39. See Antoinette Sutto, *Loyal Protestants and Dangerous Papists: Maryland and the Politics of Religion in the English Atlantic, 1630–1690* (Charlottesville: University of Virginia Press, 2015).
40. "Instructions to the Colonists by Lord Baltimore," in *Narratives of Early Maryland, 1633–1684*, ed. Clayton Colman Hall (New York: Charles Scribner's Sons, 1910), 17–18.
41. J. Thomas Scharf, *History of Maryland from the Earliest Period to the Present Day* (Baltimore: John B. Piet, 1879), 1:103–4; Fausz, "Merging and Emerging Worlds," 67.
42. Claiborne, "Petition of Colonel William Claiborne," 5:20–22.
43. J. Mills Thornoton III, "The Thrusting Out of Governor Harvey: A Seventeenth-Century Rebellion," *Virginia Magazine of History and Biography* 76, no. 1 (January 1968): 21.
44. Andrew White, "A Briefe Relation of the Voyage unto Maryland," in Hall, ed., *Narratives of Early Maryland*, 39–40. Claiborne, "Petition of Colonel William Claiborne," 5:165.
45. Andrew White, "Briefe Relation of the Voyage unto Maryland," 39–41.
46. "Letter of Governor Leonard Calvert to Lord Baltimore, 1638," in Hall, ed., *Narratives of Early Maryland*, 154.
47. Claiborne, "Petition of Colonel William Claiborne," 5:166.
48. Fausz, "Present at the 'Creation,'" 15.
49. Claiborne, "Petition of Colonel William Claiborne," 5:167. The Marylanders may also have misinterpreted Pasptanzie, an Algonquian town on the Potomac River. For a recent analysis of this passage in the context of

the Fleet-Claiborne feud, see Jeffrey Glover, *Paper Sovereigns: Anglo-Native Treaties and the Law of Nations, 1604–1664* (Philadelphia: University of Pennsylvania Press, 2014).

50. "Mr. R.[ichard] Bennet and Mr. S.[amuel] Mathew to Secretary Thurloe," 10 October 1656, in *A Collection of the State Papers of John Thurloe*, ed. Thomas Birch (London: Fletcher Gyles, 1742), 5:487.
51. Claiborne, "Petition of Colonel William Claiborne," 5:207; Walsh, *Motives of Honor, Pleasure, and Profit*, 78.
52. "Henry Ewbank's Account of His Capture," *The Calvert Papers*, ed. John Wesley Murray Lee (Baltimore: Maryland Historical Society, 1889), 1:148.
53. Claiborne, "Petition of Colonel William Claiborne," 5:165.
54. Ames, ed., *County Court Records of Accomack-Northampton, Virginia, 1632–1640*, 57.
55. "A Relation of Maryland," in Hall, ed., *Narratives of Early Maryland*, 88.
56. Ibid., 90.
57. "Instructions to the Colonists by Lord Baltimore," 19–20.
58. "Henry Ewbank's Account of His Capture," 147–48.
59. "Governor Leonard Calvert to Lord Baltimore," 25 April 1638, in Lee, ed., *The Calvert Papers*, 1:179, 184.
60. "Extract from a Letter of Captain Thomas Yong to Sir Toby Matthew," in Hall, ed., *Narratives of Early Maryland*, 54–56.
61. "Zouch" to Sir John Zouch, 5 May 1635, in Sainsbury and Fortescue, eds., *Calendar of State Papers, Colonial*, 9:76–79.
62. "Thomas Smith's Account of His Capture," in Lee, ed., *The Calvert Papers*, 1:148.
63. Fausz, "Merging and Emerging Worlds," 71.
64. Claiborne, "Petition of Colonel William Claiborne," 5:231–34.
65. "Letter of Governor Leonard Calvert to Lord Baltimore," in Hall, ed., *Narratives of Early Maryland*, 150.
66. Ibid., 150–51.
67. "Proceedings and Acts of the General Assembly January 1637/8–September 1664," in Browne et al., eds., *Archives of Maryland*, 1:12.
68. Commission to Giles Brent, 12 January 1641, in Browne et al., eds., *Archives of Maryland*, 3:101. Claiborne's financial backers in England replaced him with Marylander Robert Evelyn, who sent his son to live with the Patawomecks and learn an Algonquian language to become an interpreter. Fausz, "Middlemen in Peace and War," 62.
69. "Proceedings and Acts of the General Assembly, April 1666–June 1676," in Browne et al., eds., *Archives of Maryland*, 2:21.

70. Claiborne, "Petition of Colonel William Claiborne," 5:211; "Proceedings and Acts of the General Assembly, April 1666–June 1676," in Browne et al., eds., *Archives of Maryland*, 2:27.
71. Kruer, *Time of Anarchy*, 42; Jennings, "Glory, Death, and Transfiguration," 20, 26.
72. "A Description of the Province of New Albion," in Force, ed., *Tracts and Other Papers*, 2:6.
73. Rice, *Nature and History*, 104.
74. Rountree and Seib make the argument that attitudes toward Indigenous people hardened in Maryland during and after Ingle's Rebellion. Rountree and Seib, *Indians of Southern Maryland*, 77–78.
75. For example, "The Opinion Delivered by the Honorable Director General Petrus Stuyvesant in the Case of Fiscal van Dyck against Jochom Pietersen and Melyn," 16 July 1647, in *New York Historical Manuscripts: Dutch*, vol. 4, *Council Minutes, 1638–1649*, ed. Arnold J. F. Van Laer (Baltimore: Genealogical Publishing, 1974), 406; Christian J. Koot, "The Merchant, the Map, and Empire: Augustine Herrman's Chesapeake and Interimperial Trade, 1644–73," *William and Mary Quarterly*, 3rd series, 67, no. 4 (October 2010): 611.
76. Council Minutes, 27 February 1643, in Van Laer, ed., *New York Historical Manuscripts*, 187.
77. Council Minutes, 23 August 1640, in ibid., 91.
78. "Decisions of the General Court," *Virginia Magazine of History and Biography* 5, no. 3 (1898): 237.
79. Ibid., 237–38. For childrens' escapes to Native towns, see p. 199.
80. "Annual Letter of the Jesuits," *Narratives of Early Maryland*, ed., Colman, 120; Ames, ed., *County Court Records of Accomack-Northampton, Virginia, 1640–1645*, 354; "Commission to Mr Neale to Apprehend Edward Robins, Daniel Duffill and Thomas," 12 June 1644, in Browne et al., eds., *Archives of Maryland*, 4:280. Duffield appeared before the Maryland governor in 1642 to argue against his forced return to Virginia and served with the Marylanders in an expedition to Kent Island against the Susquehannocks later that year. By 1644, other planters accused him of attempting to leave the colony of Maryland to avoid debt, but he may have also been escaping Ingle's Rebellion. "Court and Testementary Business," 1644; "An Assessmt Made by the Lieutent Grall and Counsell," 25 November 1642; "Court and Testementary Business," 1644, in Browne et al., eds., *Archives of Maryland*, 4:125; 3:120; 4:279. Perhaps he escaped to New Netherland or elsewhere; the *Archives of Maryland* have no further references to him after 1644.

81. Council Minutes, 13 April 1642, in Van Laer, ed., *New York Historical Manuscripts*, 143.
82. Henry Norwood, "A Voyage to Virginia," in Force, ed., *Tracts and Other Papers*, 3:30.
83. Ibid., 3:23–28.
84. Ibid., 3:29.
85. Ibid., 3:43.
86. Ibid., 3:41, 48.

5. TRADE, PROPERTY, AND THE MEANING OF ALGONQUIAN PLACES

1. Edward Bland, "The Discovery of New-Brittaine," in *Narratives of Early Carolina, 1650–1708*, ed. Alexander S. Salley Jr. (New York: Charles Scribner's Sons, 1911), 13–14.
2. I refer here to the "shatter zone" and its effects on Virginia covered in Shefveland's *Anglo-Native Virginia* and Robin Beck's *Chiefdoms, Collapse, and Coalescence in the Early American South*. Beck and Shefveland trace the long-term and geographically long-ranging effects of Native slavery throughout the seventeenth-century Piedmont. Focusing specifically on the Coastal Plain, I build on their work here to first add that Virginian reactions to that instability cannot be disentangled from their own sloppily handled local politics, suppression of labor, and infighting. Second, the amount of movement and violence in the Piedmont and down Native roads near English settlements encouraged an obsession with bounding but, more importantly, patrolling plantation and colony boundaries. Robin Beck, *Chiefdoms, Collapse, and Coalescence in the Early American South* (Cambridge: Cambridge University Press, 2013); Shefveland, *Anglo-Native Virginia*. For more on the shatter zone across the southeast, see Robbie Ethridge, *From Chicaza to Chickasaw: The European Invasion and the Transformation of the Mississippian World, 1540–1715* (Chapel Hill: University of North Carolina Press, 2010); and Robbie Ethridge and Susan Shuck-Hall, eds., *Mapping the Mississippi Shatter Zone: The Colonial Indian Slave Trade and Regional Instability in the American South* (Lincoln: University of Nebraska Press, 2009). See also Hayley Negrin, "Possessing Native Women and Children: Slavery, Gender, and English Colonialism in the Early American South, 1670–1717," PhD diss., New York University, 2018. The understanding of this shift in orientation from water to land is supported by political and legal histories of the seventeenth-century Virginian government, notably John Kukla, who argued that Claiborne's faction led this orientation away from Kent Island to tobacco profits in the 1630s in "Order and Chaos in Early America: Political and Social

Stability in Pre-Restoration Virginia," *American Historical Review* 90, no. 2 (1985): 286.
3. Walsh, *Motives of Honor, Pleasure, and Profit*, 131.
4. Lois Green Carr and Russell R. Menard, "Immigration and Opportunity: The Freedmen in Early Colonial Maryland," in Tate and Ammerman, eds., *Chesapeake in the Seventeenth Century*, 208; Horn, *Adapting to a New World*, 151, 184.
5. John C. Coombs, "The Phases of Conversion: A New Chronology for the Rise of Slavery in Early Virginia," *William and Mary Quarterly*, 3rd series, 68, no. 3 (2011): 345–46. The status of these Africans was often contested in the seventeenth century and accordingly is often contested now. Many scholars accept that the initial "20. And odd Negroes" were considered enslaved for life, but records are vague about the status of Africans in the following decades. Michael Guasco argues that the vague language is intentional, while most recently, John C. Coombs has argued that the ability to reduce someone to slavery, rather than the person's actual status, was key to the conversion to African slavery. Throughout, I attempt to be as specific as possible about an individual's status but use the word "African" when references to "Negro" arise. See John C. Coombs, "Others Not Christians in the Service of the English: Interpreting the Status of Africans and African Americans in Early Virginia," *Virginia Magazine of History and Biography* 127, no. 3 (2019): 212–38; Morgan, "Virginia Slavery in Atlantic Context"; Michael Guasco, *Slaves and Englishmen: Human Bondage in the Early Modern World* (Philadelphia: University of Pennsylvania Press, 2014); Coombs, "The Phases of Conversion," 332–60; and John K. Thornton and Linda M. Heywood, *Central Africans, Atlantic Creoles, and the Foundation of the Americas, 1585–1660* (Cambridge: Cambridge University Press, 2007).
6. See Ibram X. Kendi and Keisha N. Blain, eds., *Four Hundred Souls: A Community History of African America, 1619–2019* (New York: One World, 2021), esp. Nakia Parker, "1654–1659: Unfree Labor," 30–35, and Walsh, *Motives of Honor, Pleasure, and Profit*, 140.
7. Hening, ed., *Statutes at Large*, 1:262.
8. Lois Green Carr, Russell R. Menard, and Lorena S. Walsh, *Robert Cole's World: Agriculture and Society in Early Maryland* (Chapel Hill: University of North Carolina Press, 1991), chapter 3.
9. Anderson, "Animals into the Wilderness," 389; "An Act for Fencing of Ground," October 1640, in Browne et al., eds., *Archives of Maryland*, 1:96.
10. Willie Graham et al., "Adaptation and Innovation: Archaeological and Architectural Perspectives on the Seventeenth-Century Chesapeake," *William and Mary Quarterly*, 3rd series, 64, no. 3 (2007): 464.

11. Timothy Silver, "A Useful Arcadia: European Colonization as Biotic Factors in Chesapeake Forests," in *Discovering the Chesapeake: The History of an Ecosystem,* ed. Philip D. Curtin, Grace S. Brush, and George W. Fisher (Baltimore: Johns Hopkins University Press, 2001), 154.
12. Allan Kulikoff, *Tobacco and Slaves: The Development of Southern Cultures in the Chesapeake, 1680–1800* (Chapel Hill: University of North Carolina Press, 1986), 7.
13. Carr, Menard, and Walsh suggest that land claimed by Maryland was less densely settled in the 1660s than in the 1620s, before colonists arrived. Carr, Menard, and Walsh, *Robert Cole's World,* 21.
14. Morgan, *American Slavery, American Freedom,* 171–73.
15. Stephen Fonzo, *Mapping the Rappahannock Path: Colonial Land Patents and Indigenous Cultural Landscape in Virginia's Middle Peninsula* (Annapolis, MD: Captain John Smith Chesapeake National Historic Trail, National Park Service, 2022), 40, 70.
16. Russell Menard, *Economy and Society in Early Colonial Maryland* (New York: Garland, 1985), 41–44.
17. Ibid., 23–24; Russo and Russo, *Planting an Empire,* 47, 50; "Land Notes, 1634–1655," *Maryland Historical Magazine* 5, no. 3 (1910): 269–70.
18. McIlwaine, ed., *Minutes of the Council and General Court of Colonial Virginia,* 466–67.
19. "An Act against Fugitives," 26 March 1642, in Browne et al., eds., *Archives of Maryland,* 1:124; Hening, ed., *Statutes at Large,* 1:254–55; Billings, "The Law of Servants and Slaves in Seventeenth-Century Virginia," 45–62. Billings argued that these punishments were in line with English vagrancy laws.
20. Hening, ed., *Statutes at Large,* 1:255.
21. Gwynn's neighbors, who shared a boundary line with him, recorded nearby Native occupation, including an agreement with the werowance of Kiskiak to settle. George Ludlow, 12 March 1652 land grant, Land Office Patents Reel 2, No. 3, 23; Gilbert Metcalfe, 25 September 1664 land grant, Land Office Patents Reel 5, No. 5, 455. See also Kevin P. Kelly, "'In Dispers'd Country Plantations': Settlement Patterns in Seventeenth-Century Surry County, Virginia," in Carr, Morgan, and Russo, eds., *Colonial Chesapeake Society,* 183.
22. Lois M. Feister, "Linguistic Communication between the Dutch and Indians in New Netherland 1609–1664," *Ethnohistory* 20, no. 1 (1973): 25–38.
23. Council Minutes, 27 February 1643, in Van Laer, ed., *New York Historical Manuscripts,* 187. Given the date, the "massacre" referenced by the Dutch could be the 1622 attack. "Court and Testamentary Business," 1642, in Browne et al., eds., *Archives of Maryland,* 4:177.

24. "Coppie of a Letter Written to Our Govr to Govr of Virginiea," n.d.; "Instructions to Capt Henry Ffleete," n.d., in Browne et al., eds., *Archives of Maryland*, 3:106, 149; Rountree and Davidson, *Eastern Shore Indians of Virginia and Maryland*, 45. The fur traders in question, Rowland Williams and John Angood/Angud, were both active in the trade of beaver pelts on the Virginian Eastern Shore in the 1630s, although Angood's estate appears to have been settled in Maryland after his death. Ames, ed., *County Court Records of Accomack-Northampton, Virginia, 1640–1645*, 13, 18; Jennings, "Glory, Death, and Transfiguration," 20.
25. Hening, ed., *Statutes at Large*, 1:255; "Proclamacon," 2 January 1643, in Browne et al., eds., *Archives of Maryland*, 3:144.
26. "Court and Testementary Business," 1643, in Browne et al., eds., *Archives of Maryland*, 4:210.
27. William Berkeley, "Order Concerning Runaway Servants," 5 June 1643, in Billings and Kimberly, eds., *Papers of Sir William Berkeley*, 58.
28. Ames, ed., *County Court Records of Accomack-Northampton, Virginia, 1640–1645*, 273.
29. Lionel Gatford, *Publick Good without Private Interest; or, A Compendious Remonstrance of the Present Sad State and Condition of the English Colonie in Virginiea* (London: Henry Maersh, 1657), 9.
30. Russell R. Menard and Lois Green Carr, "The Lords Baltimore and the Colonization of Maryland," in *Early Maryland in a Wider World*, ed. David B. Quinn (Detroit: Wayne State University Press, 1982), 209; Ames, ed., *County Court Records of Accomack-Northampton, Virginia, 1640–1645*, 317.
31. "A Perfect Description of Virginia" in Force, ed., *Tracts and Other Papers*, 2:8.
32. Joseph Frank, "News from Virginny, 1644," *Virginia Magazine of History and Biography* 65, no. 1 (1957): 86.
33. Keith, *History of the British Plantations*, 144.
34. In 1642, for example, Stephen Gill was granted 2,500 acres of land on Rosewell Creek in what is now Gloucester County. Stephen Gill, 18 November 1642 patent, Land Office Patents Reel 2, No. 2, 160; Rountree, *Pochatonas, Powhatan, Opechancanough*, 227–29.
35. Gleach, *Powhatan's World and Colonial Virginia*, 175.
36. Gatford, *Publick Good without Private Interest*, 6.
37. William Castell, *A Short Discoverie of the Coasts and Continents of America* (London, 1644), 24–25.
38. Keith, *History of the British Plantations*, 144.
39. Ibid., 144.
40. John Oldmixon, *The British Empire in America, Containing the History of the Discovery, Settlement, Progress and State of the British Colonies on the*

Continent and Islands of America (New York: Augustus M. Kelley, 1969), 1:373–74.
41. "A Perfect Description of Virginia," 2:11.
42. Hening, ed., *Statutes at Large,* 1:347.
43. William Berkeley, "Treaty of Peace with 'Necotowance King of the Indians' Successor to Opechancanough, Jamestown," 5 October 1646, in Billings and Kimberly, eds., *Papers of Sir William Berkeley,* 71.
44. McIlwaine, ed., *Minutes of the Council and General Court of Colonial Virginia,* 502.
45. William Berkeley, "Letter from Richard Kemp," 27 February 1644/5, in Billings and Kimberly, eds., *Papers of Sir William Berkeley,* 62–65.
46. Timothy B. Riordan, *The Plundering Time: Maryland and the English Civil War* (Baltimore: Maryland Historical Society, 2004), 35–43.
47. Rice, *Nature and History,* 104. According to Virginian records, Ingle had just before the attack changed the name of the ship to the *Recovery.* Ames, ed., *County Court Records of Accomack-Northampton, Virginia, 1640–1645,* 331.
48. Assembly Proceedings, April 1662, in Browne et al., eds., *Archives of Maryland,* 1:432–33.
49. For more on Ingle's Rebellion, see Noeleen McIlvenna, *Early American Rebels: Pursuing Democracy from Maryland to Carolina, 1640–1700* (Chapel Hill: University of North Carolina Press, 2020), chapter 1.
50. Francis Moryson, "A Letter Written to Sir William Jones, the Kings Attorney Generall Prefatory to the Present State of Affairs in Virginia," October 1676, in *Samuel Wiseman's Book of Record: The Official Account of Bacon's Rebellion in Virginia,* ed. Michael Leroy Oberg (Lanham, MA: Lexington Books, 2005), 127.
51. Hening, ed., *Statutes at Large,* 1:285, 292.
52. Ibid., 1:292. See also Brown, *Good Wives, Nasty Wenches, and Anxious Patriarchs,* 116–20.
53. Based on US Geological Survey maps and Anthony Langford's circa 1650 map of the Pamunkey River, I believe this to be near the Horseshoe on the Pamunkey River. See Martha W. McCartney, "The Draft of York River in Virginia: An Artifact of the Seventeenth Century," *Southeastern Archaeology* 3, no. 2 (Winter 1984): 97–110.
54. Richard Lee, 20 August 1646 land grant, Land Office Patents Reel 2, No. 2, 62; Berkeley, "Letter from Richard Kemp Jamestown, 27 February 1644/5," 65; Hening, ed., *Statutes at Large,* 1:318.
55. Hening, ed., *Statutes at Large,* 1:318.
56. Oldmixon, *British Empire in America,* 1:374.
57. Beverley, *History and Present State of Virginia,* 52–53.

58. Dylan Ruediger, "'Neither Utterly to Reject Them, nor Yet to Drawe Them to Come In': Tributary Subordination and Settler Colonialism in Virginia," *Early American Studies* 18, no. 1 (2020): 17.
59. Berkeley, "Treaty of Peace with 'Necotowance King of the Indians,'" 71.
60. Rountree and Turner, *Before and after Jamestown*, 170.
61. Sayers, *A Desolate Place*, 105–7.
62. Philip Ludwell, "The Examination of Nick Majr. & Sevll Other of ye Old Men of ye Meherrin Indians," 3 October 1710, Lee Family Papers, Mss. 1 L51 f24, Virginia Museum of History and Culture, Richmond.
63. Stephen R. Potter, "Ethnohistory and the Owings Site: A Re-Analysis," *Archaeological Society of Virginia Quarterly Bulletin* 31, no. 4 (June 1977): 169.
64. Hening, ed., *Statutes at Large*, 1:481–82.
65. Rountree, *Pocahontas, Powhatan, Opechancanough*, 233. Thanks to Martha McCartney for clarifying that Tangier was called the "Western Island" in contemporary patents.
66. Thomas Wilkinson, 18 October 1650 land grant, Land Office Patents Reel 2, No. 2, 257.
67. Rountree, *Pocahontas, Powhatan, Opechancanough*, 233; "Court and Testamentary Business," 1649, in Browne et al., eds., *Archives of Maryland*, 4:512; Kristalyn Marie Shefveland, "The Many Faces of Native Bonded Labor in Colonial Virginia," *Native South* 7 (2014): 71, 74. Brewster was on the Wood expedition. See Bland, "The Discovery of New-Brittaine," 8.
68. In historian Michael Guasco's words, "Indian slavery may have been valued less at this time for its ability to provide laborers and more for its ability to facilitate Anglo-American colonialism." Guasco, "To 'Doe Some Goode upon Their Countrymen': The Paradox of Indian Slavery in Early Anglo-America," *Journal of Social History* 42, no. 2 (Winter 2007): 399.
69. Warren Billings, "Some Acts Not in Hening's 'Statutes': The Acts of Assembly, April 1652, November 1652, and July 1653," *Virginia Magazine of History and Biography* 83, no. 1 (January 1975): 64–65.
70. Morgan, *American Slavery, American Freedom*, 149.
71. Hening, ed., *Statutes at Large*, 1:249, 269.
72. Berkeley, "Treaty of Peace with 'Necotowance King of the Indians,'" 71.
73. "Authorization for a Bodyguard," 12 October 1648, in Billings and Kimberly, eds., *Papers of Sir William Berkeley*, 82; McCartney, "The Draft of York River in Virginia," 104.
74. Gatford, *Publick Good without Private Interest*, 7–8.
75. Morgan, *American Slavery, American Freedom*, 136.

76. Ibid., 244; Castell, *A Short Discoverie*, 24; Menard, *Economy and Society in Early Colonial Maryland*, 157.
77. H. Trawick Ward and R. P. Stephen Davis Jr., *Indian Community on the North Carolina Piedmont, AD 1000 to 1700* (Chapel Hill, NC: Research Laboratories of Archaeology, 1993), 131–39.
78. John D. Krugler, *English and Catholic: The Lords Baltimore in the Seventeenth Century* (Baltimore: Johns Hopkins University Press, 2004), 180; "Non-Exportation of Corn, &c.," 10 November 1647, in Browne et al., eds., *Archives of Maryland*, 3:194.
79. Levy, "'A New Look at an Old Wall,'" 226–65.
80. Hening, ed., *Statutes at Large*, 1:327; "A Description of the Province of New Albion," 2:6.
81. Hening, ed., *Statutes at Large*, 1:315.
82. Rountree, *Pocahontas, Powhatan, Opechancanough*, 233; Schmidt, *Divided Dominion*, 151.
83. Manwarring Hamon, 15 March 1649 land grant, Land Office Patents Reel 2, No. 2, 195; Major John Lewis, 15 October 1653 land grant, Land Office Patents Reel 2, No. 3, 59; George Smith, 8 September 1657 land grant, Land Office Patents Reel 4, No. 4, 162; Strickland, King, and McCartney, *Defining the Greater York River Indigenous Cultural Landscape*, 162.
84. Hantman, *Monacan Millennium*, 143–44. Other archaeologists have suggested that some trading towns were reoriented toward trade with Fort Henry on the Appomattox River. Jane M. Eastman, "The Sara and Dan River Peoples: Siouan Communities in North Carolina's Interior Piedmont from AD 1000 to AD 1700," PhD diss., University of North Carolina at Chapel Hill, 1999, 298.
85. Conway Robinson, ed., "Notes from the Council and General Court Records, 1641–1664," *Virginia Magazine of History and Biography* 8, no. 2 (October 1900): 164; George Smith, 8 September 1657 land grant, Land Office Patents Reel 4, No. 4, 162; William Lewis, 14 October 1653 land grant, Land Office Patents Reel 2, No. 3, 59.
86. Jennings, "Glory, Death, and Transfiguration," 25; Rountree and Davidson, *Eastern Shore Indians of Virginia and Maryland*, 66; Orders, 10 May 1651, in *Northampton County, Virginia, Orders, Deeds, and Wills, 1651–1654*, ed. Frank V. Walczyk (Coram, NY: Peter's Row, 1998), 4:17, 31.
87. Hening, ed., *Statutes at Large*, 1:377.
88. Commission to Henry Fleete, 18 June 1644, in Browne et al., eds., *Archives of Maryland*, 3:148.
89. Shefveland, *Anglo-Native Virginia*, 23.
90. Briceland, *Westward from Virginia*, 14–16.

91. Trader Richard Traunter found the travel through multiple towns unacceptable enough that he found new ways to ford two rivers himself and proudly reported back that he cut off hundreds of miles from his route. Richard Traunter, "The Travels of Richard Traunter on the Main Continent of America from Appomattox River in Virginia to Charles Town in South Carolina" (1701), Mss. 5L9 T6945, 1–2, Virginia Museum of History and Culture; Bland, "The Discovery of New-Brittaine," 16; Benjamin Harrison, affidavit, 15 November 1707, Lee Family Papers, section 66.
92. Reverend John Blair, "Mission to North Carolina, 1704," in Salley, ed., *Narratives of Early Carolina*, 214.
93. Francis Louis Michel, "Report of the Journey of Francis Louise Michel from Berne, Switzerland, to Virginia, October 2, 1701–December 1, 1702, Part II," *Virginia Magazine of History and Biography* 24, no. 2 (April 1916): 125; Samuel Wilson, "An Account of the Province of Carolina, 1682," in Salley, ed., *Narratives of Early Carolina*, 169.
94. H. R. McIlwaine, *Journals of the House of Burgesses of Virginia, 1659/60–1693* (Richmond: Virginia State Library, 1914), 17.
95. Rice, *Nature and History*, 106.
96. Rountree, *Pocahontas, Powhatan, Opechancanough*, 43, 199, 221.
97. Charles Edgar Gilliam, "The Appomatoc Tribe of Powhatan Algonkians: A Preliminary Outline of Its History from 1607 to 1723," *Archaeological Society of Virginia Quarterly Bulletin* 2, no. 4 (June 1948): 4.
98. There is some debate over whether the farthest point of the expedition was modern-day Clarksville, which would eventually become Occaneechi territory about eighty miles from Fort Henry, or modern-day Roanoke Rapids, which was south along the fall line by sixty miles. The fall line was historically an area for trade and hunting for different Native polities (such as the Algonquian-speaking Appamattucks and the Siouan-speaking Nottoway and Meherrin), and perhaps the expedition followed these zones of interaction. See Briceland, *Westward from Virginia*, and Hantman, *Monacan Millennium*.
99. Bland, "The Discovery of New-Brittaine," 18.
100. Ibid., 9–11.
101. Govert Loockermans to "Uncle and Assoc.," 26 March 1648, in *Govert Loockermans Correspondence and Papers: Stuyvesant-Rutherfurd Papers*, Box 23, transl. Wim Vanraes (Albany, NY: New Netherland Institute, 2014), 32.
102. Bland, "The Discovery of New-Brittaine," 8–9.
103. Ibid., 16.

104. Mary Ellen N. Hodges, *Archaeological Addendum to the Camden National Historic Landmark, Caroline County, Virginia* (Richmond: Division of Historic Landmarks, 1986), 6, fig. 6. Thanks to Martha McCartney for bringing this example to my attention.
105. Greer, *Property and Dispossession*, 317–19; see Carville Earle, *The Evolution of a Tidewater Settlement System: All Hallow's Parish, Maryland, 1650–1783* (Chicago: University of Chicago, Department of Geography Research Paper Series, 1975).
106. Allan Greer discusses the unstable and sometimes nonsensical application of property lines in the seventeenth century in *Property and Dispossession*, 314. This chapter, and the maps throughout this book, align with his assertion (and increasing numbers of data visualizations in the field mapping the relationships between Atlantic World residents) that first, overseas empires are "webs and nodes rather than . . . solid blocks of territory" (6), and second, that property lines are attempts to divide colonists and Native people socially and politically as well as spatially.
107. Andrew McRae, *Literature and Domestic Travel in Early Modern England* (Cambridge: University of Cambridge Press, 2011), 7.
108. Steven Hindle, "Beating the Bounds of the Parish: Order, Memory, and Identity in the English Local Community, c. 1500–1700," in *Defining Community in Early Modern Europe*, ed. Karen E. Spierling and Michael J. Halvorson (New York: Routledge, 2008), 206; Ilana Krausman Ben-Amos, *The Culture of Giving: Informal Support and Gift-Exchange in Early Modern England* (Cambridge: Cambridge University Press, 2009). "Perambulations," as they called their ritual walks, also might set parishioners at odds with landlords, who sought to map and fence their holdings beginning in the early modern period. Alexandra Walsham, *The Reformation of the Landscape: Religion, Identity, and Memory in Early Modern Britain and Ireland* (New York: Oxford University Press, 2011), 534–35. Protestant reformers also altered traditional forms of bounding land, looking to eliminate pre-Reformation understandings of local wells, trees, and springs as sites imbued with religious meaning.
109. Assembly Proceedings, March 1638/9; Assembly Proceedings, August 1642; Assembly Proceedings, September 1642; Commission to Giles Brent, 12 January 1641, in Browne et al., eds., *Archives of Maryland*, 1:59, 163, 194; 3:101.
110. Hening, ed., *Statutes at Large*, 1:116, 125, 173, 262; Greer, *Property and Dispossession*, 346.
111. Greer, *Property and Dispossession*, 313.

112. Tristam Nosworthy, 5 June 1639 land grant, Land Office Patents Reel 1, No. 1, 656; Richard Preston, 11 May 1639 land grant, Land Office Patents Reel 1, No. 1, 645; Charles Harmer, 4 June 1635 land grant, Land Office Patents Reel 1, No. 1, 245.
113. Richard Lee, 20 August 1646 land grant, Land Office Patents Reel 2, No. 2, 62; John Thomas, 7 February 1649 land grant, Land Office Patents Reel 2, No. 2, 188; Walter Broadhurst, 17 October 1650 land grant, Land Office Patents Reel 2, No. 2, 249.
114. Edmund Scarburgh, 29 September 1663 land grant, Land Office Patents Reel 4, No. 4, 581.
115. "Petition of Richard Young," Gloucester County, 19 June 1675, Virginia (Colony), Colonial Papers, State Government Records Collection, Accession 36138, Library of Virginia.
116. Philip Levy, "Middle Plantation's Changing Landscape: Persistence, Continuity, and the Building of Community," 191; "Will of Thomas Goodrich," 15 March 1678/9, in *(Old) Rappahannock County, Virginia Deed and Will Book Abstracts, 1677–1678/9*, ed. Ruth Sparacio and Sam Sparacio (Arlington, VA: Antient Press, 1990), 36; Ludwell, "Examination of Nick Majr."
117. For more on livestock and conflict in early colonial contexts, see Virginia DeJohn Anderson, "King Philip's Herds: Indians, Colonists, and the Problem of Livestock in Early New England," *William and Mary Quarterly*, 3rd series, 51, no. 4 (October 1994): 601–24.
118. Walsh, *Motives of Honor, Pleasure, and Profit*, 104.
119. Northampton County Deeds, Wills, Etc., No. 4 (1651–54), Reel 3, 106, Library of Virginia.
120. Over the course of a two-year period, John Bedford was sentenced to an additional year under David Fox in 1669. William Steward stole hogs and then ran away from David Fox in 1668 and was referred to the court at James City. Richard Higby stole three hogs from John Carter and was sentenced to six years. Another servant of John Carter's was sentenced to eighty lashes instead. Ruth Sparacio and Sam Sparacio, eds., *Lancaster County, Virginia, Order Book Abstracts, 1666–1669* (Arlington, VA: Antient Press, 1993), 46–47, 71, 101. Specifically, there are 104 documented, twentieth-century marshes along the Corotoman River, the largest waterway in Lancaster County. Gene M. Silberhorn, "Lancaster County Tidal Marsh Inventory," Special Report no. 45 (1973; reprint, Gloucester Point: Virginia Institute of Marine Science, 1982), 34; David Fox, 1 November 1653 land grant, Land Office Patents Reel 2, No. 3, 22; John Carter, 19 October 1653 land grant, Land Office Patents Reel 2, No. 3, 88.

121. Ames, ed., *County Court Records of Accomack-Northampton, Virginia, 1640–1645*, 205.
122. Brown, *Good Wives, Nasty Wenches, and Anxious Patriarchs*, 139.
123. Billings, "The Growth of Political Institutions in Virginia," 230, 237.
124. "Second Petition of John Edwards," 15 June 1675, in Billings and Kimberly, eds., *Papers of Sir William Berkeley*, 471.
125. Hening, ed., *Statutes at Large*, 1:370.

6. NEIGHBORS, LOCAL AUTHORITY, AND LOCAL VIOLENCE

1. Rountree, *Pocahontas's People*, 120; Richard White, 12 December 1654 land grant, Land Office Patents Reel 2, No. 3, 310.
2. (Old) Rappahannock County, Records, 1656–1664, Reel 19, 153–54, Library of Virginia. This Rappahannock County is "extinct," and the current Rappahannock County, Virginia, is in a different geographical location. (Old) Rappahannock County was split to form Essex and Richmond Counties in 1692.
3. Berkeley, "A Discourse and View of Virginia," 162.
4. (Old) Rappahannock County, Records, 1656–1664, Reel 19, 153–54.
5. Ibid.
6. Hening, ed., *Statutes at Large*, 1:456–57; Billings, "Some Acts Not in Hening's 'Statutes,'" 72; Seib and Rountree, *Indians of Southern Maryland*, 93; Flick and King, "'We Can Fly No Farther,'" 24. For more on the reserve system, see Martha W. McCartney, "Last Refuge: Tribal Preserves in Eastern Virginia," 222–43. The Virginian preserves were created during the governorship of Samuel Mathews established due to the takeover of Parliamentarians in England.
7. Ruediger, "'Neither Utterly to Reject Them,'" 19. See, for example, the Rappahannock Nation boundaries set in (Old) Rappahannock County, Records, 1656–1664, Reel 19, 257.
8. Rountree, *Pocahontas's People*, 94.
9. Flick and King, "'We Can Fly No Farther,'" 24–25; Assembly Proceedings, April–May 1666, in Browne et al., eds., *Archives of Maryland*, 2:26; Francis Jennings, "Indians and Frontiers in Seventeenth-Century Maryland," in Quinn, ed., *Early Maryland in a Wider World*, 224.
10. Julia A. King, Mary Kate Mansius, and Scott Strickland, "'What Towne Belong You To?' Landscape, Colonialism, and Mobility in the Potomac River Valley," *Historical Archaeology* 50, no. 1 (2016): 7, 18.
11. Strickland, King, and McCartney, *Defining the Greater York River Indigenous Cultural Landscape*, 55; Gallivan, *The Powhatan Landscape*, 19; Hantman, *Monacan Millennium*, 51.

12. Stafford County, Records, 1664–1668, Reel 7, 1, Library of Virginia.
13. Walsh, *Motives of Honor, Pleasure, and Profit*, 140.
14. Darrett B. Rutman and Anita H. Rutman, *A Place in Time: Middlesex County, Virginia, 1650–1750* (New York: Norton, 1984), 73.
15. Menard, *Economy and Society in Early Colonial Maryland*, 157.
16. Ibid., 323; Lorena Walsh, "Servitude and Opportunity in Charles County, Maryland, 1658–1705," in *Law, Society, and Politics in Early Maryland*, ed. Aubrey C. Land, Lois Green Carr, and Edward C. Papenfuse (Baltimore: Johns Hopkins University Press, 1977), 123–26.
17. Noeleen McIlvenna, *A Very Mutinous People: The Struggle for North Carolina, 1660–1713* (Chapel Hill: University of North Carolina Press, 2009), 17–28. See also Jonathan Edward Barth, "'The Sinke of America': Society in the Albemarle Borderlands of North Carolina, 1663–1729," *North Carolina Historical Review* 87, no. 1 (2010): 1.
18. Morgan, *American Slavery, American Freedom*, 136.
19. Coombs, "The Phases of Conversion," 332–60.
20. Ibid., 351; Peter H. Wood, "The Changing Population of the Colonial South: An Overview by Race and Region, 1685–1790," in Waselkov, Wood, and Hatley, eds., *Powhatan's Mantle*, 60–62; Henings, ed., *Statutes at Large*, 2:260.
21. R. P. Stephen Davis Jr., ed., "The Travels of James Needham and Gabriel Arthur through Virginia, North Carolina, and Beyond, 1673–1674," *Southern Indian Studies* 39, no. 1 (1990): 40.
22. Castell, *A Short Discoverie*, 24–25; Mooney, "The Powhatan Confederacy, Past and Present," 134; Hening, ed., *Statutes at Large*, 2:274–75.
23. Laura J. Galke, "Perspectives on the Use of European Material Culture in Two Mid-to-Late 17th-Century Native American Sites in the Chesapeake," *North American Archaeologist* 25, no. 1 (2004): 108; James Harmon et al., "Archaeological Investigations at the Posey Site (18CH281) and 18CH282 Indian Head Division, Naval Surface Warfare Center, Maryland," *Jefferson Patterson Park and Museum Occasional Papers* 7 (1999): 147–51.
24. Strickland et al., *Defining the Rappahannock Indigenous Cultural Landscape*, 33–34; Hening, ed., *Statutes at Large*, 2:274–75.
25. Menard and Carr, "The Lords Baltimore and the Colonization of Maryland," 197. For a recent discussion of the shifts in planning of towns and construction of planters' relationship to the idea of the plantation during this period, see Musselwhite, "Naming Plantations," 741–74.
26. Graham et al., "Adaptation and Innovation," 451–522.
27. Michael Leroy Oberg discussed at length the land claims of elites on the Eastern Shore and on the Northern Neck in *Dominion and Civility: English*

Imperialism and Native America, 1585–1685 (Ithaca, NY: Cornell University Press, 1999), 190.
28. (Old) Rappahannock County, Records, 1668–1672, Reel 20, 166–67.
29. Ibid., 107, 225. It is also worth noting that a ship with the same name as one of Shepheard's, the *Exchange,* entered the service of the Royal African Company in 1676, suggesting that the large number of headrights may have resulted from his share in a ship involved in the trade in enslaved Africans. "Ships Entertained by ye Royall Affrican Company since Xtmas 1674," 17 June 1676, CO 1/24, No. 50.
30. Hening, ed., *Statutes at Large,* 1:468.
31. (Old) Rappahannock County, Records, 1668–1672, Reel 4, 257–58.
32. (Old) Rappahannock County, Deeds & C., 1663–1668, Reel 19, No. 3, 425–26.
33. Ibid., 282, 356.
34. C. G. Chamberlayne, ed., *The Vestry Book of Christ Church Parish, Middlesex County, Virginia, 1663–1767* (Richmond, VA: Old Dominion Press, 1927), 5.
35. Fonzo, *Mapping the Rappahannock Path,* 87.
36. Philip Levy, "Middle Plantation's Changing Landscape: Persistence, Continuity, and the Building of Community," in Bradburn and Coombs, eds., *Early Modern Virginia,* 191.
37. Northumberland County Record Book, 1658–1666, Reel 2, 169, Library of Virginia. See also (Old) Rappahannock County, Records, 1656–1664, Reel 19, 116, and John Benson, 10 April 1667 land grant, Land Office Patents Reel 6, No. 6, 72; Fonzo, *Mapping the Rappahannock Path,* 26.
38. Arthur Pierce Middleton, *Tobacco Coast: A Maritime History of the Chesapeake Bay in the Colonial Era* (Newport News, VA: Mariner's Museum, 1953), 32.
39. Hening, ed., *Statutes at Large,* 2:261.
40. Northampton County, Deeds, Wills, Etc., 1651–1654, Reel 3, 194, Library of Virginia.
41. Stafford County, Court Records, 1689–1693, Reel 7, 45.
42. Middlesex County, Deeds, Etc., 1679–1694, Reel 2, No. 2, 325.
43. (Old) Rappahannock County, Records, 1671–1676, Reel 20, 152–53. In this land sale from Richard White to Bartholomew Wood in 1672, the destination of the path was also called "Chicacus." This path may have been a different one than the one George took ten years before to reach Richard White's plantation house.
44. Michel, "Report of the Journey," 134.
45. Seib and Rountree, *Indians of Southern Maryland,* 82.
46. Clement Herbert, 21 April 1657 patent, Land Office Patent Book Reel 4, No. 4, 45.

47. (Old) Rappahannock County, Records, 1656–1664, Reel 19, 17.
48. Hening, ed., *Statutes at Large*, 1:382.
49. Gilbert Chinard, ed., *Durand de Dauphine, voyages d'un Francois exile pour la Religion* (New York: Press of the Pioneers, 1934), 145–57; "Sale of Land from Henry Chicheley to Ralph Wormeley," 25 December 1674, in Sparacio and Sparacio, eds., *(Old) Rappahannock County Virginia Deed Book Abstracts, 1673/4–1676*, ed. Ruth Sparacio and Sam Sparacio (Arlington, VA: Antient, 1999), 88; Hening, ed., *Statutes at Large*, 2:138–43.
50. R. G., *Virginia's Cure; or, An Advisive Narrative Concerning Virginia* (London: W. Godbid, 1662), 6.
51. John Clayton, "A Letter from the Revd Mr. John Clayton (Afterwards Dean of Kildare in Ireland) to Dr. Grew, in Answer to Several Queries Relating to Virginia, Sent to Him by That Learned Gentleman, A.D. 1687," *Royal Society Philosophical Transactions* 41, no. 454 (31 October 1739): 144.
52. Rice, *Nature and History*, 112.
53. D. Brad Hatch, "Venison Trade and Interaction between English Colonists and Native Americans in Virginia's Potomac River Valley," *Northeast Historical Archaeology* 41, no. 1 (2012): 18–49.
54. D. Brad Hatch, Lauren K. McMillan, and Barbara J. Heath, *Archaeological Reassessment of the Hallowes Site (44WM6)* (Knoxville: University of Tennessee Archaeological Reports, 2013), 120–30.
55. Hening, ed., *Statutes at Large*, 2:142.
56. George Alsop, *A Character of the Province of Maryland* (New York: William Gowans, 1869), 38–39; Durand de Dauphine, *Voyages d'un Francois Exile pour la Religion*, ed. Gilbert Chinard (New York: Press of the Pioneers, 1934), 151, 153.
57. John Hammond, *Leah and Rachel; or, The Two Fruitfull Sisters, Virginia and Mary-Land* (London: T. Mabb, 1656), 9.
58. Stanley Pargellis, "An Account of the Indians in Virginia," *William and Mary Quarterly*, 3rd series, 16, no. 2 (April 1959): 231.
59. Dugout Canoe, c. 1630, accession 1969.0001.000001A, Mariners Museum, Newport News, VA; Jacob M. Orcutt, "Mishoonash in Southern New England: Construction and Use of Dugout Canoes in a Multicultural Context," MA thesis, University of Massachusetts, Amherst, 2014, https://scholarworks.umass.edu/masters_theses_2/106.
60. Thomas Reade, "Life of Thomas Reade, Rector of Moreton, in the County of Dorcet, Written by His Own Hand, and Design'd to Be Continued by Him, so Long as God Shall Prolong It," 27, Albert and Shirley Small Special Collections Library.

61. Michel, "Report of the Journey," 31. Published in 1708, Ebeneezer Cooke's satirical poem labeled bear cub, pone, hominy, "Sider-Pap," and bacon "our Indian Country Fare" and his pipe an "Indian gun." Ebenezer Cooke, *The Maryland Muse/The Sotweed Factor*, ed. Lawrence Wroth (Worcester, MA: American Antiquarian Society, 1934), 328.
62. York County, Deeds, Orders, Wills, vol. 3, 1657–1662, Reel 2, 143, 149, Library of Virginia.
63. Hening, ed., *Statutes at Large*, 1:219; Traunter, "The Travels of Richard Traunter," 30.
64. Hening, ed., *Statutes at Large*, 1:401–2.
65. Archaeology at sites occupied for extended periods has shown that wild game and fish, popular in the seventeenth century, decreased in importance as a good source of food over time, replaced by domestic stock. The faunal remains at Clifts Plantation, a domestic site on the Potomac River occupied between the seventeenth and nineteenth centuries, demonstrate that 14 percent of animal proteins came from wild game during the mid-seventeenth century, and this proportion was even greater at other sites. Fraser D. Neiman, *Field Archaeology of the Clifts Plantation Site, Westmoreland County, Virginia* (Stratford, VA: Robert E. Lee Memorial Association, 1980), 199.
66. Northumberland County, Record Book, 1658–1666, Reel 2, 82–84, 107. The 1662 inventory of Elizabeth Colclough, administrator of Simon Oversey's estate, listed a Native girl and boy as servants, but the appraisal of Oversey's estate the following year listed a Native boy and girl as slaves. Shefveland, *Anglo-Native Virginia*, 43–48.
67. Deal, "Race and Class in Colonial Virginia," 61.
68. Shefveland, "The Many Faces of Native Bonded Labor," 79; Guasco, "To 'Doe Some Goode upon Their Countrymen,'" 399.
69. "Kent County Court Proceedings, 1656–1662," 20 December 1660, in Browne et al., eds., *Archives of Maryland*, 54:191.
70. Northumberland County, Records, 1650–1655, Reel 1, 42; Fausz, "Middlemen in Peace and War," 59; Rountree and Davidson, *Eastern Shore Indians of Virginia and Maryland*, 45.
71. Stafford County, Record Book, 1686–1693/4, Reel 7A, 80–82.
72. Rountree and Davidson, *Eastern Shore Indians of Virginia and Maryland*, 73.
73. Michael Leroy Oberg, "Introduction," in Oberg, ed., *Samuel Wiseman's Book of Record*, 7–8.
74. For an example, see (Old) Rappahannock County, Deeds & C., 1663–1668, Reel 2, 425–26, and Northumberland County, Record Book, 1652–1658, Reel 2, 101. See also Ragan, "Where the Water Ebbs and Flows," 185–87.

75. Kruer, "Bloody Minds and People Undone," 415.
76. Matthew Dennis, *Cultivating a Landscape of Peace: Iroquois-European Encounters in Seventeenth-Century America* (Ithaca, NY: Cornell University Press, 1993), 252; Provincial Court Proceedings, 1658, in Browne et al., eds., *Archives of Maryland* (Baltimore: Maryland Historical Society, 1922), 41:232.
77. Alsop, *A Character of the Province of Maryland*, 73.
78. McIlwaine, ed., *Minutes of the Council and General Court of Colonial Virginia*, 15.
79. Ibid. Wood's seat on the Appomattox River was close to profit but far from danger at that moment.
80. "Proceedings of the Council, 8 August 1663," in Browne et al., eds., *Archives of Maryland*, 3:433, 460.
81. William Berkeley to Henry Bennett, Earl of Arlington, 11 November 1667, in Billings and Kimberly, eds., *Papers of Sir William Berkeley*, 331.
82. Thomas Lynch to "Dr. Worsly," 8 July 1673, CO 1/30, No. 49, CO 389/5, 173–76.
83. "William Berkeley to Charles II and the Privy Council, Jamestown, July 1673," in Billings and Kimberly, eds., *Papers of Sir William Berkeley*, 423.
84. Oldmixon, *British Empire in America*, 1:381.
85. Berkeley, "A Discourse and View of Virginia," 164.
86. Hening, ed., *Statutes at Large*, 2:187.
87. McIlwaine, *Journals of the House of Burgesses of Virginia, 1659/60–1693*, 9, 15; Henings, ed., *Statutes at Large*, 2:152–53.
88. McIlwaine, ed., *Minutes of the Council and General Court of Colonial Virginia*, 14–15.
89. Westmoreland County, Deeds, Wills, Etc., 1661–1662, Reel 1, 71, Library of Virginia. One of these commissioners, John Carter, patented four thousand acres on the north side of the Rappahannock River in 1664, suggesting he may have had a personal investment in keeping friendly justices in place. James Rice discusses Fowke's use of fear of northern Native people in *Nature and History*, 135.
90. Hening, ed., *Statutes at Large*, 2:197.
91. William Berkeley to John Carter, Moore Fauntleroy, Henry Fleete, Henry Corbyn, and Matthew Kemp, 12 July 1660, in Billings and Kimberly, eds., *Papers of Sir William Berkeley*, 123.
92. McIlwaine, *Journals of the House of Burgesses of Virginia, 1659/60–1693*, 15.
93. William Berkeley, "Authorization for a Reservation in Accomack County," 11 October 1660, in Billings and Kimberly, eds., *Papers of Sir William Berkeley*, 133.

94. Deal, "Race and Class in Colonial Virginia," 71. See, for example, Edmund Scarburgh [Scarborough], 25 August 1642 land grant, Land Office Patents Reel 1, No. 1, 817.
95. Susie Ames, "The Reunion of Two Virginia Counties," *Journal of Southern History* 8, no. 4 (1942): 542; "Articles of Agreement," 25 June 1668, in Browne et al., eds., *Archives of Maryland*, 5:44.
96. Rice, *Nature and History*, 144.
97. "Proceedings of the Council, 1657–1660," in Browne et al., eds., *Archives of Maryland*, 3:376–80; Rice, *Nature and History*, 126.
98. Deal, "Race and Class in Colonial Virginia," 39.
99. Rountree and Davidson, *Eastern Shore Indians of Virginia and Maryland*, 70; Ames, "The Reunion of Two Virginia Counties," 537–39, 542.
100. See, for example, Petition of Captain Daniel Howe, 6 June 1654, CO 1/32, No. 7.
101. Deal, "Race and Class in Colonial Virginia," 147–50.
102. Hening, ed., *Statutes at Large*, 2:184.
103. "Proceedings of the Council, 1660–1661," in Browne et al., eds., *Archives of Maryland*, 5:474; Carr, Menard, and Walsh, *Robert Cole's World*, 16.
104. Calvert also noted that Scarborough traveled without his fellow surveyors into Maryland territory, and that Governor Berkeley disclaimed any knowledge of his actions. Charles Calvert, "Proclamation," in Browne et al., eds., *Archives of Maryland*, 3:497.
105. Hening, ed., *Statutes at Large*, 1:379.
106. "Letter from Edmund Scarborough to William Berkeley," November 1663, in Billings and Kimberly, eds., *Papers of Sir William Berkeley*, 413–17.
107. Ibid.
108. "Proceedings of the Council, 8 April 1663," in Browne et al., eds., *Archives of Maryland*, 3:474.
109. Robinson, ed., "Notes from the Council and General Court Records," 169; "Boundary Question," 3 June 1664, in Browne et al., eds., *Archives of Maryland*, 3:396–98. Secretary of the Colony Thomas Ludwell demonstrated the colony's support for the movement north of the boundary two years later when he asked the king for support of his "antientist plantation," arguing, "were wee not so invaded by your neighboring plantations who, of as much land as France, have not left us so much as Yorkshire." Thomas Ludwell to Secretary Lord Arlington, 10 April 1665, CO 1/19, No. 93.
110. McIlwaine, *Journals of the House of Burgesses of Virginia, 1659/60–1693*, 28.
111. Deal, "Race and Class in Colonial Virginia," 46.
112. Shefveland, *Anglo-Native Virginia*, 30–31; Hening, ed., *Statutes at Large*, 2:193–94; Rice, *Nature and History*, 137.

113. John Catlett to Thomas Catlett, 1 April 1664, Misc. Manuscripts, John D. Rockefeller Library, Colonial Williamsburg Foundation, Williamsburg, VA.
114. William Berkeley, "Petition of Planters from Rappahannock and Westmoreland Counties," 10 September 1663, in Billings and Kimberly, eds., *Papers of Sir William Berkeley*, 209. Original source not found. In response to their remonstrance, the assembly passed a law ordering the Patawomecks to turn over Native children hostages as insurance for goodwill, and that the werowance of the Patawomecks had to pursue the unknown Native murderers of English families, who the assembly suspected were Doegs. Hening, ed., *Statutes at Large*, 2:193–94. Because the letter mentioned "pursute of the Arickehockians" rather than Rickehockian villages or people, it is likely that this group was from the interior and frequented the area on the Maryland-Virginia border at this time, or Haudenosaunee raiders, who came south seasonally. See Rice, "Bacon's Rebellion in Indian Country."
115. John Catlett to Thomas Catlett, 1 April 1664, Misc. Manuscripts, John D. Rockefeller Library.
116. Ibid.
117. Ibid.
118. Hening, ed., *Statutes at Large*, 2:220–21. See also Edward DuBois Ragan, "'Scatter'd upon the English Seats': Indian Identity and Land Occupancy in the Rappahannock River Valley," in Bradburn and Coombs, eds., *Early Modern Virginia*, 222.
119. (Old) Rappahannock County, Records, 1656–1664, Reel 19, 367; McIlwaine, *Journals of the House of Burgesses of Virginia, 1659/60–1693*, 41; Rice, *Nature and History*, 135.
120. "The Case of the Deft., Fitzhugh vs. Fowke," Fowke/Fowlke Family Papers, Shirley and Albert Small Special Collections Library.
121. "Letter from John Catlett, Thomas Goodrich, John Weir, and Humphrey Booth, Rappahannock County to Sir William Berkeley," June 1666, in Billings and Kimberly, eds., *Papers of Sir William Berkeley*, 284.
122. "Letter from William Berkeley to Robert Smith, June 22, 1666," in ibid., 284. Rebecca Anne Goetz discusses this tactic in her work on George's people, the Nanzaticos in "The Nanziatticos and the Violence of the Archive: Land and Enslavement in Colonial Virginia," *Journal of Southern History* 85, no. 1 (2019): 33–60. Rice, *Nature and History in the Potomac Country*, 137.
123. William Berkeley, "Warrant for the Arrest of Edmund Scarborough," 12 September 1670, in Billings and Kimberly, eds., *Papers of Sir William Berkeley*, 380.

124. John Catlett to Thomas Catlett, 1 April 1664, Misc. Manuscripts, John D. Rockefeller Library.
125. Berkeley, "Warrant for the Arrest of Edmund Scarborough," 380.
126. Ibid., 380; Ames, "The Reunion of Two Virginia Counties," 537–42.

7. REBELLING BY THE BAY

1. Although this escape was planned and almost executed in 1670–71, the depositions were not taken until mid-1672. Accomack County, Deeds, Orders, and Wills, 1671–1673, Reel 2, 93, Library of Virginia. For map 5, see Devereaux Browne, 16 October 1670 land grant, Land Office Patents Reel 6, No. 6, 405; Richard Hill, 20 February 1663 land grant, Land Office Patents Reel 5, No. 5, 221; Jenkin Price, 10 March 1652 land patent, Land Office Patents Reel 2, No. 3, 191; Jenkin Price, 26 April 1655 land grant, Land Office Patents Reel 2, No. 3, 341; Thomas Teagle, 10 May 1652 land grant, Land Office Patents Reel 2, No. 3, 101; John Jenkins, 20 October 1661 land grant, Land Office Patents Reel 4, No. 4, 501; John West, 10 August 1664 land grant, Land Office Patents Reel 5, No. 5, 75; and Accomack County, Deeds, Orders, and Wills, 1671–1673, Reel 2, 95–97.
2. Accomack County, Deeds, Orders, and Wills, 1671–1673, Reel 2, 95–97.
3. Vanessa Holden discusses the role of Black women in the "continuum" between resistance and rebellion, and the role of enslaved community members in mapping human geography on overlapping landscapes of control and resistance, in *Surviving Southampton: African American Women and Resistance in Nat Turner's Community* (Urbana-Champaign: University of Illinois Press, 2021).
4. Hening, ed., *Statutes at Large*, 2:266, 273–74, 277–78.
5. Ibid., 2:94.
6. Ibid., 2:95.
7. Ibid., 2:94–97; "Inventory of Robert Pitt Estate," 8 July 1670, in *Accomack County, Virginia Court Order Abstracts*, ed. JoAnn Riley McKey (Bowie, MD: Heritage Books, 1996), 3:111. When they missed their chance with Black James, two servants from the original plot went searching for another pilot and found two more candidates at the home of a nearby yeoman.
8. Deal, "Race and Class in Colonial Virginia," 22.
9. Hening, ed., *Statutes at Large*, 2:299–300.
10. Coombs, "The Phases of Conversion," 360.
11. See Schmidt, *The Divided Dominion*, 2.
12. McIlwaine, *Journals of the House of Burgesses of Virginia, 1659/60–1693*, 101.

13. [John Cotton?], *History of Bacon's and Ingram's Rebellion* (Cambridge: John Wilson and Son, 1867), 50–51.
14. While most scholars account for reduction in available land and an increase in the number of disfranchised freedmen in the colony as components of the rebellion, historians have moved from a focus on the stability of politics in Virginian society to reinterpretations reflecting both local and continental scales. As mentioned in the introduction, earlier works like Morgan's *American Slavery, American Freedom* argued in part that the nonelites' uncontrollable behavior reflected a government with little control over them, leading to an increased reliance on African slavery and cross-class identification between white men based on race. Historians have since pushed commitment to racialized African slavery much earlier than in Morgan's work. As John C. Coombs argues persuasively, "There were not men on the verge of turning to slavery; they already had. And neither Bacon's Rebellion nor the steep decline in the availability of white servants that occurred in the years after the revolt had anything to do with it." John C. Coombs, "Beyond the 'Origins Debate': Rethinking the Rise of Virginia Slavery," in Bradburn and Coombs, eds., *Early Modern Virginia*, 249. See also Kendi and Blain, eds., *Four Hundred Souls*, for additional examples. In recent years, historians and anthropologists have pointed to Native diplomatic ruptures occurring often at great distances to the north and south of Virginia, namely in the fur and slave trades to the south, and in wars involving the Haudenosaunee to the north, producing a multisided series of conflicts among Native nations of which Virginia was only a part. See Rice, "Bacon's Rebellion in Indian Country," 730–31, and Beck, *Chiefdoms, Collapse, and Coalescence in the Early American South*. In her study of the fur trade through Virginian and Maryland boundaries, Andrea Smalley argues that the trade delegitimized borders as English fur traders crossed them to engage with Native people who threatened settlements, pitting visions of extractive and settler colonialism against one another. Smalley, *Wild by Nature: North American Animals Confront Colonialization* (Baltimore: Johns Hopkins University Press, 2017), 42. This chapter adds the long history of escaped laborers and other transgressors as discrete political actors—something historians should do more often—who heightened the stakes of Native proximity and English rebellion by flouting boundaries from the inside rather than just the outside; elite traders into the interior also protected settler colonialism in the form of plantations and chattel in their entry into Native diplomacy. Additionally, this chapter builds on the comparative analysis of county governments. Warren Billings and Brent Tarter both take a closer look at local

governments as stable, if often corrupt, loci of control. The post-rebellion county grievances against some of those officials, submitted to royal authorities, are a key explanation of the rebellion. In my focus on county and local relationships, I have followed their lead and extend this here with a look at longstanding relationships between county officials and Algonquian people outlined in the grievances. Tarter, "Bacon's Rebellion, the Grievances of the People, and the Political Culture of Seventeenth-Century Virginia," *Virginia Magazine of History and Biography* 119, no. 1 (2011): 2–41; Billings, "The Growth of Political Institutions in Virginia," 225–42.

15. Rice, *Nature and History*, 143. Rice argues that these problems were compounded by tributary status, which encouraged English settlers to see Native people as dependents on the governor.

16. Conway Robinson, ed., "Notes from the Council and General Court Records 1641–1672 (Continued)," *Virginia Magazine of History and Biography* 8, no. 3 (January 1901): 239; Robinson, ed., "Notes from the Council and General Court Records 1641–1678 (Continued)," *Virginia Magazine of History and Biography* 9, no. 1 (July 1901): 47; Hening, *Statutes at Large*, 2:141; McIlwaine, *Journals of the House of Burgesses of Virginia, 1659/60–1693*, 13; Russo and Russo, *Planting an Empire*, 85; Martha W. McCartney, "Last Refuge," 222.

17. Hening, ed., *Statutes at Large*, 2:185, 237–38.

18. McIlwaine, *Journals of the House of Burgesses of Virginia, 1659/60–1693*, 41, 51.

19. Flick and King, "'We Can Fly No Farther,'" 24–25; Ragan, "Where the Water Ebbs and Flows," 198.

20. Kruer, "Bloody Minds and Peoples Undone," 1–5.

21. Assembly Proceedings, April–May 1666, in Browne et al., eds., *Archives of Maryland*, 2:26.

22. Seib and Rountree, *Indians of Southern Maryland*, 92.

23. Strickland, Busby, and King, "Indigenous Cultural Landscapes Study for the Nanjemoy and Mattawoman Creek Watersheds," 25.

24. Flick and King, "'We Can Fly No Farther,'" 33.

25. Beck, *Chiefdoms, Collapse, and Coalescence in the Early American South*, chapter 3.

26. Rice, "Bacon's Rebellion in Indian County," 726–50.

27. Smalley, *Wild by Nature*, 71. See also Rice, "Bacon's Rebellion in Indian Country," 731–32.

28. Oberg, *Dominion and Civility*, 212.

29. Maryland Historical Trust, "Phase II and III Archaeological Database and Inventory, 18PR241," Maryland Archaeological Synthesis Project, https://mht.maryland.gov/secure/synthesis/SynthesisDetail.aspx?Class=18PR241.
30. Josias Fendall, "Complaint from Heaven with Huy and Crye and a Petition Out of Virginia and Maryland," in Browne et al., eds., *Archives of Maryland*, 5:144–45.
31. Hening, ed., *Statutes at Large*, 2:194.
32. Ibid., 2:219. The law also stipulated that if townspeople killed the chosen werowance, the English would make war on (and presumably dispossess and enslave) them. This could be the result of the Rappahannocks' rejection of a werowance approved by the English named Towerozen. He was killed sometime between when his authority was confirmed by the English in September 1653 and the following month. Lancaster County, Deed and Will Book No. 1, 1652–1657, Reel 1, 25, Library of Virginia; Lancaster Orders, 1655–1666, Reel 24, 125–26, Library of Virginia; Hening, *Statutes at Large*, 2:219.
33. "The Counties' Grievances," in Oberg, ed., *Samuel Wiseman's Book of Record*, 218, 236.
34. William Berkeley, "Address to Charles II, James Citty," 24 March 1675/6, in Billings and Kimberly, eds., *Papers of Sir William Berkeley*, 504.
35. Henry Norwood to Joseph Williamson, 17 July 1667, CO 1/21, No. 84.
36. Billings, *Sir William Berkeley and the Forging of Colonial Virginia*, 199, 226.
37. "Order-in-Council for the Defense of Virginia," 22 April 1673; "William Berkeley to Charles II and the Privy Council," July 1673, in Billings and Kimberly, eds., *Papers of Sir William Berkeley*, 417, 423.
38. D. Brad Hatch, "An Historical Archaeology of Early Modern Manhood in the Potomac River Valley of Virginia, 1645–1730," PhD diss., University of Tennessee Knoxville, 2015, 172.
39. Jennings, "Glory, Death, and Transfiguration," 32.
40. Donald Shomette, *Raid on America: The Dutch Naval Campaign of 1672–1674* (Columbia: University of South Carolina Press, 1988), 126–27.
41. "William Berkeley to Charles II and the Privy Council," July 1673, in Billings and Kimberly, eds., *Papers of Sir William Berkeley*, 423.
42. Ibid., 423.
43. Hening, *Statutes at Large*, 2:327–30.
44. Michael Leroy Oberg, "Introduction," in Oberg, ed., *Samuel Wiseman's Book of Record*, 14–15.

45. "Pardon to Mathew Swan," 23 September 1674, in Billings and Kimberly, eds., *Papers of Sir William Berkeley*, 455; Schmidt, *The Divided Dominion*, 139.
46. Brown, *Good Wives, Nasty Wenches, and Anxious Patriarchs*, 138–39.
47. Tarter, "Bacon's Rebellion, the Grievances of the People," 21.
48. Walsh, *Motives of Honor, Pleasure, and Profit*, 123–26; Jon Kukla, ed., "Some Acts Not in Hening's 'Statutes': The Acts of Assembly, October 1660," *Virginia Magazine of History and Biography* 83, no. 1 (January 1975): 95.
49. William Berkeley, "Proclamation Interdicting the Indian Trade, October 1675," in Billings and Kimberly, eds., *Papers of Sir William Berkeley*, 494.
50. Nicholas Spencer to Philip Calvert, 22 June 1677, CO 140, No. 113.
51. Graham et al., "Adaptation and Innovation," 520; John C. Coombs, "Building 'The Machine': The Development of Slavery and Slave Society in Early Colonial Virginia," PhD diss., College of William and Mary, 2003, 69–99.
52. Julia A. King and Douglas H. Ubelaker, *Living and Dying on the 17th Century Patuxent Frontier* (Crownsville: Maryland Historical Trust Press, 1996), 109–10.
53. Anna Sophia Agbe-Davies, "Up in Smoke: Pipe-Making, Smoking, and Bacon's Rebellion," PhD diss., University of Pennsylvania, 2004, 303–4.
54. "An Act Agt Runnawayes and Such Persons That Shall Give Them Entertainmt and Others That Shal Travell without Passes," April 1671, in Browne et al., eds., *Archives of Maryland*, 2:298.
55. William Berkeley to Edward Hyde, Earl of Clarendon, 28 March 1663, in Billings and Kimberly, eds., *Papers of Sir William Berkeley*, 186–87.
56. Raphael Semmes, *Crime and Punishment in Early Maryland* (Baltimore: Johns Hopkins University Press, 1938), 110.
57. (Old) Rappahannock County, Records, 1656–1664, Reel 19, 10–11.
58. "An Act Agt Runnawayes and Such Persons That Shall Give Them Entertainmt," 2:298.
59. Hening, ed., *Statutes at Large*, 2:279.
60. Ibid., 2:279, 299.
61. McIlwaine, *Journals of the House of Burgesses of Virginia, 1659/60–1693*, 55.
62. Hening, ed., *Statutes at Large*, 1:483.
63. Ibid., 2:273–74.
64. Ibid., 2:187–88. With the 1660 Treaty of Amity, the Dutch agreed to return servants who had fled to New Netherland from the English colonies. "Articles of Amity and Commerce with New Netherlands," 18 May 1660, in Billings and Kimberly, eds., *Papers of Sir William Berkeley*, 121.
65. Hening, ed., *Statutes at Large*, 2:273–74.
66. Ibid., 2:274, 278.

NOTES TO PAGES 197–202   293

67. Deeds, Wills, Etc., of Upper Northampton, 1671–1673, Accomack County, Records, 1671–1673, Reel 2, 50.
68. York County, Deeds, Order, Wills, Book 8, 1687–1691, Reel 4, 162, Library of Virginia.
69. See the grievances of Northampton and Isle of Wight Counties for examples from "The Counties' Grievances," in Oberg, ed., *Samuel Wiseman's Book of Record*, 226–36.
70. "Petition of Tabitha Browne," 18 June 1675, in Billings and Kimberly, eds., *The Papers of Sir William Berkeley*, 477.
71. Deal, "Race and Class in Colonial Virginia," 63; Rountree and Davidson, *Eastern Shore Indians of Virginia and Maryland*, 73.
72. Deeds, Wills, Etc. of Upper Northampton, Accomack County, Records, 1671–1673, Reel 2, 24.
73. Robert Pitt, 2 October 1663 land grant, Land Office Patents Reel 5, No. 5, 81.
74. Northampton County, Deeds and Wills, Book 4, 1651–1654, Reel 3, 93.
75. Ibid., 96.
76. Deal, "Race and Class in Colonial Virginia," 68; Rountree and Davidson, *Eastern Shore Indians of Virginia and Maryland*, 76–78; "Warrant for the Arrest of Edmund Scarburgh," 12 September 1670, in Billings and Kimberly, eds., *Papers of Sir William Berkeley*, 380.
77. Deal, "Race and Class in Colonial Virginia," 64; Accomack County, Deeds, Wills, Etc. of Upper Northampton, 1671–1673, Reel 2, 119.
78. "Commission to Col. William Burges," 23 March 1677, in Browne et al., eds., *Archives of Maryland*, 15:142–43. The wording is unclear, but "Amonugus" may be listed as an "Emporer of Assateague" here.
79. Robert Hutchinson, 5 May 1679 land grant, Land Office Patents Reel 6, No. 6, 683. Location of Matomkin land in the mid-1660s is based on the patent of John Dye, 10 August 1664 land grant, Land Office Patents Reel 5, no. 6, 75. Rountree and Davidson, *Eastern Shore Indians of Virginia and Maryland*, 73.
80. Deal, "Race and Class in Colonial Virginia," 68.
81. Accomack County Deeds Orders Wills of Upper Northampton, 1671–1673, Reel 2, 11.
82. "The Randolph Manuscript: Virginia Seventeenth Century Records (Continued)," *Virginia Magazine of History and Biography* 17, no. 4 (October 1909): 344. For a full account of the rebellion, see Rice, *Tales from a Revolution*.
83. Thomas Mathews, "The Beginning, Progress, and Conclusion of Bacon's Rebellion in Virginia," in Charles M. Andrews, ed., *Narratives of the Insurrections, 1675–1690* (New York: Scribner's Sons, 1915), 17.

84. "Mr. Bacon's Acct of Their Troubles in Virginia by ye Indians, June ye 18th, 1676," *William and Mary Quarterly*, 1st series, 9, no. 1 (July 1900): 9.
85. Wilcomb A. Washburn, *The Governor and the Rebel: A History of Bacon's Rebellion in Virginia* (Chapel Hill: University of North Carolina Press, 1957), 37.
86. Lyon G. Tyler, ed., "Col. John Washington: Further Details of His Life from the Records of Westmoreland Co., Virginia," *William and Mary Quarterly*, 1st series, 2, no. 1 (July 1893): 40.
87. Mathews, "The Beginning, Progress, and Conclusion of Bacon's Rebellion in Virginia," 47. Bioarchaeologist Sara K. Becker has also discussed the lack of evidence of physical violence in Susquehannock and Piscataway skeletal remains, pointing instead to a modest rise in disease rates, possible long-term diet deficiencies and acute periods of starvation at least partially related to European contact. Becker, "Health Consequences of Contact on Two Seventeenth-Century Native Groups from the Mid-Atlantic Region of Maryland," *International Journal of Historical Archaeology* 17, no. 1 (2013): 713–30. See also Kruer, *Time of Anarchy*, 56–60.
88. "Remonstrance from the Chief of the Susquehannock," February 1676, in Billings and Kimberly, eds., *Papers of Sir William Berkeley*, 499.
89. Fendall, "Complaint from Heaven with a Huy and Crye," 5:135.
90. Rice, "Bacon's Rebellion in Indian Country," 742.
91. Fendall, "Complaint from Heaven with a Huy and Crye," 5:135.
92. Address to Charles II, 24 March 1675/6, in Billings and Kimberly, eds., *Papers of Sir William Berkeley*, 504.
93. Rice, "Bacon's Rebellion in Indian Country," 738.
94. William Berkeley to Thomas Ludwell, 16 February 1675/6, in Billings and Kimberly, eds., *Papers of Sir William Berkeley*, 498. See also William Harris to Sir Joseph Williamson, 12 August 1676, Colonial Records Office, vol. 9, 441–44.
95. Governor Lord Vaughan to Secretary Coventry, 4 January 1677, in Sainsbury and Fortescue, eds., *Calendar of State Papers, Colonial*, 10:2–13.
96. Fendall, "Complaint from Heaven with a Huy and Crye," 5:134.
97. McIlvenna, *A Very Mutinous People*, 54–55. North Carolina experienced unrest in 1673 and again in 1676, resulting in an overthrow of the governor in 1677.
98. McIlwaine, ed., *Minutes of the Council and General Court of Colonial Virginia*, 98.
99. Negrin, "Possessing Native Women and Children," 117, 134, 165; Shefveland, *Anglo-Native Virginia*, 60–61. See also Shefveland, "The Many Faces of Native Bonded Labor," 68–91; C. S. Everett, "They Shalbe Slaves for

Their Lives," in *Indian Slavery in Colonial America*, ed. Alan Gallay (Lincoln: University of Nebraska Press, 2009), 67–108; and Kruer, *Time of Anarchy*, 45.
100. Abraham Wood to John Richards, 22 August 1674, in Sainsbury and Fortescue, eds., *Calendar of State Papers, Colonial*, 7:604–7.
101. Rice, *Tales from a Revolution*, 34.
102. William Berkeley to Nathaniel Bacon, 14 September 1675; Bacon to Berkeley, 18 September 1675, in Billings and Kimberly, eds., *Papers of Sir William Berkeley*, 486–87, 491.
103. Petition of William Howard, 23 November 1677; Petition of Henry West, 21 November 1677, in Sainsbury and Fortescue, eds., *Calendar of State Papers, Colonial*, 10:174–86.
104. Mathews, "The Beginning, Progress, and Conclusion of Bacon's Rebellion in Virginia," 20.
105. (Old) Rappahannock County, Records, 1677–1687, Reel 21, 82–83.
106. Moryson, "A Letter Written to Sir William Jones," 127.
107. William Travers to Giles Cale, May 13, 1676, in Sainsbury and Fortescue, eds., *Calendar of State Papers, Colonial*, 9:391.
108. Gerard Fowke, "Col. Gerard Fowke and the Indians," *William and Mary Quarterly*, 1st series, 8, no. 1 (July 1899): 25.
109. "A Narrative of the Rise, Progresse and Cesssation of the Late Rebellion in Virginia," 148.
110. (Old) Rappahannock County, Records, 1671–1676, Reel 20, 75.
111. "A Discription of the Fight between the English and the Indians in Virginia in May 1676," *William and Mary Quarterly*, 1st series, 9, no. 1 (July 1900): 2.
112. Philip Ludwell to Joseph Williamson, 28 June 1676, in "Bacon's Rebellion," *Virginia Magazine of History and Biography* 1, no. 2 (October 1893): 182–83. Kruer disputes the narrative that the Occaneechi were totally destroyed, or even dislodged from the island, in *Time of Anarchy*, 76.
113. "Journal and Relation of a New Discovery Made Behind the Apuleian Mountains to the West of Virginia," October 1671, in Sainsbury and Fortescue, eds., *Calendar of State Papers, Colonial*, 7:270–71.
114. Abraham Wood to William Berkeley, 22 March 1676, in Billings and Kimberly, eds., *Papers of Sir William Berkeley*, 522.
115. The Appamattucks and the English were also at odds after the rebellion; the commissioners did not seat the werowance because he was either harboring a murderer or was a murderer himself. If the former, it may have meant that Nessom escaped jail.
116. "A Narrative of the Rise, Progresse and Cesssation of the Late Rebellion in Virginia," 149.

117. Hening, ed., *Statutes at Large*, 2:351–52, 380.
118. Rice, *Tales from a Revolution*, 71, 77–78, 93.
119. Philip Ludwell to Joseph Williamson, 28 June 1676, in "Bacon's Rebellion," 180.
120. McIlwaine, ed., *Minutes of the Council and General Court of Colonial Virginia*, 89–90.
121. "A Narrative of the Rise, Progresse and Cesssation of the Late Rebellion in Virginia, by His Majesties Commissioners," 1677, in Oberg, ed., *Samuel Wiseman's Book of Record*, 158–60. Men, women, and children are mentioned together as captives or defenders of the homes attacked by Bacon in the Dragon Swamp. Lisa Brooks also notices this pattern in her study of Mary Rowlandson and Weetamoo's journey through New England swamps in "'Every Swamp Is a Castle': Navigating Native Spaces in the Connecticut River Valley, Winter 1675–1677 and 2005–2015," *Northeastern Naturalist* 24, special volume 7 (March 2017): 52.
122. Smith quoted in Kupperman, *Jamestown Project*, 230.
123. Washburn, *The Governor and the Rebel*, 76; "A True Narrative of the Rebellion of Virginia, by the Royal Commissioners, 1677," in Andrews, ed., *Narratives of the Insurrections*, 123–27.
124. "A List of the Names of Those Worthy Persons Whose Services and Sufferings by the Late Rebell Nathaniell Bacon Junior and His Party Have Been Reported to Us," in Oberg, ed., *Samuel Wiseman's Book of Record*, 279; Nicholas Spencer to Philip Calvert, Chancellor of Maryland, 22 June 1677, CO 1/40, No. 113.
125. John Harold Sprinkle, "Loyalists and Baconians: The Participants in Bacon's Rebellion in Virginia, 1676–1677," PhD diss., College of William and Mary, 1992, 67. Much of the rebellion's core action took place in the northern part of the colony where records are no longer extant, making it difficult to quantify the ratio or understand the spectrum of motivations of the rebels and loyalists in each region.
126. Agbe-Davies, "Up in Smoke," 60–61.
127. Sprinkle, "Loyalists and Baconians," 106.
128. "Characters of the Severall Commanders," in Oberg, ed., *Samuel Wiseman's Book of Record*, 276–77; "Questions Proposed by His Majestie and Councill, to Which I Returne This Humble Plane and True Answer," in Oberg, ed., *Samuel Wiseman's Book of Record*, 206.
129. Rice, *Tales from a Revolution*, 86–89.
130. "Journal of the Ship Young Prince, Robert Morris, Commander, during the Time She Was in the King's Service in James River," CO 1/37, No. 52, Colonial State Papers.

131. "Characters of the Severall Commanders," 276; Kelly, "'In Dispers'd Country Plantations,'" 195.
132. "Characters of the Severall Commanders," 276.
133. *A Narrative of the Indian and Civil Wars in Virginia, in the Years 1675 and 1676* (Boston: John Eliot, 1814), 44; Hening, ed., *Statutes at Large*, 2:395; "Characters of the Severall Commanders," 276.
134. Tarter, "Bacon's Rebellion, the Grievances of the People," 5.
135. McIlwaine, ed., *Minutes of the Council and General Court of Colonial Virginia*, 102.
136. Ibid., 107–8.
137. Ibid., 105.
138. Ibid., 107.
139. Ibid., 89.
140. Ibid., 88.
141. Ibid., 99.
142. Ibid., 106.
143. Mathews, "The Beginning, Progress, and Conclusion of Bacon's Rebellion in Virginia," 26; The Commissioners of Virginia to Secretary Henry Coventry, 13 April 1677, in Sainsbury and Fortescue, eds., *Calendar of State Papers, Colonial*, 10:54–72; "Charles City Grievances 1676," *Virginia Magazine of History and Biography* 3, no. 2 (October 1895): 132–60.
144. Rice, *Tales from a Revolution*, 122–29.
145. Herbert Jeffreys, John Berry, and Francis Moryson, "A Letter to the Grand Assembly," 27 February 1677, in Oberg, ed., *Samuel Wiseman's Book of Record*, 90; Moryson, "A Letter Written to Sir William Jones," 126; "A Narrative of the Rise, Progresse and Cesssation of the Late Rebellion in Virginia," 148, 171; "Notes and Other Documents Chronicling the Activities and Concerns of the Commissioners," 25 February 1676/7, in Oberg, ed., *Samuel Wiseman's Book of Record*, 191.
146. Jeffreys, Berry, and Moryson, "A Letter to the Grand Assembly," 90; Rountree, *Pocahontas's People*, 100.
147. Stephen Saunders Webb wrote about how Metacom's War in New England and Bacon's Rebellion in Virginia necessitated "English imperial remedies" and a move away from local and colonial control. Webb, *1676: The End of American Independence* (New York: Knopf, 1984), xvii.
148. "Treaty of Middle Plantation," 29 May 1677, in Oberg, ed., *Samuel Wiseman's Book of Record*, 138–39; Hening, ed., *Statutes at Large*, 2:469–70, 484.
149. McIlwaine, ed., *Minutes of the Council and General Court of Colonial Virginia*, 83. The Weyanoke werowansqua's brother, for instance, was captured by Bacon but resurfaced in London as a servant to the Culpeper family. Journal

of the Lords of Trade and Plantations, 6 December 1677, in Sainsbury and Fortescue, eds., *Calendar of State Papers, Colonial*, 10:188–89.
150. Cornelius Dabney to Francis Moryson, 29 June 1678, Letters and Papers Concerning American Plantations, Virginia Colonial Records Project, CO 1/42, f. 277.
151. Cockacoeske to Francis Moryson, June 1678, in Sainsbury and Fortescue, eds., *Calendar of State Papers, Colonial*, 10:256–68. For more on Cockacoeske's consolidation of power over Chesapeake Algonquians, see Martha W. McCartney, "Cockacoeske, Queen of Pamunkey: Diplomat and Suzeraine," in Waselkov, Wood, and Hatley, eds., *Powhatan's Mantle*, 243–66, and Ethan A. Schmidt, "Cockacoeske, Weroansqua of the Pamunkeys, and Indian Resistance in Seventeenth-Century Virginia," *American Indian Quarterly* 36, no. 3 (2012): 288–317.
152. McCartney, "Cockacoeske, Queen of Pamunkey," 249, 256; "Grievances of the Queen of Poemonkey and Her Son John West," 5 June 1678; Cockacoewe, queen of Pamunkey, to Francis Moryson, 29 June 1678, Letters and Papers Concerning American Plantations, Virginia Colonial Records Project, CO 1/42, ff. 177, 276.
153. John Banister to Robert Morrison, 6 April 1679, General Correspondence, 11:7–10, Lambeth Palace Library.
154. Hening, ed., *Statutes at Large*, 2:491–92; Negrin, "Possessing Native Women and Children," 117.
155. "Notes from the Records of Stafford County, Virginia, Order Books (Continued)," *Virginia Magazine of History and Biography* 44, no. 1 (October 1937): 277–78.
156. Strickland et al., *Defining the Rappahannock Indigenous Cultural Landscape*, 38; Rountree, *Pocahontas's People*, 104.
157. "Notes from the Records of Stafford County, Virginia, Order Books (Continued)," 278.

EPILOGUE

1. "Petition of Thomas Ballard," April 1685, Virginia (Colony), Colonial Papers, State Government Records Collection; Daniel Crafford, land grant, 24 February 1676, Land Office Patents Reel 6, No. 6, 591.
2. Nicholas Spencer to Secretary Henry Coventry, 9 July 1680, CO 1/45, No. 43, ff. 381–85; Cornelius Dabney, interpreter to the queen of Pamunkey, to Colonel Francis Moryson, 29 June 1678, CO 1/42, No. 101, f. 268.
3. Henings, ed., *Statutes at Large*, 2:283, 491. Virginia Indians were excluded through an earlier law from enslavement. See also Shefveland, *Anglo-Native Virginia*, 62–63.

4. "Proceedings of the Council, 1684–88," in Browne et al., eds., *Archives of Maryland*, 5:479–82, 517–20.
5. See Schmidt, "The Right to Violence," chapter 4, and Mallios, *The Deadly Politics of Giving*, chapter 5.
6. Smith, "A Map of Virginia," 1:146; Ludwell, "The Examination of Nick Majr."
7. Virginia archaeologist Lewis R. Binford wrote that the Weyanokes, more so than their neighbors the Nottoways and Meherrins, appreciated English material culture, trade, and farming practices, going as far as to plant orchards and build English homes despite their frequent moves. Binford, "An Ethnohistory of the Nottoway, Meherrin and Weanock Indians," 157.
8. Harrison and Ludwell, "The Examination of Great Peter."
9. Ibid. For map 6, see Bolling, "The Indians of Southern Virginia," 337–58. Beverley, *History and Present State of Virginia*, 62. Thanks to Buck Woodard for his feedback.
10. "Charter Granted by Charles II, King of England to the Lords Proprietors of Carolina," in Saunders, ed., *The Colonial Records of North Carolina*, 102–3.
11. Edward Moseley, "Testimony of Edward Smithwick," Lee Family Papers, section 66.
12. Harrison and Ludwell, "Deposition of Betty (Indian)."
13. Alexander Spotswood, "Letter to the Council of Trade," 15 December 1710, Letterbooks, vol. 1, p. 35, Alexander Spotswood Papers, Mss. 3 V8194 SP685a1, Virginia Museum of History and Culture.
14. Ibid., 35–37.
15. "Letter of Francis Foster, William Glover, Edward Moseley, Samuel Swann to Virginia Council, 17 June 1707," Lee Family Papers, 1638–1867, section 16.
16. Ludwell, "The Examination of Nick Majr."
17. Interpreter Henry Briggs added that Opechancanough chased the Weyanokes as deserters before he was captured and fought a pitched battle with them to the south of the James, a major moment that the Weyanokes themselves left out even though it would alter the history of settlement central to Ludwell's mission. Nathaniel Harrison and Philip Ludwell, "Deposition of Henry Briggs," Lee Family Papers, section 66.
18. Philip Ludwell, "A Journal of the Proceedings of Philip Ludwell Nathll Harrison Comissioners Appointed for Settling ye Limits Betwixt Virga. & Carolina Begun July ye 18th 1710," 6–10, Lee Family Papers, sections 13–14.
19. Bolling, "The Indians of Southern Virginia," 340.

20. Ludwell, "A Journal," 13.
21. William Byrd II, *The Dividing Line: Histories of William Byrd II of Westover*, ed. Kevin Joel Berland (Chapel Hill: University of North Carolina Press, 2013), 118.
22. Barr and Countryman, "Introduction," 4.

~ INDEX ~

Page numbers in italics refer to maps.

Abram, William, 98–100, 102, 124, 186
Accawmack people, 46, 71–73, 75, 79, 91–92, 166; escalating hostilities facing, 72–73, 85; network of towns, 72; trading of, 76, 260n112; werowance, 72, 115. *See also* Native peoples; Shichans, Esmy
African peoples, 10; fugitivity and mobility of, 13; as settlers, 94. *See also* enslaved Africans
agriculture: Algonquian move to, 34; clearing or draining the pocosins for, 149–50; English profits from, 64, 69, 160, 168; large-scale plantation, 162, 170; movement of laborers for English, 65, 73; of Native cornfields, 19, 23, 50. *See also* corn; tobacco
Alexander, Robert, 161
Algonquian people, 1, 4–7, 10, 13–17, 19–34, 100–102, 113, 122, 126, 216; amphibious raids on, 28, 32–33, 86; communication lines between, 21, 26–27, 42, 52, 56, 156, 178; as contesting the boundaries of English plantations, 12, 16, 80, 101, 173; control of Chesapeake resources, 69, 102, 156; cosmologies and histories of, 26, 35; Eastern Shore, 73, 91, 94, 99, 123–24, 173–74, 199–200, 221, 232n11, 241n57; English dependence on the networks and skills of, 12, 15–17, 37–39, 43–44, 47–51, 63–64, 74, 79, 87, 101, 119, 164, 186–87, 227; foraging of, 26, 140; geopolitics of, 17, 21, 26, 39, 69, 74, 87, 102–3, 126, 129, 140, 143, 221, 252n2; as guides, 104, 126, 207; methods of warfare, 20–21, 25–26, 31, 35, 87–88; migrations of, 22–23, 72, 229n4; negotiations with English landowners, 16, 101, 129; political and social relationships, 14, 32, 46, 57, 69–72, 90, 126, 129, 139; on the Potomac River, 99; relationships with waterways, 6–8, 15–27, 30–34, 38, 48, 53, 90, 99, 156, 186; Spanish attempts to colonize territory of, 28; towns, 7, 22–26, 38, 44, 199; treaties with landowners and the governor, 196; tributary, 144, 170, 192, 204. *See also* Native peoples; Powhatan chiefdom; towns; trade
Allerton, Isaac, 173, 203
Alsop, George, 164–65
Amarice, 56
Amongos, 200–201. *See also* Matomkin people
Anglicanism, 102, 110, 144. *See also* Christianity

Anglo-Dutch War, 192–93
Anglo-Powhatan War (1609–14), 38, 54–58, 70–71, 82, 86, 114
Anglo-Powhatan War (1622–32), 15, 70, 78–99, 102–4, 113–14, 145, 154, 158, 223, 256n50, 264n11
Anglo-Powhatan War (1644), 16, 127, 133–35, 139–43, 152, 154, 170, 206, 223–24, 226
anthropology, 23, 26, 30, 33, 260n112
Appamattuck people, 4, 27, 30, 44–46, 60, 125, 127, 144–45, 277n98; werowance, 295n115. *See also* Native peoples; Nessom, Jack; Pyancha
Appochaukonaugh. *See* Opechancanough
Appomattox River, 22, 125, 139, 141, 143–45, 149, 219, 276n84; English exploration of, 127
archaeology, 22, 28, 31, 49, 74–76, 91, 95, 137, 142, 156–58, 164, 190–95, 203, 236n4, 247n50, 253n4, 255n35, 261n114, 284n65. *See also* ceramics; pots
Archer, Gabriel, 44–46, 60
Argall, Captain Samuel, 35–38, 41, 48, 53, 57, 61, 73, 75
Arrohateck people, 27, 44–46, 60. *See also* Native peoples
Articles of Peace and Amity (1666). *See* Treaty of Amity (1666)
Askiminokonson, 222
Assateague people, 122–23, 174–75, 221; treaty of the Marylanders with, 157; werowance, 221. *See also* Chesapeake Bay: Eastern Shore; Native peoples

Bacon, Nathaniel, 8, 10, 188, 203, 205–14, 221, 224, 296n121
Bacon's Rebellion (1676), 9, 13, 16–17, 187–89, 192, 202–5, 209–17, 233n16, 289n14, 296n125
Bahar, Matthew, 230n6, 262n3
Baker, Hugh, 199
Barr, Juliana, 12

Bartlett, Robert, 41
Batts, Henry, 219
Beck, Robin, 270n2
Becker, Sara, 294n87
Bennett, Edward, 92
Benton, Laura, 242n7
Berkeley, Governor William, 10, 135–39, 155, 170–81, 192–96, 203–6, 214–15, 286n104; rebellion against, 202–3, 209, 211
Berkeley Hundred, 79–80
Bermuda (island), 78, 216
Bermuda Hundred, 60, 63, 76
Berry, John, 212
Beverley, Robert, 224
Biggs, John, 151
Billings, Warren, 289n14
Binford, Lewis, 299n7
Blackwater River, 137, 145, 224
Blair, James, 144
Bland, Edward, 125, 146
Blount, William, 104
Blunt Point, 93, 104
boundaries, 6–8; Algonquian notions of, 12, 21, 26, 29–30, 34, 41, 54, 69, 101, 126, 133, 149; assertions of colonial authority regarding, 8, 11–12, 14–15, 17, 38, 70, 97, 100–101, 140, 155, 166, 186–88, 217, 220, 228; enforcement of English, 38, 41, 51, 54, 56, 58–60, 65–66, 94, 97, 123–24, 155, 157, 162, 189; English notions of, 12, 15–16, 40–41, 58–63, 66, 79–80, 93, 101, 148–49, 214; mapped and legislated, 12–15, 66, 70, 75, 93, 101, 123–24, 127, 140, 147–48, 175, 187–89, 227–28; of Maryland and Virginia, 100–101, 109–26, 155, 174, 181; Native contesting of, 14, 16–17, 101, 187–88, 227; natural landscape barriers as, 26, 44, 54, 67, 94, 142, 144, 149; and notions of "frontier," 232n11; of plantations, 12–13, 16, 60, 65–66, 75, 101, 127, 166, 186; Powhatan notions of, 29, 37–38,

56, 58, 65–66, 69, 72, 80, 149; property, 94, 101, 161, 173–75, 187; transgression of, 8–15, 38, 55–58, 65–66, 70, 100–101, 112–19, 124–26, 134, 155–57, 169, 173, 183–88, 195–204, 214, 227; violence over, 9, 11, 13–14, 38, 55, 66; of Virginia and Carolina, 125, 144, 224. See also fences; laws; Powhatan chiefdom; surveyors; violence
Brent, Giles, 118–19, 129, 172, 202, 214
Brewster, Sackford, 138
Briggs, Henry, 299n17
Brooks, Lisa, 296n121; *Our Beloved Kin*, 231n9
Brown, Kathleen: *Good Wives, Nasty Wenches, and Anxious Patriarchs*, 233n16
Browne, Tabitha, 198
Bry, Theodor de: "Massacre at Jamestown, Virginia," 257n53
Bryant, Thomas, 162
Bullock, William, 83–84
Butler, John, 117
Byrd, William, I, 193, 203, 205, 210, 216

Calvert, Cecil (Lord Baltimore), 109–10, 124, 129, 191
Calvert, Governor Charles, 174, 176–77, 286n104
Calvert, Governor Leonard, 109–12, 118, 120, 124, 129, 132, 141
Calvert, Philip, 194
Calvert-Scarborough line, 174
canoes, 21–26, 44–45, 91, 103, 265n12; Algonquian, 124, 129, 165; English, 59; fleet of Powhatan, 33. See also travel
Cape Charles, 91
Capps, William, 66, 83
captive-taking, 88, 91, 113; Native looting and, 126, 140. See also Iopassus; Jackson, Anne; Pocahontas; warfare
Carolina Charter (1663), 224
Carter, John, 150, 285n89
Castell, William, 133

Catholicism, 11, 100, 102, 109–10, 118, 121, 135, 155. See also Christianity; Jesuits
Catlett, John, 10, 169, 178–80, 189, 206, 227. See also surveyors
cattle, 128, 134
ceramics, 23; Native, 49; as regional types of pottery, 28. See also archaeology; pots
Charles II, King, 214–15
Chesapeake Bay: drought and famine in the region, 28; Eastern Shore, 1, 11, 19, 28–32, 46, 63, 71–91, 98–108, 120, 154, 157, 166, 173–76, 180–83, 189, 193, 197–99, 211; ecosystems of, 22; hand-drawn maps of, 2, 3; marshes of, 22–23; natural resources of, 7, 22, 26; navigability, 7; northern, 15, 52, 101, 103, 108–9, 118–19, 191, 223; Powhatan control of, 40; southern, 24, 144, 157; tributary rivers as new Indigenous boundaries of, 21; western shore of, 1, 44, 79, 157; wetlands of, 13, 26. See also Coastal Plain; estuaries; marshlands; rivers; waterways; wetlands; woodlands
Chesapeake people, 24, 29. See also Native peoples
Chicacoan people, 137–38. See also Native peoples
Chicheley, Henry, 212
Chickahominy Fort, 142
Chickahominy people, 39, 56, 61–63, 133–34, 216; territory of, 93. See also Native peoples
Chickahominy River, 62, 71, 93, 136, 141, 219
chiefdoms, 12, 23, 26–34; English search for information about Chesapeake, 39–41; territorial limits, 41; tributary, 22–23, 27–34, 37, 50, 56, 62. See also Native peoples; Piscataway people; Powhatan chiefdom
Choptank people, 189. See also Native peoples

304 INDEX

Chounterounte, 145. *See also* Nottoway people
Chowanoke people, 125, 128. *See also* Native peoples
Christianity: baptism for enslaved Africans, 158; conversion of Native children to, 77; conversion of Native people to, 84. *See also* Anglicanism; Catholicism
Claiborne, William, 8, 75, 100–120, 124, 126–43, 148, 151, 174, 189, 193, 204, 233n16, 267n35; settlement at Kent Island, 264n11, 266n30; ships of, 116–17. *See also* surveyors
Coastal Plain, 14, 24, 31, 34, 220, 270n2. *See also* Chesapeake Bay
Cockacoeske, 210, 214, 216, 298n151. *See also* Pamunkey people
Collier, Samuel, 52
colonial officials, 4, 10–17, 75–77, 93, 101–4, 109, 115, 130, 136–37, 165, 171–72, 179–80, 187; claims on disputed land of, 142–44; contention of Native peoples with, 159, 169, 215, 227; definition and enforcement of colonial boundaries by, 220, 223–25, 232n11. *See also* colonization; county government; surveyors; Virginia
colonists. *See* settlers
colonization: European efforts of, 5, 10, 39; reliance on knowledge of the local landscape in English, 43–44, 55–56, 64, 144, 162, 187, 222–23; Spanish precedent for English, 40. *See also* colonial officials; forts; maps; Maryland; surveyors; Virginia
Commissioners on Foreign Plantations, 109
Connecticut River, 103
Coombs, John, 271n5, 289n14
Cooper, Thomas, 160
copper, 23, 27, 30–35, 45, 47, 132; ransom payment with, 53; value of, 50, 71, 92. *See also* European metal goods

corn, 22–23, 27; Algonquian corn cake, 165; English planting of, 82, 94; English raids for, 54, 79, 87–89, 94, 102, 104; English trade for, 35–36, 49, 52, 56–57, 61, 76, 103–6; feasts of wild game and, 33; Native planting of, 34, 81, 88–89, 150, 217; stones for grinding, 49; storage of, 23, 34, 51, 91; tribute, 30. *See also* agriculture
Cornwallis, Thomas, 135
Corotoman River, 150
Countryman, Edward, 12
county government, 95, 179; courts of, 16, 95, 129, 156–57, 167–69, 171, 184, 196–97, 201; justices of, 197, 209; officials of, 126, 151, 157, 171–72, 179–80, 185, 187, 194–97, 200; tensions between colonial government and, 155–57. *See also* colonial officials; English elites; laws; Maryland; Virginia
Crafford, Daniel, 219
Cromwell, Oliver, 132
Croshaw, Raleigh, 90, 102, 104
Cugley, Daniel, 115

Dale, Sir Thomas, 49, 58–64, 73, 221
Dan River, 207
Dauphine, Durand de, 164
Davies, Sir John, 41
Delaware Bay, 192
Delaware River, 103, 120; Dutch plantations along, 197
diseases, 82, 84; Algonquian, 240n46; European, 28
Doeg people, 154, 159, 177–80, 190–91, 202, 213, 287n114; werowance, 217. *See also* Native peoples
Dowd, Gregory Evans, 264n9
Dragon Swamp, 1, 130, 144, 202, 209–10, 296n121
Dubcovsky, Alejandra, 229n6, 263n4
Duffield, Daniel, 121, 124, 269n80
Dutch colonies, 174; threats to English colonies, 187, 192–93

INDEX   305

Dutch traders, 41, 98, 100, 103, 114, 120, 123, 131, 185, 265n11; forts of, 103; tobacco trade with, 121. *See also* New Netherland
Dye, John, 10

Eastern Siouan people, 26, 140. *See also* Monacan people; Native peoples
Elizabeth City, 93, 95
Elzey, John, 176
English Civil War, 132
English elites, 11, 95–96, 100, 119, 132, 151–55, 179, 195, 199; Anglo-Native relations for, 74–76, 87, 155–56, 163, 168, 169, 186–88, 199–200, 212–15, 223, 233n17; control of goods and information attempted by, 139–40, 198, 201; control of movements of Native and English people attempted by, 156, 163, 170–71, 177, 186–87, 194–200, 215, 221–22, 228; and land, 92, 95, 128, 143–44, 147, 151, 154–55, 173–75, 192, 214–15, 281n27; Native diplomacy with, 47, 69–70, 76, 87, 112; profits and investments of, 89, 92, 147, 187; seasonal warfare at harvest time as strategy of, 89; wealth of, 126, 128, 152, 158. *See also* county government; enslavers; planters
English navy, 43
English traders, 4–5, 97, 101–4, 108, 114, 126–27, 146–47, 216; fur trading of, 5, 11, 101, 170, 223; lower-class, 50–51; Native routes pursued by, 141, 170; Native trade and diplomacy with, 40, 51–54, 56, 59, 76–77, 90, 127, 140–41; unsanctioned, 76–77, 80, 82, 94, 101–4, 106, 109. *See also* European weapons; trade
enslaved Africans, 4–10, 13, 73, 78, 233n16, 271n5; arrival of, 15, 65, 119, 127, 129, 187; building of fortifications by, 171; flight of, 12, 127; legal lifetime enslavement for, 127, 158, 221; as plantation labor, 186, 195; as property, 137; rebellion of, 212; rise in the number of, 17, 127, 129, 157–58, 162, 195, 215–16; tithability of, 135. *See also* African peoples; escaped enslaved people; laborers; Middle Passage; plantations; trade in enslaved people
enslavers, 11, 65, 201. *See also* English elites; planters
escaped enslaved people, 13, 130, 137, 198–200, 220–21; community policing of, 196–97; maiming of, 66, 186, 196; to Native towns, 50–51, 57, 65, 199–200; return of, 17, 130, 134, 171, 186, 195–200, 219, 221; societies of, 234n20. *See also* enslaved Africans; indentured servants; laborers
estuaries, 24; for subsistence of Native peoples, 22, 34; and woodlands for Native foraging, 26, 34. *See also* Chesapeake Bay; rivers; waterways
European metal goods, 30, 36; and glass, 69; Powhatan raiding to obtain, 67, 69. *See also* copper; iron
European weapons, 34, 36; English trade with Native peoples in, 50–51, 103, 126, 164, 170, 199; Native acquisition of, 71, 84, 114, 140, 165. *See also* English traders; trade
Evelyn, Robert, 117–18, 268n68

Falling Creek ironworks, 69, 81
Farmer, Robert, 146
Fauntleroy, Moore, 169, 171–72, 175
Fausz, J. Frederick, 243n10, 254n16, 264n11
Felgate, Robert and Toby, 93
fences, 7, 70–71, 85, 94, 128, 135, 161, 163, 172, 278n108. *See also* boundaries
Ferris, Andrew, 264n8
Fleet, Henry, 100, 103–4, 107, 111–13, 118–19, 124, 136, 143, 151. *See also* interpreters
Flint, Lieutenant Thomas, 93

Flowerdew Hundred, 74, 254n20, 256n51
Fluvanna River, 31
Fort Algernon, 54
Fort Henry, 125, 139, 143, 145, 207, 276n84
Fort Royal, 136, 141
forts, 10–11, 14–15, 62; Native, 142; network of, 15–16, 43, 59, 141–42, 188, 193, 215–16, 227; new English, 50, 59, 141–42, 170–71, 192–93; plantations and, 10–11, 15–16, 141, 192–93; Powhatan attacks on riverside, 87; skin trade in, 140–42. *See also* colonization; palisades; settlements; soldiers
Fowke, Gerrard, 172–73, 175, 179, 285n89
Fox, David, 150
French traders, 265n11

Gallivan, Martin, 229n4, 230n8
Gates, Sir Thomas, 58–60, 63
Gingaskins, 10; land of, 189. *See also* Native peoples
glass, 35, 158
Godfrey, John, 206
Gold, Debra, 239n43
Goodrich, Thomas, 160, 198
Grandjean, Katherine, 263n5, 264n10
Great Dismal Swamp, 137, 234n20
Great Lakes, 22, 25, 31, 103, 170
Great Matomkin, 168
Greening, William, 161
Greer, Allan, 231n11, 234n19, 278n106
Gregg, Thomas, 161
Griffins, Edward, 120
Guasco, Michael, 271n5, 275n68
Gulf of Mexico, 25
Gunstocker, Edward, 207
Gwynn, Hugh, 121, 130

Hakluyt, Richard: *Divers Voyages Touching the Discoverie of America, and the Ilands Adjacent*, 43; *The Principall Navigations, Voiages, and Discoveries of the English Nation*, 43–44; promotional literature of, 43–44
Hallowes, John, 164
Hämäläinen, Pekka, 232n15
Hammond, Edward, 221
Hammond, John, 164–65
Hamor, Ralph, 64, 90
Hampton River, 93
Hantman, Jeffrey, 239n43
Harrison, Nathaniel, 223
Harvey, Governor John, 86, 93–94, 110–13, 117, 124; truce with the Chickahominies and Powhatans, 94
Hatfield, April, 231n9, 260n112
Haudenosaunee people, 169–70, 179, 187, 190–93, 217, 220; raiding of, 287n114. *See also* Native peoples
Henrico, 60, 63, 74, 81
Herbert, Clement, 163
Hill, Edward, 138, 214, 233n16
history: Algonquian cosmology and, 26; of colonial Virginia, 232n16, 235n22, 270n2; local and micro, 232n15; Native, 226–27, 233n16; of race, 233n16
Holden, Vanessa, 288n3
Hopson, John, 118
Horning, Audrey, 254n20
Horsey, Stephen, 176
Hudson River, 120
Hull, John, 160
hunting, 26, 50, 64, 96, 158, 164–68, 220, 255n35. *See also* Native peoples
Hutchinson, Robert, 200

identity: Native tribal, 163; shared Algonquian, 21, 34, 223
immigrants: continental European, 94; English, 94, 157–58
indentured servants, 6, 8, 10, 233n16; attempted control by planters of, 65, 73, 77–78, 82–83, 98, 130–32, 157, 175, 194–99; death of, 81–83; flight of, 12–13, 16–17, 65, 119–22, 130–31, 175, 183–86, 184, 194–99, 202, 220;

freedom for, 11, 98, 158, 201, 211; increase in the number of, 15, 90, 119, 127, 129, 157–58, 195; investments in, 89, 157; movements of, 13, 16–17, 78, 131, 199; return of escaped, 17, 134, 171, 186, 195–99, 201; trading of, 198–99. *See also* escaped enslaved people; laborers; plantations

Indigenous peoples. *See* Native peoples

inequality: imposition by local elites of, 228; social, 12–13; in wartime, 83

Ingle, Richard, 118, 132, 134–35, 141

Ingle's Rebellion, 118, 132, 135, 269n74, 269n80

interpreters, 51–54, 62, 97, 113, 155, 169, 221, 254n16, 260n110, 268n26, 299n17; captives and, 59; illicit traders and, 66; Powhatan control of, 53; untrustworthiness of, 78; value of, 112–13. *See also* Evelyn, Robert; Fleet, Henry; Kemps; Namontack; Poole, Robert; Savage, Thomas; Spelman, Henry

intracolonial tensions, 10, 15, 100–110, 116, 135, 195–96. *See also* Maryland; Virginia

Iopassus, 35–38, 48. *See also* captive-taking; Patawomeck people

Ireland, 40–41, 43–44, 71, 74, 246n36

iron: ironworks, 75; mining for, 57; workers skilled in working with, 67, 69, 252n1. *See also* European metal goods

Iroquois. *See* Haudenosaunee people

Isle of Wight, 95

Jackson, Anne, 88. *See also* captive-taking

James I, King, 41, 61

James City, 74, 195

James Fort, 15, 38–39, 42, 46–49, 55–58, 61, 82, 86, 141, 220–21, 247n48; Dutch or German servants at, 51, 57; Native attacks on, 39, 55; Native people in, 60, 92. *See also* Jamestown

James River, 9–11, 15–19, 24, 27–28, 32–39, 42, 48, 58, 62–64, 75, 82, 94–96, 219–20; construction of plantations and settlements along, 73–74, 93–94, 101, 105–6, 124, 128; English control of, 59, 79; English land claims and casualties in Native districts along, 66, 68, 70, 94, 101; English movement along, 69, 104; falls of, 44, 54, 67, 202, 227; fortified locations on, 53–54, 59–60, 63, 67, 69–70, 73–74, 227; navigation of, 45–46, 67; north side of, 76, 80, 135, 224; Powhatan districts along, 54, 68, 93, 101, 104; south side of, 50, 85, 93, 129–30, 133, 135, 142, 207, 256n51; west side of, 142. *See also* Powhatan River

Jamestown, 8, 35–36, 39, 42, 46–49, 52, 59, 63–64, 102; attack of Bacon's army on, 202, 207, 211–12; English founding of, 21, 39–40; officials at, 171–72; planning and urban living for, 159; Powhatan siege of, 54–56; vulnerable English position at, 44, 89. *See also* James Fort

Jeffreys, Herbert, 212

Jennings, Francis, 265n11

Jesuits, 121, 129, 135. *See also* Catholicism

jewelry and ornaments, 27, 33

Johnson, George, 176

Jones, Farmer, 199

Jones, William, 198

Kecoughtan, 19, 29, 59, 63, 74, 85, 95, 104

Kecoughtan people, 19–21, 24, 27, 47, 93; displacement of, 29. *See also* Native peoples; Pochins

Kemp, Richard, 134

Kemps, 50–51, 56. *See also* interpreters

Kent Fort, 106

Kent Island, 100–101, 105–9, 113–20, 126–29, 135, 139–43, 166, 204, 264n11, 266n30. *See also* Maryland

Kieft, Governor William, 130

"Kings Forest," 59
Kiskiak people, 46, 130, 155; land of, 189; werowance, 272n21. See also Native peoples
Koot, Christian, 263n4
Kraus map (c. 1610), 2, 3, 24
Kruer, Matthew, 235n22; *Time of Anarchy*, 233n17, 295n112
Kukla, John, 270n2
Kupperman, Karen Ordahl, 242n8

laborers: African and English, 121, 127, 129, 134, 157–58, 174, 211; escaped, 96, 120–22, 129, 131, 171, 175, 183–87, *184*, 194–202, 221; Native, 89, 127, 129, 166, 174, 186, 196–97, 199–200; networks and strategies regarding places of, 195, 198, 201, 221; physical health of, 195; plantation, 147, 157–58, 186–89, 194–99; ransoms paid to the Powhatans in return for, 88. See also enslaved Africans; escaped enslaved people; indentured servants; Native peoples; plantations
land: English disputes and negotiations over, 139–43, 173–75, 227; English legal possession of Native, 160, 169–70, 173, 179, 189, 209, 227–28; for former indentured servants, 157; large patents of, 128, 143–44, 147, 151, 154, 159–60, 285n89; precolonial Native, 230n8; value to the English of Chesapeake, 128, 157. See also maps; squatters; surveyors
language: of Algonquian dialects, 4, 22, 52, 268n68; Eastern Siouan, 28, 140; about trade goods, 262n1
laws: controlling mobility, 78, 80, 171, 186, 195–97, 201; English vagrancy, 78, 272n19; about lifetime enslavement, 127, 158, 221; about local governance, 74; about plantation locations, 74; about preserving Native land, 155, 189; about return of escaping unfree people, 130, 171, 186, 195–97, 201, 221. See also boundaries; county government
Lee, Jacob F., 229n6
Levy, Phillip, 231n9
Leyden, John, 93
London, 74, 82
Lower Peninsula, 141. See also Virginia
Ludwell, Philip, 209, 223–24, 226, 228
Ludwell, Thomas, 286n109

MacMillan, Ken, 243n9
Maddison, Captain Isaac, 88, 90
Maddison, Thomas, 162
maize. See corn
Mannahoac people, 32. See also Native peoples
maps: boundaries on, 12–13, 42, 101; of Britain, 40; county, 160; Dutch charts for mariners as, 41–42; English expeditions to host populations to catalogue and to draw up, 37, 40–41; English making of, 40–43; European, 12, 23–24, 42; Indigenous, 12, 26, 234n19; seventeenth-century and early eighteenth-century, 33, 220, 228; and titles, 12, 40–41. See also colonization; land; Speed, John; surveyors; Tindall, Robert
maroons, 137, 234n20
Marshall, Roger, 141
marshlands, 210, 279n120; Native sustenance and protection in, 21, 87, 150; stewardship of, 4. See also wetlands
Martin, John, 76–77, 84–86, 95
Martin's Hundred, 70, 73, 76, 81, 88, 254n20, 262n130
Maryland: Baltimore County, 157; boundaries of, 100–101, 124, 155, 200, 202–5, 220; competition for Virginia from the colony of, 15, 100–121, 142–43, 155; General Assembly, 134; manor system of land tenure in, 129, 155; private property model

established in, 129; rebellion of indentured servants in, 118, 132, 135, 269n80; Roman Catholic settlers of, 100; settlement of, 5, 11, 101, 109, 129, 158, 272n13; traders of, 121. *See also* colonization; county government; intracolonial tensions; Kent Island; St. Mary's City

Maryland rangers, 170

Mason, George, 202, 213

Massawomeck people, 28, 32–33, 40, 48, 240n47; raiding of, 102–3; threats to Powhatan expanding boundaries from, 32–33; trading of, 28–29, 103. *See also* Native peoples

Mathews, Governor Samuel, 143, 280n6

Mathews, Thomas, 202

Matomkin people, 200; land of, 293n79. *See also* Amongos; Native peoples; Shoes, Dick

Mattaponi people, 27, 30, 46, 159–60, 163, 209. *See also* Native peoples

Mattawoman people, 159, 167–68; werowance, 167. *See also* Native peoples

Medcalfe, Isaac, 183, 185–87, 196

Meherrin people, 32, 145–46, 207, 224, 226, 277n98, 299n7. *See also* Native peoples

Metacom's War, 204

Michel, Francis Louis, 144, 162

Middle Passage, 127. *See also* enslaved Africans

Middle Peninsula, 1, 29, 121, 189, 209, 240n50; county officials in, 144. *See also* Virginia

migration, 4, 72, 137–38, 223–27; boundaries and, 12–13; of laborers from Europe, 73; Native seasonal, 73–74. *See also* escaped enslaved people; Native peoples; travel; Weyanoke people

Monacan people, 22, 25, 28, 31–32, 45, 241n63; territory of, 42, 79. *See also* Eastern Siouan people; Native peoples; Rassawek

Monohaten, Constantine, 107–8; conjectural trade route of, *107*

Morattico people, 159. *See also* Native peoples

Morgan, Edmund: *American Slavery, American Freedom*, 232n16, 289n14

Morris, Robert, 211–12

Moryson, Francis, 212

mountains, 22; Native polities beyond the, 32; rivers and, 24

Musselwhite, Paul, 234n17

Nacotchtank people, 91, 103. *See also* Native peoples

Namontack, 52, 62. *See also* interpreters

Nandua Creek, 1, 185

Nansemond people, 24, 29, 44, 48, 54–59, 93, 104, 133, 137, 153–59, 215, 224, 226; land of, 189. *See also* Native peoples

Nansemond River, 54

Nanticoke people, 131, 174, 200; treaty of the Marylanders with, 157. *See also* Native peoples

Nanzatico people, 154, 157, 159, 179, 207, 210, 217. *See also* Native peoples

Native geographies, 9–10; Black uses of, 13; disparate spatial visions shaped by, 10; as informing English understandings of North American political geographies, 231n9; of Powhatans, 14, 44. *See also* Native peoples; travel; waterways; woodlands

Native peoples, 4, 7–11; alliances with the English of the, 91–92, 166–67, 204, 224; cartographies of, 12, 26, 234n19; dispossession and supposed disappearance of, 10–11, 140–47, 152, 155–56, 158, 173, 179, 190, 222; economic and political relationships of, 5, 10–11, 15, 21, 37–38, 42, 51–52, 57, 70–73, 90–91, 102, 170; English fear of Spanish alliances with, 40; English settlers living among, 50, 155;

Native peoples (*continued*)
  enslavement of, 83–85, 126, 129, 138, 141, 166, 170, 179–81, 190, 199–205, 212, 216, 219, 221, 270n2; as expert foragers, 22; illicit travelers in the territory of, 13, 65–66, 186, 199–201; knowledge belonging to, 4, 12, 14, 16, 40–42, 49, 50–56, 64, 69, 76, 84, 120, 125–26, 139–41, 162, 227–28; maps and descriptions of, 41–42; mobility of, 4, 11–12, 16, 21, 56, 66, 76, 156, 170, 186, 200–204, 228; of nations beyond the Chesapeake, 5–7, 16, 21, 37, 44, 52, 103, 140, 155–56, 166, 170, 215–17, 220, 289n14; "place-making" of, 230n8; raids from outsider, 17, 28, 32–33, 202–4; roads and towns of, 11, 17, 19, 38, 142, 185–86. *See also* chiefdoms; hunting; laborers; Powhatan chiefdom; roads; towns; trade; werowances; *and specific peoples*
Navirans, 45–47
Necotowance, 137–39, 142. *See also* Pamunkey people
Nemattanew, 71, 80–81
Nessom, Jack, 208. *See also* Appamattuck people
New England, 204–5, 263n5, 264n8
New Netherland, 103, 120–22, 130; massacre of Native people in, 130; traders of, 120. *See also* Dutch traders
Newport, Christopher, 44, 46–47, 52
Newport News, 85
New Sweden, 103
New York, 196
Nicholls, George, 159
Norman, Thomas, 167
North Carolina, 4, 157; boundaries of, 205, 224–26; expansion of territory of, 225; land speculators of, 226; Virginia settlers in northeastern, 224. *See also* Piedmont
Northern Neck, 124, 138, 154, 167, 177, 194, 207. *See also* Potomac River; Rappahannock River

Norwood, Colonel Henry, 122–24, 192
Nottoway people, 22, 31–32, 125–26, 144–45, 207, 215, 223–27, 277n98, 299n7; land of, 146, 217. *See also* Chounterounte; Native peoples; Oyeocker
Nottoway River, 223–24
Nuttall, John, 131

Oberg, Michael Leroy, 281n27
Occaneechi people, 126, 140, 144, 205–9, 216, 221, 295n112; attack by Bacon's army on the trading post of, 202, 205; territory of, 277n98. *See also* Native peoples; Persecles
Oldmixon, John, 171
Old Plantation Creek, 72, 91
Oliver, Roger, 131
Opechancanough, 5, 61, 69, 71–75, 116, 124–25, 206, 224; death, 136, 139; English leverage against, 87; warfare against English people, 78–91, 97, 99, 104, 129, 132–33, 136, 139, 143, 146, 206; warfare against Native peoples, 146, 299n17. *See also* Pamunkey people; Powhatan chiefdom
Opitchapam, 69, 71, 90. *See also* Powhatan chiefdom
Orapax, 71
Oyeocker, 145–46, 151–52. *See also* Nottoway people

palisades, 7, 16, 42, 46–48, 55, 71, 73–74, 85–88, 91–97, 104–5, 108, 135, 140–41, 190, 192, 227, 237n18. *See also* boundaries; forts; towns
Palmer's Island, 117, 142, 174. *See also* Susquehannock people
Pamunkey people, 27, 46, 89–90, 104, 155, 190, 202, 209, 214–16; English seasonal raids on, 89; fort (Asiskewincke) of, 142; land of, 189, 223; leadership, 136, 139; Queen of, 210; seat of, 141. *See also* Cockacoeske;

Native peoples; Necotowance; Opechancanough; Totopotomoi
Pamunkey River, 24, 31, 60–61, 86, 95, 133, 136, 274n53
Parahunt, 53
Parent, Anthony: *Foul Means,* 233n16
Parker, William, 62
Paspahegh people, 4, 46, 55–56, 113; territory of, 36, 93; werowance, 39, 55. *See also* Native peoples; Wowinchapunk
Patawomeck people, 25, 29–31, 35–37, 46–48, 61–63, 71–75, 87–91, 99, 102, 159, 173, 177–79, 190; alliance with the Powhatans, 37; English killing of allied, 90; English peace with, 57–58; territory of, 53; werowance, 36, 57, 90, 169, 172, 191, 238n27, 287n114. *See also* Iopassus; Native peoples; Wahunganoche
paths: broad horse, 200; of Native peoples, 162, 189, 245n29, 282n43; plain, 170; trading, 210; water routes and, 202. *See also* roads; trails; travel
Patuxent people, 89, 102, 109–11, 166–67; werowance, 110–14. *See also* Native peoples
Patuxent Point, 195
Patuxent River, 117; English settlements along, 128
pearls, 27, 30
Pennsylvania, 4
Pequot War, 263n5
Percy, George, 55–56
Persecles, 208. *See also* Occaneechi people
Piankatank people, 29, 46. *See also* Native peoples
Piankatank River, 130
Piedmont, 9, 15, 24, 124, 140, 152, 216, 220, 223, 270n2; English expeditions in, 16, 126, 140, 147, 207; expansion of plantations and trade in, 152, 223;

Native peoples of, 137, 140, 188, 224. *See also* North Carolina; Virginia
Pierce, William, 121
Pignell, Daniel, 169
pigs, 82, 128, 150, 158; stealing, 202
Piscataway people, 28, 46, 90, 99, 103, 111–13, 131, 190–91, 204, 260n110. *See also* Native peoples
Pitt, Robert, 185
plantations: boundaries of, 12–13, 16, 65, 84, 127, 148, 198; as changes in the landscape for Algonquian people, 69, 71, 143; English labor regimes on, 11, 65, 73, 82–83, 127, 157, 186, 195, 220; and forts, 10–11, 15–16, 141; livestock on, 157; Native access to, 141, 143; Native labor on, 127, 186, 196–97, 200; networks between, 197, 201, 227; planning of, 85, 234n17, 281n25; private, 75; as shaped by Native geopolitics, 12, 17, 64, 96; tobacco on, 5, 64, 73, 95, 119, 128, 134, 153, 157–58; transformation of Native land into, 15–17, 64, 73, 96, 147, 169, 185–87, 227. *See also* enslaved Africans; indentured servants; laborers; planters; settlements
planters, 17, 95–96, 126; attempted control of indentured servants by, 65, 73, 78, 132, 195, 199; attempted control of movements of Native people and enslaved Africans by, 65–66, 170–71; boundaries of the property of, 94, 101, 161, 173–75, 187; control of trading by, 77–79; English middling, 128, 194; English tobacco, 64, 73, 77–78, 126–28, 134; grievances of middling and elite, 212; illegal warrants for arrest by, 171–72; internal threats to, 126, 139, 175; and merchants, 75; relations of Native peoples with, 16, 65, 79, 92, 139, 164, 169, 199; small, 194. *See also* English elites; enslavers; plantations
Plowden, Edmund, 132
Pluymers, Keith, 252n1

312   INDEX

Pocahontas, 35–36, 49, 60–61, 78; as captive, 36–37; capture of, 38; Christian marriage of, 63. *See also* captive-taking; Powhatan chiefdom
Pochins, 20. *See also* Kecoughtan people
Pocomoke people, 221–23; werowance, 222. *See also* Native peoples
Pocomoke River, 199, 222
Point Comfort, 110
Poole, Robert, 78. *See also* interpreters
Pope, Nathaniel, 141
Poplar Islands, 105
Portobacco people, 159, 163–64. *See also* Native peoples
Pory, John, 64, 72
Potomac River, 11, 24–37, 46–48, 57, 71, 75, 87, 100, 102, 111, 117, 124, 143, 158–59, 182, 237n13; English settlements along, 109, 128, 138–40, 157, 164, 174, 202, 284n65; Native peoples of, 90, 103–4, 110, 172, 178, 191, 217, 267n49. *See also* Northern Neck
pots, 31, 36, 49, 158, 164. *See also* archaeology; ceramics
Potter, Stephen, 229n4, 230n8
Powhatan chiefdom, 4–7, 10, 14, 19–38, 44–45, 86, 128, 133, 136, 220, 224; boundaries of, 29, 37–38, 56, 69, 72; communication lines of, 45, 69–70, 74; control of access to waterways and river mouths, 14–15, 23–24, 34, 36–38, 40, 44, 48–49, 60, 66, 69, 242n7; control of movement of people and goods, 21, 28–29, 32, 34, 38, 46–47, 53–58, 61–63, 66, 69, 79, 92, 97; English transformation of the landscapes of, 92–93, 96; enslavement of captured people of, 83; incorporation of groups at the periphery, 28–29; invasions and migrations of, 20; knowledge about the Chesapeake, 37, 44, 50–56, 59, 84, 87, 99, 101; large size of, 23, 44; movement of knowledge and goods between English leaders and, 50–52, 79; Native peoples at the fringes of, 36, 40, 57–59, 70–72, 75, 79, 87, 89–90, 99, 102; raids on English settlements, 67, 69; trade networks, 30–34, 70; tribute to, 22–23, 27–34, 37, 50, 56, 62; violent displacement by the English, 59, 93, 127, 133–38; warfare to secure and expand the boundaries of, 20–21, 29–34, 72. *See also* Algonquian people; boundaries; chiefdoms; Native peoples; Opechancanough; Opitchapam; Pocahontas; Wahunsenacawh; werowances; Werowocomoco
Powhatan River, 21–22, 24, 29, 31, 39. *See also* James River
Powhatan's Mantle, 33–34
Price, Andrew, 199
Price, Hugh, 55
Price, Jenkin, 123, 185
Price, Thomas, 176
Proby, Peter, 219
Prynne, Nicholas, 212
puccoon, 22, 30–31
Punch, John, 121, 130, 221
Pyancha, 145, 151–52. *See also* Appamattuck people

Quakers, 174–76

Ragan, Edward, 237n20
Rappahannock people, 150, 154, 159, 171–73, 213, 240n50; arrests of, 171; rejection of werowance approved by the English, 291n32. *See also* Native peoples; Towerozen; Wachiopa
Rappahannock River, 1, 9, 19, 24, 32, 137, 143, 159–60, 163, 169, 182, 209, 212; south bank of, 153; swamps near, 144. *See also* Northern Neck
rare metals, 22
Rassawek, 31. *See also* Monacan people
Reade, Thomas, 165
Reid, Joshua, 265n12

Rice, James, 231n9, 235n22, 243n8, 252n2, 265n11, 285n89, 290n15
Richter, Daniel, 243n9, 247n48
Rickahockian people, 178, 190. *See also* Native peoples
rivers: Algonquian relationships with, 6–8, 15–27, 30–34; and Algonquian towns, 23–26, 44, 63, 67; English attempts at control of the Chesapeake's, 37, 62, 65; English descriptions of the navigability of, 41–43; fall line across the Chesapeake's, 26, 45, 73, 94, 141–42, 189, 277n98; and mountains, 24; soundings of, 220; as waterways, 22–26, 34. *See also* Chesapeake Bay; estuaries; travel; waterways
roads: Algonquian overland, 24, 26, 30, 42, 142, 144; continental Native, 25; English-controlled, 73; main fall line, 31; Native overland, 128, 130, 144, 263n5; and paths, 185–86; Piedmont, 144; plantations of elites connected by, 160–61; rivers connected to Algonquian overland, 24, 26, 30, 154; and towns, 11, 17, 19, 23–26, 185, 220; waterways and, 13–14, 30, 71, 182, 209, 227–28. *See also* Native peoples; paths; trails; travel
Roanoke colony, 39, 42–43
Roanoke River, 47, 126, 145, 202, 204, 207, 224
Robins, Obedience, 115
Rolfe, John, 60, 63–64, 71, 141
Rolfe, Thomas, 141
Rountree, Helen, 30, 230n8, 240n46, 241n62, 247n53, 269n74
Royal Society, 164
runaway slaves. *See* escaped enslaved people

Sahlins, Peter, 232n13
sailors, 12; Algonquian, 36; Caribbean, 82; English, 15, 35–37, 42, 44, 50, 92; and settlers, 50; trade between Algonquians and English, 37, 50. *See also* ships
saltworks, 75
Sandys, Edwin, 75, 84
Sandys, Sir George, 65, 82, 88–89, 93, 96
Savage, Thomas, 52–54, 62, 72–73, 79, 87, 102. *See also* interpreters
Saxine, Ian, 234n19
Saxton, Christopher, 40
Sayer, Daniel, 234n20
Scarborough, Charles, 210, 222
Scarborough, Edmund, 8, 142–43, 169, 173–77, 180–82, 188–89, 198–201, 206, 222–23, 227; as surveyor general of Virginia, 174–76, 286n104. *See also* surveyors
seafood, 22
Seib, Rebecca, 269n74
settlements: concern with defense of, 70–71, 86; expansion of English, 127, 222; fortification of core, 85; horrible conditions in Chesapeake, 12–13, 70; beyond Jamestown, 57, 65–67, 69, 75, 97, 133; on Native districts, 85–86, 91–95, 140; Native influence on patterns of English, 92, 140, 188; Native movement within the bounds of English, 77; Powhatan attacks on English, 15, 67, 69–70, 80–81, 86, 108; thinning of woodlands around, 67, 86. *See also* colonization; forts; plantations; settlers
settlers, 4–7, 10–16; accumulated knowledge of Chesapeake held by, 12, 54, 64, 187, 201, 242n8; ban on interacting with Native people for, 93–94; diplomacy and trade in the Piedmont of English, 127; English escaped, 50–51, 57, 60–61, 64, 77–78, 120–21; expansion of fields and fortifications of English, 54; feuds of English, 10, 53; pillaging of enemy towns by English, 56; as "Rangers," 220; rise in the number of English, 94, 140, 158;

settlers (*continued*)
  sailors' trade with, 50; tenants and servants as nonelite, 77, 186–87, 201; trading of lower-class English, 50; from Virginia in Maryland, 175–76. *See also* settlements
Severn River, 105
Shefveland, Kristalyn, 231n9, 270n2
shell beads, 27, 30–31, 33, 49
Shenandoah Valley, 31
Shepeard, Thomas, 160, 282n29
Shichans, Esmy, 72, 79, 84, 87, 115. *See also* Accawmack people
ships: *Abigail*, 82; advances in technology of European, 43; Algonquian guides for English, 53; Dutch, 103, 143; English, 35–37, 39, 41–43, 50, 56, 143; *Exchange*, 282n29; as loaded with tobacco, 193; *Long Taile*, 117; *Reformation*, 118; riverine travel of English, 71, 75; *Treasurer*, 65; *Tyger*, 90–91; of Virginia governor's loyalists, 203; *Virginia Merchant*, 122; *White Lion*, 65; *Young Prince*, 211–12. *See also* sailors; travel
Shirley Hundred, 63, 85
Shoes, Dick, 200. *See also* Matomkin people
Smallcomb, Thomas, 138
Smith, John, 10, 30, 33, 39–43, 47, 50–57, 62, 84, 103, 210; capture by the Powhatans, 40, 42, 240n50; exploring of, 44, 46, 48, 57, 122; mapmaking of, 41–43, 240n48
Smith, Thomas, 117–18
Smith's Hundred, 76
social mobility, 17; opportunities for, 194
soldiers, 35, 54; English, 39, 49, 74, 103–4, 108, 141. *See also* forts
Spanish Florida, 158
Spanish invaders, 28, 40, 110–12; conquests of, 39
Speed, John, 40–41. *See also* maps

Spelman, Henry, 35, 53–54, 57, 78, 87, 238n32, 249n82, 260n110. *See also* interpreters
Spencer, Nicholas, 194, 210
Spotswood, Governor Alexander, 225–26
squatters: Eastern Shore, 267n35; eviction of, 189; on Native lands, 155. *See also* land
Steponaitis, Vincas, 239n44
St. Inigoes Fort, 141
St. Mary's City, 9, 11, 100, 102, 111–17, 129, 132, 159, 221. *See also* Maryland
St. Mary's Fort, 141
St. Mary's River, 141
Strachey, William, 49, 242n73
surveyors, 5, 12, 65, 75, 104, 147–52, 189, 227; of boundaries between Virginia and Maryland, 174–76; "fixed" boundaries around Native towns by, 155; methods of, 147; Native people contending with, 16; Native roads and access according to the, 160; of property of planters, 168; Virginian, 225. *See also* boundaries; Catlett, John; Claiborne, William; colonial officials; colonization; land; maps; Scarborough, Edmund
Susquehanna River, 44
Susquehannock people, 16, 40, 48–49, 98–100, 105–18, 154, 169–70, 179, 187, 191–93, 206–9; conflict of Marylanders with, 134; English siege of the fort of, 203; hunting, 213; mobility, 131–32, 287n114; murder of five leaders of, 203–4; raiding of, 28, 32–33, 190, 203–7, 216–17; threats to Powhatan expanding boundaries of, 32–33; trading of, 28–29, 103, 105, 114–15, 118, 124, 135, 174, 260n112, 264n11; treaty of the Marylanders with, 142–43, 157. *See also* Kent Island; Native peoples; Palmer's Island
Susquehannock War, 202–4, 209

Tangier Island, 138
Tarter, Brent, 289n14

taxes, 171; county and colony, 194; land, 214–15
Thorpe, Reverend George, 79–80, 84, 256n51
Tindall, Robert, 42. *See also* maps
Tindall's Point, 42
Tindall's Shoals, 42
tobacco, 5, 96; collapse of the boom in, 266n30; export of, 60, 64, 95; merchants of, 118; Native pipes for, 31, 57, 164; planting of, 88–89, 92, 100, 122, 134, 160–61, 164, 220; safe warehouses of, 73; transition to, 69, 92, 171. *See also* agriculture
Tompkins, John, 112, 114
Totopotomoi, 142. *See also* Pamunkey people
Totuskey Creek, 1, 160
Totuskey people, 159. *See also* Native peoples
Towerozen, 291n32. *See also* Rappahannock people
towns, 7, 22–27, 31; alteration or destruction of life in Native, 126, 138–39, 158; defense of Algonquian, 48, 86, 209; disuse or consolidation of Native, 29; Eastern Shore Algonquian, 92, 123; escaped laborers to Native, 50–51, 57, 65, 199–200; manufactured goods in Algonquian, 158–59; Powhatan feasting rituals in, 27; rivers and Algonquian, 23–26, 44, 63, 67; roads and, 11, 17, 19, 185–86, 220. *See also* Algonquian people; Native peoples; palisades
trade: Atlantic, 92, 114, 185, 187; in beaver furs and other skins, 5, 15, 29, 36, 48, 63, 72, 89, 100–119, 139–42, 164, 170, 185, 192, 205, 260n112, 273n24, 289n14; in captive Native women and children, 216, 219–20; copper and beads for Algonquian, 25, 31–32, 92, 96, 140, 242n71, 254n20; corn surpluses and, 23, 103–4; and diplomacy of Native peoples, 14–16, 22–25, 30–34, 38–42, 51–54, 65–67, 70–71, 101, 130, 231n9; English maritime, 60, 69, 101, 110, 129, 131; in European weaponry and tools, 29, 36, 50–51, 114, 126, 131, 170; expansion of Native networks of, 12–16, 19, 30–34; illicit, 66, 170; long-distance Native, 23–24, 30–32, 34, 159, 170; in luxury goods by Native peoples, 30–32, 34, 38, 47, 50; Piedmont, 119, 126, 194, 203; of planters and settlers with Native people, 76–77, 80, 82, 94, 101–4, 114–16, 156, 192, 194, 225; in tobacco, 63, 69, 130; watercraft for, 24, 158; in wild game, 165. *See also* Algonquian people; English traders; European weapons; Native peoples; trade in enslaved people; travel
trade in enslaved people, 13, 65, 127, 216; in Virginia, 157. *See also* enslaved Africans; trade
trails: as "Indian paths," 162; local, 161–62; network of roads and, 160, 201. *See also* paths; roads; travel
Traunter, Richard, 277n91
travel: Algonquian riverine, 26, 34; English use of Native routes, 168, 231n9; illicit, 183–88, 194–98, 263n5; overland, 161; passports of colonists for, 64; trade and, 38, 59, 80; by watercraft, 24–26, 29, 197–98. *See also* canoes; migration; Native geographies; paths; rivers; roads; ships; trade; trails; waterways
Treaty of Amity (1666), 155–56, 190–91, 262n2, 292n64
Treaty of Middle Plantation (1677), 17, 215–16, 235n22
tribute: Algonquian, 22–23, 27–34, 37, 50, 56, 62, 136, 139, 171; English plans to collect Algonquian, 40, 61
Truett, Samuel, 232n15
Tsenacomoco, 19, 32–34, 37, 45–46, 48, 242n71

Tucker, Robin, 226
Tucker, William, 92, 127
Tuscarora people, 31, 144–46, 224, 226. *See also* Native peoples

Utie, John, 93
Uttamussak, 30; priests of the temple of, 30

Van Zandt, Cynthia: *Brothers among Nations*, 265n11
Vingboons, Johannes, 41
violence, 4, 8; over boundaries, 9–17, 66, 142–43, 155, 175, 188, 192; and English conflict with Native peoples, 11, 55–59, 67–70, 74, 80–81, 104, 118, 128, 133–35, 142–43, 155–57, 192, 202, 206, 226–27; extralegal, 8, 172–73; planter, 188–89, 202, 206; property destruction of Native people by settlers, 55, 61, 83, 86; property destruction of settlers by Native people, 5, 69, 81–82, 87, 131; race and, 17, 186; rumor of, 116, 188, 223, 264n9; vigilante, 180. *See also* boundaries; warfare
Virginia: Accomack County, 175, 213; boundaries of, 12, 16, 80, 101, 124, 155, 175, 195, 200–202, 220, 224–26; Charles City County, 74, 81, 192, 206, 210, 214, 256n51; crisis of authority in, 17, 100–101, 188; Essex County, 280n2; expansion of population of, 94, 140, 158; expansion of territory of, 11, 15–16, 58–64, 69, 80, 83–85, 101, 127, 140, 220, 225; founding of the colony of, 5, 36; General Assembly, 65, 75–78, 91, 95, 130–36, 141–43, 148, 151, 160, 163, 171–77, 186, 189, 191, 197, 215, 219, 221; General Court, 121; Gloucester County, 163, 194, 273n34; Henrico County, 192, 205–6, 210, 212, 219; Isle of Wight County, 212; James City County, 213; Lancaster County, 159, 163, 213, 279n120; Lower Norfolk County, 213; Middlesex County, 159, 162; New Kent County, 210, 219; Northampton County, 175, 181, 213; Northumberland County, 159, 167, 172, 207, 213; Old Rappahannock County, 159–60, 163, 178, 190, 196, 198, 206, 210, 213, 280n2; Richmond County, 280n2; Stafford County, 159, 161, 167, 210, 217; Surry County, 196, 212; tobacco culture of, 92; unsustainable assertions of colonial boundaries in, 14–15, 17, 84, 157; Warwick County, 219; Westmoreland County, 159, 172–73, 178, 181, 210, 213; York County, 197. *See also* colonial officials; colonization; county government; intracolonial tensions; Lower Peninsula; Middle Peninsula; Piedmont; Virginia Council
Virginia Company, 36, 48, 58, 64–65, 73–76, 82, 84; Great Charter of, 15, 64, 75, 86; land for settlers of, 88; private grants from, 75; records, 71
Virginia Council, 100. *See also* Virginia
Virginia Land Office, 5

Wachiopa, 171–72. *See also* Rappahannock people
Wahunganoche, 172, 177–80. *See also* Patawomeck people
Wahunsenacawh, 5, 10, 14, 19–34, 44–63, 72, 222, 240n46, 240n50, 263n5; control of English movements by, 66, 69; control of trade by, 47, 49–50, 56; death, 69; English leverage against, 38–40, 57–59, 61; move to Orapax, 71; Native enemies of, 40; peace of English with, 36; as werowance, 27. *See also* Powhatan chiefdom
Walsh, Lorena, 265n11
warfare: Algonquian, 20–21, 25, 31, 88–90; of English with Powhatans, 15–16, 36, 38, 54–58, 70–71, 78–90;

new strategies for English, 43, 87–89; seasonal cyclical Native, 31, 90. *See also* captive-taking; violence
Warraskoyack people, 52. *See also* Native peoples
Warren, Mary, 183
Washington, John, 173, 179, 189, 203, 233n16
wastelands, 150
Waterhouse, Edward, 83, 85
waterways, 12–14, 99; Algonquian towns located near, 23–25; and bridges, 186; conflict along, 211; English and Powhatan control of, 63–64, 69, 242n7; English exploration of, 36, 40–42, 57, 127; navigation of, 14–15, 262n3; Powhatan control over river mouths and, 14–15, 23–24, 36–37, 40, 69; rivers as, 22–24, 26, 57; and roads, 13–14, 30, 71, 182, 186, 209, 227–28; tributary, 42. *See also* Chesapeake Bay; estuaries; Native geographies; rivers; travel
Watkins Point, 175
Watts, Thomas, 185
Webb, Stephen Saunders, 297n147
werowances, 19, 22–32, 39, 46, 69, 87, 167–68, 177, 185; Accawmack, 72, 115; Appamattuck, 295n115; Assateague, 221; burial sites of, 55; Doeg, 217; Kiskiak, 272n21; lesser, 35–36, 125; locations of, 42; Mattawoman, 167; Nansemond, 72; Pamunkey, 142; Patawomeck, 36, 57, 90, 169, 172, 191, 238n27; Powhatan, 72; on the Powhatan fringe, 59, 72; Rappahannock, 169, 291n32; relations with English settlers of, 52–53, 72–73, 79; Weyanoke, 226. *See also* Native peoples; Powhatan chiefdom
werowansquas, 210, 216, 297n149
Werowocomoco, 23, 27–30, 33, 36, 40, 46, 51–52, 71. *See also* Powhatan chiefdom
West, Deputy Governor Francis, 53

West, Governor Thomas (Lord de la Warr), 56–57, 60
West, John, 200
West, Philip, 118
West Hundred, 63
West Point, 212
wetlands, 13, 26, 87, 144, 149–50, 156, 209–10, 224. *See also* Chesapeake Bay; marshlands
Weyanoke people, 19, 21–22, 30–32, 46–48, 133, 137, 144, 155, 215, 224–27, 297n149, 299n7; conjectural migration routes of, *225*; werowance, 226. *See also* Native peoples
White, Father Andrew, 111
White, Richard, 153–54, 162, 167, 178, 190, 282n43
White, Thomas, 154, 169–70, 173
Wicomiss people, 102–3, 115–16, 174. *See also* Native peoples
Wicomoco people, 137–38, 159. *See also* Native peoples
Wilcox, Matthew, 159
Wilkinson, Thomas, 138
Williamson, William, 118
Wilson, Samuel, 144
Wingfield, Edward, 57
Winsewack, 200
Witgen, Michael: *An Infinity of Nations*, 231n9
women: Algonquian, 25–26, 33, 48–50, 54, 57, 64, 92, 168, 248n65; arrival by ship of English, 90; Black, 288n3; Portobacco, 164; trade in Native, 216, 219–20; Weyanoke, 72, 223–24, 226
Wood, Abraham, 125–28, 138, 141–46, 149, 151, 170, 193, 205–7, 223
woodlands: Algonquian stewardship of, 26; bounded out as private property, 95; Native foraging in estuaries and, 26, 34; between plantations, 186; thinning around English settlements of, 66. *See also* Chesapeake Bay; Native geographies

Wormeley, Ralph, 136, 163–64
Wowinchapunk, 55. *See also* Paspahegh people
Wyatt, Governor Francis, 84, 94

Yaocomoco people, 110–13. *See also* Native peoples
Yeardley, Governor George, 65, 73–75, 92, 256n51
York River, 6, 22–24, 27–28, 33, 37, 42, 75, 90, 94, 104, 128, 197, 237n13; fortifications on, 192; north side of, 133, 137, 202; plantations along, 134; south side of, 141–42. *See also* Pamunkey River
Youghtamond people, 27, 30, 46. *See also* Native peoples

"Zúñiga Map," 42
Zúñiga, Pedro de, 42

Recent books in the series
EARLY AMERICAN HISTORIES

The Travels of Richard Traunter: Two Journeys through the Native Southeast in 1698 and 1699
Edited by Sandra L. Dahlberg

Making the Early Modern Metropolis: Culture and Power in Pre-Revolutionary Philadelphia
Daniel P. Johnson

The Permanent Resident: Excavations and Explorations of George Washington's Life
Philip Levy

From Independence to the U.S. Constitution: Reconsidering the Critical Period of American History
Douglas Bradburn and Christopher R. Pearl, editors

Washington's Government: Charting the Origins of the Federal Administration
Max M. Edling and Peter J. Kastor, editors

The Natural, Moral, and Political History of Jamaica, and the Territories thereon Depending, from the First Discovery of the Island by Christopher Columbus to the Year 1746
James Knight, edited by Jack P. Greene

Statute Law in Colonial Virginia: Governors, Assemblymen, and the Revisals That Forged the Old Dominion
Warren M. Billings

Against Popery: Britain, Empire, and Anti-Catholicism
Evan Haefeli, editor

Conceived in Crisis: The Revolutionary Creation of an American State
Christopher R. Pearl

Redemption from Tyranny: Herman Husband's American Revolution
Bruce E. Stewart

Experiencing Empire: Power, People, and Revolution in Early America
Patrick Griffin, editor

Citizens of Convenience: The Imperial Origins of American Nationhood on the U.S.-Canadian Border
Lawrence B. A. Hatter

"Esteemed Bookes of Lawe" and the Legal Culture of Early Virginia
Warren M. Billings and Brent Tarter, editors

Settler Jamaica in the 1750s: A Social Portrait
Jack P. Greene

Loyal Protestants and Dangerous Papists: Maryland and the Politics of Religion in the English Atlantic, 1630–1690
Antoinette Sutto

The Road to Black Ned's Forge: A Story of Race, Sex, and Trade on the Colonial American Frontier
Turk McCleskey

Dunmore's New World: The Extraordinary Life of a Royal Governor in Revolutionary America—with Jacobites, Counterfeiters, Land Schemes, Shipwrecks, Scalping, Indian Politics, Runaway Slaves, and Two Illegal Royal Weddings
James Corbett David

Creating the British Atlantic: Essays on Transplantation, Adaptation, and Continuity
Jack P. Greene

The Evil Necessity: British Naval Impressment in the Eighteenth-Century Atlantic World
Denver Brunsman

Early Modern Virginia: Reconsidering the Old Dominion
Douglas Bradburn and John C. Coombs, editors

www.ingramcontent.com/pod-product-compliance
Lightning Source LLC
Chambersburg PA
CBHW031756220426
43662CB00007B/430